Lecture Notes in Computer Science

Lecture Notes in Computer Science

Vol. 1: GI-Gesellschaft für Informatik e.V. 3. Jahrestagung, Hamburg, 8.–10. Oktober 1973. Herausgegeben im Auftrag der Gesellschaft für Informatik von W. Brauer. XI, 508 Seiten. 1973.

Vol. 2: GI-Gesellschaft für Informatik e.V. 1. Fachtagung über Automatentheorie und Formale Sprachen, Bonn, 9.–12. Juli 1973. Herausgegeben im Auftrag der Gesellschaft für Informatik von K.-H. Böhling und K. Indermark. VII, 322 Seiten. 1973.

Vol. 3: 5th Conference on Optimization Techniques, Part I. (Series: I.F.I.P. TC7 Optimization Conferences.) Edited by R. Conti and A. Ruberti. XIII, 565 pages. 1973.

Vol. 4: 5th Conference on Optimization Techniques, Part II. (Series: I.F.I.P. TC7 Optimization Conferences.) Edited by R. Conti and A. Ruberti. XIII, 389 pages. 1973.

Vol. 5: International Symposium on Theoretical Programming. Edited by A. Ershov and V. A. Nepomniaschy. VI, 407 pages. 1974.

Vol. 6: B. T. Smith, J. M. Boyle, J. J. Dongarra, B. S. Garbow, Y. Ikebe, V. C. Klema, and C. B. Moler, Matrix Eigensystem Routines – EISPACK Guide. XI, 551 pages. 2nd Edition 1974. 1976.

Vol. 7: 3. Fachtagung über Programmiersprachen, Kiel, 5.–7. März 1974. Herausgegeben von B. Schlender und W. Frielinghaus. VI, 225 Seiten. 1974.

Vol. 8: GI-NTG Fachtagung über Struktur und Betrieb von Rechensystemen, Braunschweig, 20.–22. März 1974. Herausgegeben im Auftrag der GI und der NTG von H.-O. Leilich. VI, 340 Seiten. 1974.

Vol. 9: GI-BIFOA Internationale Fachtagung: Informationszentren in Wirtschaft und Verwaltung. Köln, 17./18. Sept. 1973. Herausgegeben im Auftrag der GI und dem BIFOA von P. Schmitz. VI, 259 Seiten. 1974.

Vol. 10: Computing Methods in Applied Sciences and Engineering, Part 1. International Symposium, Versailles, December 17–21, 1973. Edited by R. Glowinski and J. L. Lions. X, 497 pages. 1974.

Vol. 11: Computing Methods in Applied Sciences and Engineering, Part 2. International Symposium, Versailles, December 17–21, 1973. Edited by R. Glowinski and J. L. Lions. X, 434 pages. 1974.

Vol. 12: GFK-GI-GMR Fachtagung Prozessrechner 1974. Karlsruhe, 10.–11. Juni 1974. Herausgegeben von G. Krüger und R. Friehmelt. XI, 620 Seiten. 1974.

Vol. 13: Rechnerstrukturen und Betriebsprogrammierung, Erlangen, 1970. (GI-Gesellschaft für Informatik e.V.) Herausgegeben von W. Händler und P. P. Spies. VII, 333 Seiten. 1974.

Vol. 14: Automata, Languages and Programming – 2nd Colloquium, University of Saarbrücken, July 29–August 2, 1974. Edited by J. Loeckx. VIII, 611 pages. 1974.

Vol. 15: L Systems. Edited by A. Salomaa and G. Rozenberg. VI, 338 pages. 1974.

Vol. 16: Operating Systems, International Symposium, Rocquencourt 1974. Edited by E. Gelenbe and C. Kaiser. VIII, 310 pages. 1974.

Vol. 17: Rechner-Gestützter Unterricht RGU '74, Fachtagung, Hamburg, 12.–14. August 1974, ACU-Arbeitskreis Computer-Unterstützter Unterricht. Herausgegeben im Auftrag der GI von K. Brunnstein, K. Haefner und W. Händler. X, 417 Seiten. 1974.

Vol. 18: K. Jensen and N. E. Wirth, PASCAL – User Manual and Report. VII, 170 pages. Corrected Reprint of the 2nd Edition 1976.

Vol. 19: Programming Symposium. Proceedings 1974. V, 425 pages. 1974.

Vol. 20: J. Engelfriet, Simple Program Schemes and Formal Languages. VII, 254 pages. 1974.

Vol. 21: Compiler Construction, An Advanced Course. Edited by F. L. Bauer and J. Eickel. XIV. 621 pages. 1974.

Vol. 22: Formal Aspects of Cognitive Processes. Proceedings 1972. Edited by T. Storer and D. Winter. V, 214 pages. 1975.

Vol. 23: Programming Methodology. 4th Informatik Symposium, IBM Germany Wildbad, September 25–27, 1974. Edited by C. E. Hackl. VI, 501 pages. 1975.

Vol. 24: Parallel Processing. Proceedings 1974. Edited by T. Feng. VI, 433 pages. 1975.

Vol. 25: Category Theory Applied to Computation and Control. Proceedings 1974. Edited by E. G. Manes. X, 245 pages. 1975.

Vol. 26: GI-4. Jahrestagung, Berlin, 9.–12. Oktober 1974. Herausgegeben im Auftrag der GI von D. Siefkes. IX, 748 Seiten. 1975.

Vol. 27: Optimization Techniques. IFIP Technical Conference. Novosibirsk, July 1–7, 1974. (Series: I.F.I.P. TC7 Optimization Conferences.) Edited by G. I. Marchuk. VIII, 507 pages. 1975.

Vol. 28: Mathematical Foundations of Computer Science. 3rd Symposium at Jadwisin near Warsaw, June 17–22, 1974. Edited by A. Blikle. VII, 484 pages. 1975.

Vol. 29: Interval Mathematics. Procedings 1975. Edited by K. Nickel. VI, 331 pages. 1975.

Vol. 30: Software Engineering. An Advanced Course. Edited by F. L. Bauer. (Formerly published 1973 as Lecture Notes in Economics and Mathematical Systems, Vol. 81) XII, 545 pages. 1975.

Vol. 31: S. H. Fuller, Analysis of Drum and Disk Storage Units. IX, 283 pages. 1975.

Vol. 32: Mathematical Foundations of Computer Science 1975. Proceedings 1975. Edited by J. Bečvář. X, 476 pages. 1975.

Vol. 33: Automata Theory and Formal Languages, Kaiserslautern, May 20–23, 1975. Edited by H. Brakhage on behalf of GI. VIII, 292 Seiten. 1975.

Vol. 34: GI – 5. Jahrestagung, Dortmund 8.–10. Oktober 1975. Herausgegeben im Auftrag der GI von J. Mühlbacher. X, 755 Seiten. 1975.

Vol. 35: W. Everling, Exercises in Computer Systems Analysis. (Formerly published 1972 as Lecture Notes in Economics and Mathematical Systems, Vol. 65) VIII, 184 pages. 1975.

Vol. 36: S. A. Greibach, Theory of Program Structures: Schemes, Semantics, Verification. XV, 364 pages. 1975.

Vol. 37: C. Böhm, λ-Calculus and Computer Science Theory. Proceedings 1975. XII, 370 pages. 1975.

Vol. 38: P. Branquart, J.-P. Cardinael, J. Lewi, J.-P. Delescaille, M. Vanbegin. An Optimized Translation Process and Its Application to ALGOL 68. IX, 334 pages. 1976.

Vol. 39: Data Base Systems. Proceedings 1975. Edited by H. Hasselmeier and W. Spruth. VI, 386 pages. 1976.

Vol. 40: Optimization Techniques. Modeling and Optimization in the Service of Man. Part 1. Proceedings 1975. Edited by J. Cea. XIV, 854 pages. 1976.

Vol. 41: Optimization Techniques. Modeling and Optimization in the Service of Man. Part 2. Proceedings 1975. Edited by J. Cea. XIII, 852 pages. 1976.

Vol. 42: James E. Donahue, Complementary Definitions of Programming Language Semantics. VII, 172 pages. 1976.

Vol. 43: E. Specker und V. Strassen, Komplexität von Entscheidungsproblemen. Ein Seminar. V, 217 Seiten. 1976.

Vol. 44: ECI Conference 1976. Proceedings 1976. Edited by K. Samelson. VIII, 322 pages. 1976.

Vol. 45: Mathematical Foundations of Computer Science 1976. Proceedings 1976. Edited by A. Mazurkiewicz. XI, 601 pages. 1976.

Vol. 46: Language Hierarchies and Interfaces. Edited by F. L. Bauer and K. Samelson. X, 428 pages. 1976.

Vol. 47: Methods of Algorithmic Language Implementation. Edited by A. Ershov and C. H. A. Koster. VIII, 351 pages. 1977.

Vol. 48: Theoretical Computer Science, Darmstadt, March 1977. Edited by H. Tzschach, H. Waldschmidt and H. K.-G. Walter on behalf of GI. VIII, 418 pages. 1977.

Lecture Notes in Computer Science

Edited by G. Goos and J. Hartmanis

67

Theoretical Computer Science
4th GI Conference

Aachen, March 26–28, 1979

Edited by K. Weihrauch

Springer-Verlag
Berlin Heidelberg New York 1979

Editor
Klaus Weihrauch
Lehrstuhl für Informatik I
RWTH Aachen
Büchel 29–31
5100 Aachen/BRD

Library of Congress Cataloging in Publication Data

GI-Fachtagung Theoretische Informatik, 4th, Aachen, 1979.
Theoretical computer science.

(Lecture notes in computer science ; 67)
English, French, or German.
Bibliography: p.
Includes index.
1. Machine thoery--Congresses. 2. Formal languages
--Congresses. I. Weihrauch, Klaus, 1943-
II. Gesellschaft für Informatik. III. Title.
IV. Series.
QA267.G18 1979 001.6'4 79-9707

AMS Subject Classifications (1970): 68-XX, 94-XX, 02-XX, 05-04
CR Subject Classifications (1974): 5.0; 5.1

ISBN 3-540-09118-1 Springer-Verlag Berlin Heidelberg New York
ISBN 0-387-09118-1 Springer-Verlag New York Heidelberg Berlin

Printing and binding: Beltz Offsetdruck, Hemsbach/Bergstr.
2145/3140-543210

VORWORT

Der vorliegende Band faßt alle Vorträge zusammen, die auf der 4. GI-Fachtagung Theoretische Informatik vom 26. - 28. März 1979 in Aachen gehalten wurden. Diese Tagung setzt die Reihe der Vorgängertagungen über Theoretische Informatik, ehemals Automatentheorie und Formale Sprachen, fort. Wie bisher wurden auch dieses Mal keine Parallelsitzungen abgehalten. Daher bot das Programm außer den 6 Hauptvorträgen nur noch für 26 weitere Vorträge Raum. Dem Programmkomitee fiel die schwere Aufgabe zu, diese aus 79 eingereichten Vorträgen auszuwählen. Die Arbeiten wurden dabei nicht formal referiert, und es wurde davon ausgegangen, daß viele auch der nicht angenommenen Arbeiten evtl. in überarbeiteter Form in einer wissenschaftlichen Zeitschrift veröffentlicht werden.

An dieser Stelle danken die Veranstalter den Vortragenden, den Teilnehmern und allen, die zum Gelingen der Tagung beigetragen haben, insbesondere Frau I. Prost, die einen großen Teil der anfallenden Aufgaben übernommen hat. Das Bundesministerium für Forschung und Technologie hat durch seine finanzielle Förderung die Durchführung der Tagung ermöglicht. Für großzügige Unterstützung danken wir der RWTH Aachen und den Spendern aus der Wirtschaft.
Schließlich gilt unser Dank dem Springer Verlag und den Herausgebern der Lecture Notes in Computer Science für die Aufnahme des Tagungsberichtes in diese Reihe.

Aachen, im März 1979 K. Weihrauch

INHALTSVERZEICHNIS

H a u p t v o r t r ä g e

V o r t r ä g e (in alphabetischer Reihenfolge)

CONTEXT-FREE SETS OF INFINITE WORDS

L. Boasson

Abstract

In this paper we give some new results about context-free sets of infinite words. The presentation will be a generalization of McNaughton's approach in [7], where he analyzed regular sets of infinite words. However, our extension to the regular case is not straightforward and thus distinguishes from the approach given in [4].

Some of the results given below originate from two papers by Nivat [9,10], others are unpublished supplementary results due to Nivat and Boasson.

We recall from [9] that to each context-free grammar G one can associate an operator $\hat{G}$, which has a unique fixed point over finite words and a greatest fixed point over finite and infinite words, each of them being the vector of languages generated by the non-terminals of G.

We then show that any context-free set of infinite words can be obtained by a substitution of some context-free languages into a regular set of infinite words.

In the sequel the notions of adherence and center of context-free languages are introduced and analyzed to establish a link between the infinite words and the language generated by a grammar.

Nous nous proposons de présenter ici quelques résultats récents concernant l'étude des ensembles algébriques de mots infinis, soit aussi des ensembles de mots infinis engendrés par une grammaire algébrique. Ceux-ci prennent place dans une nouvelle présentation du problème général posé par l'extension au cas algébrique des études de McNaughton menées dans le cas rationnel [7]. Elle n'apparait pas cependant comme une extension directe de ces dernières et se sépare ainsi tout de suite des travaux de [4]. Les résultats donnés ci-dessous sont issus de deux articles de M. Nivat [9, 10] ; ils sont complétés de résultats originaux encore non publiés obtenus conjointement par M. Nivat et l'auteur de ces lignes.

Avant d'entrer dans le vif du sujet, nous voudrions brièvement présenter l'origine de ces travaux. En effet, on saisira mieux ainsi quelles peuvent être les raisons qui conduisent à une telle étude.

Les problèmes posés par la définition de la sémantique des programmes ont conduit bon nombre d'informaticiens à la notion de Schéma de Programme et d'Interprétation (voir par exemple [5]). On a alors développé beaucoup d'énergie pour préciser et utiliser aisément la notion de calcul réalisé par schéma. Très tôt, on a vu que le concept le plus commode permettant les traitements ultérieures (interprétation, évaluation, simplification, ...) était celui d'arbre infini : On peut en effet trouver un tel arbre représentant tous les calculs possibles du schéma (voir [8] par exemple). Les calculs effectifs du schéma interprété sont alors donnés par les sous arbres initiaux (approximant l'arbre infini) de l'arbre ainsi associé au schéma. Lorsque le problème s'est posé de traiter les schémas non-déterministes, on a bien sur songé à procéder de façon semblable, c'est-à-dire à trouver une forêt d'arbres infinis associée au schéma non-déterministe. Le problème s'est vite montré fort délicat (voir [2, 6] par exemple). La plupart des manipulations concernant les schémas (avant interprétation) étant tout à fait similaires à celles concernant les grammaires algébriques, il est tentant de chercher à associer à ces dernières des mots infinis pouvant alors donner une idée de ce que l'on doit faire dans le cas des schémas non déterministes. Cette idée, à l'origine de l'étude ci-dessous, a d'ailleurs déjà porté ses fruits, puisque le théorème 3 énoncé plus loin s'étend aux arbres et permet de définir une sémantique dénotationnelle des programmes récursifs non déterministes [1].

Nous terminerons cette brève présentation en notant que la plupart des résultats présentés (en particulier ceux de notre dernière partie) soulèvent de nombreuses questions concernant la théorie des langages algébriques classiques.

Cet article est divisé en quatre parties. La première précise nos notations et rappelle les résultats élémentaires concernant les mots infinis. La deuxième présente la méthode utilisée pour associer à une grammaire algébrique un ensemble de mots infinis. La troisième propose une méthode associant un tel ensemble de mots à un langage ordinaire. Les relations existant entre les deux ensembles obtenus ainsi sont éclaircis. La dernière partie enfin associe à un langage ordinaire un second langage rendant compte de l'extension infinie du premier fournie par le paragraphe précédent.

Préliminaires :

Etant donné un alphabet fini X, nous notons X^* l'ensemble des mots finis sur X (monoïde libre), par X^ω l'ensemble des mots infinis sur X et par X^∞ l'ensemble des mots finis ou infinis sur X, soit $X^\infty = X^* \cup X^\omega$.

Nous considérons les mots infinis comme des applications de N dans X et pour chaque entier n, nous désignons par $u(n)$ la $n^{\text{ième}}$ lettre du mot infini $u = u(1)\, u(2) \ldots u(n) \ldots$. Le mot fini $u(1)\, u(2) \ldots u(n)$ est alors le facteur gauche de longueur n du mot infini u. L'ensemble $FG(u)$ des facteurs gauches finis d'un mot infini u constitue un langage infini sur X. (Le terme de langage reste ici réservé aux seules parties de X^*).

Si l'on définit sur X^* l'ordre partiel $\leqslant$ par $u \leqslant v$ si u est facteur gauche de v, on voit que ce langage est totalement ordonné. On vérifie sans peine qu'un langage infini totalement ordonné défini un mot infini unique.

On peut munir X^∞ d'un produit interne associatif ; c'est celui de X^* si les deux mots sont finis, il est ainsi défini sinon :

- $u \in X^\omega$, $v \in X^*$ vu est donné par

$1 \leqslant i \leqslant |v|$ $vu(i) = v(i)$ ($i^{\text{ème}}$ lettre de v)

$|v| < i$ $vu(i) = u(i - |v|)$.

($|v|$ désigne la longueur du mot v.)

- $u \in X^\omega$, $v \in X^\infty$ $uv = u$.

X^∞ étant doté d'un produit, on peut étendre celui-ci aux parties de X^∞ et définir une opération $*$ comme on le fait pour les parties du monoïde libre - En outre, on définit l'opération ω en posant :

$A \subset X^\infty$, $A^\omega = \{u \in X^\omega \mid \exists$ une suite de mots (non vides) de A , $v_1, v_2, \ldots, v_n, \ldots$ telle que $v_1 v_2 \ldots v_n \ldots = u$.$\}$

Notons que $\{1\}^\omega = \emptyset$ (où 1 désigne le mot vide de X^*).

Enfin, si $A \subset X^\infty$, nous désignons par A^{fin} le langage sur X , $A^{fin} = A \cap X^*$ et par A^{inf} l'ensemble $A \cap X^\omega$ des mots infinis de A . Ainsi $A = A^{fin} \cup A^{inf}$.

Exemples :

- Si l'on considère le mot infini u donné par

$u(3i + 1) = a$, $u(3i + 2) = b$, $u(3i + 3) = b$ pour $i \geqslant 0$,

On peut "l'écrire" :

$u = abbabbabb \ldots$

ou $u = (abb)^\omega$

On vérifie alors que $FG(u) = (abb)^* (1 \cup a \cup ab)$.

- Si l'on considère maintenant le langage "ordonné par facteur gauche" $L = (ab)^*$, il définit le mot infini $u' = (ab)^\omega$ ou $u' = abab \ldots ab \ldots$ ou, précisément $u'(2i + 1) = a$ $u'(2i + 2) = b$ $(i \geqslant 0)$.

- Si A désigne l'ensemble $b \cup a^\omega$, on a

$A^{fin} = b$ $A^{inf} = a^\omega$ et $A^\omega = b^\omega \cup a^\omega \cup b^* a^\omega$ alors que

$A^* = a^\omega \cup b^* a^\omega \cup b^*$.

II - Grammaires et Dérivations :

L'ensemble des résultats présentés dans ce paragraphe est issu de [9] où l'on trouvera les preuves complètes de ceux-ci.

Une grammaire algébrique sur X est donnée par un triple $G = \langle X, V, P \rangle$ où V désigne l'alphabet des variables ou non-terminaux (disjoint de X) et P l'ensemble des règles. Une grammaire algébrique est faiblement de Greibach si aucun membre droit de règle n'est dans V^* (i.e. tout membre droit contient au moins une lettre terminale). Elle est sous forme normale de Greibach si chaque membre droit de règle commence par une lettre terminale. Nous utiliserons les notations classiques $\rightarrow$ et $\overset{*}{\rightarrow}$ concernant les dérivations usuelles. Si v est une variable, on note L(G, v) le langage engendré par la grammaire G avec v pour axiome.

Etant donné un mot t sur $X \cup V$, nous désignerons par FGT(t) le plus long facteur gauche de t qui soit dans X^* .

a) Dérivations de mots finis :

Etant donnés une grammaire algébrique $G = \langle X, V, P \rangle$ avec $V = \{v_1, v_2, \ldots, v_n\}$, un vecteur de parties de $(X \cup V)^*$ $\vec{Q} = \langle Q_1, Q_2, \ldots, Q_n \rangle$ et un mot t de $(X \cup V)^*$, on définit $t[\vec{Q}/\vec{V}]$ comme l'ensemble des mots obtenus en substituant à chaque occurence de v_i dans t le langage Q_i pour $i = 1, \ldots, N$. Désignant alors par P_i l'ensemble (fini) des nombres droits des règles de G issues de v_i , on pose

$$\hat{G}(\vec{Q}) = \langle P_1[\vec{Q}/\vec{V}], \ldots, P_N[\vec{Q}/\vec{V}] \rangle .$$

et $$\hat{G}_\infty(\vec{Q}) = \bigcup_{i \geq 0} G^i(Q) .$$

On sait alors :

<u>Théorème 1</u> (Schützenberger [11]) : <u>L'opérateur $\hat{G}$ admet un plus petit point fixe $\hat{G}_\infty(\vec{\emptyset})$ qui satisfait</u>

$$\hat{G}_\infty(\vec{\emptyset}) = \langle L(G, v_1), \ldots, L(G, v_N) \rangle .$$

De la même façon, on peut montrer :

<u>Théorème 2</u> : <u>Si G est une grammaire faiblement de Greibach, $\hat{G}$ admet un plus grand point fixe $\hat{G}_\infty(X^*)$ qui satisfait</u>

$$\hat{G}_\infty(X^*) = \langle L(G, v_1), \ldots, L(G, v_N) \rangle .$$

Ainsi une grammaire faiblement de Greibach définit-elle un opérateur n'ayant qu'un seul point fixe (sur les mots finis) qui n'est autre que le vecteur des langages engendrés par chaque non-terminal.

b) Dérivations de mots infinis :

On appelle dérivation infinie dans G toute suite (infinie) de mots de $(X \cup V)^*$ donc chacun dérive directement au sens usuel du précédent. Une telle dérivation $t_1, t_2, \ldots, t_i, \ldots$ est terminale si et seulement si $\bigcup_{i \geq 1} FGT(t_i)$ est infini (Ceci signifie que la longueur du facteur gauche terminal du mot t_i tend vers l'infini avec i) . Comme il est clair que $FGT(t_i)$ est facteur gauche de $FGT(t_{i+1})$, on voit que le langage $\bigcup_{i \geq 1} FGT(t_i)$ définit alors un mot infini t unique. Ce mot est alors dit être engendré par la dérivation infinie terminale $t_1, t_2, \ldots, t_i, \ldots$.

On notera $L^{\infty}(G, v)$ l'ensemble des mots finis et infinis engendrés par G avec v pour axiome.

On peut alors établir le :

Théorème 3 : Si G est une grammaire de Greibach, $\hat{G}$ admet un plus grand point fixe dans X^{∞} qui satisfait
$\hat{G}_{\infty}(X^{\infty}) = < L^{\infty}(G, v_1), \dots, L^{\infty}(G, v_N) >$.

Remarquons que le plus petit point fixe de $\hat{G}$ dans X^{∞} reste évidemment celui trouvé dans X^* !!

Exemples :

Soit $X = \{a, b\}$, $V = \{S\}$ et la grammaire donnée par $S \rightarrow aSb + ab$.
On sait que $L(G, S) = \{a^n b^n \mid n \geq 1\}$.
On vérifie que la seule dérivation infinie d'origine S possible est terminale : elle s'écrit : $S, aSb , a^2Sb^2 , \dots, a^nSb^n, \dots$ et
$\bigcup_{n \geq 0} FGT(a^nSb^n) = \bigcup_{n \geq 0} a^n = a^*$ définit l'unique mot infini a^{ω} . Ainsi
$L^{\infty}(G, S) = \{a^n b^n \mid n \geq 1\} \cup a^{\omega}$.

III - Adhérence d'un langage :

Nous nous proposons ici d'établir un lien entre les mots infinis engendrés par une grammaire et le langage usuel qu'on lui associe. Ce lien met en évidence que la plupart des transformations classiques que l'on sait pouvoir faire subir à une grammaire sans changer le langage engendré ne sont plus du tout sans effet sur les mots infinis. C'est de là que proviennent d'ailleurs les phénomènes paradoxaux relevés dans [4] .

Nous commençons par associer à un langage L , un ensemble de mots infinis que nous appelons son adhérence en posant
$Adh(L) = \{u \in X^{\omega} \mid$ Tout facteur gauche fini de u est facteur gauche d'un mot de L .$\}$
(Remarquons qu'évidemment L et l'ensemble de ses facteurs gauches $FG(L)$ ont même adhérence !)

Exemple : Si $L = \{a^n b^n \mid n \geq 1\}$, $Adh(L) = \{a^{\omega}\}$.
On peut alors établir un premier

Théorème 4 [10] : Etant donnée une grammaire algébrique G sous forme normale de Greibach, pour chaque variable v
$L^{\infty}(G, v) = L(G, v) \cup Adh(L(G, v))$.

On peut alors vouloir caractériser les ensembles algébriques de mots finis et infinis engendrables par une grammaire sous forme normale de Greibach. Ces ensembles algébriques peuvent en effet être définis directement ainsi :

- Une partie A de X^{∞} est dite amène si $A^{inf} = Adh(A^{fin})$ - Elle est dite algébrique si elle est engendrable par une grammaire algébrique.
On peut alors énoncer :

Théorème 5 [10] : Pour toute partie de X^{∞} amène et algébrique A , il existe une grammaire algébrique sous forme normale de Greibach telle que $L^{\infty}(G) = A$.

Nous terminerons ce paragraphe en présentant une construction clef utile à la preuve de tous ces résultats ainsi qu'un dernier théorème caractérisant les ensembles algébriques de X^{∞} .

Etant donnée une grammaire algébrique $G = \langle X, V, P \rangle$, on lui associe la grammaire $\bar{G} = \langle X \cup V, \bar{V}, \bar{P} \rangle$ où
- $\bar{V}$ est une copie de V : $\bar{V} = \{\bar{v}_i \mid v_i \in V\}$
- $\bar{P}$ est donné par
$\bar{v}_i = \bar{p}_i$ avec $\bar{p}_i = \{m_1 \bar{v} \mid m_1 \in (X \cup V)^* \exists m_2$ tel que $v_i \to m_1\, v\, m_2\}$
On notera que $\bar{G}$ d'une part est linéaire unilatère, d'autre part sans règle terminale.

Elle n'engendra donc aucun mot fini. Cependant, elle engendre un ensemble rationnel de mots infinis exactement de la nature de ceux étudiés dans [7] . Cette grammaire $\bar{G}$ est essentielle ici à cause de

Théorème 5 [10]: $L^{inf}(G, v) = L^{inf}(\bar{G}, \bar{v})\ [\vec{L}(G) / \vec{V}]$.

Ce dernier résultat admet pour

Corollaire [10] : Tout ensemble algébrique A de X^{ω} est obtenu par substitution de langages algébriques dans un ensemble rationnel de mots infinis.

Remarque : Il faut bien voir que la famille des ensembles algébriques amènes est strictement contenue dans celle des ensembles algébriques :

Soit $G = \langle X, V, P \rangle$ donnée par

$S \to T_1 T_2$
$T_1 \to T_1 a + a$
$T_2 \to b\, T_2 + b$

$L(G, T_1) = a^+$ $\qquad$ $L^{\infty}(G, T_1) = a^+$
$L(G, T_2) = b^+$ $\qquad$ $L^{\infty}(G, T_2) = b^+ \cup b^{\omega}$
$L^{\infty}(G, S) = a^+b^+ \cup a^+b^{\omega}$ qui est donc un ensemble algébrique.
Comme il n'existe clairement aucun langage dont a^+b^{ω} ne soit adhérence, il est hors de question de $L^{\infty}(G, S)$ soit amène !

IV - Centre d'un langage :

Reprenant la notion d'adhérence définie ci-dessus, on s'aperçoit facilement que deux langages distincts peuvent avoir même adhérence. Ainsi, par exemple, les langages L et FG(L) ont-ils toujours même adhérence. Très vite, on s'assure que, parmi tous les langages stables par facteur gauche ayant même adhérence, il en est un minimal vis à vis de l'inclusion : le langage forme de facteurs gauches finis des mots infinis de l'adhérence considérée. On appellera alors centre du langage L le langage $\mathring{L} = FG(Adh(L))$.

Exemple : Si $L = \{a^n b^n \mid n \geq 1\}$, $Adh(L) = a^\omega$ et donc $\mathring{L} = a^*$.
Un langage L égal à son centre sera dit central.
On peut vérifier

Proposition 1 [2] : Le centre d'un langage algébrique est algébrique.

L'opération de "passage au centre" n'est cependant pas simple puisque (cf. l'exemple ci-dessus) un langage non rationnel peut avoir un centre rationnel et qu'au contraire, un langage non générateur peut avoir un centre générateur (voir [3]) . On peut néanmoins établir assez facilement quelques propriétés concernant les langages centraux.

Propriété 1 : Tout langage algébrique est rationnellement équivalent à un langage central.

Propriété 2 : Les langages centraux sont fermés par union, produit et étoile.

Pour ce qui concerne les clotures par morphisme, le problème est fort délicat. Nous commencerons par expliquer pourquoi à l'aide de remarques simples qui montrent bien les difficultés sous-jacentes :

- Tout langage central contient ses facteurs gauches. On ne peut donc espérer une fermeture par morphisme non alphabétique !

- Tout langage central est infini - On ne peut donc espérer une fermeture par morphisme si celui-ci peut "effacer" des lettres !

Nous nous limiterons à présenter ci-dessous les premiers résultats obtenus concernant ce problème. Nous appelons application séquentielle l'opération réalisée par un automate fini déterministe "incomplet" muni d'une fonction de sortie (le plus souvent de signé comme un "g.s.m.").

Exemple : Si l'on considère $X = \{a, b\}$ et l'automate avec sortie 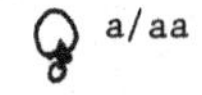

, on réalise l'application séquentielle γ

$\forall n \quad \gamma(a^n) = a^{2n}$

$\forall f \in X^* b X^* \quad \gamma f = \emptyset$

Nous dirons qu'une application séquentielle est fidèle (= "ε.limited") si, quelque soit le mot h , Card $\{\gamma^{-1} h\}$ est fini. Elle est totale si, quelque soit le mot f, $\gamma f \neq \emptyset$.

On entend une application séquentielle γ aux mots infinis en posant

$\forall u \in X^{\omega}$ $\bar{\gamma} u = \gamma u$ si γu est un mot infini

$= \emptyset$ sinon

(Notons que si l'application γ est fidèle, on peut sans inconvénient confondre γ et $\bar{\gamma}$.)

On peut alors énoncer :

Proposition 2 : Si A est une adhérence algébrique et γ une application séquentielle fidèle, $\bar{\gamma} A$ est une adhérence algébrique.

Corollaire : Etant données une adhérence algébrique A et une adhérence rationnelle R, $A \cap R$ est une adhérence algébrique.

Corollaire : Les adhérences algébriques sont fermées par morphisme continu. (= "ε.free").

Revenant alors aux langages centraux, on peut prouver la

Proposition 3 : Si L est un langage central et γ une application séquentielle fidèle et totale, $FG(\gamma L)$ est un langage central.

Nous terminerons cet article en présentant un dernier résultat qui pose beaucoup de questions concernant les langages algébriques classiques et laisse entrevoir quelques nouvelles possibilités de classifications :

Théorème 6 a : A toute adhérence algébrique A, on peut associer un entier n et une application séquentielle fidèle γ tels que

$$A = \bar{\gamma}(Adh(D'^{*}_{n})).$$

(D'^{*}_{n} désigne le langage de Dyck restreint sur $2n$ lettres). On a donc un théorème de Chomsky-Schützenberger concernant les adhérences algébriques. Or, on sait bien que l'on peut coder D'^{*}_{n} dans D'^{*}_{2}. Ce code utilisé étant en outre préfixe, on en déduit immédiatement

Théorème 6 b : A toute adhérence algébrique A, on peut associer une application séquentielle γ telle que

$$A = \bar{\gamma}(Adh(D'_{2})^{*}).$$

On voit donc que l'adhérence du langage de Dyck joue le rôle d'adhérence génératrice. Il est alors naturel de chercher d'autres adhérences de même nature. En particulier, on peut se demander si l'adhérence du langage E_1 engendré par la grammaire $\langle S \rightarrow aSbSc + d \rangle$ jouit d'une propriété semblable.

1 - A. Arnold et M. Nivat : Non deterministic Recursive Program Schemes.
Fundamentals of Computation Theory
Lecture Notes in Computer Science N°56 p. 12-21 - Springer Verlag (1977)

2 - J.W. de Bakker : Semantics of Infinite Processes Using Generalized Trees
dans Mathematical Foundations of Computer Science
Lecture Notes in Computer Science N° 53, p. 240-246 - Springer Verlag (1977)

3 - L. Boasson : Un langage algébrique particulier.
A paraître dans la R.A.I.R.O. - Informatique Théorique.

4 - R. Cohen et A. Gold : Theory of ω-Languages - Part. I : Characterization of ω Context-Free Languages.
J. Comp. Syst. Sciences, 15 (1977), p. 169-184.

5 - S. Greibach : Theory of Program Structures : Schemes, Semantics, Verification.
Lecture Notes in Computer Sciences n° 36 - Springer Verlag (1975).

6 - M. Hennessy et E.A. Ashcroft : On Proofs of Programs for Synchronization.
dans Automata, Languages and Programming - 3rd International Colloquium
ed. S. Michaelson et R. Milner, p. 478-493 (1976).

7 - R. McNaughton : Testing and Generationg Infinite Sequences by a Finite Automaton.
Inf. and Control, 9 (1966), p. 521-530.

8 - M. Nivat : On the Interpretation of Recursive Polyadic Schemes.
Symposia Mathematica - Vol. 15 - Bologne (1975).

9 - M. Nivat : Mots Infinis Engendrés par une Grammaire Algébrique.
R.A.I.R.O. Informatique Théorique, 11 , N° 4 (1977), p. 311-327.

10 - M. Nivat : Sur les Ensembles de Mots Infinis Engendrés par une Grammaire Algébrique.
A paraître dans R.A.I.R.O. Informatique Théorique.

11 - M.P. Schützenberger : Push-down Automata and Context-Free Languages.
Inf. and Control, 6 (1963), p. 246-264.

NEW ASPECTS OF HOMOMORPHISMS

H. Maurer

Abstract

Homomorphisms have played an important role throughout the development of language theory. In the last years, new areas of language theory have been developed based on homomorphisms. We survey some recent results in such areas: Starting with the DOL equivalence problem we first mention the notions of homomorphism equivalence and equality sets, and their application to homomorphic representation theorems. We then use lengthpreserving homomorphisms to define grammatical similarity and discuss some striking results from the fast growing area of grammar forms and L forms.

1. Introduction

Homomorphisms have been a basic tool in language theory for a long time. Typical well-known results involving homomorphisms are the following.

R_1: The class $\mathcal{L}_{RE}$ of recursively enumerable languages can be obtained by applying homomorphisms to the languages of $\mathcal{L}_{CS}$, the class of context-sensitive languages.

R_2: Each language $L \in \mathcal{L}_{RE}$ can be written as $L = h(L_1 \cap L_2)$ where L_1 and L_2 are two languages of $\mathcal{L}_{CF}$, the class of context-free languages, and where h is a homomorphism.

R_3: (Chomsky-Schützenberger Theorem) Each language $L \in \mathcal{L}_{CF}$ can be written as $L=h(R\cap D)$, where R is a languages in $\mathcal{L}_{Reg}$, the class of regular languages, where D is a language in $\mathcal{L}_{D}$, the class of Dyck languages, and where h is a homomorphism.

R_4: (Greibach's hardest language theorem) There exists a certain (explicitly specifiable) context-free language $\hat{L}$ such that for every L in $\mathcal{L}_{CF}$ and some homomorphism h, $L = h^{-1}(\hat{L})$ holds. (Here h^{-1} denotes the inverse of homomorphism h, as usual).

In addition to results such as the above, two of the major developments in language theory in the last ten years can also be considered as based on homomorphisms.

The first major area is the theory of parallel rewriting, in particular the theory of L systems as initiated in [L]. The second is the theory of grammatical similarity, in particular the theory of grammar forms and L forms as initiated in [CG], [N] and [MSW1].

In this paper, we will not try to survey the theory of L systems. (We refer the interested reader to the introductory book [HR], the monograph [SS], the survey paper [RS1] or the forthcoming book [RS2]). We will just mention one of the most important problems of L systems theory which has recently been resolved in [CF]. The solution of this problem of deciding the equivalence of DOL system, has led to the notions of homomorphism equivalence and equality sets. These notions yield, among other things, powerful representation theorems somewhat analogous to the results R_3 and R_4.

Concerning the theory of grammar forms and L forms, we report on a number of striking results obtained in one particular area of that theory. Space and time constraints do not allow us to cover other equally important aspects of grammatical similarity. (We refer the interest reader to the references quoted in the sequel, to the recent bibliography [W2], to the survey [G] of a rather different aspect of grammar form theory, and to the forthcoming monography [W]).

Throughout this paper we assume familiarity with the basics of language theory. For the notions not explicitly defined and for further details the books [S], [M] of [H] may be consulted.

2. Homomorphic definition of language families

One of the most basic notions of L systems theory is the notion of a DOL system.

A DOL system G consists of an alphabet Σ, a homomorphism $h: \Sigma^* \to \Sigma^*$ and a word $w \in \Sigma^+$ designated as axiom, $G = (\Sigma, h, w)$. A DOL system G defines a DOL sequence E(G) and a DOL language L(G) by $E(G) = w, h(w), h^2(w), h^3(w), \ldots$ and $L(G) = \{h^{(i)}(w) \mid i \geq 0\}$.

The DOL equivalence problem is the problem of deciding of any two given DOL systems G and H whether or not $E(G) = E(H)$.

For quite a long time the decidability of the DOL equivalence problem was open and was considered one of the most important unresolved problems of L systems theory. The problem was finally shown decidable in [C] and [CF]. (That the problem is equivalent to deciding $L(G) = L(H)$ was already shown in [N2]; that the problem is decidable for DOL systems with "polynomially bounded length sequences" was demonstrated in [K]). A simpler proof of the decidability of the DOL equivalence problem was later given in [ER] and an extension to the ultimate equivalence problem for DOL systems in [C2]. An excellent account of the ideas involved in the proof of the sequence equivalence problem is given in [S2] and will not be repeated here. However, it is important to note that the solution of the DOL equivalence problem has suggested (see [S2]) a systematic study of the new notions of homomorphism equivalence and equality set.

The notion of homomorphism equivalence was first introduced in [CS]: let L be a language over some alphabet Σ and let h_1, h_2 be homomorphisms on Σ^*. Then h_1, h_2 are homomorphism equivalent on L if for all $x \in L$, $h_1(x) = h_2(x)$.

The homomorphism equivalence problem for a language family $\mathcal{L}$ is the problem of deciding for arbitrary L in $\mathcal{L}$ and arbitrary homomorphisms h_1 and h_2 whether or not h_1 and h_2 are equivalent on L.

It is important to note that the homomorphism equivalence problem for a language family $\mathcal{L}$ is quite different from the problem of deciding for arbitrary L in $\mathcal{L}$ and homomorphisms h_1 and h_2 whether or not $h_1(L) = h_2(L)$ holds. (If h_1 and h_2 are homomorphism equivalent on L, then we have $h_1(L) = h_2(L)$. The converse is not true, in general: homomorphism equivalence requires more than equivalence of the whole language, it requires equivalence on each word of the language individually.)

Whether homomorphism equivalence is decidable for $\mathcal{L}_{DOL}$ (the family of DOL languages) is still open. (In [CS] that problem is shown to be equivalent to the sequence equivalence problem for HDOL systems: an HDOL system $\hat{G}$ is a DOL system $G = (\Sigma, w, h)$ together with a further homomorphism $h_1: \Sigma^* \to \Sigma_1^*$. The sequence $E(\hat{G})$ generated by $\hat{G}$ is defined by $h_1(w)$, $h_1(h(w))$, $h_1(h^2(w))$, $h_1(h^3(w))$, ...).

However, it is established in [CS] that homomorphism equivalence is decidable for every "smooth" family of languages ("smoothness" is already defined in [C]) and is also decidable for $\mathcal{L}_{CF}$, despite the fact that $\mathcal{L}_{CF}$ is not a "smooth" family.

This last result is particularly interesting since for arbitrary L in $\mathcal{L}_{CF}$ and arbitrary homomorphisms h_1 and h_2 the validity of $h_1(L) = h_2(L)$ can be shown to be undecidable.

The notion of equality set explicitly appears first in [S3] but is already implicitly present in [C]: Let h_1, h_2 be homomorphisms mapping words over some alphabet Σ into words over some alphabet Δ. The <u>equality set of h_1, h_2,</u> in symbols $E(h_1, h_2)$, is defined by $E(h_1, h_2) = \{w \in \Sigma^* \mid h_1(w) = h_2(w)\}$.

Consider two n-tuples of words $(x_1, x_2, \ldots, x_n)$ and $(y_1, y_2, \ldots, y_n)$ over some alphabet Δ. Consider, further, an alphabet Σ consisting of n symbols, $\Sigma = \{1,2,\ldots,n\}$, and define $h_1(i) = x_i$, $h_2(i) = y_i$. Then $E(h_1, h_2)$ is the set of solutions of the instance $(x_1, x_2, \ldots, x_n)$, $(y_1, y_2, \ldots, y_n)$ of the Post correspondence problem.

While the undecidability of the Post correspondence problem (and thus the infinity problem of equality sets) has been a basic tool for proving problems in language theory undecidable, it was only suggested by the solution of the DOL equivalence problem to study equality sets in their own right.

As one of the main results in [S3] the following result R_5 was established.

R_5: For every L in $\mathcal{L}_{RE}$ one can find homomorphisms h_1 and h_2 and a deterministic gsm mapping g such that $L = g(E(h_1,h_2))$.

In the sequal, a number of additional results concerning the representation of $\mathcal{L}_{RE}$ have been obtained, extending or strengthening R_5.

In [C3] minimal equality sets have been introduced as important modification of modification of equality sets: let h_1, h_2 be homomorphisms mapping words over some alphabet Σ into words over some alphabet Δ. The <u>minimal equality set of h_1, h_2,</u> in symbols $e(h_1, h_2)$, is defined by $e(h_1, h_2) = \{w \in \Sigma^+ \mid h_1(w) = h_2(w)$ and for every nonempty proper prefix u of w, $h_1(u) \neq h_2(u)\}$.

Based on the notion of minimal equality set the following representation theorem R_6 for $\mathcal{L}_{RE}$ is obtained in [C3]:

R_6: For each L in $\mathcal{L}_{RE}$ one can effectively find homomorphisms h_0, h_1 and h_2 such that $L = h_0(e(h_1,h_2))$.

It is indeed shown that the alphabets involved need not depend on L but just on the alphabet of L, and that h_0 can be chosen to be an erasing, i.e. a homomorphism mapping each symbol either into itsself or into ε. It is also shown in [C3] that $\mathcal{L}_{Reg}$ can be similarly characterized by imposing natural restrictions on the homomorphisms h_1 and h_2 involved.

In [ER2] a somewhat different approach is taken to obtain an elegant representation theorem for $\mathcal{L}_{RE}$ analogous to R_3: Let α be some (possibly partial) mapping, $\alpha: \Sigma^* \to \Delta^*$. The fixed point language of α is the set $\{x \in \Sigma^* \mid x = \alpha(x)\}$. It is established in [ER2] that each L in $\mathcal{L}_{RE}$ can be obtained by an erasing from the fixed point language of a deterministic gsm mapping. It is then shown that each such fixed point language can be obtained by an erasing from the intersection of a so-called twin shuffle T_Σ and a regular set: let Σ be an alphabet and $\overline{\Sigma} = \{\overline{a} \mid a \in \Sigma\}$ be a "barred version" of Σ; the twin shuffle T_Σ is defined by $T_\Sigma = \{x \in (\Sigma \cup \overline{\Sigma})^* \mid x = x_1 \overline{y_1}\, x_2 \overline{y_2} \ldots x_n \overline{y_n},\ x_i \in \Sigma^*, \overline{y_i} \in \overline{\Sigma}^*,\ x_1 x_2 \ldots x_n = y_1 \ldots y_n\}$.

Based on above two results R_7 is obtained in [ER2]:

R_7: For each L in $\mathcal{L}_{RE}$ one can effectively find an erasing h, a twin shuffle T_Σ and a regular set R such that $L = h(T_\Sigma \cap R)$.

The result R_7 is particularly insteresting since twin shuffles appear to be "simple" and certainly easily specifyable languages. According to the proof of R_7 in [ER2], the alphabet Σ of the twin shuffle T_Σ depends on L (i.e. on how L is generated). That Σ can be made to depend only on the alphabet of L is e.g. shown, extending methods used for proving R_6, in [CM]. It is also shown in [CM] that a result analogous to R_7 not only holds for $\mathcal{L}_{RE}$ but indeed for every full principal AFL:

R_8: Let $\mathcal{L}$ be a full principal AFL. There exists a language $L_\Sigma \in \mathcal{L}$ such that for each $L \in \mathcal{L}$, L over some alphabet $T \subseteq \Sigma$, there exists an erasing h and a regular set R such that $L = h(L_\Sigma \cap R)$.

Also in [CM], a result analogous to Greibach's hardest language theorem R_4 is obtained for both $\mathcal{L}_{CS}$ and $\mathcal{L}_{RE}$, yielding the probably "simplest" representation theorems possible for these language classes:

R_9: There exists a language $U \subseteq \{0,1\}^*$ in $\mathcal{L}_{RE}$ (in $\mathcal{L}_{CS}$, respectively) such that every L in $\mathcal{L}_{RE}$ (in $\mathcal{L}_{CS}$, respectively) can be written as $L = h_2^{-1}(U)$ for some suitable homomorphisms h_L.

The results R_4 and R_9 show that each of $\mathcal{L}_{RE}$, $\mathcal{L}_{CS}$ and $\mathcal{L}_{CF}$ can be obtained as inverse homomorphic images of some universal language. This is not true for $\mathcal{L}_{Reg}$. Indeed, even a combination of homomorphism and inverse homomorphism is not sufficient as is readily seen (cf. [CM]):

R_{10}: For every regular R there exists a regular R' such that $R' \neq g(h^{-1}(R))$ for all homomorphisms g and h.

3. Homomorphisms and grammatical similarity

In language theory it is often costumary to specify the homomorphism h in a DOL system $G = (\Sigma,h,w)$ explicitly by means of a finite set of productions P, $P = \{a \to h(a) \mid a \in \Sigma\}$.

This terminology is closer to the terminology of grammars and rewriting systems. We write $x \Rightarrow y$ (and say x directly derives y) iff $y = h(x)$, or equivalently, following the traditional grammar-like definition, iff: $x = a_1a_2 \ldots a_n$, $y = y_1y_2 \ldots y_n$ $(a_i \in \Sigma,\ y_i \in \Sigma^*)$ and $a_i \to y_i \in P$ for all i. Defining $\overset{*}{\Rightarrow}$ as usual, we may write $L(G) = \{x \mid w \overset{*}{\Rightarrow} x\}$. In this way, we interpret a DOL system G as a parallel rewriting system without nonterminals, henceforth. We will further write $G = (\Sigma,P,w)$, instead of $G = (\Sigma,h,w)$, where P is the set of productions as explained above. We will always assume that G is reduced in the sense that every symbol of Σ is reachable from w.

Somewhat analogous to [N], we call two DOL systems G_1 and G_2 similar if there is a "master" DOL system G such that both G_1 and G_2 can be mapped onto G by using codings, i.e. letter-to-letter homomorphisms.

More precisely, let $G_1 = (\Sigma_1,P_1,w_1)$ and $G_2 = (\Sigma_2,P_2,w_2)$ be DOL systems, G_1 and G_2 are similar iff:
$\Sigma = f_1(\Sigma_1) = f_2(\Sigma_2)$, $w = f_1(w_1) = f_2(w_2)$ and $P = \{f_1(a) \to f_1(x) \mid a \to x \in P_1\} = \{f_2(b) \to f_2(y) \mid b \to y \in P_2\}$ holds for some DOL system $G = (\Sigma,P,w)$ and some codings f_1 and f_2.

A DOL system $G_1 = (\Sigma_1,P_1,w_1)$ is an interpretation of a DOL system $G = (\Sigma,P,w)$ iff for some coding f we have: $\Sigma = f(\Sigma_1)$, $w = f(w_1)$ and $P = \{f(a) \to f(x) \mid a \to x \in P_1\}$.

Thus, G_1 and G_2 are similar iff they are interpretations of one DOL system G, such G then usually called DOL form to emphasize its role as "master" DOL system.

Instead of defining G_1 as interpretation of G by means of "reducing" G_1 to G by applying a coding, it is more costumary in the literature to "obtain" G_1 from G by using a dfl-substitution, such a dfl-substitution being the mathematical inverse of a coding. (Thus, a dfl - substitution maps symbols into sets of symbols and different symbols into disjoint sets).

We thus can reword the definition of interpretation as follows:

A DOL form is a DOL system $G = (\Sigma,P,w)$. A DOL system $G' = (\Sigma',P',w')$ is an interpretation of G modulo μ, in symbols $G' \lhd G(\mu)$, iff μ is a dfl substitution defined on Σ such that

(i) $\Sigma' = \mu(\Sigma)$,
(ii) $w' \varepsilon \mu(w)$,
(iii) $P' \subseteq \{b \to y \mid b \varepsilon \mu(a),\ y \varepsilon \mu(x),\ a \to x \varepsilon P\}$.

The family of DOL systems defined by G is denoted by $\mathcal{G}(G)$ and defined by $\mathcal{G}(G) = \{G' \mid G' \triangleleft G(\mu)\}$. The family of languages defined by G is denoted by $\mathcal{L}(G)$ and defined by $\mathcal{L}(G) = \{L(G') \mid G' \varepsilon \mathcal{G}(G)\}$.

We believe that above definition of $\mathcal{G}(G)$ is a meaningful definition of the notion of a family of structurally related DOL systems. For a more detailed discussion of this matter we refer to [MSW1].

It is easy to see that the validity of $\mathcal{G}(G_1) = \mathcal{G}(G_2)$ is decidable for arbitrary DOL systems G_1 and G_2, and that $G_1 \triangleleft G_2$ implies $\mathcal{L}(G_1) \subseteq \mathcal{L}(G_2)$. This suggests to consider the question of form equivalence of DOL systems G_1 and G_2, i.e. to consider whether $\mathcal{L}(G_1) = \mathcal{L}(G_2)$ holds. Language equivalence (i.e. $L(G_1) = L(G_2)$) does not imply form equivalence ($\mathcal{L}(G_1) = \mathcal{L}(G_2)$), nor conversely. It is still unknown whether form equivalence is decidable for arbitrary DOL systems. That form equivalence is decidable for arbitrary PDOL systems (propagating DOL systems, i.e. DOL systems without productions of the type $a \to \varepsilon$) is established by a sequence of complex theorems in [MOS] and [CMORS].

We conclude this discussion by listing the productions of two pairs (F_1,F_2) and (G_1,G_2) of PDOL forms with axiom ab such that $L(F_1) = L(F_2)$, $\mathcal{L}(F_1) \neq \mathcal{L}(F_2)$ and $L(G_1) = L(G_2)$, $\mathcal{L}(G_1), = \mathcal{L}(G_2)$.

F_1: $a \to aba$, $b \to bab$;
F_2: $a \to ab$, $b \to abab$;
G_1: $a \to cdc$, $b \to dcd$, $c \to cd$, $d \to ddc$;
G_2: $a \to cd$, $b \to cdcd$, $c \to cd$, $d \to ddc$.

It should be instructive to the reader to try to see why $\mathcal{L}(F_1) \neq \mathcal{L}(F_2)$ holds.

We now turn our attention to the question of similarity of context-free grammars (just called grammars in the sequel). A grammar form G is a grammar $G = (V,\Sigma,P,S)$; V is the total alphabet, $\Sigma \subseteq V$ is the set of terminals, $P \subseteq (V-\Sigma) \times V^*$ the finite set of productions, and $S \varepsilon V - \Sigma$ the startsymbol.

A grammar $G' = (V',\Sigma',P',S')$ is an s-interpretation of a grammar form $G = (V,\Sigma,P,S)$ modulo μ, in symbols $G' \triangleleft_s G(\mu)$ iff μ is a dfl substitution defined on V such that (i) - (iv) hold:

(i) $V' - \Sigma' \subseteq \mu(V - \Sigma)$

(ii) $\Sigma' \subseteq \mu(\Sigma)$

(iii) $S' \in \mu(S)$

(iv) $P' \subseteq \mu(P)$, $\mu(P) = \{B \to y \mid A \to x \in P,\ B \in \mu(A),\ y \in \mu(x)\}$.

In analogy to DOL forms we define the family of grammars $\mathcal{G}_s(G)$ and family of languages $\mathcal{L}_s(G)$ generated by G, and talk about s-form equivalent grammar forms G_1 and G_2 provided $\mathcal{L}_s(G_1) = \mathcal{L}_s(G_2)$ holds.

Our definition of s-interpretation differs from the one introduced in the pioneering paper [CG] which we like to call g-interpretation significantly: in a g-interpretation, μ is a dfl substitution on $V - \Sigma$ only, and is an arbitrary substitution on Σ, with condition (ii) replaced by: $\mu(\Sigma)$ is a finite subset of Σ'^*.

We denote the grammar and language families corresponding to g-interpretation by $\mathcal{G}_g(G)$ and $\mathcal{L}_g(G)$. It is shown in [MSW2] that for every G generating an infinite language there exists a $\hat{G}$ such that $\mathcal{L}_g(G) = \mathcal{L}_s(\hat{G})$, but not conversely, and that for any two "nontrivial" grammars G_1, G_2 with $\mathcal{L}_g(G_1) \subsetneq \mathcal{L}_g(G_2)$ there are infinitly many language families $\mathcal{L}_s(G)$ such that $\mathcal{L}_s(G)$ is strictly between $\mathcal{L}_g(G_1)$ and $\mathcal{L}_g(G_2)$. Thus, the structure of language families is considerably richer under s-interpreatations. In what follows we will only be concerned with s-interpretations and for convenience we will drop the letter s in the term s-interpretation, and in the notations $\triangleleft_s$, $\mathcal{G}_s$ and $\mathcal{L}_s$.

One of the most important notions of form theory is the notion of completeness introduced in [MSW1]:

Let $\mathcal{L}$ be a family of languages. A (grammar) form G is called $\mathcal{L}$-complete iff $\mathcal{L}(G) = \mathcal{L}$.

Consider the following grammar forms $G_1 - G_8$ specified by their respective production sets:

G_1: $S \to SS$, $S \to a$.

G_2: $S \to aS$, $S \to aSS$, $S \to a$.

G_3: $S \to aSaSa$, $S \to a^i$ $\quad (i = 1,2,3,4)$

G_4: $S \to aS$, $S \to a$.

G_5: $S \to aSa$, $S \to a$.

G_6: $S \to aS$, $S \to Sa$, $S \to a$.

G_7: $S \to A$, $S \to B$, $A \to AA$, $A \to a^2$, $B \to aB$, $B \to a$.

G_8: $S \to aA$, $S \to A$, $S \to a$, $A \to AA$, $A \to a^2$.

G_1 is $\mathcal{L}_{CF}$ complete by the Chomsky normal form theorem. (Here and in the sequel, languages and language families are considered equal up to ε). G_2 is $\mathcal{L}_{CF}$ complete by the Greibach normal form theorem. Thus, normal form theorems for a language family $\mathcal{L}$ usually lead to completeness results. And any form shown to be $\mathcal{L}$-complete defines a normal form for the family $\mathcal{L}$. The study of completeness is thus a systematic study of normal forms. The results below seem to indicate that this point of view is contributing significantly to our understanding of generative processes.

That G_3 is also $\mathcal{L}_{CF}$ complete is a consequence of R_{11} below. G_4 is clearly $\mathcal{L}_{Reg}$ complete, G_6 can be seen to be $\mathcal{L}_{Lin}$ complete ($\mathcal{L}_{Lin}$ being the class of linear languages). However, G_5 is <u>not</u> $\mathcal{L}_{Lin}$ complete. G_7 is <u>not</u> $\mathcal{L}_{CF}$ complete by [MSW3], but G_8 is.

In [MSW4] the following "supernormal form result" (combining and generalizing Chomsky - and Greibach normal form) is obtained:

R_{11}: If $G = (\{S, a\}, \{a\}, P, S)$ is a grammar form such that
(i) $S \overset{*}{\Rightarrow} a^i$ for all $i \geq 1$, and
(ii) for some production $S \rightarrow x$ of P the right side x contains at least two S,
then G is $\mathcal{L}_{CF}$ complete.

In [MSW2] and [MSW3] the theory of complete grammar forms is systematically developed. It is shown that for $\mathcal{L}_{Reg}$ and $\mathcal{L}_{Lin}$ completeness and exhaustive and easily decidable characterization can be given and that even $\mathcal{L}_{CF}$ completeness is decidable provided the following conjecture C_1 holds:

C_1: Let (k,l,m) be an arbitrary triple of nonnegative integers and L a context-free language. Then L can be generated by productions of the type $A \rightarrow x B y C z$ where A,B,C are nonterminals, x,y,z are terminal words with $|x| = k$, $|y| = l$, $|z| = m$, and by productions $A \rightarrow w$ where w is a terminal word of length equal to some word of L.

Note that except for the last condition on the length of w, C_1 directly follows from R_{11}.

The fact that $\mathcal{L}_{Reg}$, $\mathcal{L}_{Lin}$ and (if C_1 holds) also $\mathcal{L}_{CF}$ completeness is decidable is surprising in as much, as the form equivalence problem for grammar forms is not known to be decidable (indeed we believe it <u>is</u> not; the form equivalence problem for g-interpretations is decidable by [G]). On the other hand, e.g. the $\mathcal{L}_{Lin}$ completeness of G_6 above and the decidability of $\mathcal{L}_{Lin}$ completeness implies that for arbitrary grammar forms G the validity of $\mathcal{L}(G_6) = \mathcal{L}(G)$ is decidable!

Another important notion of form theory is the question of reducibility: given an arbitrary form G find a "simpler" form F which is form equivalent.

Some of the usual constructions leading to normal forms give rise to reducibility results, others - somewhat surprisingly - do not. We mention two such "opposite" results proven in [MSW2]:

R_{12}: For every grammar form G there exists a form equivalent grammar form $F = (V,\Sigma,P,S)$ with $P \subseteq (V-\Sigma) \times ((V-\Sigma)^2 \cup \Sigma^*)$. There exists a grammar form G such that no grammar form $F = (V,\Sigma,P,S)$ with $P \subseteq (V-\Sigma) \times (\Sigma(V-\Sigma)^2\Sigma \cup \Sigma^*)$ is formequivalent to G.

The second half of R_{12} is in interesting contrast to R_{11}: although we can construct a grammar $F = (V,\Sigma,P,S)$ with $P \subseteq (V-\Sigma) \times (\Sigma(V-\Sigma)^2\Sigma \cup \Sigma^*)$ with $L(F) = L(G)$ for every G by R_{11}, $\mathcal{L}(F) \neq \mathcal{L}(G)$ by R_{12}.

We conclude this paper by mentioning some results on EOL forms, as introduced in [MSW1] and investigated in a number of papers since, cf. [W2].

An EOL form G is an EOL system $G = (V,\Sigma,P,S)$. V,Σ and S are as for context-free grammars. P is a finite subset of $V \times V^*$ with a production for every symbol $\alpha \in V$ (i.e. including terminals). In contrast to grammars, derivations in EOL systems proceed in parallel as in DOL systems.

All notions concerning grammar forms are carried over to EOL forms in the obvious manner. In particular, for some EOL system (form) G we may speak of its interpretations, we may consider $\mathcal{G}(G)$ and $\mathcal{L}(G)$ and discuss completeness and reducibility results.

Since EOL systems are more powerful generative devices than grammars, a systematic treatment of completeness is less developed than in the case of grammars.

For example, although the EOL form F_1 with productions F_1: $S \to aS$, $S \to a$, $a \to a$ is known to be $\mathcal{L}_{Reg}$ complete, we do not yet have a characterization of all $\mathcal{L}_{Reg}$ complete EOL forms. We do know by [AM] that no $\mathcal{L}_{CF}$ complete EOL form exists. (This very fact has been one of the main reasons for studing interpretation machanisms under which $\mathcal{L}_{CF}$ is obtainable, as e.g. under uniform interpretations introduced in [MSW5] and further investigated e.g. in [MSW6] and [AMR]). $\mathcal{L}_{EOL}$ completeness ($\mathcal{L}_{EOL}$ being the class of all EOL languages) has been investigated must thoroughly starting in [MSW1] and continuing in [CM2] and [CMO].

$F_2 - F_5$ are a number of examples of complete EOL forms.

F_2: $S \to a$, $S \to S$, $a \to S$, $S \to SS$;
F_3: $S \to a$, $S \to S$, $a \to S$, $S \to aS$;
F_4: $S \to a$, $S \to S$, $S \to SS$, $a \to a$, $S \to Sa$, $a \to SS$;
F_5: $S \to a$, $a \to S$, $a \to a$, $S \to SS$;
F_6: $S \to a$, $a \to S$, $a \to aa$, $a \to aS$, $S \to aS$, $S \to aa$.

The completeness of $F_2 - F_4$ is comparatively easy to establish based on results in [MSW1]. The proof of the completeness of F_5 requires the proof of a strong normal form theorem for EOL languages in [CM2] (establishing that every EOL language can be generated by an EOL system all of whose derivation trees are strictly increasing from level to level); to show the completeness of F_6 requires the above mentioned normal form result and tricky "simulation" arguments.

A characterization of all $\mathcal{L}_{EOL}$ complete EOL forms even of those involving just one nonterminal S and one terminal a is still missing.

Reducibility results for EOL forms are particularly intriguing, since many constructions converting some EOL system G into a simpler EOL system F retaining language equivalence $L(G) = L(F)$ do not result in form equivalent systems.

Some reducibility results which do carry over from language equivalence are already obtained in [MSW1] and summarized in R_{13}. A number of "antireducibility" results are listed in R_{14}, some of them having been obtained quite recently.

R_{13}: For every EOL form G a form equivalent EOL form $F = (V,\Sigma,P,S)$ with $P \subseteq V \times (\{\varepsilon\} \cup V \cup V^2)$ can be obtained. For every synchronized EOL form G a form equivalent EOL form $F = (V,\Sigma,P,S)$ with $P \subseteq (V-\Sigma) \times (V \cup (V-\Sigma)^2) \cup \Sigma \times (V-\Sigma)$ can be obtained.

R_{14}: (i) There exists an EOL form G such that no synchronized EOL form F is form equivalent to G.

(ii) There exists an EOL form G such that no propagating EOL form F is form equivalent to G.

(iii) There exists an interpretation G' of G: $S \to aS$, $S \to S$, $a \to a$ such that no interpretation F' of F: $S \to Sa$, $S \to S$, $a \to a$ is form equivalent to G.

(iv) There exists an EOL form G such that no EOL form $F = (V,\Sigma,P,S)$ containing no production $A \to \varepsilon$ with $A \in V - \Sigma$ is form equivalent to G.

Of the statements in R_{14}, (i) is already shown in [MSW1]; (ii) is proven in [MSW7]. The surprising result (iii), that left- and right linear productions do not behave alike if considered part of an EOL form, is shown in [MSW8]; (iv) is proven in [AM2].

Result (iv) states that ε-productions for nonterminals are more powerful than ε-productions for terminals in EOL forms: it is shown in [MSW7] that for every EOL form G a form equivalent F which is interpretation of the form with productions: $S \to S$, $S \to SS$, $S \to a$, $S \to \varepsilon$, $a \to S$ exists. By (iv), no such result is possible if $S \to \varepsilon$ is replaced by $a \to \varepsilon$, even if other productions are added.

References

[AM] Albert,J., Maurer,H.: The class of context-free languages is not an EOL family; Information Processing Letters 6 (1977), 190 - 195.

[AM2] Ainhirn,W., Maurer,H.: On ε-productions in EOL forms; IIG-Technical University of Graz, Manuscript (1978).

[AMR] Albert,J., Maurer,H., Rozenberg,G.: Simple EOL forms under uniform interpretation generating CF languages; Fundamenta Informatica (to appear).

[C] Culik II,K.: On the decidability of the sequence equivalence problem for DOL systems; Theoretical Computer Science 3 (1977), 75 - 84.

[C2] Culik II,K.: The ultimate equivalence problem for DOL systems; Acta Informatica 10 (1978), 79 - 84.

[C3] Culik II, K.: A purely homomorphic characterization of recursively enumerable sets; Journal of the ACM (to appear).

[CF] Culik II,K., Fris,I.: The decidability of the equivalence problem for DOL systems; Information and Control 35 (1977), 20 - 39.

[CG] Cremers,A.B., Ginsburg,S.: Context-free grammar forms; Journal of Computer and Systems Sciences 11 (1975), 86 - 119.

[CM] Culik II,K., Maurer,H.: On simple representations of language families; University of Waterloo Report CS-78-41 (1978).

[CM2] Culik II,K., Maurer,H.: Propagating chain-free normal forms for EOL systems; Information and Control 36 (1978), 309 - 319.

[CMO] Culik II,K., Maurer,H., Ottmann,Th.: On two symbol complete EOL forms; Theoretical Computer Science 6 (1978), 69 - 92.

[CMORS] Culik II,K., Maurer,H., Ottmann,Th., Ruohonen,K., Salomaa,A.: Isomorphism, form equivalence and sequence equivalence of PDOL forms; Theoretical Computer Science 6 (1978), 143 - 173.

[CS] Culik II,K., Salomaa,A.: On the decidability of homomorphism equivalence for languages; University of Waterloo Report CS-77-26 (1977).

[ER] Ehrenfeucht,A., Rozenberg,G.: Elementary homomorphisms and a solution of the DOL sequence equivalence problem; Theoretical Computer Science 7 (1978), 169 - 183.

[ER2] Engelfriet,J., Rozenberg,G.: Fixed point languages, equality languages and representations of recursively enumberable languages; FOCS (1978), 123 - 126.

[G] Ginsburg,S.: A survey of grammar forms - 1977; Manuscript (1977).

[G] Ginsburg,S.: Private communication (1977).

[H] Harrison,M.: Introduction to formal language theory; Addison Wesley, Reading (1978).

[HR] Herman,G.I., Rozenberg,G.: Developmental systems and languages; North Holland, Amsterdam (1975).

[K] Karhumäki,J.: The decidability of the equivalence problem for polynomially bounded DOL sequences; RAIRO, Ser. Rouge 11 (1977), 17 - 28.

[L] Lindenmayer,A.: Mathematical Models for cellular interactions in development; Journal of Theoretical Biology 18 (1968), 280 - 315.

[M] Maurer,H.: Theoretische Grundlagen der Programmiersprachen - Theorie der Syntax; BI, Mannheim (1969).

[MOS] Maurer,H., Ottmann,Th., Salomaa,A.: On the form equivalence of L forms; Theoretical Computer Science 4 (1977), 199 - 225.

[MSW1] Maurer,H., Salomaa,A., Wood,D.: EOL forms; Acta Informatica 8 (1977), 75 - 96.

[MSW2] Maurer,H., Salomaa,A., Wood,D.: Context-free grammar forms with strict interpretations; IIG-Technical University of Graz, Report 19 (1978).

[MSW3] Maurer,H., Salomaa,A., Wood,D.: Strict context-free grammar forms: completeness and decidability; IIG-Technical University of Graz, Report 20 (1978).

[MSW4] Maurer,H., Salomaa,A., Wood,D.: On generators and generative capacity of EOL forms; IIG-Technical University of Graz, Report 5 (1978).

[MSW5] Maurer,H., Salomaa,A., Wood,D.: Uniform interpretations of L forms; Information and Control 36 (1978), 157 - 173.

[MSW6] Maurer,H., Salomaa,A., Wood,D.: Synchronized EOL forms under uniform interpretation; McMaster University Report 78-CS-11 (1978).

[MSW7] Maurer,H., Salomaa,A., Wood,D.: On good EOL forms; SIAM Journal on Computing 7 (1978), 158 - 166.

[MSW8] Maurer,H., Salomaa,A., Wood,D.: Relative goodness of EOL forms; RAIRO, series rouge (to appear).

[N] Nivat,M.: Extensions et restrictions des grammaires algebriques; In: Formal Languages and Programming (ed.R.Aguilar) North Holland, Amsterdam (1976) 83 - 96.

[N2] Nielsen,M.: On the decidability of some equivalence probelems for DOL systems; Information and Control 25 (1974), 166 - 193.

[R] Rozenberg,G.: L systems, sequences and languages; Lecture Notes in Computer Science 34 (1975), 71 - 84

[RS1] Rozenberg,G., Salomaa,A.: The mathematical theory of L systems; In: Advances in Information Systems Sciences (J.Tou, Ed.) 6 (1976), 160 - 200.

[RS2] Rozenberg,G., Salomaa,A.: The mathematical theory of L systems; forthcoming.

[S] Salomaa,A.: Formal languages; Academic Press (1973).

[S2] Salomaa,A.: DOL equivalence: the problem of iterated morphisms; EATCS Bulletin 4 (1978), 5 - 12.

[S3] Salomaa,A.: Equality sets for homomorphisms of free monoids; Acta Cybernetica (to appear).

[SS] Salomaa,A., Soittola,M.: Automata theoretic aspects of formal power series; Springer Verlag (1978).

[W] Wood,D.: Grammar and L forms (in preparation).

[W2] Wood,D.: Bibliography of grammatical similarity; EATCS Bulletin 5 (1978), 15 - 22.

CAN PARTIAL CORRECTNESS ASSERTIONS SPECIFY PROGRAMMING LANGUAGE SEMANTICS?

Irene Greif

Albert R. Meyer*

The thesis that a programming language semantics could be specified by giving all the "before-after" assertions true of programs has been espoused by Dijkstra [1975, 1976]. An effort by Hoare and Wirth [1973] to specify the semantics of a fragment of PASCAL using partial correctness assertions supports the practical applicability of this thesis. Our desire to investigate this general thesis motivates our definition and analysis of <u>partial correctness semantics</u> of programming languages.

With each program, $\underline{a}$, or more precisely with each possible <u>relational semantics</u> which might be assigned to $\underline{a}$, we consider the set $PC(\underline{a})$ of partial correctness assertions true for $\underline{a}$. Conversely, given any set $\mathscr{P}$ of partial correctness assertions about $\underline{a}$, we let $\max(\mathscr{P})$ be the largest input-output relation on program states which could be assigned to $\underline{a}$ and preserve the truth of all the assertions in $\mathscr{P}$.

It is easy to show that if $R_{\underline{a}}$ is the input-output relation assigned to $\underline{a}$, then $R_{\underline{a}} = \max(PC(\underline{a}))$. In other words, given the set of all true partial correctness assertions about a program, one can in fact exactly determine the input-output behavior of that program.

But suppose we add the sensible restriction that the predicates used in the partial correctness assertions be, not arbitrary predicates on program states, but only those expressible in some familiar formal notation - such as the first or second order statements in the language appropriate to program states?

Several situations can now arise, even for a very trivial class of <u>while</u>-programs, depending on the choice of expressible predicates. Let $\mathscr{E}$ be the set of true, <u>espressible</u>, partial correctness assertions about program $\underline{a}$ when $\underline{a}$ is assigned the input-output relation $R_{\underline{a}}$. Some possible situations are:

(i) $\max(\mathscr{E}) = R_{\underline{a}}$, but no "effective" subset $\mathscr{E}'$ of $\mathscr{E}$ suffices to determine R_a in this way;

(ii) $\max(\mathscr{E}') = R_a$ for some "effective" subset $\mathscr{E}'$ of $\mathscr{E}$;

(iii) $\max(\mathscr{E}) \neq R_a$, but there is another natural sense in which $\mathscr{E}$ uniquely determines the behavior of the program $\underline{a}$;

(iv) $\mathscr{E}$ does not determine the behavior of the program in any straightforward way;

*The second author is on partial leave at Harvard University for the academic year 1978-1979. This research was supported in part by NSF Grants MCS 77-19754 A03 and MCS 78-17698 and Advanced Research Projects Agency Contract N00014-75-C-0661.

We present examples illustrating each of these possibilities.

We conclude, as might be expected, that the possibility of understanding a program from assertions made about it depends critically on the class of notations allowed for expressing assertions.

Dijkstra, E.W.D. 1975. Guarded Commands, Non-determinacy and Formal Derivation of Programs. CACM 18, 8. pp 453-457.

Dijkstra, E.W.D. 1976. *A Discipline of Programming*, Prentice-Hall, Englewood Cliffs, N.J., 217 pp.

Greif, I. and Meyer, A.R. Specifying Programming Language Semantics: A Tutorial and Critique of a Paper by Hoare and Lauer, December, 1978, submitted for publication.

Hoare, C.A.R. and Wirth, N. 1973. An Axiomatic Definition of the Programming Language PASCAL. *Acta Informatica 2*, pp 335-355.

Schwartz, J.S. 1974. Semantics of Partial Correctness Formalisms. Ph.D. Thesis, Syracuse University. Syracuse, N.Y. 126pp.

Cambridge, U.S.A. Dec. 11, 1978.

AN ALGEBRAIC THEORY FOR SYNCHRONIZATION

R. Milner

1. Introduction

The purpose of this short paper is to present, in condensed form but with intuitive motivation, an algebraic approach to the theory of communicating systems. The broad aim of the approach is to be able to write and manipulate expressions which not only denote - under some choice of interpretation - the behaviour of composite communicating systems, but also may reveal in their form the physical structure of such systems. This goal has been achieved to some extent in sequential programming; an applicative (i.e. non-imperative) program not only reflects in its form the structures by which it may be implemented, but also denotes a mathematic function - i.e. the intended behaviour of the program. Landin [2] was one of the first to explore this type of programming, and the recent work of Backus [1] is a further step in the same direction. In pursuing the same aim for parallel (concurrent, distributed) programming, we hope at the same time to achieve a calculus for describing hardware systems (at some level of abstraction) and also indeed non-computer systems.

The work described here is in strong contrast to the theory of concurrency developed in the Net Theory of Petri [9]. Petri takes the notion of concurrency as primitive, and derives from it an elegant thoery of processes. We tentatively regard this as an intensional study; this view would be justified if we could argue that concurrency is a property of systems which is certainly valuable to their analysis, but may not be directly observed. Much clarification is needed to support this view - if indeed it is valid - and we do not attempt it here. However, we believe that a theory which is more obviously extensional will play a useful role. To this end, we want to take something akin to observation as our central notion. More precisely, we take the meaning of a system to depend only upon what may occur when we communicate with it; further, the collaboration of separate components of a system is to be described in terms of their communication with each other.

Fuller expositions of our approach, and its technical formulation, can be found in other papers [5,6,7,8]. What follows is not fully formal; in particular, we purposely use the word 'process' in a way which sometimes refers to a physical agent, and sometimes to the behaviour of an agent. Even more, the notion of behaviour is not fully determined. We propose some algebraic laws which naturally induce a congruence among expressions (or among agents), but wish to leave open the possibility of further laws which will identify more expressions and so correspond to a more abstract notion of behaviour.

2. An algebra of processes

We imagine a process as a black box with a finite number of ports on its border, through which it may communicate with other black boxes, or with us as observers. It may be pictured in this way

with blobs standing for ports. But we wish to distinguish among the ports, to determine for each of them which ports of other processes may join in communication with it.

To this end, we introduce an infinite set $\Delta = \{\alpha,\beta,\gamma,\ldots\}$ of names, and a set $\bar{\Delta} = \{\bar{\alpha},\bar{\beta},\bar{\gamma},\ldots\}$ of conames, disjoint from Δ . $\Lambda = \Delta \cup \bar{\Delta}$ is the set of labels, and we use λ,μ to range over Δ . For $\alpha \in \Delta$, α and $\bar{\alpha}$ are complementary labels. The complement of λ is written $\bar{\lambda}$; thus $\bar{\bar{\alpha}} = \alpha$.

Further, any finite $L \subseteq \Lambda$ is called a sort. A process of sort L is one whose ports are labelled by the members of L ; for $L = \{\lambda_1,\lambda_2,\lambda_3\}$ it may be pictured

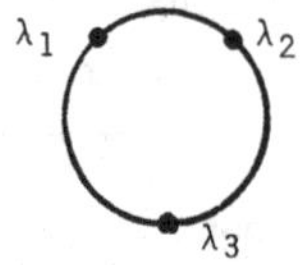

We denote by P_L the class of processes of sort L ; the family $\{P_L \mid L \text{ is a sort}\}$ is the carrier of our sorted process algebra. Now a process p of sort L is to be thought of as a collection of capabilities for communication. Each capability is associated with one of the ports, i.e. with a member λ of L, and specifies a renewal process p' which describes the possible future behaviour (i.e. future capabilities) which may follow a communication at the port labelled λ . We write this capability as

$$\lambda : p'$$

The sort L' of p' must be a subset of L, since the sort L of p specifies the labels by which p may communicate both immediately and at all future times. The notation we have adopted for a capability emphasizes that (in this presentation) a communication carries no values (e.g. integers) into or out of the process; a communication is merely the realization of two capabilities, one of form $\lambda : p'$ and another (in a different process q) of form $\bar{\lambda} : q'$, enabling them to proceed simultaneously to their renewals p' and q' .

A process p , then, is just the sum of its capabilities, and we may write it as

$$p = \sum_i \lambda_i : p_i$$

Now the class of all finite processes may be built by three operations in a many-sorted algebra of processes. The first operation is a nullary one

Nullity $\quad$ $NIL \in P_{\emptyset}$,

the process with no capabilities. Second is the binary operation

Ambiguity $\quad$ $+ \in P_L \times P_M \to P_{L \cup M}$;

$p + q$ has exactly the capabilities of p and of q.

Third, the unary operation (one for each λ)

Guarding $\quad$ $\lambda: \in P_L \to P_{L \cup \{\lambda\}}$

builds the single-capability process $\lambda:p$ from the process p .

We postulate the following laws

Laws (1) $\quad$ + is commutative and associative, with NIL as an identity. This, ignoring sorts, $(P; +, NIL)$ is an Abelian Monoid.

Under these laws only, P_L is isomorphic to the set ST_L of synchronization trees of sort L ; that is, ST_L is the set of finite, rooted, unordered trees whose arcs are labelled with members of L. Thus the process $\alpha:(\beta:NIL + \beta:\alpha:NIL) + \beta:NIL$ is represented by the tree

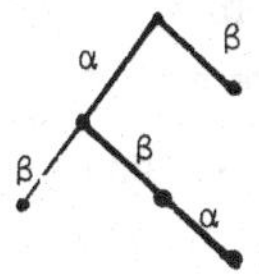

We do not postulate the distributivity $\lambda:(p+q) = \lambda:p + \lambda:q$, nor the idempotency $p + p = p$, though some useful interpretations of our algebraic theory may indeed satisfy additional laws such as these.

We now turn to the parallel composition of two processes $p \in P_L$ and $q \in Q_M$, i.e. the binary operation

Composition $\quad$ $| \in P_L \times P_M \to P_{L \cup M}$.

$p|q$ may be understood as follows: p and q are placed side by side, and allowed to communicate both with their joint environment and also (whenever they have complementary capabilities) with each other. Thus, for capabilities $\lambda:p'$ of p and $\mu:q'$ of q the composite has capabilities $\lambda:(p'|q)$ and $\mu:(p|q')$. But in the case that $\mu = \bar{\lambda}$ the composite has also a capability which we write

$$\tau : (p'|q')$$

which represents the possibility of communication of p with q. We assume that the special label τ is not a member of Λ , and that $\bar{\tau}$ is never used. But we allow the guarding operation

$$\tau : \in P_L \to P_L$$

and we allow $\lambda,\mu,\ldots$ to range over $\Lambda \cup \{\tau\}$. We may think of $\tau : p$ as representing a capability which requires no complementary capability for its realization.

The description of composition is embodied in the following

Laws(2)	Let $p = \sum_i \lambda_i : p_i$, $q = \sum_j \mu_j : q_j$. Then
$p|q = \sum_i \lambda_i : (p_i|q) + \sum_j \mu_j : (p|q_j) + \sum_{\mu_j = \bar{\lambda}_i} \tau : (p_i|q_j)$	

For finite processes we can deduce the following property of composition, but we state it as a law since we wish to postulate it for all interpretations of our algebraic theory:

Laws(3)	$(P \,;\, |, \text{NIL})$ is an Abelian Monoid

Indeed, there is considerable interest in interpretations which satisfy this law but not the previous one, since Laws(2) embodies the assumption that it is sufficient to represent independent communications by p and q as occurring interleaved in either order in the composite $p|q$. We believe that this assumption is justified for some purposes, though it certainly runs counter to the view that concurrency is a key fundamental notion - as exemplified by Petri's Net Theory. To adopt the assumption allows considerable algebraic power which we have not yet achieved without it.

Two further operations, with less important semantic content than the others, are needed for an expressive algebra of processes. The first is, for each name α , a postfixed operation

Restriction $\quad \backslash\alpha \in P_L \to P_{L - \{\alpha,\bar{\alpha}\}}$

The process $p\backslash\alpha$ is gained from p by removing all capabilities of the form $\alpha : p'$ or $\bar{\alpha} : p'$ both from p and from all its renewals (and renewals of renewals, etc). Clearly, in the tree representation of finite processes, it corresponds to removing all branches entered by an arc labelled α or $\bar{\alpha}$. An important use of restriction is combined with composition; for example if $p = \alpha : p'$ and $q = \bar{\alpha} : q'$, then

$$p|q = \alpha : (p'|q) + \bar{\alpha} : (p|q') + \tau : (p'|q'),$$

while

$$(p|q)\backslash\alpha = \tau : ((p'|q')\backslash\alpha) \ .$$

What has happened is that the ports α of p and $\bar{\alpha}$ of q have been restricted to communication between p and q .

Our last operation concerns relabelling of ports. We only permit, as relabelling, a bijection $S : L \to M$ such that if $\lambda, \bar{\lambda} \in L$ then $\overline{S(\lambda)} = S(\bar{\lambda})$; then we have the postfixed operation

Relabelling $\quad [S] \in P_L \to P_{S(L)}$

The process $p[S]$ is gained from p by replacing each $\lambda \in L$ by $S(\lambda)$ throughout its future. The effect on the trees representation of finite processes is obvious.

It remains to characterize the meaning of these operations by laws. The laws are mostly distributive ones:

<u>Laws(4)</u>

$$(p+q)[S] = p[S] + q[S] \; ; \; (p+q)\backslash\alpha = p\backslash\alpha + q\backslash\alpha \; ;$$

$$(\lambda : p)[S] = S(\lambda) : (p[S]) \; ;$$

$$(\lambda : p)\backslash\alpha = \begin{cases} \text{NIL} & \text{if } \lambda \in \{\alpha, \bar{\alpha}\} \\ \lambda : (p\backslash\alpha) & \text{otherwise} \end{cases} \; ;$$

<u>Laws(5)</u> (Assume $p \in P_L, q \in P_M$. [] stands for an identity relabelling)

$$(p|q)[S] = p[S\restriction L] \mid q[S\restriction M] \; ;$$

$$(p|q)\backslash\alpha = (p\backslash\alpha) \mid (q\backslash\alpha) \text{ when } \alpha, \bar{\alpha} \notin L \cap \bar{M} \; ;$$

$$p[\,] = p \; ; \; p[S_1][S_2] = p[S_2 \circ S_1] \; ;$$

$$p\backslash\alpha = p \text{ when } \alpha, \bar{\alpha} \notin L \; ; \; p\backslash\alpha\backslash\beta = p\backslash\beta\backslash\alpha \; ;$$

$$p\backslash\alpha[S] = p[S \cup \{\alpha \mapsto \lambda\}]\backslash\beta \text{ where } \lambda \in \{\beta, \bar{\beta}\} \text{ and } \beta, \bar{\beta} \text{ are not in the range of } S \, .$$

3. Discussion of the algebra

The first important property of our algebraic theory is the following:

NORMAL FORM LEMMA. Every expression built from the six operator families (nullity, ambiguity, guarding, composition, restriction, relabelling) is equivalent by the laws to an expression involving only nullity, ambiguity and guarding.
That is, every expression e has a normal form

$$\sum \lambda_i : e_i$$

where in turn each e_i is in normal form. From this it is a short step to show that, among all possible interpretations of the theory, the finite tree interpretation is distinguished. An interpretation P of the theory consists of a family $\{P_L \mid L \text{ is a sort}\}$ of sets, together with operations which satisfy the laws, and we call P a synchronisation algebra. In particular the algebra ST of synchronization trees [8] is a synchronization algebra.

PROPOSITION ST is initial in the category whose objects are synchronization algebras and whose morphisms are homomorphisms.

Our operations fall naturally into two classes when we consider their intuitive meaning. Ambiguity and guarding concern a particular event in time (in the first case the resolution of ambiguity in some way which is not specified, and in the second case a synchronizing communication). On the other hand, the four other operations are time-independent in nature; e.g. composition means establishing a permanent linkage between processes. If we restrict ourselves to NIL, composition, restriction and relabelling, and the Laws (3),(5) which concern them, then we have an algebraic theory of the static structure of communicating processes. This theory was studied in [6] (though without NIL, which requires only slight adjustment). We called the interpretations of this theory Flow Algebras, and proved a corresponding initiality result for the algebra G of flowgraphs:

PROPOSITION The algebra G of flowgraphs is free, over an arbitrary generator set Γ, in the category of Flow Algebras whose morphisms are homomorphisms.

In both the theories one naturally wishes to use recursion to define infinite objects; in particular, in synchronization algebra one wishes to define processes with infinite behaviour, represented by synchronization trees with infinite paths. A trivial example is to define a binary semaphore (after Dijkstra); it will have sort $\{\bar{\pi},\bar{\phi}\}$ and its definition is just

$$s = \bar{\pi} : \bar{\phi} : s$$

Less trivial examples may be found in [7,8]. The initiality results extend naturally, though we shall not give precise details here (see [6] for the case of Flow Algebras). Here our full set of operations gains importance; the Normal Form Lemma shows that the operations of composition, relabelling and restriction may be eliminated from any expression for a <u>finite</u> process, but this cannot be done for expressions which involve recursively defined processes (unless indeed one admits infinite expressions!).

4. An example

We illustrate the expressive power of our algebra by constructing a simple scheduling process from elementary components.

Suppose that for $1 \le i \le n$, p_i is a process which requests (at port α_i) permission to start a certain action, and signals (at port β_i) that it has completed the action. We want to design a scheduling process to communicate with these ports, thereby enforcing the following constraints upon sequences σ of requests and termination signals:

(i) The restriction of σ to $\{\alpha_i \mid 1 \le i \le n\}$ must be the sequence

$\alpha_1\alpha_2 \ldots . \alpha_n\alpha_1\alpha_2 \ldots . \alpha_n\alpha_1 \ldots .$

(requests are in cyclic order, starting with p_1).

(ii) For each i, the restriction of σ to $\{\alpha_i, \beta_i\}$ must be the sequence

$\alpha_i\beta_i\alpha_i\beta_i\alpha_i \ldots .$

(requests and termination signals must alternate, for each process p_i)

Our scheduler will be of sort $\{\bar{\alpha}_1, \bar{\beta}_1 \ldots ., \bar{\alpha}_n, \bar{\beta}_n\}$. It is built in the form

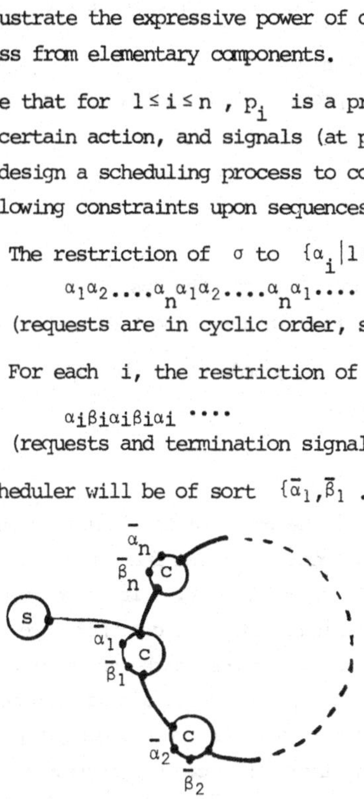

using n copies of a 'cycler' module c, and a 'starter' module s. The cycler has sort $\{\alpha, \beta, \gamma, \delta\}$

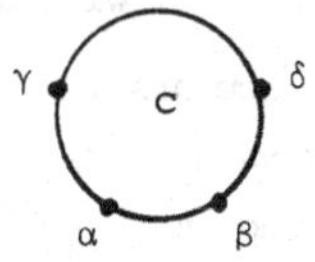

and it functions as follows. On being enabled at γ, by its left neighbour, it can receive a request at α; then it can receive a termination signal at β and enable its right neighbour through δ, in either order; it then waits to be enabled again at γ.

$$c = \gamma : \alpha : (\beta : \delta : \gamma : c + \delta : \beta : \gamma : c)$$

The sole function of s, of sort $\{\gamma_1\}$, is to supply one communication and then die:

$$s = \gamma_1 : \mathrm{NIL}$$

The scheduler is then

$$sch = (s \mid c_1 \mid \ldots\ldots \mid c_n)\backslash\gamma_1\ldots\backslash\gamma_n$$

where $c_i = c[\bar{\alpha}_i/\alpha, \bar{\beta}_i/\beta, \gamma_i/\gamma, \bar{\gamma}_{i+1}/\delta]$. (We are using the notation $[\lambda_1/\alpha_1, \ldots, \lambda_n/\alpha_n]$ for a relabelling S in which $S(\alpha_j) = \lambda_j$). The whole scheduled system is

$$(sch \mid p_1 \mid \ldots \mid p_n)\backslash\alpha_1\backslash\beta_1 \ldots\backslash\alpha_n\backslash\beta_n$$

It may also be constructed by attaching each process first to its cycler

$$q_i = (p_i \mid c_i)\backslash\alpha_i\backslash\beta_i$$

and then assembling the results:

$$(s \mid q_1 \mid \ldots \mid q_n)\backslash\gamma_1\ldots\backslash\gamma_n \ .$$

The algebraic laws verify that these two expressions for the system are equivalent; such restructuring of systems is indeed important in analysing their behaviour.

It is plausible that our construction of the scheduler can be closely matched by the construction of corresponding hardware.

5. Discussion of applications

It is not possible to convince oneself of the power of a calculus by one simple example such as we have given. Let us first comment on one feature of our example. At its centre is the recursive definition of c, the cycler. It indeed cycles; it restores itself after a small number of communications. It can therefore be represented by a physical device of fixed size, and as a result the physical structure of our scheduler is fixed throughout time. But the calculus allows much more; we have only to use the composition operator "|" in a recursive process to gain systems whose physical structure must evolve through time; they can bifurcate, and parts may die if NIL occurs anywhere. How to reflect this in hardware is an open question - but such power already exists in sequential programming languages (compare the full power of recursion, and its implementation with stacks, with mere iteration).

A simple example of such evolving processes appears in [7] . In that paper, we also deal with the more general algebra in which values are transmitted by communications, allowing the renewal of a process to depend upon the value received.

Other applications which have been reported are (1) the demonstration of freedom from deadlock in a system [8] , (2) a general approach to scheduling problems [4], (3) verification that a hardware device meets its specification [3] .

References

1. J. Backus, "Can programming be liberated from the von Neumann style? A functional style and its algebra of programs", C.ACM 21,8,1978,pp613-641.

2. P.J. Landin, "The mechanical evaluation of expressions", Computer Journal 6,4, 1964, pp308-320.

3. G.J. Milne, "A mathematical model of concurrent computation", Ph.D. Thesis, CST-4-78, Computer Science Dept, Edinburgh University, 1977.

4. G.J. Milne, "Scheduling within a process model of computation", to appear in Proc. 1st European Conference on Parallel and Distributed Processing, Toulouse, France, Feb. 1979.

5. G.J. Milne and R. Milner, "Concurrent processes and their syntax", to appear in J.ACM, 1979. Also CSR-2-77, Computer Science Dept, Edinburgh University, 1977.

6. R. Milner, "Flowgraphs and flow algebras", CSR-5-77, Computer Science Dept, Edinburgh University, 1977. (submitted for publication).

7. R. Milner, "Synthesis of communicating behaviour", Proc. 7th MFCS Symposium (Zakopane, Poland), Lecture Notes in Computer Science 64, Springer Verlag, 1978, pp 71 - 83.

8. R. Milner, "Algebras for communicating systems", Proc AFCET/SMF Joint Colloquium in Applied Mathematics (Palaiseau, France), 1978. Also CSR-25-78, Computer Science Dept, Edinburgh University, 1978.

9. C.A. Petri, "Nichtsequentielle Prozesse", Interner Bericht 76-6, GMD, Bonn, 1976.

STORAGE MODIFICATION MACHINES

A. Schönhage

Abstract. In 1970 the author introduced a new machine model (cf. [11]) now called storage modification machine (SMM) and posed the intuitive thesis that (among all models of an atomistic nature) this model possesses extreme flexibility. In the meantime some progress has been made in comparing SMMs with other machine models by investigating the possibility of real time reductions. Here we give a survey of our present knowledge of SMMs.
We briefly explain the notion of Δ-structures (which serve as storage devices), the instruction set of an SMM, the related successor RAM model and its real time equivalence to the SMM model. Then we discuss the relationship between SMMs and Kolmogorov Uspenskii machines (KUM) introduced in [7]. In spite of the obvious similarities KUMs are different from SMMs; they are certainly not stronger but perhaps weaker than SMMs.

Any multidimensional Turing machine (mdTM) can be simulated in real time by a suitable SMM (cf. [12]). In view of the result in [3] that KUMs are definitely stronger than mdTMs we therefore have that SMMs are stronger than mdTMs.

Finally we present our most recent result that there exists an SMM which can perform integer-multiplication in linear time. The underlying algorithm is still based upon the FFT, now combined with the more general observation that with the SMM model savings are possible in simulating the work of a multitape Turing machine applied to many different inputs simultaneously. As a corollary we obtain the existence of a successor RAM which multiplies n-bit numbers at logarithmic cost O(n log n).

References.

[1] A.V. Aho, J.E. Hopcroft and J.D. Ullman, The Design and Analysis of Computer Algorithms (Addison-Wesley, Reading, MA, 1974).
[2] A. Church, An Unsolvable Problem of Elementary Number Theory, Amer. J. Math. 58 (1936) 345-363.

[3] D.Yu. Grigoryev, Kolmogorov algorithms are stronger than Turing machines, in: Matijasevič, Slisenko, eds., Investigations in constructive mathematics and mathematical logic VII (Russian; Izdat. Nauka, Leningrad, 1976) 29-37.

[4] J.E. Hopcroft, W.J. Paul and L.G. Valiant, On time versus space and related problems, Proc. 16th Ann. IEEE Symp. Foundations Comp. Sci., Berkeley (1975) 57-64.

[5] D.E. Knuth, The Art of Computer Programming vol. 2, Semi-numerical Algorithms (2nd ed., Addison-Wesley, Reading, MA, 1971)

[6] D.E. Knuth, The Art of Computer Programming, vol. 3, Sorting and Searching (Addison-Wesley, Reading, MA, 1973).

[7] A.N. Kolmogorov and V.A. Uspenskii, On the definition of an algorithm, Uspehi Mat. Nauk 13 (1958) 3-28; AMS Transl. 2nd ser. vol. 29 (1963) 217-245.

[8] M.V. Kubinec, Recognition of the self-intersection of a plane trajectory by Kolmogorov's algorithm, in: Matijasevič, Slisenko, eds., Investigations in constructive mathematics and mathematical logic V (Russian; Izdat. Nauka, Leningrad, 1972) 35-44.

[9] W.J. Paul, Komplexitätstheorie (Teubner, Stuttgart, 1978).

[10] C.P. Schnorr, Rekursive Funktionen und ihre Komplexität (Teubner, Stuttgart, 1974).

[11] A. Schönhage, Universelle Turing Speicherung, in: Dörr, Hotz, eds., Automatentheorie und Formale Sprachen (Bibliogr. Institut, Mannheim, 1970) 369-383.

[12] A. Schönhage, Real-time simulation of multidimensional Turing machines by storage modification machines, Technical Memorandum 37, M.I.T. Project MAC, Cambridge, MA (1973).

[13] A. Schönhage and V. Strassen, Schnelle Multiplikation großer Zahlen, Computing 7 (1971) 281-292.

NEGATIVE RESULTS ON COUNTING

L.G. Valiant

1. Introduction

Numerous problems in the mathematical and physical sciences can be reduced to questions of counting solutions in combinatorial structures. Much effort has been put into developing analytic techniques for doing this effectively for the various problems that arise most frequently. A glance at the literature, however, suggests that the search for positive results has had only very limited success, and that for the majority of questions we still cannot count exactly in any effective sense.

In this paper we aim to survey recent techniques that enable negative results to be proved. Three classes of problems are defined that contain many of the best known problems. On historical grounds membership in each of these classes can be interpreted as overwhelming evidence of intrinsic intractability, in the same sense as NP-completeness for combinatorial search problems. In some areas we are able to classify most of the previously open problems as intractable in this sense, thereby confirming that the known positive techniques go as far as they can. In other cases, however, the resulting classification leaves the large gaps in our knowledge virtually untouched.

For uniformity we shall restrict ourselves to graph-theoretic problems. Other discrete structures, such as Boolean functions, can be treated similarly.

We shall assume that graphs are undirected, except where otherwise stated. The particular problems on which we focus are the following. The dimer problem is that of counting the number of perfect matchings in a graph. It is motivated by its several applications in the physical sciences [12,19]. The monomer-dimer problem counts matchings of arbitrary size and is similarly motivated. Self-avoiding walks are paths that do not go through any node more than once. Discussions of applications are given by Frisch and Hammersley [10] and Barber and Ninham [4]. A self-avoiding walk that goes through every node is a Hamiltonian path. Counting spanning trees first appeared in connection with electrical flow (Kirchhoff [20]), and of unlabelled trees in chemistry (Cayley [8]). An Eulerian path is one that contains every edge exactly once. Counting the number of subgraphs of a graph that connect a given pair of nodes corresponds to a reliability problem. In regular lattice graphs varieties of it appear as percolation problems [10,32]. A complete subgraph is a maximal clique if it is a complete subgraph that is not properly contained in a larger one. It is a k-clique if it has cardinality k.

Our first two notions of intractability, #P-completeness and $\#P_1$-completeness, concern the runtime of discrete computations and the non-existence of algorithms that run in polynomial time. The third notion, completeness over field F, is an algebraic one. It refers to the generating polynomials associated with the counting problem. Its implications include not only the complexity of algebraic programs in the sense of [6,p6] but also, we believe, the nonexistence of analytic techniques for solving these problems within a certain class [30]. The three classes will be defined informally in the next section. Examples of their members will be given in sections 3,4 and 5.

The three notions correspond to the different levels of effectiveness at which we may hope to count substructures in a graph. Suppose graph G is defined by the pair (V,E) when V is the set of nodes, and $E = \{e_1,\ldots,e_r\}$ the set of edges. Let $M = \{E_1,E_2,\ldots,E_m\}$ be the set of subsets of E that correspond to the occurrences of the substructures (e.g. M may be the set of perfect matchings or the set of self-avoiding walks.) Then the full polynomial for M over field F is

$$\sum_{j=1}^{m} \prod_{e_i \in E_j} x_i$$

regarded as a polynomial over indeterminates $\{x_1,\ldots,x_r\}$ with coefficients from the field F. If this polynomial can be computed and manipulated easily then we are in an excellent position not only to count the number of solutions, by substituting the identity for the indeterminates, but also to get further information, such as the asymptotic behaviour. If this polynomial is not easily computable itself there may still be a fast discrete algorithm for the counting problem itself. A third still weaker situation arises when such algorithms do not exist for arbitrary graphs but do for one special graph of each size. For example if we want to know how many labelled graphs on n nodes have some property, then we can rephrase this by asking how many subgraphs of the complete graph K_n on n nodes have the property. A second common example is the restriction of the graph to rectangular lattice grids, as is often sufficient for physical applications. When none of the three levels of counting is possible we may hope for approximate techniques, or for asymptotic results. For many of the structures defined above even these questions are problematic although much research has been done on them.

In section 6 an application of counting in computer science is discussed. In the final section brief mention is made of the problems that arise in counting when we wish to identify classes of objects according to some equivalence relation, typically isomorphism. This is often referred to as unlabelled enumeration to distinguish it from labelled enumeration which is the subject of the other sections.

2. Definitions

For discrete computations we assume that all objects are encoded over finite alphabets Σ,Γ. The size of an object x is $|x|$, the number of symbols required to represent it. Suppose $X \subseteq \Sigma^*$ and $Y \subseteq \Gamma^*$ are sets of encoded objects. A mapping f from X to subsets of Y is a *search function* if

(i) $\exists k \ \forall x \in X \ \forall y \in f(x) \cdot |y| < |x|^k$ (unless $|x| = 1$)

and (ii) there is a polynomial time algorithm that, given a pair (x,y) as input, will determine whether $y \in f(x)$.

In the present context X will be a class of graphs, and Y a class of candidate *solutions* to the problem in question. The set f(x) will be the actual solutions for graph x. Condition (i) guarantees that the size of a solution is bounded polynomially in the size of a graph. The second condition says that the validity of a candidate solution can be checked in polynomial time. It is easy to verify that all the counting problems given in the previous section can be formulated as search functions.

A computational problem P is *p-reducible* to problem Q if there is a program for P that besides elementary operations involves subroutine calls for a program for Q, and runs in polynomial time if each subroutine call is notionally charged as one elementary step. This is essentially the notion used by Cook [9]. For a discussion of its model-independence see [1].

The *existence* problem for a search function f is that of determining whether f(x) is empty given any x. The *counting* problem is that of determining the cardinality of f(x).

Definitions Search function f is *NP-complete* if the existence problem for every other search function is p-reducible to the existence problem for f. It is *#P-complete* if the counting problem for every other search function is p-reducible to the counting problem for f.

It is easy to verify that the NP-complete sets in the sense of Cook [9] are just those that can be characterized by the nonemptiness of some search function. The #P-complete functions of [28] are just those that are the counting problem for some search function.

Clearly, for any search function counting must be at least as difficult as existence. For most natural NP-complete search functions counting is easily proved to be #P-complete. The following, however, is open:

Problem Are all NP-complete search functions also #P-complete?

In [29] DNP and D#P are defined as the class of predicates that can be computed in polynomial time with respect to oracles for the existence and counting problems respectively of arbitrary search functions. It is evident that DNP ⊆ D#P ⊆ SPACE.

Problem Is DNP = D#P, or D#P = PSPACE?

Although the resolution of these questions appears to be beyond present proof techniques relativised results in the style of Baker, Gill and Solovay [3] do yield some insights. Angluin [2] has shown that with respect to some oracle DNP is strictly contained in D#P.

Problem Can D#P and PSPACE be distinguished relative to some oracle?

For counting problems for which there are few instances of each size we have the notion of $\#P_1$:

Definition A search function $f : X \to 2^Y$ is $\#P_1$-complete iff X is over a singleton alphabet (i.e. card $(\Sigma) = 1$) and the counting problem for every other search function with card $(\Sigma) = 1$ is p-reducible to it.

Our third notion of intrinsic difficulty is the algebraic one defined in [30]. Let F be any field and $F[x_1,\ldots,x_n]$ the ring of polynomials over indeterminates $\{x_1,\ldots,x_n\}$ with coefficients from F. A formula f over $F[x_1,\ldots,x_n]$ is any expression of the form (i) "c" for some $c \in F$, or (ii) "x_i" for some i, $1 \le i \le n$, or (iii) "$(f_1 + f_2)$" where f_1, f_2 are expressions, or (iv) "$(f_1 \times f_2)$" where f_1, f_2 are expressions. The formula size $|f|$ is the number of operations (i) - (iv) required to define f.

Suppose $P_i \in F[x_1,\ldots,x_i]$ and $Q_j \in F[y_1,\ldots,y_j]$. P_i is a projection of Q_j if for some substitution mapping σ

$$\sigma : \{y_1,\ldots,y_j\} \to \{x_1,\ldots,x_i\} \cup F$$

Q_j^σ equals P_i. (Q_j^σ denotes substitution for $y_1,\ldots,y_j$ in the obvious manner.)

Let P denote an infinite family $\{P_i \mid P_i \in F[x_1,\ldots,n_i]\}$ of polynomials, and similarly Q. Then P is a p-projection of Q if there is a polynomial h over the integers s.t.

$$\forall i \quad P_i \text{ is a projection of } Q_j \text{ for some } j \le h(i).$$

This is a very restricted notion of reduction. Note that if $P = \{P_i = \sum_1^i x_k\}$ and $Q = \{Q_j = \prod_1^j x_k\}$ then neither is a p-projection of the other.

Definition A polynomial family P is p-definable over F if either (i) for each i there is a polynomial Q_i with formula size polynomially bounded by i such that

$$P_i(x_1,\ldots,x_i) = \sum_{\sigma \in S} Q_i^\sigma(y_1,\ldots,y_i) \prod_{\sigma(y_k)=1} x_k$$

where S is the set of 2^i substitutions $\sigma : \{y_1,\ldots,y_i\} \to \{0,1\}$, or (ii) it is a p-projection of such a p-definable family.

It can be verified that the full polynomials of all the counting problems defined in the introduction are p-definable. Furthermore some of them are maximal in this class in the following strong sense:

Definition A polynomial family P is complete over F iff every Q that is p-definable is a p-projection of P.

We note that here the notion of reduction is simple substitution. Hence the complete problems will be equivalent in difficulty for any property that is preserved under it. Computational complexity is just one application.

Problem Would we get the same classes of complete problems if in the definition of p-definability "formula size" were replaced by "straight-line program complexity"?

3. Counting Substructures of Arbitrary Graphs

A few problems can be counted for arbitrary graphs or for a significant exponentially large subset, such as planar graphs. Polynomial time discrete algorithms are known for the following:

(3.1) Spanning trees (Kirchhoff [20])

(3.2) Directed spanning trees (Tutte [27])

(3.3) Eulerian circuits in directed graphs (van Aardenne Ehrenfest, de Bruijn [31])

(3.4) Perfect Matchings in planar graphs (Kasteleyn [17])

Expositions of these are also given by Berge [5] and Kasteleyn [19] .

In the above search functions the existence problems are necessarily polynomial time computable. For the numerous other well-known problems for which existence is polynomial time computable but no fast counting method is known, it turns out they can be proved to be #P-complete. The following are examples from [29]:

(3.5) Perfect matchings (even in bipartite graphs).

(3.6) Matchings (even in bipartite graphs)

(3.7) Self-avoiding walks

(3.8) Subgraphs that connect two given vertices

(3.9) Maximal cliques

(3.10) Subtrees in directed graphs

An obvious ommission from the two lists, whose status is unresolved, is

(3.11) Subgraphs that connect all vertices

As noted before, for NP-complete problems such as Hamiltonian paths or k-cliques, #P-completeness can usually be proved via standard proofs of NP-completeness [16] or variations on them.

Finally we note that the problem of listing all solutions to a search function efficiently has also been given much attention. We say that a problem is p-enumerable if the listing can be done in time N.p(n) where p(n) is some polynomial in the input size, and N the number of solutions found. Search functions with easy existence questions are often p-enumerable for trivial reasons, irrespective of whether they are easy to count or not [28]. Getting good upper bounds on p(n) does however require particular analysis. See Tarjan [26], Gabow [11] and Itai et al. [15] for examples.

4. Substructures in Sparse Sets of Graphs

Harary and Palmer [14] list several score open problems of the form "how many graphs on n nodes have property X ? " Since there is just one question of each these are, if anything, candidates for being $\#P_1$-complete. Unfortunately $\#P_1$-completeness has been established so far for one problem only, called "patterns" [29]. This concerns connected subgraphs with various additional highly contrived but easily checked local properties.

For the well-known open problems we have as yet no such evidence of difficulty. An embarrassing example is that of counting the number of subgraphs of the complete graph that contain Hamiltonian circuits. Since checking a subgraph for this property is NP-complete itself we do not expect that this problem can be posed as a search function even. We have, however, no clue as to the reason for its difficulty when we restrict ourselves to the complete graph of each size.

We note, on the other hand, that some problems appear to become computationally easier under such restrictions of inputs. For example counting connected subgraphs of K_n can be done in polynomial time [14], as can counting Hamiltonian circuits in rectangular grids with a certain pattern of orientations [18].

Problems that have resisted concerted attempts at a positive solution and are significant open problems include:

(4.3) Self-avoiding walks in 2-dimensional rectangular lattice

(4.4) Perfect matchings in 3-dimensional rectangular lattice

(4.5) Matchings in 2-dimensional rectangular lattice

Obtaining even the dominant asymptotic behaviour has proved elusive in these cases [13].

5. Generating Polynomials

The reason for regarding the computation of full polynomials as a counting process is simply that the known discrete techniques for counting are frequently algebraic in nature and based on the fact that the generating functions themselves can be computed fast. Examples of problems that can be computed by polynomial length straight-line programs [6] over any field F of constants are the natural full polynomials for (3.1), (3.2) and (3.3). The references given in §3 to these establish these stronger facts.

Fortunately negative results in this algebraic case are much easier to establish than for the discrete one. For example, the following is complete for any F such that $\mathrm{char}(F) \neq 2$ [30]:

(5.1) Perfect matchings in $2 \times n \times n$ rectangular lattice

Examples that are complete for any field F, or are derivable from one that is, are [30]:

(5.2) Self-avoiding walks in 2-dimensional rectangular directed lattice

(5.3) Connected components in 2-dimensional rectangular lattice

Such results establish that no positive algebraic techniques for the corresponding discrete problems of the previous section should be expected. An interesting problem for which even this has yet to be established is the monomer-dimer problem:

(5.4) Counting matchings in 2-dimensional rectangular lattice

Finally we observe that if we identify or fix some of the indeterminates in the full polynomial, we get other generating functions for the same problem, that contain less information. They can become computationally easier in the process.

6. Counting as Runtime Prediction

Combinatorial problems for which no fast-in-the-worst-case algorithm is known have to be attacked in practice by heuristics. We argue that algorithms whose performance is well-understood are more within our control than those that are not. A strong sense in which an algorithm could be in our control is that for any input its runtime can be predicted in much less time than would be required to run it. A collection of heuristics, each efficient on a different class of inputs and each having runtime that can be predicted in low polynomial time, would be obviously a desirable asset.

For many combinatorial problems there are simple heuristics that essentially search through an enumeration of easy-to-find objects in order to discover a hard-to-find solution. As examples consider the following methods of finding a Hamiltonian path:

Algorithm I : (i) List all the spanning trees of G
(ii) Test for each one whether it is a Hamiltonian path

Algorithm II: Denote the set of all self-avoiding walks of length i in G by X_i
(i) For i:=1 step 1 until n-1 deduce X_i from X_{i-1}
(ii) Test X_{n-1} for emptiness

As far as runtimes the two algorithms are incomparable in that example graphs can be found to demonstrate the superiority of either one over the other. From what we have said previously, however, the number of steps of I can be predicted exactly in polynomial time, whereas the same problem, in a natural interpretation, is #P-complete for II.

Whether there is hope that we can always restrict attention to heuristics with polynomial time predictable runtimes, without any penalties, appears to be a significant practical question. Of course, approximate predictions may be sufficient. In that direction Knuth [21] has proposed a Monte-Carlo method that performs well on certain branch-and-bound algorithms.

7. Compensating for Isomorphisms

A major branch of enumeration theory springs from Polya's theorem [25]. It provides an algebraic technique of counting that identifies objects that are isomorphic or are related by some other equivalence relation. Descriptions of the theory can be found in [7,14,22] .

While the number of labelled spanning trees of a graph can be counted fast, no analogous method is known for counting them up to isomorphism. It would be interesting to obtain results that confirm that counting in the latter sense can be intrinsically more difficult.

Algebraic problems arise in connection with the "cycle index", which is fundamental to Polya's theory. Little appears to be known about the maximal difficulty of computing these polynomials.

Counting the actual number of isomorphic embeddings of one graph into another is p-reducible to the corresponding existence problem [23]. This suggests that this question has the anomalous position that, while no polynomial time algorithm is known for testing for solutions, the counting problem is not expected to be #P-complete.

References

[1] A.V. Aho, J.E. Hopcroft and J.D. Ullman. The Design and Analysis of Computer Algorithms. Addison-Wesley, Reading, Mass. (1974).

[2] D. Angluin. On counting problems and the polynomial time hierarchy, to appear (1978).

[3] T. Baker, J. Gill and R. Solovay. Relativizations of the P = ? NP question. SIAM J. Comput. 4(1975) 431-442.

[4] M.N. Barber and B.W. Ninham. Random and restricted walks. Gordon and Breach, New York (1970).

[5] C. Berge. Graphs and Hypergraphs. North-Holland, Amsterdam (1973).

[6] A. Borodin and I. Munro. The Computational Complexity of Algebraic and Numeric Problems. American Elsevier, New York (1975).

[7] N.G. De Bruijn. Polya's theory of counting. In Applied Combinatorial Mathematics, E.F. Beckenbach (ed), Wiley, New York (1964).

[8] A. Cayley. On the theory of the analytical form called trees. Collected Works, Vol.3, Cambridge Univ. Press (1890) 243-246.

[9] S.A. Cook. The complexity of theorem proving procedures. Proc. 3rd ACM Symp. on Theory of Computing (1971) 151-158.

[10] H.L. Frisch and J.M. Hammersley. Percolation processes and related topics. J.SIAM Appl. Math. 11 (1963) 894-918.

[11] H.N. Gabow. Finding all spanning trees of undirected and directed graphs. Tech. Report, Univ. of Colorado, Boulder (1977).

[12] H.S. Green and G.A. Hurst. Order-Disorder Phenomena. Interscience. London (1964).

[13] J.M. Hammersley and D.J.A. Welsh. Further results on the rate of convergence to the connective constant of the hypercubical lattice. Quart. J. Math. Oxford Ser.2, 13 (1962) 108-110.

[14] F. Harary and E.M. Palmer. Graphical Enumeration. Academic Press. (1973).

[15] A. Itai, M. Rodeh and S.L. Tanimoto. Some matching problems for bipartite graphs. JACM 25 (1978) 517-525.

[16] R.M. Karp. Reducibility among combinatorial problems. In Complexity of Computer Computations, R.E. Miller and J.W. Thatcher (eds). Plenum Press, New York (1972).

[17] P.W. Kasteleyn. Dimer statistics and phase transitions. J.Math. Phys. 4 (1963) 287-293.

[18] P.W. Kasteleyn. A soluble self-avoiding walk problem. Physica 29 (1963) 1329-1337.

[19] P.W. Kasteleyn. Graph theory and crystal physics. In Graph Theory and Theoretical Physics. F. Harary (ed.) Academic Press (1967).

[20] G. Kirchhoff. Über die Ausflosung der Gleichungen, auf welche man bei der Untersuchung der linearen Verleilung galvanischer Ströme gefuhrt wird. Ann. Phys. Chem. 72 (1847) 497-508.

[21] D.E. Knuth. Estimating the efficiency of backtrack algorithms. Math. Comp. 29 (1975) 121-136.

[22] C.L. Liu. Introduction to Combinatorial Mathematics. McGraw Hill, New York (1968).

[23] R. Mathon. A note on the graph isomorphism counting problem, to appear (1977).

[24] J.K. Percus. Combinatorial Methods. Springer-Verlag, New York (1971).

[25] G. Pólya. Kombinatorische Anzahlbestimmungen für Gruppen, Graphen und chemische Verbindungen. Acto Math 68 (1937) 145-154.

[26] R.E. Tarjan. Enumeration of the elementary circuits of a directed graph. SIAM J. on Comput 2 (1973) 211-216.

[27] W.T. Tutte. The dissection of equilateral triangles into equilateral triangles. Proc. Cambridge Phil. Soc. 44 (1948) 463-482.

[28] L.G. Valiant. The complexity of computing the permanent. Tech. Rep. CSR-14-77, Edinburgh Univ. (1977). Also, TCS, to appear.

[29] L.G. Valiant. The complexity of enumeration and reliability problems. Tech. Rep. CSR-15-77, Edinburgh Univ. (1977). Also, SIAM J. on Comput. to appear.

[30] L.G. Valiant. Completeness classes in algebra (1978), to appear.

[31] T. van der Aardenne-Ehrenfest and N.G. de Bruijn. Circuits and trees in oriented line graphs. Simon Stevin 28 (1951) 203-217.

[32] D.J.A. Welsh. Percolation and related topics. Sci. Prog. Oxf. (1977) 64, 65-83.

STRONG NON-DETERMINISTIC CONTEXT-FREE LANGUAGES

Joffroy Beauquier

Introduction.

The notion of rational transduction is a valuable tool to compare structures of different languages, in particular context-free languages. The explaination of this is a powerful property of rational transductions with respect to iterative pairs [4] (or systems of iterative pairs [1]), in a context-free language. This property is the so-called Transfer Theorem (Cf.[3]), whose terms are : Let A and B be two context-free languages and let T be a rational transduction, such that TB = A. If A has a non-degenerated system of iterative pairs σ , then B has a non-degenerated system of iterative pairs σ', of the same type than σ.

That means that some systems of iterative pairs in the target language by a rational transduction, must appear, in an other form, in the source language.

The structure complexity of a language can be mesured by the kind of iterative pairs it contains and the way they are combined. So, the use of the preorder relation : "B $\geq$ A if and only if there is a rational transduction T such that TB = A" (and its corresponding equivalence, called rational equivalence), allows a good classification of context-free languages. We could define the structure of a language as its rational equivalence class. But, two rationally equivalent languages may be rather different and we need to define a more precise notion. In fact, we connect any context-free language L with the set of the languages of the form $L \cap K$, where K is a regular set, such that $L \cap K$ is rationally equivalent to L. That allows us to separate with regular intersection, the unsignificant and significant parts of a language L.

In these conditions, we do not study properties of languages on the languages themselves, but on the sets, that represent their structures. Let us see on an example what this new way of acting consists in.

Let us consider
the context-free generators case (generators of the rational cone or, equivalently, of the full-AFL of context-free languages). The question of the existence of an inherently ambiguous context-free generator can be easily solved in a positive

manner : we can do the disjoint union of an arbitrary generator with an inherently ambiguous language and we obtain an ambiguous context-free generator.

But different is the following question : may the structure of a context free generator be ambiguous? With our definitions, this question is : does there exist a context-free generator G, such that, for any regular set K satisfiyng : "$G \cap K$ is a context-free generator", $G \cap K$ is an ambiguous language ? In this particular case, we know the answer is negative [1]. Acting this way, we may connect any property on context-free languages, with another property on structures of context-free languages, which we call "strong property". A precise definition is :

Let P be a property of languages (If the language L satisfies P, we note P(L)). The strong property P_s connected with P is defined by :

$$P_s(L) \Leftrightarrow \forall K \in \text{Reg such that } L \cap K \approx L, \text{ then } P(L \cap K)$$

(Reg is the family of regular sets).

In the same way, we can define the "very strong properties" by :
Let P be a property of languages. The very strong property P_{vs}, connected with P, is defined by :

$$P_{vs}(L) \Leftrightarrow \forall L' , L' \approx L \text{ then } P(L')$$

Remark.

$P_{vs}(L)$ implies $P_s(L)$, which implies itself $P(L)$.

In this paper, we first study two examples of strong properties that are both context-free languages properties : ambiguity and non-determinism. In the two cases, we will point out that all the classical examples are not strong examples.

In the third part, we try to build a general theory of strong properties. The idea of this part is to prove, under certain hypothesis, general theorems, valid for any strong property satifying these hypothesis. Then we obtain particular results for particular strong properties as corollaries.

Part I. Strong ambiguity.

Definition 1.

Let L be a context-free language. L is strong ambiguous, if and only if, for any regular set K such that $L \cap K$ is rationally equivalent to L, $L \cap K$ is an inherently ambiguous context-free language.

Definition 2.

Let L be a context-free language. L is very strong ambiguous, if and only if, for any context-free language L' such that L' is rationally equivalent to L, L' is an inherently ambiguous context-free language.

Proposition 1 [3]

Let L_1, L_2, L_3, L_4, L_5 be the following languages :

$$L_1 = \{a^n \# a^m \# a^n \# a^p \mid n,m,p \in \mathrm{N}\} \cup \{a^m \# a^n \# a^p \# a^n \mid n,m,p \in \mathrm{N}\}$$
(Parikh - 1966)

$$L_2 = \{a^n b^m c^p \mid p \leq n \text{ or } p \leq m\}$$ (Haines - 1966)

$$L_3 = \{a^{n_1} b a^{n_2} b \ldots a^{n_k} b \mid k \in \mathrm{N}_+ ,\ n_i \in \mathrm{N} \text{ for } i = 1,\ldots,k ,\ \exists i = n_i\}$$
(Ogden - 1967)

$$L_4 = \{f \# u \tilde{f} v \mid f,u,v \in X^* ,\ \# \notin X,\ \tilde{f} \text{ is the mirror-image of } f\}$$ (Shamir-1971)

$$L_5 = \{f_1 \tilde{f}_1 f_2 \tilde{f}_2 \mid f_1, f_2 \in X^*\}$$ (Crestin - 1973)

None of them is strong ambiguous.

Proposition 2 [3]

Let L_6 be the context-free language defined by :

$$L_6 = \{a^n b^m c^p \mid p \geq n \text{ or } p \geq m\}$$

1. For any regular set K , $L \cap K$ is either regular or rationally equivalent to L.

2. If $L \cap K$ is rationally equivalent to L then $L \cap K$ is ambiguous.

Corollary 1.

L_6 is a strong ambiguous language.

Proposition 3 [3].

Let L_7 be the context-free language defined by :

$$L_7 = \{a^n \# a^m \# a^p \# a^q \mid (n \geq q \text{ and } m \geq p) \text{ or } (n \geq m \text{ and } p \geq q)\}$$

L_7 is a very strong ambiguous language.

Part II. Strong non-determinism.

An ambiguous context-free language is necessarily non-deterministic. So the problem is to find strong non-deterministic context-free languages that are not strong ambiguous. We first try with the classical examples of non-deterministic languages.

Definition 3.

Let L be a context-free language. L is strong (resp. very strong) non-deterministic, if and only if, for any regular set K (resp. context-free language L') such that $L \cap K$ (resp. L') is rationally equivalent to L, $L \cap K$ (resp. L') is a non-deterministic context-free language.

Proposition 4.

Let L_8 be the context-free language defined by :

$$L_8 = \{a^n b^n | n \in N\} \cup \{a^n b^{2n} | n \in N\}$$

L_8 is not strong non-deterministic.

If we try to generalize this example, we obtain :

Proposition 5.

Let $m_1, m_2, \ldots, m_k, n_1, n_2, \ldots, n_k, p_1, p_2, \ldots, p_k, q_1, q_2, \ldots, q_k$ be positive integers and let L_9 be the context-free language defined by :

$$L_9 = \{a^{m_1+n_1 . i} b^{p_1+q_1 . i} | i \in N\} \cup \{a^{m_2+n_2 . i} b^{p_2+q_2 . i} | i \in N\}$$
$$\cup \ldots \cup \{a^{m_k+n_k . i} b^{p_k+q_k . i} | i \in N\} .$$

L_9 is not strong non-deterministic.

Another classical example of an unambiguous, non-deterministic language is the language L_{10} .

Proposition 6.

Let L_{10} be the context-free language defined by :

$$L_{10} = \{f \tilde{f} | f \in X^* , \tilde{f} \text{ is the mirror-image of } f\} \ (\text{card } X \geq 2)$$

L_{10} is not strong non-deterministic.

Now, we establish the existence of strong non-deterministic languages with the :

Proposition 7.

Let L_{11} be the context-free language :

$$L_{11} = \{a^n b^m \mid \exists \ell_0 > k_0 > 1 \text{ , } n \leq k_0 \text{ . } m \quad \text{or} \quad n \geq \ell_0 \text{ . } m\}$$

L_{11} is strong non-deterministic.

Proposition 8.

Let K be a regular set. $L_{11} \cap K$ is either a regular set or is rationally equivalent to L_{11}.

L_{11} is an unambiguous language. Let us give now an example of a strong non-deterministic language, that is ambiguous, but not strong ambiguous.

Proposition 9.

Let L_{12} be the context-free language defined by :

$$L_{12} = L_{11} \cup \{x^n y^m z^p \mid p = n \quad \text{or} \quad p = m\}$$

(i). L_{12} is inherently ambiguous.

(ii). L_{12} is not strong ambiguous.

(iii). L_{12} is strong non-deterministic.

Summary

The results of the first two parts allow us to fulfill the following diagram :

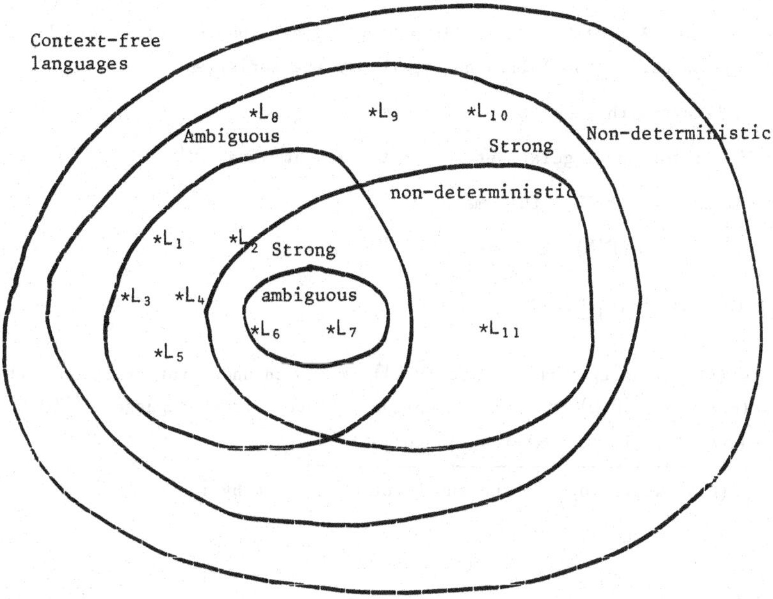

Part III - Strong properties.

In this third part we try to built a general theory of strong properties. The idea is to prove, under certain hypothesis, general theorems, valid for any strong (or very strong) property satisfying these hypothesis. Then particular results, for particular strong (or very strong) properties, are obtained as corollaries.

Notation.

We design by $\square$ any operator between languages, choosed in the set : {syntactic substitution [+], disjoint product, insertion}(cf.[12]).

Definition.

We say that a language $L_1 \subset X_1^*$ is consistant with respect to a language $L_2 \subset X_2^*$ $(X_1 \cap X_2 = \emptyset)$ for the operator $\square$, if and only if, for any regular set K : $L_1 \square L_2 \approx (L_1 \cap K) \square L_2$ implies $L_1 \approx L_1 \cap K$.

Example [4]

The language S_2 (generated by the grammar : $V \to a\, V\, \bar{a}$; $V \to b\, V\, \bar{b}$; $V \to \varepsilon$) is consistant with respect to the language D'^*_1 (the restricted Dyck set over the alphabet {(,)}) for the syntactic substitution.

Theorem 1.
Let $L_1 \subset X_1^*$ and $L_2 \subset X_2^*$ be two languages over disjoint alphabets, and let P be a property of languages. If the following hypothesis are satisfied :

(i). L_1 is consistant with respect to L_2 for $\square$.

(ii). P satisfies : for any regular set L , $P(L \cap K)$ implies $P(L)$.

(iii). P is compatible with $\square$, that means :

$$P(L) \text{ or } P(M) \text{ implies } P(L \square M)$$

then $P_{vs}(L_1)$ implies $P_s(L_1 \square L_2)$

Remark1.
The hypothesis (ii) means that the set $\{L \mid \neg P(L)\}$ is closed under intersection with regular sets (Examples : $P(L) \Leftrightarrow$ "L is an ambiguous context-free language", $P(L) \Leftrightarrow$ "L is a non-deterministic context-free language").

+ $L_1 \square L_2 = \sigma_{L_2}(L_1)$, where σ_{L_2} is the substitution defined by :

$$\forall x \in X_1 \quad \sigma_{L_2}\, x = xL_2 \quad .$$

Remark 2.

For any operator $\square$, $L_1 \square L_2$ is greater, by rational preorder relation, than L_1. So theorem 1 allows to obtain more complicated examples of strong languages from basic examples.

Proof of theorem 1.

Without loss of generality, we can suppose that $\varepsilon \in L_2$ (ε is the empty word). Let K be a regular set such that : $(L_1 \square L_2) \cap K \approx L_1 \square L_2$.

We have to prove : $P((L_1 \square L_2) \cap K)$.

Let be $K_1 = \mathrm{Proj}_{X_1} K$ the projection of K onto X_1^*; we have :

$$(L_1 \square L_2) \cap K = ((L_1 \cap K_1) \square L_2) \cap K$$

Then : $((L_1 \cap K_1) \square L_2) \cap K \approx L_1 \square L_2$ and

$$((L_1 \cap K_1) \square L_2) \approx L_1 \square L_2$$

since : $L_1 \square L_2 \geq (L_1 \cap K_1) \square L_2$

From the hypothesis (i) : $L_1 \approx L_1 \cap K_1$

Then : $P_{vs}(L_1) \Rightarrow P_s(L_1) \Rightarrow P(L_1 \cap K_1)$

Let $A = \langle X_1 \cup X_2, E, q_0, \ldots, F\rangle$ a finite automaton recognizing K. For every states $q, q' \in E$, we define :

$$_qK_{q'}^{(1)} = \{f \mid f \in X_1^*, \ q.f = q'\}$$

and $$_qK_{q'}^{(2)} = \{f \mid f \in X_2^*, \ q.f = q'\}$$

Let $\{_q m_{q'}\}$ be the set containing the smallest word $_q m_{q'}$, in $_qK_{q'}^{(2)} \cap L_2$ (recall that $\varepsilon \in L_2$) if $_qK_{q'}^{(1)} \cap X_1 = \emptyset$ or the empty set if $_qK_{q'}^{(1)} \cap X_1 \neq \emptyset$.

Now, we build a finite automaton $A' = \langle X_1 \cup X_2, E, q_0, *, F\rangle$, recognizing a regular set K', where the transition function $*$ is defined by :

$$\forall p', p'' \in E, \{f \mid p' * f = p''\} = \{f \mid \exists k \in \mathbb{N}, \ \exists p_0 = p', p_1, \ldots, p_k = p'' \in E,$$

$$\exists f_1, f_2, \ldots, f_k \in (X_1 \cup X_2)^* \text{ with } f = f_1 f_2 \ldots f_k$$

$$\text{and } f_i \in (_{p_{i-1}}K_{p_i}^{(1)} \cap X_1) \cup \{_{p_{i-1}} m_{p_i}\} \text{ for } i = 1, 2, \ldots, k\}$$

We set :

$$L_1' = (L_1 \square L_2) \cap K'$$

Clearly, for any operator $\square$, there are a morphism $\Psi : (X_1 \cup X_2)^* \to X_1^*$, a regular set $R_\square$, such that :

$$\Psi^{-1} L_1 \cap R_\square = L_1'$$

$$\Psi \; L_1' = L_1$$

So, L_1 and L_1' are rationally equivalent and :

$$P_{vs}(L_1) \text{ implies } P(L_1')$$

Now : $L_1' = [(L_1 \square L_2) \cap K] \cap K'$ since $K' \subset K$.

From the hypothesis (ii) :

$$P(L_1') \text{ implies } P((L_1 \square L_2) \cap K)$$

$\square$

Remark.

By adding the hypothesis *(iv)* :

(iv) . $(P(L_1)$ and $L_1' = \Psi^{-1} L_1 \cap K)$ implies $P(L_1')$

we have proved :

$$P_s(L_1) \Rightarrow P_s\,(L_1 \square L_2)$$

and we can enounce :

Theorem 2 :

Let $L_1 \subset X_1^*$ and $L_2 \subset X_2^*$ be two languages over disjoint alphabets, and let P be a property of languages. If the following hypothesis are satisfied :

(i) L_1 is consistant with respect to L_2 for $\square$.

(ii) P satisfies : for any regular set K , $P(L \cap K)$ implies $P(L)$.

(iii) $P(L)$ or $P(M)$ implies $P(L \square M)$

(iv) L_1 and P satisfy : for any regular set K, for any morphism Ψ such that: $L_1' = \Psi^{-1} L_1 \cap K_1$, $L_1 = \Psi L_1'$, then $P(L_1)$ implies $P(L_1')$.

Then : $P_s(L_1)$ implies $P_s(L_1 \square L_2)$

Let us give now two applications of these theorems.

Application 1.

P : to be ambiguous.

$L_1 = \{a^n \# a^m \# a^p \# a^q \mid (n \geq q \text{ and } m \geq p) \text{ or } (n \geq m \text{ and } p \geq q)\}$

$L_2 = D_1'^*$

We can easily verify that P satisfies the hypothesis (ii) of Theorem 1 and that P is compatible with any $\square$.

The only thing to prove is that L_1 is consistant with respect to L_2 , for $\square$. But, in the same way than in the propositions 2 or 7, we can prove :

Proposition 10.

Let K be a regular set. Then $L_1 \cap K$ either is rationally equivalent to L_1 , either is rationally equivalent to $L_1' = \{a^n \# a^m \mid n \geq m\}$, or is a regular set. Then, the consistancy of L_1 with respect to $D_1'^* = L_2$ is easy to prove.

From Theorem 1 we have :

$L_1 \square D_1'^*$ is a strong ambiguous language.

So, by using Theorem 1, we can build chains of strictly increasing ($L_1 \square D_1'^* \gneq L_1$) principal full semi-AFL's (resp.rational cones, according Eilenberg's terminology [8]), generated by strong ambiguous languages.

Application 2.

P : to be non-deterministic.

$L_1 = \{a^n b^m \mid \exists l_0 > k_0 > 1 \quad , n \leq k_0 \, . \, m \quad \text{or} \quad n \geq l_0 \, . m\}$

$L_2 = S_2$

P satisfies the hypothesis (ii) and (iii) of Theorem 2. One can verify that L_1 and P satisfy the hypothesis (iv). From proposition 8 we can deduce that L_1 is consistant with respect to S_2 , for any operator $\square$. Then, from Theorem 2, we have:

$L_1 \square S_2$ is a strong non-deterministic language. So, we can build chains of strictly increasing ($L_1 \square S_2 \gneq L_1$) principal full semi-AFL's (resp. rational cones), generated by strong non-deterministic languages.

Final Remark.

In fact, strong properties are not properties of languages, but properties of languages families, finite or infinite.

If we note C(F) the least rational cone containing F (rational cone generated by F), we can define :

Definition :

Let $F = (L_1, L_2, \ldots, L_p, \ldots)$ be an infinite family of languages. F satisfies the strong property P_s , if and only if, for any infinite sequence $(K_1,K_2,\dots,K_p,\dots)$ of regular sets, such that : $C(F) = (L_1 \cap K_1, L_2 \cap K_2, \dots, L_p \cap K_p, \dots)$ then there exists an integer r with :

$$P(L_r \cap K_r)$$

In these conditions, we have :

Theorem 3 [1]

Any family generating the rational cone of derivation bounded languages [10] is not strong ambiguous.

Open Problem

If P is the property : "to be ambiguous" do the hypothesis *(i)*, *(ii)*, *(iii)* in Theorem 1 imply : $P_s(L_1) \Rightarrow P_s(L_1 \,\square\, L_2)$?

Bibliography

[1] *BEAUQUIER J.* - 1977 - Contribution à l'Etude de la Complexité Structurelle des langages Algébriques, Thèse de Doctorat d'Etat - Université Paris VII.

[2] *BEAUQUIER J.* - 1978 - Générateurs Algébriques et Systèmes de Paires Itérantes- To appear in Theoretical Computer Science.

[3] *BEAUQUIER J.* 1978 - Ambiguïté forte. In proceedings of the 5th I.C.A.L.P. - Udine-Italy, Lecture Notes in Computer Science 62, p. 52-62.

[4] *BEAUQUIER J.* - Substitutions de langages linéaires et de langages à compteur. Submitted to the Jour. of Comp. and Syst. Sciences.

[5] *BERSTEL J.* - 1979 - Transductions and Context-Free Languages. Teubner Verlag.

[6] *BOASSON L.* - 1976 - Langages Algébriques, Paires Itérantes et Transductions Rationnelles - Theoretical Computer Science 2, p.209-223.

[7] *CRESTIN J.P.* - 1972 - Sur un language non-ambigu dont le carré est d'ambiguïté inhérente non-bornée. Actes du Colloque I.R.I.A.

[8] *EILENBERG S.* - 1970 - Communication au Congrès International des Mathématiciens Nice - France.

[9] *GINSBURG S.* - 1966 - The Mathematical Theory of Context-Free Languages. Mc Graw Hill

[10] *GINSBURG S.* and *SPANIER E.H.* - 1968 - Derivation Bounded Languages, Journ. of Comp. and Syst. Sciences 2, p. 228-250.

[11] *GREIBACH S.* - 1970 - Chains of full AFL'S - Math. System Theory 4, p. 231-242.

[12] *GREIBACH S.* - 1972 - Syntactic Operators on full Semi-AFL's. Journ. of Comp. and Syst. Sciences 6, p. 30-76.

[13] *HAINES L.H.* 1965 - Generation and Recognition of Formal Languages. Doctoral Dissertation. M.I.T.

[14] *OGDEN W.* 1967 - A helpful Result for Proving Inherent Ambiguity - Math. System Theory 2, p. 191-194.

[15] *PARIKH R.J.* - 1966 - On Context-Free Languages. J.A.C.M. 13, p. 570-581.

[16] *SHAMIR E.* - 1961 - Some Inherently Ambiguous Context-Free Languages, Information and Control 18, p. 355-363.

INFORMATION CONTENT CHARACTERIZATIONS OF COMPLEXITY THEORETIC PROPERTIES

Victor L. Bennison

1. Introduction and notation

It is intuitively appealing to suppose that if one is given an appropriate measure of the information content of a computable set then the more information the set contains the more difficult the set should be to compute. In this paper we shall furnish some evidence that this intuitive notion is accurate. We shall consider the complexity theoretic notions of nonspeedability, effective speedability, levelability, effective levelability, and complexity sequences, and we shall show that each has a characterization in terms of levels of information as measured in various natural ways. "Easy to compute" sets such as nonspeedable sets, nonlevelable sets and sets with complexity sequences will be shown to have low levels of information and "hard to compute" sets such as effectively speedable sets and effectively levelable sets will be shown to have high levels of information content.

Our notation will be primarily that of Rogers [12] and Blum [4]. Let $\{\phi_i : i \in \omega\}$ be an acceptable numbering of the partial recursive (p.r.) functions, and for every i let W_i be the domain of ϕ_i. Let R^n denote the class of all total recursive functions mapping $\omega^n \longrightarrow \omega$. "$\exists^\infty_x$" is an abbreviation for "there exist infinitely many x," and "$\forall^\infty_x$" and "a.e." are both abbreviations for "for all but finitely many x." We write $A \subseteq^* B$ if A-B if finite and $A =^* B$ if $A \subseteq^* B$ and $B \subseteq^* A$.

We say $\Phi = \{\Phi_i : i \in \omega\}$ is a complexity measure (for some fixed acceptable numbering of the p.r. functions) if Φ satisfies the following two axioms of Blum:

$$(\forall i)(\forall x)[\Phi_i(x) \text{ is defined} \Longleftrightarrow \phi_i(x) \text{ is defined}]$$

$$(\exists M \in R^3)(\forall i,x,m)[M(i,x,m) = 1 \text{ if } \Phi_i(x) = m$$
$$= 0 \text{ otherwise}]$$

In this paper we shall assume a fixed enumeration of r.e. sets and shall denote by $W_{i,s}$ the elements of W_i enumerated by stage s. We use the following index set notation:

$$\text{FIN} = \{i : W_i \text{ is finite}\} = \overline{\text{INF}}$$
$$\text{COF} = \{i : W_i \text{ if cofinite}\} = \overline{\text{COINF}}$$
$$H_A = \{i : W_i \cap A \neq \emptyset\}.$$

This work was partially supported by NSF grant MCS 77-02192.

2. Definitions of Complexity Theoretic Properties

Loosely speaking, a set is nonspeedable if there is a fastest program for computing it. By "fastest" we mean faster modulo some fixed total recursive function than any other program for computing the set.

Definition 2.1 (Blum). An r.e. set A is nonspeedable if there is an $h \in R^2$ and an e such that $W_e = A$ and

$$(\forall i)[W_i = A \Longrightarrow \Phi_e(x) \leq h(x,\Phi_i(x)) \text{ a.e.}].$$

Nonspeedable sets have been extensively studied and classified by Blum [6], Marques [6,9], Soare [13], Morris [11], and others. Soare's characterization will be considered in section 4. Sets which are not nonspeedable are called speedable sets.

Some speedable sets are "effectively" speedable. Not only do they have no fastest program but there is an effective procedure for finding programs that are faster, by any recursive amount, than any program claiming to be fastest.

Definition 2.2 (Blum). An r.e. set A is effectively speedable if there is a recursive function $\sigma \in R^2$ such that for every i and e, if $W_i = A$ and ϕ_e is total, then $W_{\sigma(i,e)} = A$ and

$$(\overset{\infty}{\exists} x)\,[\Phi_i(x) > \phi_e(x,\Phi_{\sigma(i,e)}(x))].$$

Blum and Marques [6] showed that the effectively speedable sets were the same as the subcreative sets.

Though a speedable set A has no fastest program, it might possess a computable sequence of programs which form upper and lower bounds on the running times of all programs for A. Complexity sequences have been extensively studied by Blum [5], Meyer and Fischer [10], Bennison [1], and others. Bennison modified a definition of Blum to obtain the following definitions of type 0, type 1, and type 2 r.e. complexity sequences.

Definition 2.3. An r.e. set A has a type 0 (type 1) (type 2) r.e. complexity sequence if there is a $\sigma \in R^1$ and an $h \in R^2$ such that for every i:

1) $W_{\sigma(i)} = A \quad (W_{\sigma(i)} =^* A) \quad (W_{\sigma(i)} \supseteq A)$

2) $W_i = A \Longrightarrow (\exists j)[\Phi_{\sigma(j)}(x) \leq h(x,_{\sigma i}(x)) \text{ a.e.}]$, and

3) $(\exists k)[W_k = A \text{ and } \Phi_k(x) \leq h(x,\Phi_{\sigma(i)}(x)) \text{ a.e. on } A]$.

He then found recursion theoretic characterizations for sets possessing each kind of sequence. These results will be mentioned in Section 4.

Another well known complexity theoretic property is that of levelability. As with speedable sets, levelable sets have no fastest program, but in a stronger way. Namely, for each program i for A there will be a faster program j for A which itself behaves very well (i.e., runs less than a fixed recursive function r) in infinitely many places where i is being very slow to compute (i.e., is running slower than an arbitrary recursive function h).

Definition 2.4 (Blum). An r.e. set A is levelable if there is a recursive function $r \in R^1$ such that for all i and for all recursive functions $h \in R^1$, if $W_i = A$ then there exists a j such that $W_j = A$ and

$$(\overset{\infty}{\exists} x)[\Phi_i(x) > h(x) \text{ and } \Phi_j(x) \leq r(x)].$$

Definition 2.5 (Blum). An r.e. set A is effectively levelable if there is an $r \in R^1$ and an $\ell \in R^2$ such that for all i and e, if $W_i = A$ and ϕ_e is a total recursive function then $W_{\ell(i,e)} = A$ and

$$(\overset{\infty}{\exists} x)[\Phi_i(x) > \phi_e(x) \text{ and } \Phi_{\ell(i,e)}(x) \leq r(x)].$$

Blum and Marques [6] and Soare [13] gave recursion theoretic characterizations of levelable sets. Soare's characterization will be considered in Section 5. Filotti [7] showed that the effectively levelable sets are the same as the undercreative sets.

3. The Weak Jump Operator

In [2] and [3] recursion theoretic characterizations are given for nonspeedable sets and for sets with different kinds of complexity sequences. These results indicate that there is a strong connection between the computational complexity of a set and its information content as measured by various index sets. The information a set contains with respect to the Turing degrees seems to correspond in a weaker fashion to the set's computational complexity than does its information content with respect to the 1-degrees. For example, if $A \leq_1 B$ then B nonspeedable implies A nonspeedable, and A effectively speedable implies B effectively speedable, whereas $A \leq_T B$ yields neither implication.

The jump A' of a set A is defined by $A' = \{x : x \in W_x^A\} \equiv_1 \{x : W_x^A \neq \emptyset\}$. This jump operation can be iterated in the following way, for $n \geq 0$ (see Rogers [12, p. 256]):

$$A^{(0)} = A$$

$$A^{(1)} = A' \text{ , and in general}$$

$$A^{(n+1)} = (A^{(n)})'.$$

$A^{(n)}$ is called the nth jump of A. The information an r.e. set A contains with respect to the Turing degrees can be measured by considering, for various values of n, the nth jump of A. The set A is said to be low_n if $A^{(n)}$ has the same Turing degree as $\emptyset^{(n)}$, and high_n if $A^{(n)}$ has the same Turing degree as $\emptyset^{(n+1)}$.

An analogous iterated operation can be defined on the 1-degrees. For $n \geq 0$ let

$$A^{<0>} = A$$

$$A^{<1>} = H_{\bar{A}} = \{i : W_i \cap \bar{A} \neq \emptyset\}, \text{ and in general}$$

$$A^{<n+1>} = H_{\overline{A^{<n>}}} = \{i : W_i \cap \overline{A^{<n>}} \neq \emptyset\}.$$

$A^{<n>}$ will be called the nth weak jump of A. Hartmanis and Lewis [8] show that for all n, $\emptyset^{(n)} \equiv_1 \emptyset^{<n>}$. So in particular we know that $K \equiv_1 \emptyset^{<1>}$, $FIN \equiv_1 \emptyset^{<2>}$, and $COF \equiv_1 \emptyset^{<3>}$. Lemma 3.1 shows that for an r.e. set $A \neq \omega$, the various n^{th} weak jumps of A behave on the 1-degrees in a manner analogous to the behavior of the nth jumps of A on the Turing degrees. (Note that for $A = \omega$, $A^{<n>} = \emptyset$ for all $n \geq 1$.)

Lemma 3.1. If A is an r.e. set different from ω then for all $n \geq 1$,

$$\emptyset^{<n>} \leq_1 A^{<n>} \leq_1 \emptyset^{<n+1>}.$$

Proof. The proof can be found in [1] and will appear elsewhere.

We can now measure the information on r.e. set A contains with respect to the 1-degrees by considering the various n^{th} weak jumps of A. We will say that A is weak low_n if $A^{<n>} \equiv_1 \emptyset^{<n>}$, and strong $high_n$ if $A^{<n>} \equiv_1 \emptyset^{<n+1>}$. This terminology, though designed to be intuitive, might seem confusing at first glance. The weak jump of a set is "weak" because it does not necessarily result in a set as high in the Turing degrees as the full jump of the set. Therefore a set which is weak low_n is not necessarily low_n and a set which is $high_n$ is not necessarily strong $high_n$.

We shall show that the nonspeedable sets are exactly those r.e. sets which are weak low_2, and that the effectively speedable sets are exactly those r.e. sets which are strong $high_1$. First we want to consider the index set $FIN_{\bar{A}} = \{i : W_i \cap \bar{A} \text{ is finite}\}$. The set $FIN^A = \{i : W_i^A \text{ is finite}\}$ is recursively isomorphic to $A'' = A^{(2)}$, the full double jump of A. $FIN_{\bar{A}}$ could then be looked upon as a form of weak double jump of A. The next lemma shows that for coinfinite r.e. sets A, $FIN_{\bar{A}}$ indeed exists in the appropriate range of 1-degrees to be so considered, and that, in addition, $FIN_{\bar{A}} \leq_1 A^{<2>}$. (Note that for A cofinite $FIN_{\bar{A}} = \omega$.) However, in the discussion following Theorem 4.1, it will be shown that $FIN_{\bar{A}} \not\equiv_1 A^{<2>}$ in general and is therefore a different variety of weak double jump (a weaker variety) than the the one we have been considering.

Lemma 3.2. If A is a coinfinite r.e. set then

$$\emptyset^{<2>} \leq_1 FIN_{\bar{A}} \leq_1 A^{<2>} \leq_1 \emptyset^{<3>}.$$

Proof. The proof can be found in [1] and will appear elsewhere.

4. Characterizations of Nonspeedable and Effectively Speedable Sets

Before presenting the information content characterizations of nonspeedable and effectively speedable sets, it is appropriate to consider some results on r.e. complexity sequences. Bennison [1] showed that the sets possessing type 0 r.e. complexity sequences are exactly the nonspeedable sets and these will therefore be dealt with momentarily. He also showed that an r.e. set A has a type 1 r.e. complexity sequence if and only if $FIN_{\bar{A}} \equiv_1 FIN$. So a coinfinite r.e. set A has a type 1 r.e. complexity sequence if and only if $FIN_{\bar{A}} \equiv_1 \emptyset^{<2>}$, or in other words, if and only if $FIN_{\bar{A}}$ has the lowest possible 1-degree. The property of having a type 1 r.e. complexity sequence thus corresponds to one type of lowness property on the 1-degrees. No good information content characterization has yet been found for the type 2 r.e. complexity sequences.

Theorem 4.1. An r.e. set A different from ω is nonspeedable if and only if $A^{<2>} \equiv_1 \emptyset^{<2>}$ (i.e., A is weak low_2).

Proof. The proof can be found in [1] and will appear elsewhere.

In Lemma 3.2 we showed that $FIN_{\bar{A}} \leq_1 A^{<2>}$. That there exist coinfinite r.e. sets A for which $A^{<2>} \not\leq_1 FIN_{\bar{A}}$ follows from Theorem 4.1 and from the fact that there are speedable sets which have type 1 r.e. complexity sequences [3] and therefore have $FIN_{\bar{A}} \equiv_1 \emptyset^{<2>}$ but $A^{<2>} \not\equiv_1 \emptyset^{<2>}$.

Theorem 4.2. An r.e. set A is effectively speedable if and only if $A^{<1>} \equiv_1 \emptyset^{<2>}$ (i.e., A is strong $high_1$).

Proof. The proof can be found in [1] and will appear elsewhere.

Thus nonspeedable sets and sets with type 1 r.e. complexity sequences exhibit the "lowness" properties $A^{<2>} \equiv_1 \emptyset^{<2>}$ and $FIN_{\bar{A}} \equiv_1 \emptyset^{<2>}$, respectively, and effectively speedable sets exhibit the "highness" property $A^{<1>} \equiv_1 \emptyset^{<2>}$. It is trivial to show that the r.e. sets A for which $A^{<1>} \equiv_1 \emptyset^{<1>}$ (i.e., the weak low_1 sets) are the recursive sets and those for which $A^{<0>} \equiv_1 \emptyset^{<1>}$ are the creative sets. We have not yet discovered any complexity theoretic (or even any well-studied recursion theoretic) properties corresponding either to the condition $A^{<2>} \equiv_1 \emptyset^{<3>}$ or to the condition $A^{<3>} \equiv_1 \emptyset^{<3>}$.

5. Characterizations of Nonlevelable and Effectively Levelable Sets

Blum and Marques [6] and Soare [13] have studied the complexity theoretic property of levelability. Their results tend to confirm that, though all levelable sets are speedable, the notions of levelability and speedability are quite dissimilar. For example Blum and Marques show that there are effectively nonlevelable sets which are nonetheless effectively speedable. This means that there are nonlevelable (even effectively nonlevelable) sets which do not even have type 2 r.e. complexity sequences (the least restrictive kind of complexity sequence). Bennison [2] showed, on the other hand, that there are levelable sets which do have type 2 r.e. complexity sequences. It would be reasonable to expect, therefore, that to characterize levelability our measure of information content will have to be modified. Soare [13] defined such an alternate measure and used it to find an information content characterization of the nonlevelable sets. Instead of looking at the information contained in the index set $H_{\bar{A}} = \{i : W_i \cap \bar{A} \neq \emptyset\}$, he looked at the index sets $\{i : R_i \cap \bar{A} \neq \emptyset\}$ where R_i is a uniformly recursive array.

Definition 5.1. A sequence $\mathcal{R} = \{R_i\}_{i \in \omega}$ of recursive sets is a:

(1) recursively enumerable array if there is a recursive function σ such that $R_i = W_{\sigma(i)}$ for all i;

(2) uniformly recursive array if there is a recursive function σ such that $\phi_{\sigma(i)}$ is the characteristic function of R_i for all i.

In the latter case if $\sigma = \phi_e$ we call e an index for $\mathcal{R}$. Note that as a jump operator $\{i : R_i \cap \bar{A} \neq \emptyset\}$ is ill-behaved. As an extreme example, if A = K where K is the halting problem and if for every i, $R_i = \omega$ then $\{i : R_i \cap \bar{A} \neq \emptyset\} = \omega$ and contains no information. We will therefore not try to iterate the operation. However, by looking at all possible uniformly recursive arrays and their corresponding index sets we can arrive at useful characterizations.

Theorem 5.2 (Soare [13, p. 26]). An r.e. set A is nonlevelable if and only if $\{i : R_i \cap \bar{A} \neq \emptyset\} \leq_T \emptyset'$ for every uniformly recursive array $\{R_i\}_{i \in \omega}$.

Since for every r.e. set A, $\{i : R_i \cap \bar{A} \neq \emptyset\} \leq_1$ FIN for every uniformly recursive array, it follows that for r.e. sets A, A is nonlevelable if and only if $\{i : R_i \cap \bar{A} \neq \emptyset\} \leq_1$ INF for every uniformly recursive array $\{R_i\}_{i \in \omega}$. This is analogous to Soare's result [13] that an r.e. set A is nonspeedable if and only if $EMP_{\bar{A}} \leq_1$ FIN, as the latter condition is directly equivalent to $H_{\bar{A}} \leq_1$ INF. This says that an r.e. set is nonlevelable if the information in $\{i : R_i \cap \bar{A} \neq \emptyset\}$ is low for all uniformly recursive arrays. The highest information level achievable by $\{i : R_i \cap \bar{A} \neq \emptyset\}$ for any uniformly recursive array is that of FIN. We now show that an r.e. set is effectively levelable if and only if this level is reached for some such array. We will use Filotti's characterization of the effectively levelable sets.

Definition 5.3 (Filotti [7]). An r.e. set A is undercreative if there exists a uniformly recursive array $\{W_{\sigma(i)}\}_{i \in \omega}$ such that for all j

$$W_j \cap A \text{ finite} \implies W_{\sigma(j)} \subseteq \overline{W_j - A} \quad \text{and}$$
$$W_{\sigma(j)} \cap \overline{(W_j \cup A)} \neq \emptyset.$$

Theorem 5.4 (Filotti [7]). An r.e. set A is effectively levelable if and only if it is undercreative.

Theorem 5.5. An r.e. set A is effectively levelable if and only if there exists a uniformly recursive array $\{R_i\}_{i \in \omega}$ such that $\{i : R_i \cap \bar{A} \neq \emptyset\} \leq_1 \text{FIN}$.

Proof. We need only show that A is effectively levelable if and only if $\text{FIN} \leq_1 \{i : R_i \cap \bar{A} \neq \emptyset\}$ for some uniformly recursive array $\{R_i\}_{i \in \omega}$, since for any such array

$$\{i : R_i \cap \bar{A} \neq \emptyset\} \leq_1 \{i : W_i \cap \bar{A} \neq \emptyset\} = H_{\bar{A}} \leq_1 \text{FIN}.$$

($\Longrightarrow$). Since A is effectively levelable it is undercreative and we have the uniformly recursive array $\{W_{\sigma(i)}\}_{i \in \omega}$ given to us by Definition 5.3. We define a function $\delta \in R^1$ which will be used later to obtain the desired 1-1 reduction. For every i, let $W_{\delta(i)} = W_{\sigma(j)}$ where j is effectively found from i using implicit recursion as follows:

$$W_j = \begin{cases} W_i & \text{if } W_j \cap W_{\sigma(j)} \cap \bar{A} = \emptyset \\ \text{finite} & \text{otherwise} \end{cases}$$

In other words, elements of W_i will be enumerated into W_j while there are no candidates for membership in $W_j \cap W_{\sigma(j)} \cap \bar{A}$, i.e., an element of $W_j \cap W_{\sigma(j)}$ which has not yet appeared in A. When such a candidate x appears, enumeration of W_i ceases until x is shown to be in A, at which time at least one new element of W_i is enumerated into W_j (should such an element exist) before enumeration can be blocked again by another candidate. We claim that $W_j = W_i$. Clearly if W_j is infinite then $W_j = W_i$, whereas W_j finite implies $W_j \cap A$ finite implies by the definition of σ that $W_{\sigma(j)} \subseteq \overline{W_j - A}$, which directly implies $W_j \cap \bar{A} \cap W_{\sigma(j)} = \emptyset$ so that again $W_j = W_i$ by the definition of W_j.

It follows from the above that for every i

$$W_i \cap W_{\delta(i)} \cap \bar{A} = \emptyset$$

which is the same as saying that for every i

$$W_{\delta(i)} \subseteq \overline{W_i - A}\ .$$

Define $\alpha \in R^1$ by

$$W_{\alpha(i)} = \begin{cases} N & \text{if } W_i \text{ is infinite} \\ \text{finite} & \text{otherwise} \end{cases}$$

Then

$$\begin{aligned} W_i \text{ infinite} &\Longrightarrow W_{\alpha(i)} = N \\ &\Longrightarrow W_{\delta(\alpha(i))} \subseteq \overline{W_{\alpha(i)} - A} = \overline{N - A} = A \\ &\Longrightarrow W_{\delta(\alpha(i))} \cap \bar{A} = \emptyset \end{aligned}$$

$$\begin{aligned} W_i \text{ finite} &\Longrightarrow W_{\alpha(i)} \text{ finite} \\ &\Longrightarrow W_{\alpha(i)} \cap A \text{ finite} \end{aligned}$$

$$\Longrightarrow W_{\delta(\alpha(i))} \cap \overline{W}_{\alpha(i)} \cap \bar{A} \neq \emptyset$$

$$\Longrightarrow W_{\delta(\alpha(i))} \cap \bar{A} \neq \emptyset.$$

Therefore FIN $\leq_1 \{i : R_i \cap \bar{A} \neq \emptyset\}$ via α where for every i, $R_i = W_{\delta(i)}$.

($\Longleftarrow$). We are given a uniformly recursive array $\{R_i\}_{i \in \omega}$ and a $\sigma \in R^1$ such that for every j

$$W_j \text{ is finite } \Longleftrightarrow R_{\sigma(j)} \cap \bar{A} \neq \emptyset.$$

We shall find an effective subarray of this array which will satisfy the definition of undercreativity. For each i we shall use implicit recursion to effectively find an index j such that our desired array will be defined by $W_{\delta(i)} = R_{\sigma(j)}$. The index j will be constructed in stages. At stages s, we shall say that an integer x is a _good candidate_ if

$$x \in R_{\sigma(j),s} \cap \bar{A}_s \cap \overline{W}_{i,s}$$

and a _bad candidate_ if

$$x \in R_{\sigma(j),s} \cap \bar{A}_s \cap W_{i,s}.$$

Notice that if x is a bad candidate at stage s then x cannot become a good candidate at a later stage though x can cease to be a candidate. A good candidate can become bad or cease to be a candidate.

Construction of W_j.

Stage s.

(1) If there is at least one good candidate at stage s and no bad candidates then go to stage s+1.

(2) If there is a bad candidate at stage s then let $W_{j,s} = W_{j,s-1} \cup A_s$ and go to stage s+1.

(3) If there are no candidates then let $W_{j,s} = W_{j,s-1} \cup (W_{i,s} \cap A_s)$ and go to stage s+1.

It is easy to show that under the original hypothesis A must be infinite. If, therefore, $W_i \cap A$ is finite (the only case in which we are interested) then step (2) can be executed at only finitely many stages. Otherwise $W_j \supseteq A$ and is therefore infinite making $R_{\sigma(j)} \cap \bar{A} = \emptyset$. This in turn would mean that infinitely many bad candidates had ceased to be candidates by becoming members of $W_i \cap A$, a contradiction. Now consider what happens beyond the last stage at which step (2) is executed. By examining steps (1) and (3) we see that since $W_i \cap A$ is finite so is W_j and therefore $R_{\sigma(j)} \cap \bar{A} \neq \emptyset$. Say $x \in R_{\sigma(j)} \cap \bar{A}$. Then x must become a permanent candidate (of necessity good) at some stage beyond which step (3) can never again be executed. Beyond that stage only step (1) will be executed. We may conclude that if $W_i \cap A$ is finite then beyond some stage there is at least one permanent good candidate and there are no bad candidates. Letting $W_{\delta(i)} = R_{\sigma(j)}$ we have

$$W_i \cap A \text{ finite} \Longrightarrow W_{\delta(i)} \subseteq \overline{W_i - A} \text{ and}$$

$$W_{\delta(i)} \cap (\overline{W_i \cup A}) \neq \emptyset.$$

So A is effectively levelable.

References.

[1] V. Bennison, On the computational complexity of recursively enumerable sets, Ph.D. Dissertation, University of Chicago, 1976.

[2] ________, Recursively enumerable complexity sequences and measure independence, preprint to appear.

[3] V. Bennison and R.I. Soare, Some lowness properties and computational complexity sequences, J. Theoretical Computer Science 6 (1978) 233-254.

[4] M. Blum, A machine-independent theory of the complexity of recursive functions, J. Assoc. for Computing Machinery 14 (1967), 322-336.

[5] ______, On defining the complexity of partial recursive functions, preprint.

[6] M. Blum and I. Marques, On complexity properties of recursively enumerable sets, J. Symbolic Logic 38 (1973), 579-593.

[7] I. Filotti, On effectively levelable sets, Recursive Function Newsletter No. 2 (1972), 12-13.

[8] J. Hartmanis and F.D. Lewis, The use of lists in the study of undecidable problems in automata theory, J. Computer and Systems Science 5 (1971), 54-66.

[9] I. Marques, Complexity properties of recursively enumerable sets, Ph.D. Dissertation, University of California, Berkeley, 1973.

[10] A.R. Meyer and P.C. Fischer, Computational speed-up by effective operators, J. Symbolic Logic 37 (1972), 55-68.

[11] P.H. Morris, Complexity theoretic properties of recursively enumerable sets, Ph.D. Dissertation, University of California, Irvine, 1974.

[12] H. Rogers, Jr., Theory of recursive functions and effective computability, McGraw-Hill, New York, 1967.

[13] R.I. Soare, Computational complexity, speedable and levelable sets, J. Symbolic Logic 42 (1977), 545-563.

MITTLERE ANZAHL VON REBALANCIERUNGSOPERATIONEN IN GEWICHTSBALANCIERTEN BÄUMEN

Norbert Blum
Kurt Mehlhorn

Kurzfassung: Es wird gezeigt, daß die mittlere Anzahl von Balancierungsoperationen (Rotationen und Doppelrotationen) bei gewichtsbalancierten Bäumen konstant ist.

Abstract: It is shown that the average number of rebalancing operations (rotations and double rotations) in weight-balanced trees is constant.

I. EINLEITUNG

Balancierte Bäume sind eine populäre Methode für die Speicherung von Information in einem Computer. Die Basisoperationen Zugriff, Einfügen und Streichen können bei einer Menge von n Items in einer Zeit von O(log n) ausgeführt werden.

Sämtliche bekannten Arten von balancierten Bäumen lassen sich auf zwei Grundtypen zurückführen: Höhenbalancierte Bäume (AVL-Bäume [AVL], 2-3-Bäume [AHU], Bruder-Bäume [OS],...) und gewichtsbalancierte Bäume. Bei den ersteren balanciert man entweder Höhen der Teilbäume (AVL-Bäume) oder die Anzahl der Söhne eines Knotens (2-3 Bäume, Bruder-Bäume). Hier werden wir uns mit den gewichtsbalancierten Bäumen näher befassen. Gewichtsbalancierte Bäume wurden von Nievergelt und Reingold [NR] eingeführt.

Ein Knoten in einem binären Baum hat entweder zwei Söhne oder keinen Sohn. Knoten ohne Söhne werden Blätter genannt.

Definition: Sei T ein binärer Baum. Ist T ein einfaches Blatt, dann ist die Wurzelbalance $\rho(T)$ gleich 1/2. Im anderen Fall definieren wir:

$\rho(T) = \frac{|T_\ell|}{|T|}$, wobei $|T_\ell|$ die Anzahl der Blätter im linken Teilbaum von T und $|T|$ die Anzahl der Blätter in T ist.

Definition: Sei $0 \leq \alpha \leq 1/2$. Ein binärer Baum T heißt von beschränkter Balance α oder in $BB[\alpha]$, genau dann, wenn gilt:

1) $\alpha \leq \rho(T) \leq 1-\alpha$

2) T ist Blatt oder beide Teilbäume sind von beschränkter Balance α.

Bemerkung: Beachte, daß $\frac{|T_r|}{|T|} = 1-\rho(T)$. Indem wir eventuell den linken und rechten Teilbaum austauschen, können wir oBdA annehmen, daß $\rho(T) \leq 1/2$.

Balancierte Bäume haben viele Eigenschaften gemeinsam:

1) Die Tiefe ist durch $O(\log |T|)$ beschränkt.

2) Nach Einfügen oder Streichen eines Blattes sind höchstens $O(\log|T|)$ Balancierungsoperationen nötig, um den Baum zu rebalancieren. Die Rebalancierungsoperationen sind begrenzt auf den Suchpfad. In allen bekannten Beispielen von balancierten Bäumen ist es einfach, ein Beispiel zu konstruieren, in welchem jeder Knoten entlang dem Suchpfad rebalanciert werden muß.

Beispiel: Betrachte folgenden 2-3 Baum

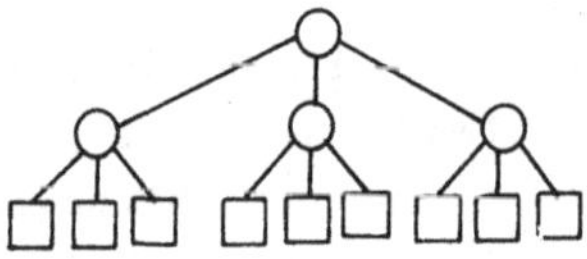

Das Einfügen eines Knotens im linken Teilbaum verursacht folgende Folge von Balancierungsoperationen.

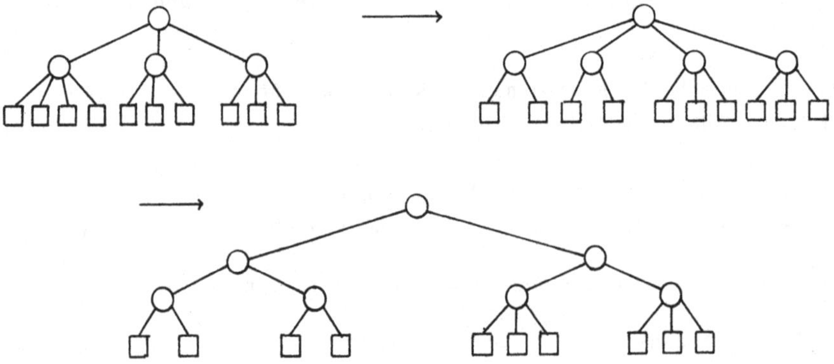

<u>Beachte:</u> Erneutes Einfügen eines Blattes verursacht höchstens eine Balancierungsoperation. Dies liegt nahe, daß im Mittel (gemittelt über eine Zufallsfolge von Einfügen und Streichen) eine kleinere Anzahl von Balancierungsoperationen genügen. Beachte auch, daß Streichen des am weitesten links liegenden Blattes die obige Folge umkehrt und den ursprünglichen Baum wiederherstellt.

3) Simulationsresultate zeigen, daß im Mittel eine konstante Anzahl von Operationen genügen. Karlton und andere [KFSK] berichten, daß im Mittel 0,46 (0,23) Balancierungsoperationen (Rotationen und Doppelrotationen) erforderlich sind, um einen AVL-Baum nach Einfügen (Streichen) eines Blattes zu rebalancieren. Plausibilitätsargumente stützen den empirischen Befund [F,KN Seite 462, NR].

Diese Plausibilitätsargumente basieren auf der ungerechtfertigten Annahme, daß die Balancen (Höhendifferenz zwischen linkem und rechtem Teilbaum in AVL-Bäume, Wurzelbalancen in BB[α]-Bäumen) unabhängige Zufallsvariablen sind. Diese Plausibilitätsbetrachtungen liefern Konstanten, die nahe bei den empirischen Befunden liegen.

Wir werden beweisen, daß die mittlere Anzahl der Balancierungsoperationen in BB[α]-Bäumen durch eine Konstante beschränkt ist. Wir beweisen sogar noch ein stärkeres Resultat, nämlich:

Es gibt eine Konstante c (abhängig von α) sodaß: Die Gesamtzahl der Balancierungsoperationen, die bei Ausführung einer beliebigen Folge von n Einfüge- und Streiche-Operationen in einem anfänglich leeren BB[α]-Baum erforderlich sind, ist durch $c \cdot n$ begrenzt.

Wir mitteln nicht über <u>viele</u> Folgen von Einfüge- und Streiche-Operationen, sondern nur über die Einfüge- und Streich-Operationen einer einzigen beliebigen Folge (im Gegensatz zu den Simulationen). Unsere Konstante ist viel größer als die empirischen Befunde nahelegen (über 27 für α = 1/4). Wir behaupten nicht, daß unsere Konstante die bestmögliche ist.

Zusätzlich korrigieren wir einen ernsthaften Fehler in der Originalarbeit von Nievergelt und Reingold über BB[α]-Bäume.

II. DER EFFEKT VON ROTATION UND DOPPELROTATION IN GEWICHTSBALANCIERTEN BÄUMEN

BB[α]-Bäume werden durch Rotation und Doppelrotation balanciert. Folgendes Bild ist aus [NR] genommen. Vierecke stehen für Knoten, Dreiecke für Teilbäume. Die Wurzelbalancen sind neben den Knoten angegeben. Symmetrische Varianten der Operationen existieren.

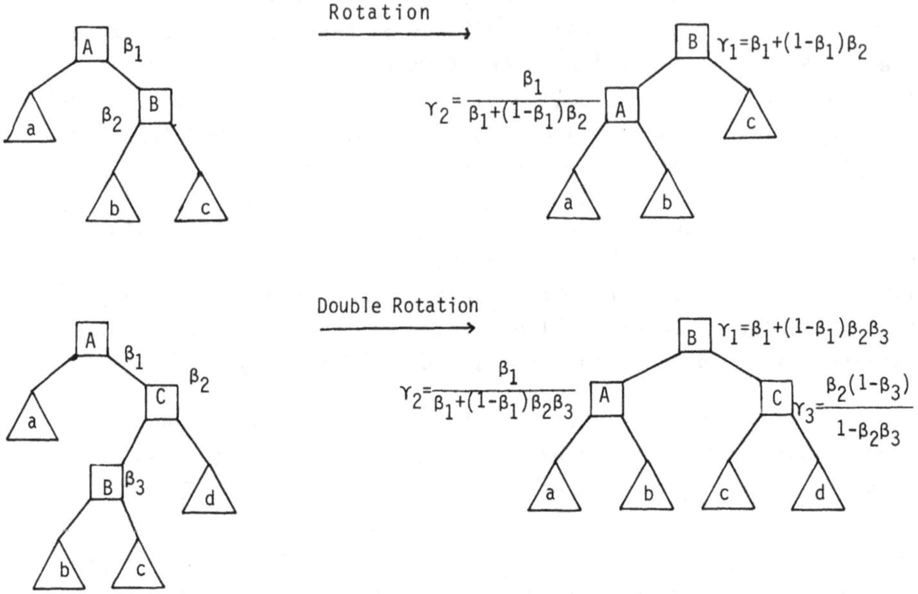

Bild 1:

Nievergelt und Reingold geben in [NR] folgenden Satz ohne Beweis

Theorem 4: If $\alpha \leq 1-\sqrt{2}/2$ and the insertion or deletion of a node in a tree in BB[α] causes a subtree T of that tree to have root-balance less than α, T can be rebalanced by performing one of the two transformations shown above. More precisely, let β_2 denote the balance of the right subtree of T after the insertion or deletion has been done. If $\beta_2 < (1-2\alpha)/(1-\alpha)$, then a rotation will rebalance T, otherwise a double rotation will rebalance T.

Dieser Satz ist falsch. Betrachte folgendes Gegenbeispiel:
$\alpha = 2/11$. Die Blätter sind nicht eingezeichnet.

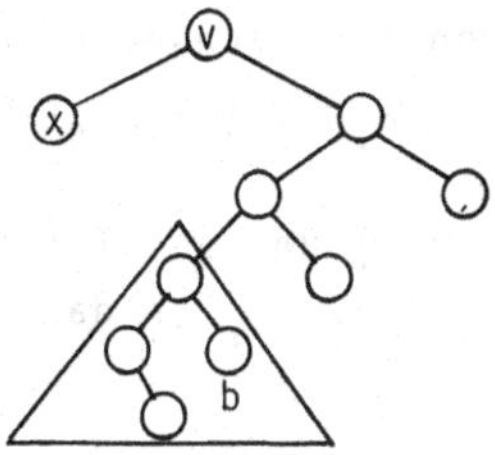

Die Wurzel v dieses Baumes hat Balance $\rho(v) = 2/11$. Nach Streichen eines Blattes mit Vater x ist $\rho(v) = 1/10$. Die Wurzel muß daher rebalanciert werden. Eine Doppelrotation liefert:

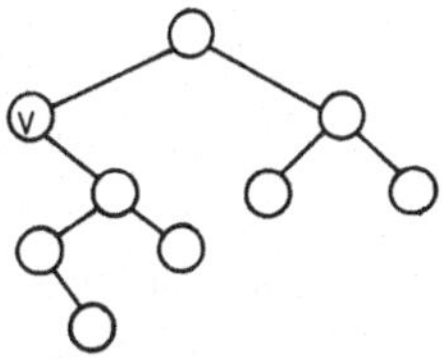

Knoten v hat Balance $1/6 < 2/11$. Nach einer Rotation erhalten wir folgenden Baum

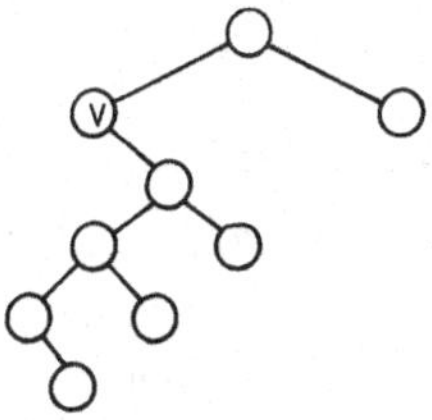

Die Balance von v ist hier noch schlechter.

Dieses Gegenbeispiel zeigt, daß der "Satz" in [NR] für $1/6 < \alpha \leq 2/11$ falsch ist. Für jedes α mit $0 < \alpha \leq 1/6$ erhält man ein analoges Gegenbeispiel, indem man den Teilbaum b vergrößert.

Wir werden zeigen, daß eine stärkere Version des obigen Satzes für $2/11 < \alpha \leq 1-\sqrt{2}/2$ gilt. Wir werden noch mehr beweisen. Wir werden nicht nur zeigen, daß Rotation und Doppelrotation genügen, um den Baum zu rebalancieren, sondern auch dazu ausreichen, die Balancen in das Intervall $[(1+\delta)\alpha, 1-(1+\delta)\alpha]$ für kleines δ zu bewegen. Diese Beobachtung wird uns im nächsten Abschnitt erlauben zu zeigen, daß die mittlere Anzahl der Balancierungsoperationen konstant ist.

Satz 1: Es gibt eine stetige monoton wachsende Funktion

$c : [0,0.01] \to R$ mit $c(0) = 0$, $c(0{,}01) = 0{,}0043$ so daß gilt:

Sei $\alpha \in R$, $2/11 < \alpha \leq 1-\sqrt{2}/2 - c(\delta)$ und sei T ein binärer Baum mit linken und rechten Teilbäumen T_ℓ bzw. T_r so daß gilt:

1) T_ℓ und T_r sind in $BB[\alpha]$

2) $|T_\ell|/|T| < \alpha$ und entweder

2.1) $|T_\ell|/(|T|-1) \geq \alpha$

(T wurde durch Einfügen eines Blattes im rechten Teilbaum erhalten)

oder

2.2) $(|T_\ell|+1|)/(|T|+1) \geq \alpha$

(T wurde durch Streichen eines Blattes von linkem Teilbaum von T erhalten)

Dann genügen Rotation und Doppelrotation, um T derart zu balancieren, so daß für $\gamma_1,\gamma_2,\gamma_3$ bezüglich Bild 1 gilt:

$$\gamma_1,\gamma_2,\gamma_3 \in [(1+\delta)\alpha,\ 1-(1+\delta)\alpha] \quad \text{für } 1/4 < \alpha \leq 1-\sqrt{2}/2 - c(\delta)$$

$$|T| > 10 \text{ und } \gamma_1,\gamma_2,\gamma_3 \in [\alpha, 1-\alpha] \qquad \text{sonst.}$$

Bemerkung: Für $\delta = 0$ ist dies die korrekte Version des Satzes von Nievergelt und Reingold.

Beweis: Mühevolle, aber einfache Rechnungen (siehe hierzu [BM]).

III. DIE MITTLERE ANZAHL DER BALANCIERUNGSOPERATIONEN

Bevor wir unser Haupttheorem zeigen können, benötigen wir einige Begriffe:

Eine Transaktion ist entweder eine Einfüge- oder eine Streiche-Operation. Eine Transaktion geht durch einen Knoten v, falls v auf dem Suchpfad zu dem Blatt liegt, das eingefügt bzw. gestrichen wurde.

Ein Knoten v nimmt an einer Balancierungsoperation teil, falls er einem der in Bild 1 bezeichneten Knoten entspricht. Ein Knoten v verursacht eine Balancierungsoperation, falls er der Wurzel eines in Bild 1 auf der linken Seite gezeichneten Baumes entspricht.

Betrachte eine Folge von Transaktionen. Wir starten mit einem Baum T_0 und wenden die erste Transaktion auf ihn an. Dann wird der Baum rebalanciert und wir erhalten als Resultatsbaum T_1. Die nächste Transaktion wird auf T_1 angewandt, T_1 wird rebalanciert ... .

Sei $T_0, T_1, T_2, \ldots, T_m, \ldots$ eine solche Folge von BB[α]-Bäumen.

Lemma 1: Sei $0 \leq \delta \leq 0{,}01$, $2/11 < \alpha \leq 1-\sqrt{2}/2 - c(\delta)$ und v ein Knoten. Falls

1) v verursacht eine Balancierungsoperation in T_m (nachdem eine Transaktion auf T_m angewandt wurde) und
2) entweder v nahm schon vorher an einer Balancierungsoperation teil oder v war nicht schon ein Knoten im Anfangsbaum T_0 und
3) n ist die Anzahl der Blätter des Teilbaumes mit Wurzel v in T_m und $n > 11$ falls $\alpha \leq 1/4$

Dann gingen mindestens $\lceil \delta\alpha n \rceil$ Transaktionen durch v seit v zum letzten Mal an einer Balancierungsoperation teilgenommen hat oder, falls v noch an keiner Balancierungsoperation teilgenommen hat, seitdem v kreiert wurde.

Beweis: Sei $j < m$ so daß gilt:

v nahm an einer Balancierungsoperation in T_j teil, aber nicht in $T_{j+1}, \ldots, T_{m-1}$ oder v existierte nicht in T_j aber in $T_{j+1}, \ldots, T_{m-1}$ und nahm niemals an einer Balancierungsoperation teil. Im zweiten Fall ist die Wurzelbalance $\rho(v)$ des Knotens v in T_{j+1} gleich 1/2. Im ersten Fall liegt die Wurzelbalance $\rho(v) = t'/n'$ des Knotens v in T_{j+1} in

$[(1+\delta)\alpha,\ 1-(1+\delta)\alpha]$ oder $\alpha \leq 1/4$ und $n' \leq 10$. Dies folgt unmittelbar aus Satz 1.

Die Balance $\rho(v) = t/n$ des Knotens v in T_m liegt außerhalb des Intervalls $[\alpha,1-\alpha]$. Sei oBdA $t/n < \alpha$.

In den Bäumen $T_{j+1},\ldots,T_{m-1}$ waren $d_\ell(i_\ell)$ Streiche-(Einfüge-)Operationen im linken Teilbaum von v und d_r (i_r) Streiche-(Einfüge-) Operationen im rechten Teilbaum von v durchgeführt worden.

Also gilt:

$$t = t' - d_\ell + i_\ell$$

$$n = n' - d_\ell - d_r + i_\ell + i_r$$

Die Anzahl der Transaktionen, die durch v gehen, beträgt $d\ +d_r+i_\ell\ +i_r$. Wir benötigen eine untere Schranke für diese Zahl. Sicher ist $|n-n'|$ eine untere Schranke. Deswegen sind wir im Fall $n' \leq 10\ \wedge$ $\alpha \leq 1/4$ fertig. Sei also $n' > 10 \vee \alpha > 1/4$ und daher auch $t'/n' \in [(1+\delta)\alpha,\ 1-(1+\delta/\alpha]$.

Anm.: Die Behauptung stimmt nicht und daher $d_\ell+d_r+i_\ell+i_r<\delta\alpha n$ dann gilt:

$$t'/n' - (1+\delta)\alpha =$$

$$\frac{t+d_\ell-i_\ell}{n+d_\ell+d_r-i_\ell-i_r} - (1+\delta)\alpha$$

$$\leq \frac{t+d_\ell}{n+d_\ell-i_r} - (1+\delta)\alpha$$

$$\leq \frac{t+\delta\alpha n}{n+\delta\alpha n} - (1+\delta)\alpha \qquad \text{da } 0 \leq d_\ell + i_r \leq \delta\alpha n$$

$\frac{t+d_\ell}{n+d_\ell-i_r}$ monoton wachsend in d_ℓ und $\frac{t+\delta\alpha n-i_r}{n+\delta\alpha n-2i_r}$ für

$2/11 < \alpha \leq 0{,}3,\ 0 \leq \delta \leq 0{,}01$ monoton fallend in i_r

$$\leq \frac{\alpha n+\delta\alpha n}{n+\delta\alpha n} - (1+\delta)\alpha$$

$$= - \frac{(1+\delta)\delta\alpha^2}{1+\delta\alpha} < 0$$

Widerspruch

□

Lemma 1 zeigt, daß zwischen zwei Zeitpunkte, in welchen v an einer Balancierungsoperation teilnimmt, viele Transaktionen durch v gehen. Um den Beweis zu beenden, benötigen wir nur nooch eine gescheite Art, die Transaktionen und die Balancierungsoperationen zu zählen.

Jeder Knoten v erhält Zähler

Transaktionszähler	$TA_i(v)$	
Balancierungsoperationszähler	$BO_i(v)$	$i \in N_0$

Weiterhin gibt es noch einen speziellen Zähler S. Alle Zähler haben anfangs den Wert 0.

Sei T_0 ein Baum in BB[α] und sei $T_0, T_1, \ldots, T_m, \ldots$ eine Transaktionsfolge von BB[α]-Bäumen.

Sei v ein Knoten in T_m und n die Anzahl der Blätter des Teilbaumes in T_m mit Wurzel v. Sei i so gewählt,daß gilt:

$(1/1-\alpha)^i \leq n < (1/1-\alpha)^{i+1}$. Da $n \geq 2$ ist, gilt $i \geq 1$.

Falls die auf T_m angewandte Transaktion durch Knoten v geht, zählen wir eine Einheit zu den Transaktionszählern $TA_{i-1}(v)$, $TA_i(v)$ und $TA_{i+1}(v)$.

Falls v eine Balancierungsoperation in T_m verursacht, zählen wir eine Einheit zu

$BO_i(v)$. falls v schon vorher an einer Balancierungsoperation teilnahm oder nicht schon im Anfangsbaum T_0 war

S sonst.

Da für jeden Knoten v im Anfangsbaum T_0 höchstens eine Einheit zu S gezählt wird, gilt

$$S \leq |T_0| - 1.$$

Wir müssen noch die Inhalte der Balancierungsoperationszähler $BO_i(v)$ zusammenzählen.

Wann immer eine Einheit zum Zähler $BO_i(v)$ addiert wird, sind wir in einer Situation, in welcher Lemma 2 anwendbar ist: Ist $n \geq 11$ oder

$\alpha > 1/4$, dann gingen mindestens $\delta\alpha n$ Transaktionen durch v, seitdem v zum letzten Mal an einer Balancierungsoperation teilgenommen hat (falls v dies jemals tat) oder v kreiert wurde. Da (betrachte Bild 2) $n - [1/(1-\alpha)]^{i-1} \geq \delta\alpha n$ und $[1/(1-\alpha)]^{i+2} - n \geq \delta\alpha n$

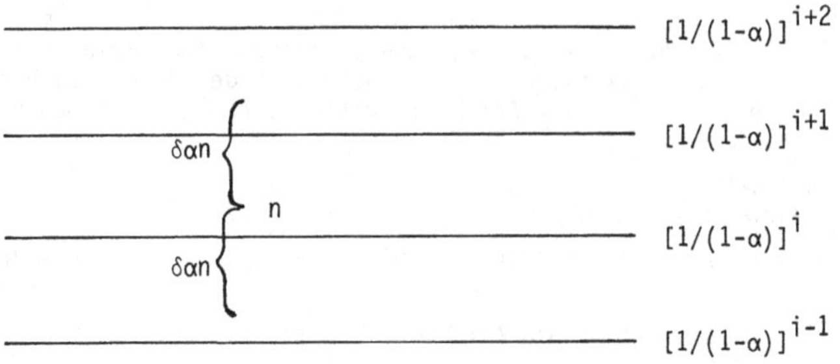

Bild 2:

wissen wir , daß mindestens $\delta\alpha n$ Einheiten zu $TA_i(v)$ addiert wurden, seitdem v zum letzten Mal an einer Balancierungsoperation teilgenommen hat oder kreiert wurde. Also gilt:

$$BO_i(v) \leq \frac{1}{\delta\alpha n} TA_i(v) \leq \frac{(1-\alpha)^i}{\delta\alpha} TA_i(v) \qquad \text{falls } \alpha > 1/4 \text{ oder } [1/(1-\alpha)]^i \geq 11$$

Da $\alpha > 2/11$, ist dies sicher der Fall für $i \geq 12$.

Wir können nun die Anzahl A der für die ersten m Transaktionen benötigten Balancierungsoperationen abschätzen.

Es gilt:

$$A = S + \sum_v \sum_i BO_i(v)$$

$$= S + \sum_v \sum_{i<k} BO_i(v) + \sum_v \sum_{i \geq k} BO_i(v)$$

Da $S \leq |T_0| - 1$,

$$\sum_v \sum_{i \geq k} BO_i(v)$$

$$\leq 1/\delta\alpha \sum_v \sum_{i \geq k} (1-\alpha)^i \, TA_i(v)$$

$$\leq [3(1-\alpha)^k/\delta\alpha^2]\cdot m$$

und

$$\sum_{v} \sum_{i<k} BO_i(v)$$

$\leq$ max. Tiefe eines BB[α]-Baumes mit $[1/(1-\alpha)]^k$ Blättern]·m

$\leq$ (k-1)·m

wie einfache Rechnungen ergeben (siehe [BM]) gilt:

$$\leq |T_0|-1 + \min_{\substack{k\in N \\ k\geq 12}} [\, k-1+3(1-\alpha)^k/\delta\alpha^2]\cdot m$$

Wir haben damit folgenden Satz bewiesen:

Satz 2: Sei $0 < \delta \leq 0{,}01$ und $2/11 < \alpha \leq 1-\sqrt{2}/2 - c(\delta)$, wobei c wie in Satz 1 definiert ist. Dann gibt es eine Konstante d, so daß gilt: Sei T_0 ein Baum in BB[α]. Höchstens $|T_0|-1+d\cdot m$ Balancierungsoperationen sind bei der Durchführung einer beliebigen Folge von m Einfüge- und Streiche-Operationen mit Anfangsbaum T_0 erforderlich.

Korollar: Es gibt eine Konstante d mit folgender Eigenschaft: Es genügen d·m Balancierungsoperationen zur Ausführung von m Einfüge- und Streiche-Operationen in einem anfänglich leeren Baum.

Wir wollen nun für ein konkretes Beispiel die Konstante d bestimmen.

Sei $\alpha = 1/4$ und $\delta = 0{,}01$.

Sei K = 25. Dann gilt $\frac{3(1-\alpha)^k}{\alpha 2} \approx 3{,}61$.

Ein BB[1/4]Baum mit $\leq (4/3)^{25} \approx 1329$ Blättern hat maximale Tiefe 23,87 (vergleiche [M,NR]).

Also gilt $d \leq 27{,}48$.

BIBLIOGRAPHY

[AHU] Aho, Hopcroft, Ullman: The Design and Analysis of Computer Algorithms, Addison Wesley, 1974

[AVL] Adel'son-Velskii, Laudis: An algorithm for the organization of information, Soviet. Math. Dokl, 3, 1259-1262, 1962

[BM] Blum N., Mehlhorn, K.: On the average number of rebalancing operations in weight-balanced trees, Technischer Bericht A-78/06, FB 10 der Universität des Saarlandes, 1978

[BS] Bayer, Schkolnik: Concurrency of Operations on B-Trees, Acta Informatica, Vol. 9, Fasc. 1, 1977, S. 1-22

[F] Foster: Information Storage and Retrieval using AVL-trees, Proc. ACM Nat. Conf. 20, 192-2o5, 1965

[KFSK] Karlton, Fuller, Scroggs, Kaehler: Performance of Height Balanced Trees, ACM, Jan. 1976, Vol. 19/1, S. 23-28

[M] Mehlhorn, K.: Effiziente Algorithmen, Teubner Verlag, Studienbücher Informatik, 1977

[NR] Nievergelt, Reingold: Binary Search Trees of Bounded Balance, SIAM, J. Comput., Vol. 2, No. 1, March 1973

[OS] Ottman, Six: Eine neue Klasse von ausgeglichenen Bäumen, Angewandte Informatik, Heft 9, S. 395-4oo, 1976

[Y] Yao: On Random 2-3 Trees, Acta Informatica, Vol. 9, Fasc. 2, 1978, S. 159-17o

[KN] Knuth: The Art of Computer Programming, Vol. III: Sorting and Searching, Addison Wesley Publishing Company

A NEW RECURSION INDUCTION PRINCIPLE

Gérard Boudol

Abstract : In this paper, a new recursion induction principle is formulated, by means of the "parallel outermost" computation rule, which allows us to validate a scheme of transformations and a method for proving strong equivalences.

Introduction

In the area of programs verifications and programs transformations, the main question is : how to prove properties of programs, how to prove equivalences which ensure the correctness of transformations ? Some powerful proof techniques are well-known for recursive procedures : These are inductive methods, such as "structural induction" ([2]) and "recursion inductions"([8], [16]. For an overview, see [14]). In the last methods, properties are proved by induction on the level of recursion or, to be more precise, by induction on the number of applications of a correct computation rule. It must be seen that, in all these recursion induction techniques, the underlying computation rule is the "full substitution"one. But there is at least another computation rule known to be (universally) correct : the "parallel outermost" rule (see [20],[9]).

We present here a recursion induction principle, which is an induction on the number of applications of this rule, and derive from it a correct transformation scheme, and a method for proving strong equivalences. We achieve this in the framework of the "algebraic semantics" of recursive programs, originated by M. Nivat ([17],[18],[6]). Two reasons for this choice : we believe that the formal distinction between syntactic and semantic aspects of programs leads to more perspicuous analysis of proofs (see [1]) - and that "algebraic" (or syntactic) proofs may be easier automatically performed. On the other hand, our inductive method seems to be especially convenient to prove strong equivalence (ie equivalence of terms under all interpretations), which is nicely expressed in algebraic semantics ([18]).

As an illustration of the proposed method, let us see the following example : the system Σ of recursive definitions of (monadic) procedure symbols φ, Ψ is given by

$$\begin{cases} \varphi(x)=f(x,\varphi(\Psi(x))) \\ \Psi(x)=f(\varphi(x),\Psi(\Psi(x))) \end{cases}$$

(where f is a base function symbol). Our induction principle asserts that, in order to prove the strong equivalence of the terms $\varphi(\varphi(x))$ and $\Psi(x)$, we only have to verify that

$$\varphi(\varphi(x))=\Psi(x) \Rightarrow f(\varphi(x),\varphi(\Psi(\varphi(x))))=f(\varphi(x),\Psi(\Psi(x)))$$

(where the second equality is obtained by applying to each member of the first the parallel outermost rule), which is obvious. The reader may convince himself that the corresponding proof with the usual recursion induction principle is not so easy (see [7], and [1] for an analysis of this example). Moreover, we emphasize another difference with the usual formulation of induction principle : the meaning of the implication from induction hypothesis at induction step is explicit in our formulation (see below, and [1] for consequences of this design in the usual principle).

1 - Algebraic Framework

In the two first sections, we briefly introduce the formalism and results of algebraic semantics that we need. For more details, see [5] and [6].

In order to built recursive program schemes - systems of recursive definitions -, we need sets of function symbols, that is sets F given with an arity function p (for each $f \in F$, the non-negative integer p(f) is the number of arguments of f, and we denote by F_k the set of elements of F of arity k).The terms obtained by composition of these symbols and applied to variables are particular cases of (finite) trees, and the set of (finite or infinite) trees is itself, as we shall see, a special case of F-magma (or F-algebra, cf [10]) ie structure $M=\langle D_M, \{f_M / f \in F\}\rangle$ where for each $f \in F$, f_M is a mapping from $D_M^{p(f)}$ to D_M (the domain of M). An ordered F-magma is a structure $M=\langle D_M, \leq_M, \bot_M, \{f_M / f \in F\}\rangle$ where $\langle D_M, \{f_M / f \in F\}\rangle$ is an F-magma, and $\leq_M$ is an order relation on D_M such that $\bot_M$ is the least element of D_M, and the functions f_M are monotonic (for the product order). A complete ordered F-magma (see also [10]) is the same, with the supplementary assumptions that D_M is complete for $\leq_M$ and that the f_M's are continuous - ([15])

Let $V=\{x_n / n \in N \text{ and } n \geq 1\}$ be a denumerable set of variables, disjoint from F, and let

$$W_F=\{(f,n) / f \in F_k, k \geq 1 \text{ and } 1 \leq n \leq k\}$$

An F-well-formed tree on V (abreviated F-tree on V) is a mapping t from $dom(t) \subseteq W_F^*$ (the free monoïd generated by W_F) to $F \cup V$ such that

$$w(f,i) \in dom(t) \Rightarrow w \in dom(t), \ t(w)=f \text{ and}$$
$$(dom(t)/w) \cap W_F \subseteq \{(f,n) \ / \ 1 \leq n \leq p(f)\}$$

(where, for $L \subseteq X^*$ and $w \in X^*$ = $L/w=\{u / u \in X^* \text{ and } wu \in L\}$.)

The set $M_F^\infty(V)$ of F-trees on V is ordered by $t \leq t' \Leftrightarrow dom(t) \subseteq dom(t')$ and $w \in dom(t) \Rightarrow t'(w)=t(w)$ (the restriction order)

For this order, the empty tree (whose domain is empty), denoted Ω, is the least element. Let $M_F(V)$ (resp. $\overline{M}_F(V)$) be the set of finite F-trees on V (whose domain is finite. Resp. the set of $\leq$-maximal finite F-trees on V: the terms). Each $f \in F_k$ obviously defines a continuous function f_H from $M_F^\infty(V)^k$ to $M_F^\infty(V)$ (see [5]), and we have :

Proposition 1 ([5])

The structure $\langle M_F(V), \{f_H / f \in F\}\rangle$,
$\langle M_F(V), \leq, \Omega, \{f_H / f \in F\}\rangle$ and

$H=\langle M_F^\infty(V), \leq, \Omega, \{f_H / f\in F\}\rangle$ are resp. free F-magma, the free ordered F-magma, the free complete ordered F-magma generated by V.

This essentially means that, for any complete ordered F-magma M and mapping $\nu : V \to D_M$ there exists one and only one continuous morphism $\nu_M^\infty : M_F^\infty(V) \to D_M$ such that $\nu_M^\infty(x)=\nu(x)$ for $x\in V$ and (by definition)

$\nu_M^\infty(f_H(t_1,\ldots,t_k))=f_M(\nu_M^\infty(t_1),\ldots,\nu_M^\infty(t_k))$ for $f\in F_k$. In the case M=H, this morphism is denoted by ν^* and called a substitution and, if for $t\in M_F(V)$, $var(t)=\{x_{i_1},\ldots,x_{i_q}\}$ is the least (w.r.t. set inclusion) subset of V such that $t\in M_F(var(t))$, then $\nu^*(t)$ is denoted by $[t_1/x_{i_1}\ldots tq/x_{i_q}]t$ if $\nu(x_{i_j})=t_j$.

We shall use, for $w\in \underline{dom}$ (t) where $\underline{dom}$ $(t)=\{w(f,i) \mid w\in dom(t)$ and $t(w)=f$, $1\leq i\leq p(f)\}$, the classical notions of subtree (t/w) of t at node w and subtree replacement t[t'/w] of (t/w) by t' in t (see [19], [12] with different notations).

A _precongruence_ is a preorder (reflexive and transitive binary relation) R on $M_F(V)$ such that, for all $m\in M_F(V)$ $w\in\underline{dom}(m)$ and $\nu\in M_F(V)^V$:

$$(t,t')\in R \Rightarrow (m[\nu^*(t)/w],\ m[\nu^*(t')/w])\in R$$

A _congruence_ is a symetric precongruence (thus an equivalence relation). For any binary relation $R\subseteq M_F(V)^2$, the precongruence generated by R is $\xrightarrow[R]{*}$, the reflexive and transitive closure of $\xrightarrow[R]{}$:

$$m \xrightarrow[R]{} m' \Leftrightarrow \exists (t,t')\in R\ \exists w\in \underline{dom}(m)\ \exists \nu\in M_F(V)^V : \quad m=m[\nu^*(t)/w] \text{ and } m'=m[\nu^*(t')/w]$$

while $\xleftrightarrow[R]{*}$ is the congruence generated by R, where $\xleftrightarrow[R]{}$ is the symetric closure of $\xrightarrow[R]{}$.

2 - Recursive program schemes and their semantics

A _recursive program scheme_ (RPS in short) is a triple $\Sigma=(A,\Phi,R_\Sigma)$ where A is the base function symbols' alphabet, $\Phi=\{\varphi_1,\ldots,\varphi_k\}$ (with $\varphi_i\in\Phi_{n_i}$) the procedure symbols' alphabet, disjoint from A, and R_Σ a functional binary relation (ie $(\theta,\theta')\in R_\Sigma$ and $(\theta,\theta'')\in R_\Sigma \Rightarrow \theta'=\theta''$) over $\overline{M}_{A\cup\Phi}(V)$ such that :

$(\theta,\theta')\in R_\Sigma \Rightarrow \exists i(1\leq i\leq k) : \theta=\varphi_i x_1\ldots x_{n_i}$ (here we adopt the prefixed polish notation for terms) and $var(\theta')\subseteq\{x_1,\ldots,x_{n_i}\}$.

For sake of simplicity, we denote $\xrightarrow[R_\Sigma]{}$ by $\xrightarrow[\Sigma]{}$, and present an RPS as an equational system :

$$\Sigma \left\{ \begin{array}{l} \varphi_i x_1\ldots x_{n_i} = \tau_i \\ \\ 1\leq i\leq k \end{array}\right.$$

(it is allways implicitely assumed that R_Σ is "total", that is for each i, there exists τ_i s.t. : $(\varphi_i x_1\ldots x_{n_i},\tau_i)\in R_\Sigma$) .

We denote $\Sigma \subseteq \Sigma'$ if $\Sigma=(A,\Phi,R_\Sigma)$, $\Sigma'=(A,\Phi',R_{\Sigma'})$ and $\Phi\subseteq\Phi'$ and $R_\Sigma\subseteq R_{\Sigma'}$.

An interpretation of an RPS $\Sigma=(A,\Phi,R_\Sigma)$ is a complete ordered A-magma. Since $M_A^\infty(V)$ is free over V, for each $t\in M_A^\infty(V)$ and interpretation M, one can define a continuous function t_M from D_M^V (the set of "data mappings") to D_M by $t_M(\nu)=\nu_M^\infty(t)$.
Let $\pi: \overline{M}_{A\cup\Phi}(V) \rightarrow M_A(V)$ be :

$$\begin{cases} \pi(x)=x \text{ for } x\in V \\ \pi(am_1\dots m_k)=a\pi(m_1)\dots\pi(m_k) \text{ for } a\in A_k \text{ and} \\ \pi(\varphi_i m_1\dots m_{n_i})=\Omega \end{cases}$$

$\pi(m)$ is the direct - ie without any computation - symbolic approximation of m. The fundamental following property holds :

<u>lemma</u> 1 (Nivat [17])
for all RPS $\Sigma=(A,\Phi,R_\Sigma)$, $m\in\overline{M}_{A\cup\Phi}(V)$ and interpretation M the set $\{\pi(t)_M / m \xrightarrow[\Sigma]{*} t\}$ is directed w.r.t $\leq_M$

(where $\leq_M$ denotes as well the natural extension of $\leq_M$ to the set of mappings from D_M^V to D_M).

The algebraic semantics defines the function computed by $m\in\overline{M}_{A\cup\Phi}(V)$ in an RPS $\Sigma=(A,\Phi,R_\Sigma)$ and interpretation M as the least upper bound $m_{<\Sigma,M>}$ of the set $\{\pi(t)_M / m \xrightarrow[\Sigma]{*} t\}$. When M is the free interpretation H, this function is simply noted m_Σ and can be considered, as pointed out by M. Nivat ([18]), as a tree of $M_A^\infty(V)$ such that $(m_\Sigma)_M = m_{<\Sigma,M>}$.

Our interest here is the preorder $\leq_{<\Sigma,C>}$ and equivalence $\equiv_{<\Sigma,C>}$ on $\overline{M}_{A\cup\Phi}(V)$ where C is a class (in the sense of set theory) of interpretations :

$m \leq_{<\Sigma,C>} m' \Leftrightarrow \forall M\in C \;\; m_{<\Sigma,M>} \leq_M m'_{<\Sigma,M>}$

$m \equiv_{<\Sigma,C>} m' \Leftrightarrow \;\; m \leq_{<\Sigma,C>} m'$ and $m' \leq_{<\Sigma,C>} m$

especially in the case of classes C_S of interpretations satisfying some relation $S\subseteq M_A(V)^2$, expressing properties of base functions ($M\in C_S \Leftrightarrow (t,t')\in S \Rightarrow t_M = t'_M$), in which case the relations above are denoted by $\leq_{<\Sigma,S>}$ and $\equiv_{<\Sigma,S>}$ resp. One has :

<u>Proposition</u> 2 ([6])
for all RPS $\Sigma=(A,\Phi,R_\Sigma)$ and class C of interpretations of Σ, the relations $\leq_{<\Sigma,C>}$ and $\equiv_{<\Sigma,C>}$ are resp. a precongruence and a congruence of $\overline{M}_{A\cup\Phi}$ (V)

Moreover it can be seen, from results of M. Nivat ([17],[18]) that $\leq_{<\Sigma,C>}$ always contains $\xleftrightarrow[\Sigma]{*}$ (thus if $R\subseteq\leq_{<\Sigma,C>}$ then $(\xleftrightarrow[\Sigma]{} \cup \xrightarrow[R]{})^* \subseteq \leq_{<\Sigma,C>}$).

Our work relies on the two following theorems, the first due to I. Guessarian ([11], see also [6],[5]), which generalizes the fundamental theorem of M. Nivat ([18]), and states, if we denote by $\leq_S$ the precongruence $(\leq \cup \xrightarrow[S]{})^*$ of $M_A(V)$ (for $S\subseteq M_A(V)^2$) :

<u>theorem</u> 1 (I. Guessarian [11])

for all RPS $\Sigma=(A,\Phi,R_\Sigma)$, m,m' trees of $\bar{M}_{A\cup\Phi}(V)$ and $S\subseteq M_A(V)^2$:

$m\leq_{<\Sigma,S>}m' \Leftrightarrow \forall t: m \xrightarrow[\Sigma]{*} t\ \exists t' : m' \xrightarrow[\Sigma]{*} t'$ and $\pi(t)\leq_S\pi(t')$

This implies $\xleftrightarrow[\Sigma\cup S]{*} \subseteq \equiv_{<\Sigma,S>}$, a property on which is based the transformational system of R. Burstall and J. Darlington ([3]), and which we shall generalize later. The second theorem, due to J. Vuillemin ([20], see also [9]), asserts that the parallel outermost computation rule is universally correct. Let us formalize this rule, applied to an RPS $\Sigma=(A,\Phi,R_\Sigma)$ as the mapping α_Σ over $\bar{M}_{A\cup\Phi}(V)$:

$$\begin{cases} \alpha_\Sigma(x)=x \text{ for } x\in V \\ \alpha_\Sigma(am_1\ldots m_k)=a\alpha_\Sigma(m_1)\ldots\alpha_\Sigma(m_k) \text{ if } a\in A_k \\ \alpha_\Sigma(\varphi_i m_1\ldots m_{n_i})=[m_1/x_1\ldots m_{n_i}/x_{n_i}]\tau_i \text{ if } (\varphi_i x_1\ldots x_{n_i},\tau_i)\in R_\Sigma \end{cases}$$

<u>theorem</u> 2 (J. Vuillemin [20])

for all RPS $\Sigma=(A,\Phi,R_\Sigma)$, $m\in\bar{M}_{A\cup\Phi}(V)$ and interpretation M, $m_{<\Sigma,M>}$ is the least upper bound of $\{\pi\alpha_\Sigma^n(m)_M/n\in N\}$ (where $\alpha_\Sigma^0(m)=m$ and $\alpha_\Sigma^{n+1}(m)=\alpha_\Sigma(\alpha_\Sigma^n(m))$.)

As a corollary of these two results, we get a sufficient condition for S-equivalence (with the same notations as above)

<u>Proposition</u> 3

<u>If</u> $\forall n\in N$: $\pi\alpha_\Sigma^n(m) \xleftrightarrow[S]{*} \pi\alpha_\Sigma^n(m')$ <u>then</u> $m\equiv_{<\Sigma,S>}m'$

3 - <u>The Recursion Induction Principle</u>

Let be given an RPS $\Sigma=(A,\Phi,R_\Sigma)$ with $\Phi=\{\varphi_1,\ldots,\varphi_k\}$ and $\varphi_i x_1\ldots x_{n_i} \xrightarrow[\Sigma]{} \tau_i$ for all this section. In order to formulate our induction principle, we need to express a technical restriction on relations between trees : let us say that $R\subseteq M_{A\cup\Phi}(V)^2$ "separates the variables" iff, for each $(t,t')\in R$, a variable occurring in t or t' has, in t as well as in t', occurrences only below base functions symbols or only below some procedure function symbol. To formalize this : if, for $t\in M_{A\cup\Phi}(V)$ and $T\subseteq M_{A\cup\Phi}(V)$: $occ(t,T)=\{w/\ \exists t'\in T: w\in \underline{dom}(t') \text{ and } t=(t'/w)\}$ then $R\subseteq M_{A\cup\Phi}(V)^2$ <u>separates the variables</u> iff

$$(t,t')\in R \text{ and } x\in V \Rightarrow occ(x,\{t,t'\})\subseteq W_A^* \text{ or } occ(x,\{t,t'\})\cap W_A^*=\emptyset$$

For any mapping $\Psi: M_{A\cup\Phi}(V) \longrightarrow M_{A\cup\Phi}(V)$ and relation R : $\Psi\times\Psi(R)=\{(\Psi(t),\Psi(t'))\ /\ (t,t')\in R\}$. We can now establish :

<u>Theorem 3</u> (The induction principle)

for all RPS $\Sigma'=(A,\Phi',R_{\Sigma'})$ such that $\Sigma\subseteq\Sigma'$, for all $S\subseteq M_A(V)^2$ and $R\subseteq\bar{M}_{A\cup\Phi'}(V)^2$:

<u>if</u> R separates the variables and satisfies :

(base) $\pi\times\pi(R)\subseteq \xleftrightarrow[S]{*}$ and (induction step) $\alpha_{\Sigma'}\times\alpha_{\Sigma'}(R) \subseteq \xleftrightarrow[R\cup S]{*}$

<u>then</u>, for all m,m' in $\bar{M}_{A\cup\Phi}(V)$: $m \xleftrightarrow[R\cup S\cup\Sigma']{*} m' \Rightarrow m\equiv_{<\Sigma,S>}m'$

We say, by definition, that R is $<\Sigma',S>$-stable iff $\pi\times\pi(R) \subseteq \overset{*}{\underset{S}{\longleftrightarrow}}$ and $\alpha_{\Sigma'}\times\alpha_{\Sigma'}(R) \subseteq \overset{*}{\underset{R\cup S}{\longleftrightarrow}}$

Proof : We first remark that for $m\in\bar{M}_{A\cup\Phi}(V)$, $m_\Sigma = m_{\Sigma'}$ since $\Sigma\subseteq\Sigma'$. Thus the theorem is proved if we show that $\overset{*}{\underset{R\cup S\cup\Sigma'}{\longleftrightarrow}} \subseteq \equiv_{<\Sigma',S>}$. From the previous results, we only have to prove that $R\cup S \subseteq \equiv_{<\Sigma',S>}$. We show the following points :

1 - $\tau \overset{*}{\underset{R\cup S}{\longleftrightarrow}} \tau' \Rightarrow \pi(\tau) \overset{*}{\underset{S}{\longleftrightarrow}} \pi(\tau')$

2 - $\tau \overset{*}{\underset{R\cup S}{\longleftrightarrow}} \tau' \Rightarrow \alpha_{\Sigma'}(\tau) \overset{*}{\underset{R\cup S}{\longleftrightarrow}} \alpha_{\Sigma'}(\tau')$

which imply, by an obvious induction on n :

$\tau \overset{*}{\underset{R\cup S}{\longleftrightarrow}} \tau' \Rightarrow \forall n \in N : \pi\, \alpha^n_{\Sigma'}(\tau) \overset{*}{\underset{S}{\longleftrightarrow}} \pi\, \alpha^n_{\Sigma'}(\tau')$

whence the theorem (by prop. 3)

(1) Since the predicate $P(\tau,\tau') \Leftrightarrow \pi(\tau)\overset{*}{\underset{S}{\longleftrightarrow}}\pi(\tau')$ is reflexive, symetric and transitive, it suffices to show $:\tau \underset{R\cup S}{\longrightarrow} \tau' \Rightarrow \pi(\tau) \overset{*}{\underset{S}{\longleftrightarrow}} \pi(\tau')$

$\tau \underset{R\cup S}{\longrightarrow} \tau' \Leftrightarrow \exists (t,t')\in R\cup S,\ \exists \nu\in\bar{M}_{A\cup\Phi}(V)^V,\ \exists\, w \in \underline{dom}(\tau) :\ \tau=\tau[\nu^*(t)/w]$ and $\tau'=\tau[\nu^*(t')/w]$

Let $x\in V\text{-var}(\tau)$ ($var(\tau)$ is finite) and $\bar{\tau} = \tau[x/w]$. We can write $: \tau = [\nu^*(t)/x]\bar{\tau}$ and $\tau'=[\nu^*(t')/x]\bar{\tau}$. And one easily verifies that

$\pi(\tau)=[(\pi\circ\nu)^*(\pi(t))/x]\ \pi(\bar{\tau})$ and $\pi(\tau')=[(\pi\circ\nu)^*(\pi(t'))/x]\ \pi(\bar{\tau})$

Since $\pi\times\pi(R\cup S) \subseteq \overset{*}{\underset{S}{\longleftrightarrow}}$, we have $\pi(\tau)\overset{*}{\underset{S}{\longleftrightarrow}}\pi(\tau')$

(2) Here again since the relation $P'(\tau,\tau') \Leftrightarrow \alpha_{\Sigma'}(\tau)\overset{*}{\underset{R\cup S}{\longleftrightarrow}} \alpha_{\Sigma'}(\tau')$ is an equivalence, to show the second point, it suffices to prove :

$\tau \underset{R\cup S}{\longrightarrow} \tau' \Rightarrow \alpha_{\Sigma'}(\tau) \overset{*}{\underset{R\cup S}{\longleftrightarrow}} \alpha_{\Sigma'}(\tau)$

With the same notations as above :

$\tau=\tau[\nu^*(t)/w]$ and $\tau'=\tau[\nu^*(t')/w]$ for some $(t,t')\in R\cup S$.

We distinguish between two cases :

2-1 If $w\in W^*_A$, then one may verify that $w\in\underline{dom}(\alpha_{\Sigma'}(\tau))$ and $\alpha_{\Sigma'}(\tau)=\alpha_{\Sigma'}(\tau)[\alpha_{\Sigma'}(\nu^*(t))/w]$ and $\alpha_{\Sigma'}(\tau')=\alpha_{\Sigma'}(\tau)[\alpha_{\Sigma'}(\nu^*(t'))/w]$

Since R separates the variables, $R\cup S$ also does, and there exist disjoint subsets V' and V" of V such that

$$\begin{cases} x\in V' \Rightarrow occ(x,\{t,t'\})\subseteq W^*_A \\ x\in V'' \Rightarrow occ(x,\{t,t'\})\cap W^*_A = \emptyset \end{cases}$$

We then have :

$\alpha_{\Sigma'}(\tau)=\alpha_{\Sigma'}(\tau)[\bar{\nu}^*(\alpha_{\Sigma'}(t))/w]$ and $\alpha_{\Sigma'}(\tau')=\alpha_{\Sigma'}(\tau)[\bar{\nu}^*(\alpha_{\Sigma'}(t'))/w]$ where $\bar{\nu}(x)=\nu(x)$ if $x\in V''$ and $\bar{\nu}(x)=\alpha_{\Sigma'}(\nu(x))$ if $x\in V'$

Since $\alpha_{\Sigma'}\times\alpha_{\Sigma'}(R\cup S)\subseteq \overset{*}{\underset{R\cup S}{\longleftrightarrow}}$, we have $\alpha_{\Sigma'}(\tau) \overset{*}{\underset{R\cup S}{\longleftrightarrow}} \alpha_{\Sigma'}(\tau')$

2-2 If $w\notin W^*_A$, we can write, for some $x\in V\text{-var}(\tau)$: $\tau=[\nu^*(t)/x]\bar{\tau}$ and $\tau'=[\nu^*(t')/x]\bar{\tau}$ where $\bar{\tau}=\tau[x/w]$. In this case : $\alpha_{\Sigma'}(\tau)=[\nu^*(t)/x]\alpha_{\Sigma'}(\bar{\tau})$ and $\alpha_{\Sigma'}(\tau')=[\nu^*(t')/x]\alpha_{\Sigma'}(\bar{\tau})$, thus $\alpha_{\Sigma'}(\tau) \overset{*}{\underset{R\cup S}{\longleftrightarrow}} \alpha_{\Sigma'}(\tau')$ ■

Remark : the technical restriction that R separates the variables may be avoided by using a computation rule α^R_Σ (which is α_Σ if R separates the variables). But this modification is irrelevant for the purpose of this paper, see next section.

As first example of application of the proposed proof method, we show that in the RPS (where, for clarity, arguments of monadic functions are not enclosed by parenthesis) :

$$\Sigma \begin{cases} \chi x = h(x,a,k(k(fx,gx),\chi dx) \\ \theta x = k(\varphi x, \Psi x) \\ \varphi x = h(x,a,k(fx,\varphi dx)) \\ \Psi x = h(x,a,k(gx,\Psi dx)) \end{cases}$$

with $A=\{h,a,k,f,g,d\}$ and $\Phi=\{\chi,\theta,\varphi,\Psi\}$, we have $\chi x=\theta x$ for a suitable set of properties of base functions expressed by :

$$S \begin{cases} k(\Omega,\Omega)=\Omega \\ k(h(x,y,z),h(x,y',z'))=h(x,k(y,y'),k(z,z')) \\ k(a,a)=a \\ k(k(x,y),k(x',y'))=k(k(x,x'),k(y,y')) \end{cases}$$

We prove that the relation $R=\{(k(\varphi x,\Psi x),\chi x)\}$ is $<\Sigma,S>$-stable (R obviously separates the variables), for we then have : $\theta x \xrightarrow[\Sigma]{} k(\varphi x,\Psi x) \xrightarrow[R]{} \chi x$.

$\pi\times\pi(R) \subseteq \overset{*}{\underset{S}{\longleftrightarrow}}$ since $\pi\times\pi(R)=\{(k(\Omega,\Omega),\Omega)\}$

$$\begin{aligned} \alpha_\Sigma(k(\varphi x,\Psi x)) &= k(h(x,a,k(fx,\varphi dx)),h(x,a,k(gx,\Psi dx))) \\ &\underset{S}{\rightarrow} h(x,k(a,a),k(k(fx,\varphi dx),k(gx,\Psi dx))) \\ &\underset{S}{\rightarrow} h(x,a,k(k(fx,\varphi dx),k(gx,\Psi dx))) \\ &\underset{S}{\rightarrow} h(x,a,k(k(fx,gx),k(\varphi dx,\Psi dx))) \\ &\underset{R}{\rightarrow} h(x,a,k(k(fx,gx),\chi dx))=\alpha_\Sigma(\chi x) \end{aligned}$$

This example is taken, (with a slight modification in S), from [4], and validates a transformation performed in the system of R. Burstall & J. Darlington [3] (applied to the sum of two scalar products). As in [4] we only have checked equations, but in contrast we do not need any hypothesis on S (such as termination, confluence...). Another example shows that we can prove some facts that the method of B. Courcelle [4] cannot handle :

$$\Sigma \begin{cases} \varphi = f\varphi \\ \Psi = g\varphi \\ \theta = h(\varphi,\Psi) \end{cases} \qquad S \begin{cases} fgx=gfx \\ g\Omega=\Omega \\ h(x,x)=gx \end{cases}$$

with $A=\{f,g,h\}$ and $\Phi=\{\varphi,\Psi,\theta\}$ (procedure symbols without parameters). We have $\theta \equiv_{<\Sigma,S>} \varphi$ since the relation $R=\{(g\varphi,\varphi)\}$ is $<\Sigma,S>$-stable and $\theta \underset{\Sigma}{\rightarrow} h(\varphi,\Psi) \underset{\Sigma}{\rightarrow} h(\varphi,g\varphi) \underset{R}{\rightarrow} h(\varphi,\varphi) \underset{S}{\rightarrow} g\varphi \underset{R}{\rightarrow} \varphi$.

The last example of this section suggests a "transformation scheme" : the addition (over non-negative integers) is well-known to be recursively defined by

$\varphi(x,y)=$ <u>if</u> $x=0$ <u>then</u> y <u>else</u> $1+\varphi(x-1,y)$

In scheme :

$\Sigma\ \{\varphi(x,y)=h(x,y,s\varphi(px,y))$

But one can also propose the "iterative" equivalent form :

$\Sigma'\{\varphi'(x,y)=h(x,y,\varphi'(px,sy))$

Under the assumptions :

$$S\begin{cases} s\Omega = \Omega \\ sh(x,y,z)=h(x,sy,sz)\end{cases}$$

it is easily seen that the relation $R=\{(S\varphi(x,y),\varphi(x,sy))\}$ is $<\Sigma,S>$-stable. But how can we use this equivalence $s\varphi(x,y)\equiv_{<\Sigma,S>}\varphi(x,sy)$ to transform Σ ?

It can be shown that, if, for an RPS $\Sigma\begin{cases}\varphi_i\, x_1\dots x_{n_i} = \tau_i \\ 1\le i\le k\end{cases}$

and $S\subseteq M_A(V)^2$, a relation $R\subseteq\bar{M}_{A\cup\Phi}(V)^2$ separates the variables and is $<\Sigma,S>$-stable, then for all RPS :

$$\Sigma'\begin{cases}\varphi'_i x_1\dots x_{n_i} = \bar{\tau}'_i \\ 1\le i\le k\end{cases}$$

where $\bar{\tau}'_i$ is, for all i, obtained by replacing each occurrence of φ_j by φ'_j in a $\bar{\tau}_i\in\bar{M}_{A\cup\Phi}(V)$ such that $\bar{\tau}_i \overset{*}{\underset{R\cup S}{\longleftrightarrow}} \tau_i$, we have $(\varphi_i x_1\dots x_{n_i})_\Sigma \equiv_S (\varphi'_i x_1\dots x_{n_i})_{\Sigma'}$

This allows us to transform, in the last example, Σ in Σ', and this transformation is correct. It must be pointed out that this kind of transformation cannot be achieved in the system of R. Burstall & J. Darlington [3] (here we generalize the "folding"operation and ensure correctness, which is not so obvious, see [13]).

4 - Application to Strong Equivalence

We study in this section the strong equivalence $\equiv_\Sigma$ (that is $\equiv_{<\Sigma,I>}$, for the class I of all interpretations of Σ), restricting our attention to standard RPS's, which are $\Sigma=(A,\Phi,R_\Sigma)$ such that, for each $(\varphi x_1\dots x_n,\tau)\in R_\Sigma$ $var(\tau)=\{x_1,\dots x_n\}$ and there exists an $a\in A_k$ and $m_1,\dots,m_k$ in $\bar{M}_\Phi(V)$ such that $\tau=am_1\dots m_k$. In these schemes, the following property holds :

lemma 2

Let $\Sigma=(A,\Phi,R_\Sigma)$ be a standard RPS, $m\in\bar{M}_{A\cup\Phi}(V)$ and $t\in M_A(V)$. If there exists θ s.t. $m \overset{*}{\underset{\Sigma}{\rightarrow}} \theta$ and $t\le\pi(\theta)$ then there exists one and only one $\hat{m}(t)\in\bar{M}_{A\cup\Phi}(V)$ such that $m \overset{*}{\underset{\Sigma}{\rightarrow}} \hat{m}(t)$ and $\{m'/m \overset{*}{\underset{\Sigma}{\rightarrow}} m'$ and $t\le\pi(m')\} = \{m'/\ \hat{m}(t) \overset{*}{\underset{\Sigma}{\rightarrow}} m'\}$

The proof (by induction on t) is omitted. If $m=\varphi_i x_1\dots x_{n_i}$, the term $\hat{m}(t)$ will be denoted by $\hat{\varphi}_i(t)$.

Let us see an example of strong equivalence, in a standard scheme, taken from [7]:

$$\begin{cases}\varphi_1 x=f(x,\varphi_1 x,\varphi_1\varphi_1 x)\\ \varphi_2 x=f(x,\varphi_2 x,\varphi_3 x)\\ \varphi_3 x=f(\varphi_2 x,\varphi_3 x,\varphi_4 x)\\ \varphi_4 x=f(\varphi_3 x,\varphi_4 x,\varphi_4\varphi_1 x)\end{cases}$$

To prove that $\varphi_1 x\equiv_\Sigma\varphi_2 x$, it suffices to see that $R=\{(\varphi_1 x,\varphi_2 x), (\varphi_1\varphi_1 x,\varphi_3 x), (\varphi_1\varphi_1\varphi_1 x,\varphi_4 x)\}$ is Σ-stable. The corresponding proof with the usual induction principle is not so easy (see [7]). But the way to get a Σ-stable relation which solves the problem is not allways obvious :

$$\Sigma \begin{cases} \varphi_1 x = h(\varphi_2(\varphi_1 x,x),\varphi_1 x,x) \\ \varphi_2(x,y) = f(\varphi_2(\varphi_2(x,y),y),x,\varphi_1 y) \\ \varphi_3 x = h(\varphi_4(\varphi_3 x,\varphi_3 x),\varphi_3 x,x) \\ \varphi_4(x,y) = f(\varphi_4(\varphi_4(x,y),y),x,y) \end{cases}$$

To prove $\varphi_1 x \equiv_\Sigma \varphi_3 x$, we have here to "invent" the lemma : $\varphi_2(x,y) \equiv_\Sigma \varphi_4(x,\varphi_3 y)$ and then verify that $R = \{(\varphi_1 x,\varphi_3 x),\ (\varphi_2(x,y),\ \varphi_4(x,\varphi_3 y))\}$ is Σ-stable.

We now develop a "method"(not entirely effective)to get such lemmas. The main idea is to associate - whenever possible - to each pair (φ_i,φ_j) a new procedure symbol $\varphi_{<i,j>}$ - together with its definition in an RPS - such that $\varphi_{<i,j>}$ is a "min" for φ_i and φ_j : there exist substitutions γ and δ making $\varphi_i x_1 \ldots x_{n_i}$ and $\gamma^*(\varphi_{<i,j>} x_1 \ldots x_{n_{<i,j>}}$ $\gamma^*(\varphi_{<i,j>} x_1 \ldots x_{n_{<i,j>}})$, $\varphi_j \dot{x}_1 \ldots x_{n_j}$ and $\delta^*(\varphi_{<i,j>} x_1 \ldots x_{n_{<i,j>}})$ resp. equivalent. From these equivalences, we may deduce some information about $\equiv_\Sigma$ and especially infer some auxiliary lemmas. We first need a lot of technical definitions, a standard RPS $\Sigma = (A,\Phi,R_\Sigma)$, with $\Phi = \{\varphi_1,\ldots,\varphi_k\}$, being given from now on.

- the partial function μ from $M_{A\cup\Phi}(V)$ to $M_A(X)$, where $X = V \times M_{A\cup\Phi}(V) \cup M_{A\cup\Phi}(V) \times V$, (analoguous to a part of the "glb for subsumption ordering" of G. Huet [12]) is defined by :

$(m,m') \in dom(\mu)$ <u>iff</u>

$m = \Omega = m'$ and then $\mu(m,m') = \Omega$ <u>or</u>

$(m,m') \in X$ and then $\mu(m,m') = (m,m')$ <u>or</u>

$m = \varphi_i m_1 \ldots m_{n_i}$ and $m' = \varphi_j m'_1 \ldots m'_{n_j}$ and then $\mu(m,m') = \Omega$ <u>or</u>

$m = am_1 \ldots m_k$ and $m' = am'_1 \ldots m'_k$ and $1 \le i \le k \Rightarrow (m_i,m'_i) \in dom(\mu)$ and then $\mu(m,m') = a\mu(m_1,m'_1)\ldots\mu(m_k,m'_k)$

$\bar{\pi} : M_A(X) \to M_A(\emptyset)$ is given by

$\bar{\pi}(z) = \Omega$ if $z \in X \cup \{\Omega\}$

$\bar{\pi}(am_1 \ldots m_k) = a\bar{\pi}(m_1)\ldots\bar{\pi}(m_k)$ for $a \in A_k$.

- if, for all $i (1 \le i \le k)$ and $n \in N$ $\tau_i^n = \pi\alpha_\Sigma^n(\varphi_i x_1 \ldots x_{n_i})$ then we say that φ_i and φ_j are <u>compatible at order n</u> <u>iff</u> $(\tau_i^n,\tau_j^n) \in dom(\mu)$

- for each $\tau \in M_A(X)$ let $\{Z_1,\ldots,Z_q\}$ be the set of all the $Z \in X$ such that $1 \le h < l \le q \Rightarrow \exists w \in occ(Z_h,\tau)\ \forall w' \in occ(Z_l,\tau) : w \le_{lex} w'$ where $<_{lex}$ is the strict lexicographic partial order on W_A^* defined by the strict partial order $<$ on W_A: $(a,i) < (a',j) \Leftrightarrow a' = a$ and $i < j$). We define $\chi(\tau) \in M_A(V)$ as $\nu^*(\tau)$ where $\nu(Z_h) = x_h$ for all $h\ (1 \le h \le q)$.

We finally define inductively sequences $(Yn)_{n\in N}$, $(\Psi n)_{n\in N}$ of sets of function symbols in such a way that $\Psi n \subseteq Yn \subseteq Y$ where $Y = \{\varphi_{<i,j>} / 1 \le i < j \le k\}$) together with arity functions Pn (for each $\varphi_{<i,j>} \in Yn$: $Pn(\varphi_{<i,j>}) = p_n^{<i,j>}$) and sequence $(Rn)_{n\in N}$ of relations $R_n \subseteq \bar{M}_{\Phi\cup Y}(V)^2$:

1 - $Yo = Y$ and $p_o^{<i,j>} = 0$ for all i,j

$\Psi_o = \emptyset$ and $R_o = \emptyset$.

2 - For $n > 0$, let us suppose that Y_{n-1}, Ψ_{n-1}, P_{n-1} and R_{n-1} are built.

2.1. $\varphi_{<i,j>} \in Y_n \iff \varphi_{<i,j>} \in Y - \Psi_{n-1}$ and φ_i and φ_j are compatible at order n.

For $\varphi_{<i,j>} \in Y_n$, if $g_n^{<i,j>} = \hat{\varphi}_i(\bar{\pi}(\mu(\tau_i^n, \tau_j^n)))$ and $d_n^{<i,j>} = \hat{\varphi}_j(\bar{\pi}(\mu(\tau_i^n, \tau_j^n)))$,

we let : $p_n^{<i,j>} = \text{card}\ (\text{var}\ (\chi(\mu(g_n^{<i,j>}, d_n^{<i,j>}))))$

2.2. For $\varphi_{<i,j>} \in Y_n$, the substitutions $\gamma_n^{<i,j>}$ and $\delta_n^{<i,j>}$ are given by $\gamma_n^{<i,j>}(x_h) = (g_n^{<i,j>}/w)$ and $\delta_n^{<i,j>}(x_h) = d_n^{<i,j>}/w)$ iff $1 \le h \le p_n^{<i,j>}$ and $x_h = (\chi(\mu(g_n^{<i,j>}, d_n^{<i,j>}))/w)$.

For $\Psi \subseteq Y_n$, let :

$$R_n(\Psi) = R_{n-1} \cup \{(\varphi_i\, x_1 \ldots x_{n_i}, \gamma_n^{<i,j>*}(\varphi_{<i,j>}\, x_1 \ldots x_{p_n^{<i,j>}}))\ /\ \varphi_{<i,j>} \in \Psi\}$$
$$\cup \{(\varphi_j\, x_1 \ldots x_{n_j}, \delta_n^{<i,j>*}(\varphi_{<i,j>}\, x_1 \ldots x_{p_n^{<i,j>}}))\ /\ \varphi_{<i,j>} \in \Psi\}$$

and we say that Ψ is <u>definable</u> (at order n) iff $\varphi_{<i,j>} \in \Psi \implies$ $\exists \sigma_n^{<i,j>} \in \bar{M}_{F_n(\Psi)}(\{x_1, \ldots, x_{p_n^{<i,j>}}\})$ where $F_n(\Psi) = A \cup \Phi \cup \Psi_{n-1} \cup \Psi$ s.t. $\gamma_n^{<i,j>*}(\sigma_n^{<i,j>}) \overset{*}{\underset{R_n(\Psi)}{\longleftrightarrow}} \sigma_i$ and $\delta_n^{<i,j>*}(\sigma_n^{<i,j>}) \overset{*}{\underset{R_n(\Psi)}{\longleftrightarrow}} \sigma_j$.

To achieve the construction, Ψ_n will be $\Psi_{n-1} \cup \bar{\Psi}_n$ where $\bar{\Psi}_n$ is the greatest (w.r.t. set inclusion) definable subset of Y_n, and $R_n = R_n(\bar{\Psi}_n)$.

<u>Claim</u>

If $R = \bigcup_{n\in N} R_n$ then $\overset{*}{\underset{R \cup \Sigma}{\longleftrightarrow}} \subseteq \equiv_\Sigma$

<u>Proof</u> : clear since for all $n \in N$ there exists a Σn such that $\Sigma \subseteq \Sigma_n$ and R_n-stable (Σn defines all the $\varphi_{<i,j>}$'s definable at level p, less than n, by $\sigma_p^{<i,j>}$) ∎

Application to the last example : we get $Y_1 = \{\varphi_{<1,3>}, \varphi_{<2,4>}\} = \Psi_1$ with

$$R_1 \begin{cases} \varphi_1\, x = \varphi_{<1,3>}\, x \\ \varphi_3\, x = \varphi_{<1,3>}\, x \\ \varphi_2(x,y) = \varphi_{<2,4>}(x, \varphi_1\, y) \\ \varphi_4(x,y) = \varphi_{<2,4>}(x,y) \end{cases}$$

$\varphi_{<1,3>}$ being definable by $h(\varphi_{<2,4>}(\varphi_{<1,3>}\, x,x), \varphi_{<1,3>}\, x, x)$ and $\varphi_{<2,4>}$ by $f(\varphi_{<2,4>}(\varphi_{<2,4>}(x,y), y), x, y)$. ($R = R_1$ since $Y_n = \emptyset$ for $n > 1$) and we have :

$$\varphi_1\, x \overset{*}{\underset{R}{\longleftrightarrow}} \varphi_3\, x \quad \text{and} \quad \varphi_2(x, y) \overset{*}{\underset{R}{\longleftrightarrow}} \varphi_4(x, \varphi_3\, y), \quad \text{qed.}$$

At this point, it should be mentionned that, for all examples I know, the $\sigma_n^{<i,j>}$ defining $\varphi_{<i,j>}$ (if it exists) can be obtained as described in the following.

For $\varphi_{<i,j>} \in \bigcup_{n\in N} \Psi_n = \Psi$, let q be the least non-negative integer such that $\varphi_{<i,j>} \in \Psi_q$: we say that $\varphi_{<i,j>}$ is q-definable, and $p_n^{<i,j>}$, $\delta_n^{<i,j>}$ are resp. $p_q^{<i,j>}$, $\gamma_q^{<i,j>}$, $\delta_q^{<i,j>}$ for all $n \geq q$.

Let $\hat{\mu}_n$ be a partial mapping from $\bar{M}_{A \cup \Phi}(V)$ to $\bar{M}_{A \cup \Phi \cup \Psi}(Z)$ (where $Z = V \times \bar{M}_\Phi(V) \cup \bar{M}_\Phi(V) \times V)$ such that :

$(m, m') \in \text{dom}(\hat{\mu}_n) \iff$

$(m, m') \in Z$ and then $\hat{\mu}_n(m, m') = (m, m')$ <u>or</u>

$m = f\, m_1 \ldots m_k$, $m' = f\, m'_1 \ldots m'_k$ $(f \in (A \cup \Phi)_k)$ and $1 \leq i \leq k \implies$

$(m_i, m'_i) \in \text{dom}(\hat{\mu}_n)$ and then $\hat{\mu}_n(m, m') = f\, \hat{\mu}_n(m_1, m'_1) \ldots \hat{\mu}_n(m_k, m'_k)$ <u>or</u>

$m = \varphi_i\, m_1 \ldots m_{n_i}$, $m' = \varphi_j\, m'_1 \ldots m'_{n_j}$ and $j < i$ and $(m', m) \in \text{dom}(\hat{\mu}_n)$ and then $\hat{\mu}_n(m, m') = \hat{\mu}_n(m', m)$ <u>or</u>

$m = \varphi_i\, m_1 \ldots m_{n_i}$, $m' = \varphi_j\, m'_1 \ldots m'_{n_j}$, $i < j$ and $\varphi_{<i,j>} \in Y_n \cup \Psi_{n-1}$ and $1 \leq h \leq p_n^{<i,j>} \implies (t_h, t'_h) \in \text{dom}(\hat{\mu}_n)$ where

$t_h = [m_1/x_1 \ldots m_{n_1} - /x_{n_i}]\, \gamma_n^{<i,j>}(x_k)$ and

$t'_h = [m'_1/x_1 \ldots m'_{n_j}/x_{n_j}]\, \delta_n^{<i,j>}(x_k)$ and then

$\hat{\mu}_n(m, m') = \varphi_{<i,j>}\, \hat{\mu}_n(t_1, t'_1) \ldots \hat{\mu}_n(t_{p_n^{<i,j>}}, t'_{p_n^{<i,j>}})$.

It seems that $\varphi_{<i,j>}$ is n-definable iff $(\sigma_i, \sigma_j) \in \text{dom}(\hat{\mu}_n)$, $\{z/z \in Z$ and $\text{occ}(Z, \hat{\mu}_n(\sigma_i, \sigma_j)) \neq \emptyset\} = \{(\gamma_n^{<i,j>}(x_h), \delta_n^{<i,j>}(x_h))/1 \leq h \leq p_n^{<i,j>}\}$ and, if $\nu(Z) = x_h$ iff $Z = (\gamma_n^{<i,j>}(x_h), \delta_n^{<i,j>}(x_h))$ then $\sigma_n^{<i,j>} = \nu^*(\hat{\mu}_n(\sigma_i, \sigma_j))$ conveniently defines $\varphi_{<i,j>}$. Moreover, in my examples again, $m \overset{*}{\underset{R_n}{\Longleftrightarrow}} m'$ (for m, m' in $\bar{M}_\Phi(V))$ iff $(m,m') \in \text{dom}(\hat{\mu}_n)$ and $\hat{\mu}_n(m,m') \in \bar{M}_{\Phi \cup \Psi}(\{(x_i, x_i)/i > 0\})$. My work is now devoted to investigate in what these facts are - or are not - allways true.

<u>Acknowledgements</u> : I thank B. Courcelle for stimulating discussions on the subject and L. Kott for helpful criticisms on a previous version of this paper.

<u>References</u> -

[1] G. BOUDOL & L. KOTT - "Recursion Induction Principle Revisited", Rapport du LITP, LA 248, CNRS & Univ. Paris VII (1978).

[2] R. BURSTALL - "Proving Properties of Programs by Structural Induction", Computer J. 12 (1969) 41-48.

[3] R. BURSTALL & J. DARLINGTON - " A Transformation System for Developping Recursive Programs", JACM 24 (1977) 44-67

[4] B. COURCELLE - "On Recursive Equations Having a Unique Solution", 19 th FOCS (1978).

[5] B. COURCELLE & M. NIVAT - "Algebraic Families of Interpretations", 17th FOCS (1876).

[6] B. COURCELLE & M. NIVAT - "The Algebraic Semantics of Recursive Program Schemes", 7th MFCS, Zakopane, Poland (1978).

[7] B. COURCELLE & J. VUILLEMIN - "Completeness Results for the Equivalence of Recursive Schemes", JCSS 12 (1976) 179-197.

[8] J. de BAKKER & D. SCOTT - "A Theory of Programs", unpublished notes (1969).

[9] P.J. DOWNEY & R. SETHI - "Correct Computation Rules for Recursive Languages", 16th FOCS (1975) 48-56.

[10] J. GOGUEN, J.W. THATCHER, E. WAGNER & J.B. WRIGHT - "Initial Algebra Semantics and Continuous Algebras", JACM 24 (1977) 68-95.

[11] I. GUESSARIAN - "Semantic Equivalence of Program Schemes and its Syntactic Characterization", 3rd ICALP, Edinburgh (1976) 189-200.

[12] G. HUET - "Confluent Reductions : Abstract Properties and Applications to Term Rewriting Systems", 18th FOCS (1977).

[13] L. KOTT - "About a Transformation System : a Theoretical Study", in "Program Transformations" (B. Robinet, Ed.), 3rd International Coll. on Programmation, Paris (1978) 232-247.

[14] Z. MANNA, S. NESS & J. VUILLEMIN - "Inductive Methods for Proving Properties of Programs", CACM 16 (1973) 491-502.

[15] R. MILNER - "Models of LCF", Stanford AI Labo Memo - AIM 184 (1973).

[16] J.H. MORRIS - "Another Recursion Induction Principle", CACM 14 (1971) 351-354.

[17] M. NIVAT - "On the Interpretation of Recursive Polyadic Program Schemes", Symposia Matematica XV, Bologna (1975) 255-281.

[18] M. NIVAT - "Interprétation Universelle d'un schéma de programmes récursif", Informatica VII, Supp. al n° 1 (1977) 9-16.

[19] B.K. ROSEN - "Tree-Manipulating Systems and Church-Rosser Theorems", JACM 20 (1973) 160-187.

[20] J. VUILLEMIN - "Correct and Optimal Implementation of Recursion in a simple Programming Language", JCSS 9 (1974) 332-354.

FINITE-CHANGE AUTOMATA

Burchard von Braunmühl
Rutger Verbeek

Introduction

Beside the question of nondeterminism the connection between time and space is the most urgent problem in automata theory. In this paper we introduce a new storage medium with properties between space and time: the finite-change tape (FC-tape), a Turing tape, on which every cell can be changed only a bounded number of times. This is an extension of both the measures considered by Hibbard (1967) and Wechsung (1976). In common with the medium time it has the limited possibility of re-using. We consider automata with one bounded FC-tape - also used as input tape - and automata with additional Turing tape. In the first chapter we summarize some simple properties which already implies the close relationship to computation time. In the second chapter we give more arguments for the position between time and space: even nondeterministic automata with linear FC-tape and $\sqrt{n}$-bounded Turing tape can be simulated by deterministic linear bounded automata; on the other hand any multitape Turing machine operating in linear time is simulated by some singletape machine which exclusively changes symbols of the original input (i.e. only once) with determinism preserved. From this follows that the class of languages accepted by automata with $f(n)$-bounded FC-tape is located between the classes of languages accepted by multitape Turing machines in time $f(n)$ and singletape Turing machines in time $(f(n))^2$. For the nondeterministic automata with linear FC-tape and $\log n$-bounded Turing tape (equivalent to multihead FC-automata) there is a lot of relations to the questions concerning P, NP, DSPACE$(\log n)$ and NSPACE$(\log n)$: these automata recognize any language in the least AFL containing NSPACE$(\log n)$; their running time is polynomial, and they can be simulated by deterministic linear bounded automata.

1. Definitions and simple properties

A f-tape bounded k-change automaton with g-bounded Turing tape ($f \geq id$) is an off-line two-tape Turing machine, which visits at most $f(n)$ cells on the first tape and $g(n)$ cells on the second and does not change any cell on the first tape more than k times during an accepting computation, where n is the length of the input. With $kC(f,g)$ we denote the class of these automata. If there is no second tape we write $kC(f)$. If $f = id$, we write kC and simply speak of a *k-change automaton* (i.e. a linear bounded automaton that prints only k times on any cell of its tape). M is called *finite-change automaton* (FC), if it is kC for some k. Corresponding to this we use FC(f,g). "Deterministic" and "nondeterministic" are indicated by D and N respectively: NFC, DFC etc. If $M \in 1C(id,g)$ and M prints on the first tape always the same symbol, we write $M \in E(g)$ *(erasing automaton)*.

As usual we denote a Turing machine T as $(Q,\Sigma,\Gamma,\delta,q_o,F)$, where Q,Σ,Γ,F are finite sets (of states, input symbols, tape symbols and accepting states), $\Sigma \subseteq \Gamma$, $F \subseteq Q$, $\delta \subseteq Q \times \Gamma^2 \times Q \times \Gamma^2 \times \{1,o,-1\}^2$ and $q_o \in Q$ (start state). A configuration of T is described by the actual state, the contents of the tapes and the position of the heads.

If M is an automaton, then L(M) is the language accepted by M; if K is a class of automata, then L(K) is the class of languages belonging to K. NT(f) (NS(f)) is the class of f-time-bounded (tape-bounded) multitape Turing machines, $NT_1(f)$ is the class of f-time-bounded singletape machines. Correspondingly we use DT(f) and DS(f). The class of nondeterministic (resp. deterministic) polynomial time-bounded Turing machines is denoted by NP (resp. P).

We write $L(K) \leq_{log} L(K')$, if every language in L(K) is many-one reducible to some language in L(K') by a transformation computable on a log-tape-bounded two-way Turing machine.

The above defined automata have some simple properties:

1. Every $M \in FC(f)$ is a $f(-)^2$-time bounded singletape Turing machine ($FC(f) \subseteq NT_1(f(-)^2)$)
2. If $T \in NT(f)$ (DT(f)) then T can be simulated by some $M \in N1C(f(-)^2)$ $(D1C(f(-)^2)$ (for a stronger result see Theorem 4)
3. L(N1C(poly)) = L(NFC(poly, log)) = NP
   L(D1C(poly)) = L(DFC(poly, log)) = P
4. For every $c \geq 1$
   $L(NFC(f,g)) = L(NFC(c\cdot f, c\cdot g))$
   $L(DFC(f,g)) = L(DFC(c\cdot f, c\cdot g))$
5. If f is nondecreasing and if for every c there is some c' such that $g(c\cdot n) \leq c'\cdot g(n)$, then L(NFCA(f,g)) forms an AFL closed under intersection. Furthermore, L(NFC(lin,g)) (L(DFC(lin,g))) is the closure of L(NE(g)) (L(DE(g))) under inverse homomorphisms. (Suppose $\Gamma = \{a_1,\ldots,a_m\}$, $L = L(M)$, $M \in NkC(id,g)$ (or DkC(id,g)), $h(a_i) = + a_i (a_1 \ldots a_m)^k$, $L' = h(L)$. Then $L' \in L(M')$, $M' \in NE(g)$ (or DE(g)) and $h^{-1}(L') = L$.
   If M changes some symbol a_j into b, then M' erases every symbol up to the next occurence of b in the corresponding block $+ \sqcap^* a_j \ldots a_k (a_1 \ldots a_k)^*$.)

L(NFC(lin,log)) includes the least AFL containing L(NS(log)).

6. L(DE) contains e.g. the Dyck-languages,
   $\{w \overleftarrow{w} \mid w \in \{a,b\}^*\}$ and $\{wcw \mid w \in \{a,b\}^*\}$.
   NEA contains e.g. $\{ww \mid w \in \{a,b\}^*\}$ and $\{v\$w \mid v$ is substring of $w\}$.
   Not so easy to show is the following:

7. Suppose $\text{lin} \frac{f(n)}{n} = o$, $M \in FC$, accepting any input of length n M prints at most on f(n) cells. Then L(M) is regular. This observation explains why we consider only $f \geq id$.

2. *Finite change automata and Turing machines with complexity*

Theorem 1

Any machine $M \in N\,1CA(f, \sqrt{f})$ can be simulated by some machine $T \in DS(f)$.

Proof: Let be $r(n) = \sqrt{f(n)} + \log(fn) + \log\sqrt{f(n)} + 7$.
T builds $\log f(n)$ blocks. The i-th block from behind (from the right side) has the length $\frac{1}{2^{i-1}} f(n) + r(n)$. A block of length $f(n) + r(n)$ is added to the end. Thus these are at most $4\,f(n)$ tape cells. T writes the initial configuration of M on the last block in the form:

$$q_o \& \underbrace{w\,\square\ldots\square}_{f(n)} \& \underbrace{\square\ldots\square}_{\sqrt{f(n)}} \& \underbrace{\beta(o)\,\square\ldots\square}_{\log f(n)} \& \underbrace{\beta(o)\,\square\ldots\square}_{\log\sqrt{f(n)}} \& \S$$

($|w| = n$, $\beta(i)$ = binary representation of i. The § of the last block means: T has marked this block). T fills the i-th block from the left with

$$\square \& \underbrace{\square\ldots\square}_{\frac{1}{2^{i-1}}f(n)} \& \underbrace{\square\ldots\square}_{\sqrt{f(n)}} \& \underbrace{\square\ldots\square}_{\log f(n)} \& \underbrace{\square\ldots\square}_{\log\sqrt{f(n)}} \& \square \qquad (i = 1,\ldots,\log f(n)).$$

T executes a nested Savitch-algorithm: We consider the $(f(n)-1)$-th configuration just before printing (from the second printing), and moreover the initial configuration and the end configuration. Let us call these $f(n)+1$ configurations the "main configurations" of the computation, and let us combine the steps between the main configurations to a main step.

By the Savitch-algorithm T is able to verify that two main configurations are connected by a main step. Moreover we can apply the Savitch algorithm to the sequence of the $f(n)+1$ main configuration, if we are able to write the actual $\log(f(n)+1)$ main configurations on the prepared $\log(f(n)+1)$ blocks. This is possible as follows: The last block always contains the initial configurations. The block on the left contains a guess of the main configuration after $\frac{1}{2}f(n)$ changes. The block again on the left contains the guessed main configuration after $\frac{1}{4}f(n)$ changes (resp. $\frac{3}{4}f(n)$ changes),

if we verify the first (resp. the second) half on the main steps. In the first case we write those cells of the first tape of M on our block which already changed are contained in the right neighbour block, since the other cells bear only redundant information. In the second case we write only the cells still unchanged in the right neighbour block (here we describe a main configuration *after* the configuration represented in the right neighbour block. Obviously, all cells changed in the latter configuration are changed in the former configurations, too. Thus we leave these out.) At every moment during our algorithm exactly these blocks are marked which represent a main configuration derivable from the initial configuration, i.e. the configuration of a marked block is prior to the configuration of the left neighbour block, but the configuration of an unmarked block later. Thus, in the one case the cells of the left neighbour block represent the cells of our block written with symbols from $\Sigma \cup \{\square\}$, in the other case the changed cells (we suppose M doesn't print any symbol from $\Sigma \cup \{\square\}$ on the first tape).
T reconstructs the respective configuration of M from the contents of a block in the following way:

(1) T writes the block on a second tape and moves to the right neighbour block, (2).

(2) T writes the block on tape 2 next to the last block. Then T copies the cells of the last block between the first two & in turns on the cells bearing symbols of $\Sigma \cup \{\square\}$ (resp. $\Gamma-(\Sigma \cup \{\square\})$) between the first two & of the block just written down if this block is marked (resp. if this block is not marked). Then T moves to the right neighbour block on tape 1, (2). But if the neighbour block is already the last block of tape 1, then the last block of tape 2 contains the reconstructed configuration.

For the rest we refer to the paper of Savitch. ⊕

Theorem 2

For any machine $M \in NFC(f, \sqrt{f})$ there exists some equivalent $T \in DS(f)$.

Proof: Any machine $M \in kC(f,g)$ can be simulated by a machine $M' \in 1C((k+2)\cdot f,g)$. First M' writes $a_1 \underbrace{\square\ldots\square}_{k}\ a_2 \underbrace{\square\ldots\square}_{k}\ a_3 \ldots\ldots a_n \underbrace{\square\ldots\square}_{k}$ on the right of the input $a_1 \ldots a_n$ and then M' simulates M on these blocks of $k+1$ cells: if M changes the i-th cell for the j-th time, then M' changes the j-th cell in the i-th block. Thus M' needs $(k+1)f(n)+n$ cells. ⊕

Theorem 3

Every f-time bounded TM T can be simulated by some $M \in FC(f)$. If T is deterministic, then M.

Proof: Suppose without loss of generality that T is a k-tape machine moving every head in every step. Let be M a (2k+1)-change machine whose tape consists of k+1 tracks: track o,...,k. The original inscription A of some cell is interpreted as $(A, \underbrace{□,....,□}_{k})$, i.e. track o holds the input.

First M prints $(*, □_r,...., □_r)$ on the cell to the left of the input. Then M simulates T step-by-step as follows:

(1) M finds out the symbol M reads on tape i: if the rightmost symbol on track i has subscript r (or l resp.), then M moves to the rightmost symbol on track i with subscript l (or r resp.). This is the symbol T reads on tape i. Then M overprints this symbol with *. If there isn't any symbol with this subscript and i > 1, then T reads □ on tape i. If i = 1 and if M doesn't find a symbol with subscript l on track 1, then T reads □ on tape 1 , too. If however i = 1 and M doesn't find a symbol with subscript r, then M moves to the leftmost symbol ≠ * on track 1 (this is the symbol T reads on tape 1) and overprints it by *.

(2) If T prints A on tape i and moves to the right (or left, resp.), then M prints A_r (or A_l resp.) to the right of the rightmost symbol on track i.

(In fact the condition that T moves every head in every step isn't necessary. If some head stays for some steps, then M remembers this in its finite memory. M doesn't print before the head of T leaves the cell). ⊕

Example:

The behaviour of T on tape i:

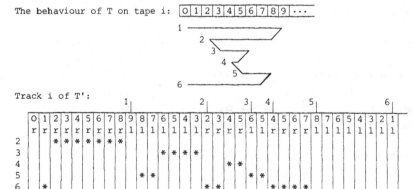

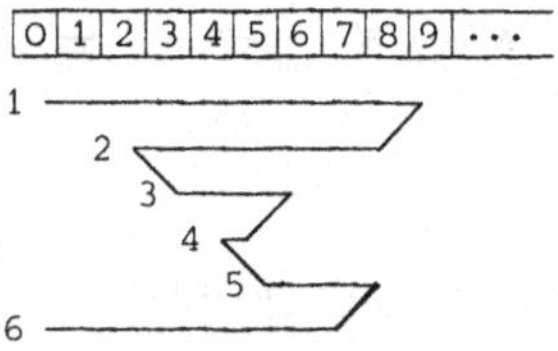

Track i of T':

										1							2				3		4				5							6
	0	1	2	3	4	5	6	7	8	9	8	7	6	5	4	3	2	3	4	5	6	5	4	5	6	7	8	7	6	5	4	3	2	1
	r	r	r	r	r	r	r	r	r	l	l	l	l	l	l	l	r	r	r	r	l	l	r	r	r	r	l	l	l	l	l	l	l	l
2			*	*	*	*	*	*	*																									
3													*	*	*	*																		
4																			*	*														
5											*	*									*	*												
6		*															*	*					*	*	*	*								

If in this proof M writes the contents of track 1,....,k on blocks of length $2\cdot k$ to the right of the input, then M needs only one track, but $n+2k\cdot f(n) \leq (2k+1)f(n)$ cells, i.e. $M \in 1C((2k+1)f)$. For any $c \in \mathbb{N}$ and any f-time-bounded TM T there is a TM T' with L(T) = L(T'), which enters a new cell on tape i at most $\frac{1}{c}f(n)$ times (after preparing the input). Analogously the f-time-bounded TM can be simulated by some $M \in FC(\max\{\frac{1}{2k+1} f,n\})$ or by some $M' \in 1C(f)$ (if f = id, M' first writes the input symbols $a_{(i-1)(2k+2)+1}, \ldots, a_{i(2k+2)}$ in the cell $i(2k+2)$ $(i = 1,\ldots,\frac{n}{2k+2})$

Theorem 4

Every f-time-bounded TM T can be simulated by some $M \in 1C(f)$. ⊕

Corollary: If L is a context-free language, then $L \in L(N\ \ C)$. ⊕

It is unlikely, that every context-free language can be accepted by some erasing automaton. The following theorem shows that an additional Turing tape of length log n - or alternatively additional heads - are sufficient. We first require a lemma concerning derivations of context-free grammars.

Lemma: Suppose G = (N,T,P,S) is a context-free grammar in Chomsky normal form. If $A \overset{*}{\in} w$ for any $A \leftarrow N$ and $w \in T^*$, then there is some derivation $A \to w_1 \to \ldots\ldots \to w_n = w$, such that the number of nonterminals in w_i $(i = 1,\ldots,n)$ is at most $m = \lfloor \log |w| \rfloor + 1$ (abbreviated $A \xrightarrow[(m)]{*} w$).

Proof: (by induction on the length of the input w)
The assertion holds for $|w| = 1$. Suppose the assertion holds for $|w| \leq 1$. Let be $m = \lfloor \log(1+1) \rfloor$, $|w| = 1+1$, $w \in T^*$, $A \to BC \xrightarrow{*} w = w_1w_2$, $B \xrightarrow{*} w_1$, $C \xrightarrow{*} w_2$ and (without loss of generality) $1 \leq |w_1| \leq |w_2|$. Then $\lfloor \log |w_1| \rfloor \leq m-1$, $|w_2| \leq 1$. From the assumption we conclude $A \xrightarrow[(2)]{} BC \xrightarrow[(m+1)]{*} w_1C \xrightarrow[(m+1)]{*} w_1w_2 = w$. ⊕

Theorem 5

The context-free languages are included in L(NE(log))

Proof: Suppose G = (N,T,P,S) is a context-free language in Chomsky normal form, $M \in NE(\log)$ simulats G-derivations as follows:

(1) If w is the input, $n = |w|$, then M constructs the work tape of length $\log n + 1 =: m$.

(2) The nonterminals resulting during the reduction correspond to the gaps on the erasing tape in the same order (if two or more nonterminals correspond to the same gap, this fact is marked on the work tape). For every $(A,v) \in P$ M may erase v on the erasing tape and insert A at the corresponding place on the work tape. If the length of the work tape exceeds m , then M does not accept. For every $(A,BC) \in P$, M may replace BC by A, if B and C correspond to the same gap.

(3) M accepts with empty erasing tape and S on the work tape.

If M happens to simulate a correct derivation $S \xrightarrow[(m)]{*} w$ (the lemma implies that for every $w \in L(G)$ there is such a derivation), M accepts w. ⊕

Corollary: If L is a derivation-bounded language, then $L \in L(NE)$.

Proof: Simulating bounded derivations, the length of the work tape is bounded. ⊕

A *f-bounded Init-automaton* M ($M \in$ Init (f)) is a machine $M \in 1C(id,f)$ that reading $a \in \Sigma$ prints $A \in \Gamma \setminus \Sigma$ and moves to the right. We can visualize $M \in$ N Init (f) as some $T \in NS(f)$ that works on the image of the input under some nondeterministic length-preserving gsm transduction. If $f \geq \log$ every $M \in$ D Init (f) is equivalent to some $T \in DS(f)$. L(N Init (f)) forms an AFL. From this we conclude

Theorem 6

L(N Init (f)) forms the least AFL containing L(NS(f)).

Corollary: The closure of L(NS(f)) under the AFL-Operations is contained in L(N1C(id,f)). ⊕

3. *log-space reducibility*

The satisfiability-problem is in L(NFC), a slight variation (padded by a homomorphism) in L(NE). The same holds for the modified knapsack-problem

$\{\beta(n_1) \underbrace{\square \ldots \square}_{\log n} \$ \ldots \$ \beta(n_k) \underbrace{\square \ldots \square}_{\log n} \$ \beta(n) \mid$ the sum of a subsequence of the n_i is $n,\ k \in \mathbb{N}\}$ ($\beta(m)$ = binary representation of m).

It is also possible to show directly that $NP \leq_{\log} NE$ and $P \leq_{\log} DE$: If $T \in DT(n^k)$ we define $f : \Sigma_T^* \to (\Sigma_T \cup \{\$\})^*$ by $w \to w \$ \square^{n^{2k}} \$$. f is computed by some machine in DS(log). f(L(T)) is accepted by $M \in DFC$; M fills the room between the \$ with a correct sequence of configurations of some w-computation of T. The same construction is possible for NP and NFC. The result for erasing automata follows by homomorphic padding.

So we conclude, if L(NE) (or L(DE) resp.) is contained in some class closed under log-space reducibility, then NP (or P resp.) is contained in this class. Such classes of languages are $L(DS(\lg^k))$, $L(DS(\log^{\log\log}))$ or $L(DS(\sqrt[h]{poly}))$ for any nondecreasing unbounded function h, all of them contained in DS(lin). (It is open, whether $P \subsetneq L(DS(lin))$.)

In particular we have the following:

$L(NE) \subseteq P \Rightarrow P = NP$

$L(NE) \subseteq L(NS(\log)) \Rightarrow L(NFC) \subseteq L(NS(\log)) = NP$

$L(NE) \subseteq L(DS(\log)) \Rightarrow L(DS(\log)) = NP$

$L(DE) \subseteq L(DS(\log)) \Rightarrow L(DS(\log)) = L(NS(\log)) = P = L(DS(\mathrm{lin})) = L(NS(\mathrm{lin}))$

As improbable as $L(NE) \subseteq P$ is $L(DS(\mathrm{lin})) = L(NFC(\mathrm{id}, \log))$, because even $L(DS(\sqrt[k]{\ })) \subseteq L(NFC(\mathrm{id},\log))$ implies $NP = L(DS(\mathrm{poly}))$. In the same way: $L(DS(\sqrt[k]{\ })) \subseteq L(DFC(\mathrm{id}, \log))$ implies $P = L(DS(\mathrm{poly}))$. Also unlikely is that $L(NS(\log))$ (or even $L(DS(\log))$) forms an AFL, for the satisfiability problem is contained in the closure of $L(DS(\log))$ unter length preserving homomorphism and hence $L(NS(\log)) = NP$ (or even $L(DS(\log)) = NP$).

Conjectures and open problems

1. $L_1 = \{u\$v \mid \text{no substring of } u \text{ of length } \log|u| \text{ is substring of } v\}$

   If the conjecture $L_1 \notin L(NFC)$ is true, we have the following consequences

   a) $L(NFC) \subset L(NFC(\mathrm{id},\log))$, $L(DS(\log)) \nsubseteq L(NFC)$

      $L(NT(\mathrm{lin})) \subset L(DS(\mathrm{lin}))$ since $L_1 \in L(DS(\log))$

   b) $L(NT(\mathrm{lin}))$ and $L(NFC)$ are not closed unter complement.

2. $L_2 = \{w_1\$ \ldots\ldots \$w_n \mid i \neq j \Rightarrow w_i \neq w_j\}$.

   If $L_2 \notin L(NT(\mathrm{lin}))$ (conjectured by Book and Greibach (197o), then

   a) $L(NT(\mathrm{lin})) \subset L(N1C)$, in particular

      $L(NT(\mathrm{lin})) \subset L(NT_1(\mathrm{lin}^2))$ because $L_2 \in L(NFC)$

      ($M \in NFC$ accepts L_2 comparing the w_i according to the lexicographical order)

   b) $L(NE) \subset L(NT(\mathrm{lin}))$, since otherwise $L(NFC)$, the least AFL containing $L(NE)$, would be contained in $L(NT(\mathrm{lin}))$.

   c) $L(DS(\log)) \nsubseteq L(NT(\mathrm{lin}))$ since $L_2 \in L(DS(\log))$.

3. Another open question concerns the classes $L(NkC) =: L_k$ $(k \in \mathbb{N})$. If any two of these classes coincide, then all, for we are able to show:

   $L_{k+1} = L_k \Rightarrow L_{k+2} = L_{k+1}$ and

   $L_{4k} = L_{2k} \Rightarrow L_{2k} = L_k$.

   On the other hand, if these classes form a hierarchy, then $L(NT(\mathrm{lin})) \subset L(N1C) \subset L(DS(\mathrm{lin}))$, since $L(NT(\mathrm{lin}))$ forms an AFL and the least AFL containing $L(N1C)$ is $L(NFC)$.

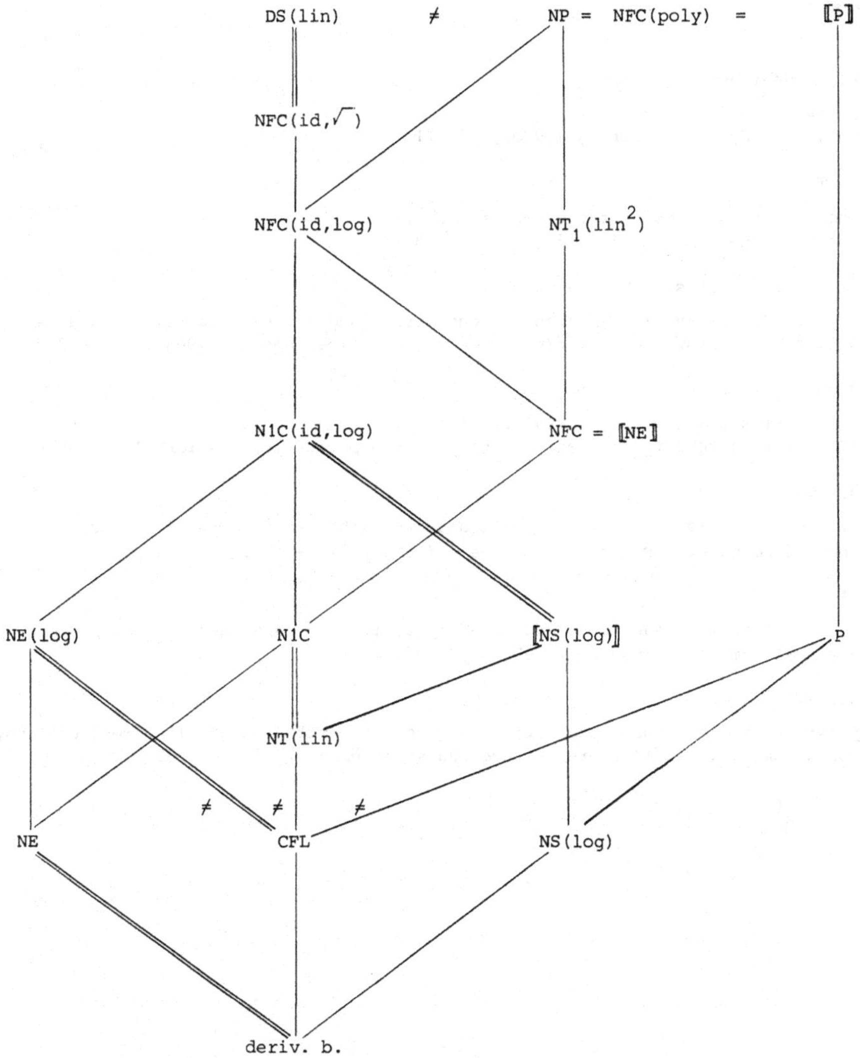

‖ : inclusion, proved in this paper,

⟦K⟧ is the least AFL containing K.

References

Book, R.V., Greibach, S.A.

Quasi-realtime languages,
Mathematical Systems Theory 4 (197o), 97-111.

Hibbard, T.N.

A generalization of context-free determinism,
Information and Control 11 (1967), 196 - 238.

Lewis II, P.M., Stearns, R.E., Hartmanis, J.

Memory bounds for the recognition of contextfree and contextsensitive languages,
IEEE Conf.Rec. on Switching Circuit Theory and Logical Design (1965), 191 - 2o2.

Karp, R.M.

Reducibilities among combinatorial problems,
in: Miller & Thatcher: Complexity of computer computations, New York 1972, 85 - 1o4.

Savitch, W.J.

Relationships between nondeterministic and deterministic tape complexities,
Journal of Computer and System Sciences 4 (197o), 177 - 192.

Springsteel, F.N.

On the pre-AFL of $\log n$ space and related families of languages,
Theoretical Computer Science 2 (1976), 295 - 3o4.

Wechsung, G.

Komplexitätstheoretische Charakterisierung der kontextfreien und linearen Sprachen,
Elektronische Informationsverarbeitung und Kybernetik 12 (1976), 289 - 3oo.

MOVE RULES AND TRADE-OFFS IN THE PEBBLE GAME

Peter van Emde Boas
Jan van Leeuwen

Abstract. The pebble game on directed acyclic graphs is commonly encountered as an abstract model for register allocation problems. The traditional move rule of the game asserts that one may "put a pebble on node x once all its immediate predecessors have a pebble", leaving it open whether the pebble to be placed on x should be taken from some predecessor of x or from the free pool (the strict interpretation). We show that allowing pebbles to slide along an edge as a legal move enables one to save precisely one pebble over the strict interpretation. However, in the worst case the saving may be obtained only at the cost of squaring the time needed to pebble the dag. It shows that one has to be very careful in describing properties of pebblings; the interpretation of the rules can seriously affect the results. As a main result we prove a linear to exponential time trade-off for any fixed interpretation of the rules when a single pebble is saved. There exist families of dags with indegrees ≤ 2 , with the property that they can be pebbled in linear time when one more pebble than the minimum needed is available but which require exponential time when the extra pebble is dropped.

1 Introduction

The pebble game has received interest in the theory of computational complexity both for practical and more theoretical goals (register alloc, network complexity, time-space trade-offs). The oldest references are Paterson & Hewitt [6] and Walker [14] (cited in [15]). The revived interest for pebbling arose from an application to Turing machine complexity by Hopcroft, Paul & Valiant [3].

The pebble game is played on directed acyclic graphs (dags). The nodes in the graph without incoming edges are called the inputs of the dag. Some other nodes are designated as the outputs of the dag. A position in the game is described by the subset of pebbled nodes. The size of this subset is the number of pebbles used in this position. Starting from an empty dag, the aim of the game is to move pebbles around according to the move rules specified below, in such a way that eventually all outputs get pebbled at least once. This should be achieved using as few pebbles as possible, or, when the number of pebbles is fixed, using as few moves as possible.

Traditionally the moves are controlled by the following rules:

(1) one can always put a pebble on an input node

(2) one can always remove a pebble from a node

(3') one can put a pebble on node x provided all immediate predecessors of x have a pebble.

The formulation of rule (3') leaves open where the pebble to be placed on x has to come from. As stated rule (3') apparently allows us to slide a pebble from a predecessor of x to x , a liberal interpretation most often used in the literature For example, the well-known result that the complete binary tree T of height n with 2^n leaves (inputs) requires n+1 pebbles is valid only if the liberal interpretation is used ; otherwise n+2 pebbles are required. The authors were reminded of this discrepancy during a live demonstration of the pebble game by J. Savage at the 1977 Fachtagung on Complexity Theory in Oberwolfach (using authentic Schwarzwalder pebbles).

Instead of following the established practice of allowing the above ambiguity in rule (3') (cf. [5, 7, 8, 9, 11]) we recognise the liberal interpretation as an additional move rule. Hence we replace (3') by the pair :

(3) one can put a free pebble on node x provided all immediate predecessors of x have a pebble

(4) if all predecessors of an empty node x have a pebble then one can slide one of these pebbles to x .

Rule (4) has been stated by Cook [2], but to our knowledge only Sethi [12] explicitly distinguished between (3) and (4) before.

We shall demonstrate that (3) and (4) should not be equivalenced ; it can have a serious impact on the complexity of pebbling whether rule (4) is allowed or not. We show that when rule (4) is allowed, then it is possible to save precisely one pebble over the minimum needed if the strict interpretation, i.e. rule (3), is used. However, in the worst case this saving may be obtained only at the price of squaring the number of moves needed.

Clearly the problem mentioned above is related to a fundamental issue in the design of machines. Should machine-instructions always deliver their result in a non-operand register (rule (3)), or should we allow that one of the operands is overwritten (rule (4)). Our result shows that the usual architectures permitting overwriting instructions may save precisely one register in the register allocation problem, at a price which has to be considered a considerable loss of speed.

The argument used to obtain the quadratic increase in time can be extended to obtain an extreme time-space trade-off result for any fixed pebbling strategy. Paul and Tarjan [7] obtained an infinite class of graphs (with indegrees ≤ 2) such that the saving of some constant fraction of the pebbles may force the time required for pebbling a graph to blow up exponentially. Lingas [5] recently obtained a similar result by saving only 2 pebbles. We show that such an explosion may even occur when just a single pebble is saved. The results of this paper are spelled out in greater detail in [13] .

The observation that rule (4) allows one to save precisely one pebble has been made independently by Gilbert and Tarjan [4]. However, their proof overlooks the crucial case (iii) below (which is responsible for the squaring of the time needed) and seems therefore incomplete. Sethi [oral comm.] has conjectured that the dags he used for the NP-hardness construction in [12] may provide examples of trade-offs similar to the one described in the paper but no specific claims have been made. Our results are unrelated to the trade-offs recently announced by Reischuk [10] and Tarjan [oral comm.].

2 Some definitions and the saving of a pebble

Let G be an arbitrary dag. Given a convention for the type of moves allowed in the game, we shall count the number of moves in which a pebble gets placed (or "moved"), i.e. we count all moves which are described by rules (1), (3) and (4) (the latter only if permitted).

Definition

$S(G)$ = the minimum number of pebbles required for pebbling G according to rules (1), (2) and (3).

$S'(G)$ = the minimum number of pebbles required for pebbling G according to rules (1), (2), (3) and (4).

$T_k(G)$ = the minimum number of counted moves required for pebbling G according to rules (1), (2) and (3) when $S(G) + k$ pebbles may be used.

$T'_k(G)$ = the minimum number of counted moves required for pebbling G according to rules (1), (2), (3) and (4) when $S'(G) + k$ pebbles may be used.

Note that S and T_k are quantities related to the "strict" interpretation of the game, S' and T'_k are the corresponding quantities for the extended move-policy. T_k and T'_k measure the "time" required for pebbling a dag if one is given k more pebbles than the minimum needed. In particular, T_0 and T'_0 measure the time required to pebble a dag with the smallest possible number of pebbles.

It is quite easy to see that for all dags G :

$$S(G) \geq S'(G) \geq S(G) - 1. \qquad (2.1)$$

The first part is trivial, the second part (which may be read as $S(G) \leq S'(G) + 1$) follows by observing that each application of rule (4) may be simulated by rules (3) and (2) if one extra pebble is provided from the start. Moves like

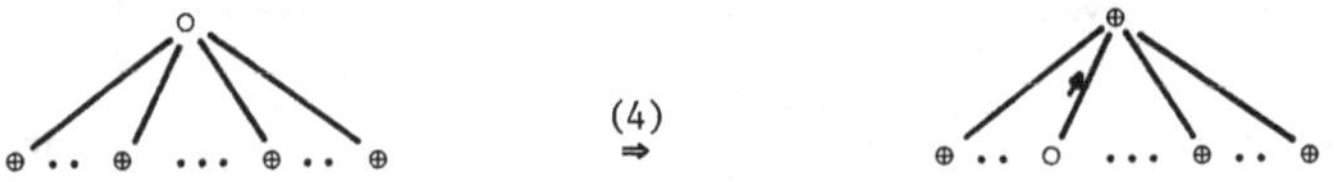

can be replaced throughout by

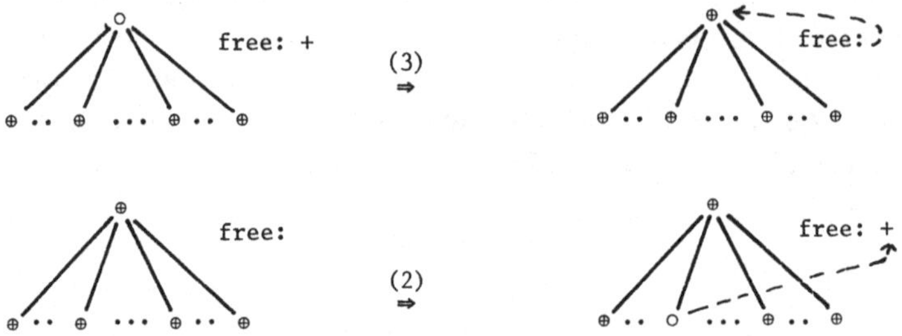

Note that the number of counted moves is not changed in the simulation.

Our first result is that rule (4) always enables one to save exactly one pebble over S(G). Observe that if G contains no edges then clearly G is pebbled by pebbling its nodes succesively using a single pebble; thus $S(G) = S'(G) = 1$.

Theorem A. For dags G with at least one edge, $S'(G) = S(G) - 1$.

Proof.

It suffices to prove that $S'(G) \leq S(G) - 1$. Consider a strategy $W = W_0, W_1, \ldots . W_N$ which uses $k = S(G)$ pebbles, with W_0 the empty position and each W_j obtained from W_{j-1} by an application of rule (1), (2) or (3). Consider the W_j where exactly k pebbles are used. In the next move some pebble must be removed, as otherwise k+1 pebbles would be present in W_{j+1}. The following possibilities arise:

(i) The pebble removed in the move W_j, W_{j+1} is not removed from a predecessor of the node pebbled during the preceding move, or from this node itself. In this situation the order of the two moves may be interchanged, thus eliminating the position involving k pebbles.

(ii) The pebble removed in the move W_j, W_{j+1} is taken from a predecessor of the node pebbled during the preceding move. In this situation the two moves may be replaced by an application of rule (4) thus eliminating the position involving k pebbles.

(iii) The pebble removed in the move W_j, W_{j+1} is the pebble which was placed during the preceding move.

Only this third case requires a non-local transformation in order to eliminate the position using k pebbles. Note that the move makes sense only if the node pebbled is an output (otherwise W_j and W_{j+1} may be eliminated alltogether). We replace W_j by a shift, provided the pebbled node has some predecessor. Otherwise we take some arbitrary pebble from the dag and use this pebble instead. In both cases the position involving k pebbles has been eliminated. However, in order to regenerate position W_{j+1}, which equals W_{j-1} in this case, it no longer suffices to take the pebble just placed from the dag ; instead we take all pebbles from the dag and repeat the entire pebbling strategy upto W_{j-1}, in this way restoring configuration W_{j+1}.

It is not hard to obtain a complete proof based upon the above transformation [13] . Always taking W_j as the first position involving k pebbles, we can use complete induction based on the number of positions in a pebbling strategy which have k pebbles on the dag. □

We should point out that the re-pebbling of portions of the dag, called for in case (iii) of the given proof, may cause a substantial increase in the time for pebbling G. The next result puts a bound on the number of extra moves needed.

Proposition B. Let G be a dag with m outputs. Then $T'_0(G) \leq m.T_0(G)$

Proof

The argument before shows that no time is lost if the dag contains only one output. If there are m outputs, then split the pebbling strategy into m strategies, starting from empty dags and each involving a single output (costing together at most $m.T_0(G)$ moves). Apply the transformation from the proof of theorem A to each strategy individually. □

Proposition B shows that the loss of time in saving one pebble with rule (4) stays within reasonable limits as long as the number of outputs of a dag is small. In general, m can be as large as $O(T_0(G))$ (whereas clearly $m \leq T_0(G)$) and proposition B learns that in worst case a squaring of the pebbling time may occur. A simple example shows that the worst case can occur and that the bound of proposition B is best possible.

Consider the dag $E_{n,1}$ defined as

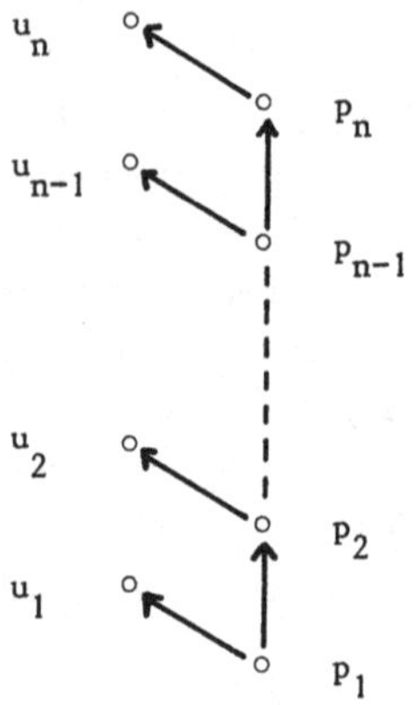

(2.2)

The reader easily verifies that $S(E_{n,1}) = 2$, $T_0(E_{n,1}) = 2n$ and $S'(E_{n,1}) = 1$, but

$$T_0'(E_{n,1}) = 2 + 3 + \ldots + (n+1) = \theta(n^2)$$

We conclude

<u>Theorem C</u>. Saving a pebble by allowing rule (4) in worst case squares the (order of magnitude of the) pebbling time in the strict interpretation.

3 <u>Extreme time-space trade-offs</u>

A pebbling strategy is called a real-time pebbling of G in case no node in G gets pebbled twice during the game. Assuming that G does not contain useless nodes (i.e. nodes which do not precede any output) this is equivalent to saying that the time needed to pebble G equals the size of G. Clearly each dag can be pebbled in real-time provided sufficiently many pebbles are available.

We noted that rule (4) can be simulated by a combination of rules (3) and (2) without changing the number of counted moves, provided one extra pebble is made available. Together with the result of theorem C, we conclude that for any dag G :

$$T_0(G)^2 \geq T_0'(G) \geq T_0(G) \geq T_1'(G) \geq T_1(G) \geq \ldots \geq T_k(G) = T_k'(G) = \text{size}(G) \quad (3.1)$$

for some $k \geq 0$ (the last equality holding only if G contains no useless nodes). From theorem C we conclude that in general :

$$T_j(G)^2 \geq T_j'(G) \tag{3.2}$$

Examining the two inequalities underscored in (3.1), we shall discover here that there can be very large (exponential) gaps between the quantities on the left-hand and right-hand sides in both. Our main goal shall be to prove the following time-space trade-off result, stated informally as

Theorem D. There is an infinite family of dags $H_n (n \geq 1)$, with indegrees bounded by 2, such that $T_0'(H_n)$ is exponentially worse than $T_1'(H_n)$ = size (H_n)

Because $T_0'(G) \leq T_0(G)^2$ and, on the other hand, $T_1(G) \leq T_1'(G)$, the same family of dags suffices to show that $T_0(G)$ can be exponentially worse than $T_1(G)$ uniformly. Thus, we need only pursue the details of the result when rule (4) is allowed. Note that it substantiates an earlier claim that, in any interpretation of the rules, the saving of a single pebble can blow up the pebbling time exponentially.

It will require a bit of "engineering" to keep the indegrees of all nodes in H_n bounded by 2. We shall ignore this constraint for the moment, so as not to obscure the idea of the construction. Let $f : N \to N$ be some function to be chosen later. Define the following auxiliary graphs:

X_n = 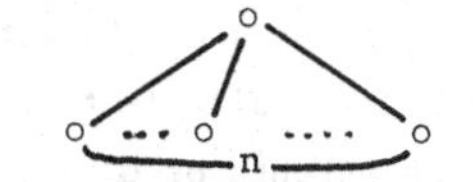

(a node with n immediate predecessors)

Y_n = 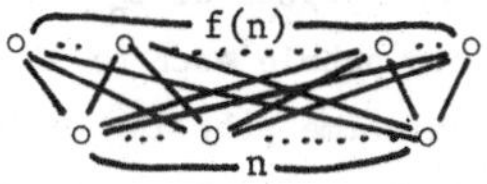

(a bipartite graph)

Now consider the family of dags $G_n (n \geq 1)$, defined inductively as follows:

G_1 =

G_n = 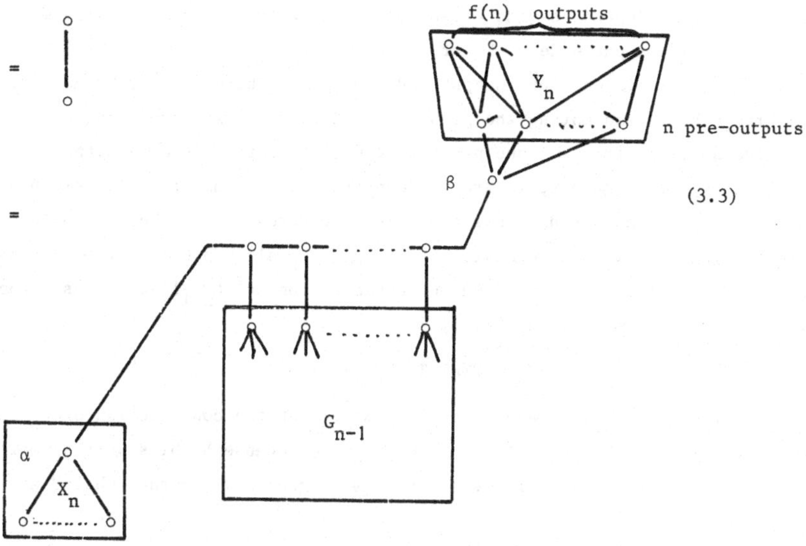

(3.3)

The size of G_n satisfies

$$\text{size } (G_1) = 2$$
$$\text{size } (G_2) = \text{size } (G_{n-1}) + 2(n+1) + f(n) + f(n-1) \qquad \text{for } n \geq 2$$

and it follows that size $(G_n) \leq 2.\ \sum_2^n f(i) + \theta(n^2)$. Likewise one can easily verify that G_n has $\theta(n^2)$ input nodes and, obviously, exactly $f(n)$ output nodes.

Clearly $S'(G_n) = n$. The following proposition makes some precise claims about the time needed to pebble G_n with n+1 or n pebbles.

Proposition E.

(i) $T_1'(G_n) = \text{size } (G_n) \leq 2.\ \sum_2^n f(i) + \theta(n^2)$

(ii) $T_0'(G_n) \geq \prod_2^n f(n)$

Proof.

(i) The simplest strategy to pebble G_n using n+1 pebbles proceeds as follows, using as an induction-hypothesis that the outputs of G_{n-1} can be pebbled (in consecutive order) using n pebbles in size (G_{n-1}) moves. First pebble α and slide its pebble along the chain to β, while pebbling the outputs of the embedded G_{n-1} in consecutive order (indeed with exactly n free pebbles available to do it!) With a pebble on β we can place a pebble on each of the n pre-outputs of G_n, which will be fixed there. Now take the pebble from β and use it to pebble each of the $f(n)$ output nodes from left to right. This actually yields a real-time pebbling of G_n.

(ii) If only n pebbles are available one must initially proceed in a similar fashion, resorting to rule (4) more often now and using that G_{n-1} can be pebbled using n-1 pebbles as an inductive assumption. Once β is reached (i.e., pebbled) things will change and we are going to see the effect of having only n pebbles to play with. In order to pebble an output node of Y_n at all one must

(a) move a pebble to each pre-output node, which can be done only by committing all n-1 free pebbles and moving the pebble from β to the last pre-output still open,

(b) slide a pebble from any one pre-output node to the designated output.

To pebble any other output, we are in deep trouble: we must get a pebble back on the one pre-output node which is now open. This requires that we get a pebble back on β first. The only way to repebble β is to pick up all n pebbles from the dag and to repebble the entire dag, including the embedded copy of G_{n-1}! So we must proceed for each output node again, and clearly

$$T_0'(G_n) \geq f(n).T_0'(G_{n-1})$$

which yields the desired estimate as stated. Note that the construction of G_n indeed forces the entire repebbling of the embedded G_{n-1}, because pebbles must appear on its outputs from left to right if we are to move a pebble along the "chain" at all. □

Choosing $f(n) = n$ we get a result as desired. The construction yields a family of dags G_n with size $(G_n) = \Theta(n^2)$ and $T_1'(G_n) = \Theta(n^2)$ but $T_0'(G_n) \geq \Theta(n!)$, an exponential blow-up by saving just one pebble! One should note, however, that the indegrees of nodes in G_n can be as large as n.

We shall modify the construction to obtain a family H_n , which exhibits the same behavior while indegrees remain bounded by 2. The idea is based on the inductive scheme of (3.3), but the sub-dags X_n and Y_n will be changed. So X_n and Y_n should now be binary, chosen such that an argument as before will go through to get an analog of proposition E.

Consider the following requirements for X_n and Y_n :

Condition I. $S'(X_n) = S'(Y_n) = n$, and n pebbles are actually required for pebbling any single output of Y_n above. Moreover X_n and Y_n can be pebbled in real-time when one extra pebble is provided.

Condition II. If Y_n is pebbled using n pebbles (without repebbling any input), then at the time one of its outputs gets pebbled there must be a pebble-free path from each of the remaining outputs to an input.

The qualifier "without repebbling any input" may seem unnatural but really isn't, considering that Y_n is embedded in H_n and the repebbling of an "input" is not just a matter of applying rule (1).

Lemma F. If X_n and Y_n satisfy conditions I and II and if the sequence of dags $\{H_n\}$ is defined according to (3.3), then:

(i) $T_1'(H_n) = \text{Size}(H_n)$, so H_n can be pebbled in real time using one extra pebble

(ii) $T_0'(H_n) \geq \prod_2^n f(n)$.

Proof. Similar to the proof of proposition E (see [13]) .

At this time it is useful to recall the structure of Cook's pyramidal dags C_m of width m ([2]):

C_m =

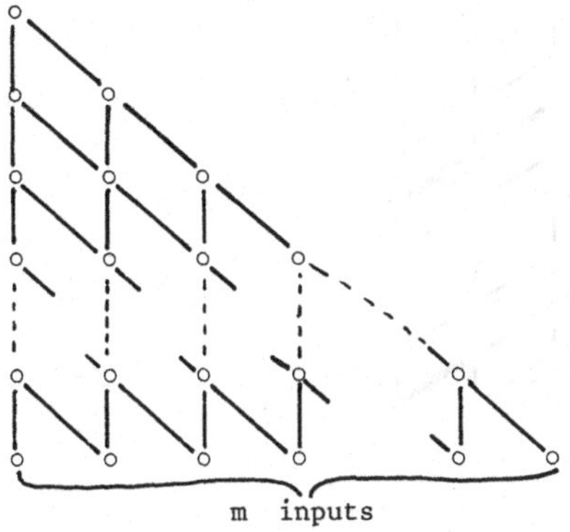

(3.4)

It is easy to see that by choosing $X_n = C_n$ the requirements of condition I are satisfied as far as X_n is concerned. To obtain the Y_n's we introduce a family of dags $E_{m,n}$. We encountered its members $E_{m,1}$ already in constructing a worst case example of the trade-off in section 2.

The structure of $E_{m,n}$ is obtained by vertical translation of a pyramid C_n over unit distance $(m-1).n$ times, leading to a "staircase" of width n and heigth n.m tapering off as a pyramid at the top. Special (unary) output nodes $u_1,\ldots,u_m$ are added on to the left side of the staircase, with u_i connected to the node at height i.n. It follows that each u_i is connected to the top of an embedded copy of C_n, denoted by P_i. Observe that the base of P_i is located at exactly one level above P_{i-1}. The structure of $E_{m,n}$ must be evident from (3.5), where $E_{m,4}$ is shown.

It is easy to verify that $S(E_{m,n}) = n+1$, and if n+1 pebbles are available then one can pebble $E_{m,n}$ in real-time (in fact, regardless of whether rule (4) is used or not).

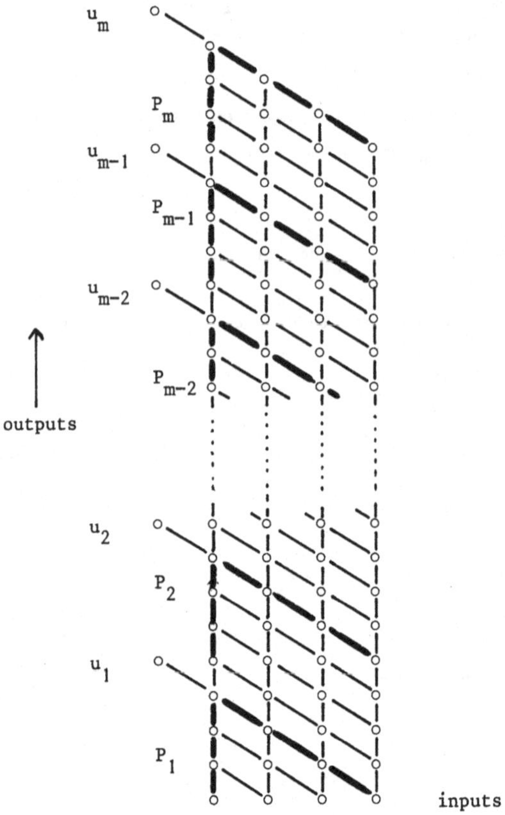

(3.5)

$$T_0(E_{m,n}) = T'_1(E_{m,n}) = \theta(m.n^2) \qquad (3.6)$$

We show that $E_{m,n}$ satisfies conditions I and II for the Y_n :

Proposition G. Let node u_i of $E_{m,n}$ be pebbled, using rules (1) to (4) and m pebbles, without pebbling any input more than once. At the time u_i gets pebbled, there must be a pebble-free path from each of the remaining outputs to some input.

Proof.

Let a configuration of pebbles on $E_{m,n}$ be called proper if each of the following conditions is satisfied:

(i) each column of $E_{m,n}$ contains a pebble (hence, all available pebbles are in use and occupy different columns),

(ii) each pebble resides at the same level or one higher than the pebble in the column immediately to its right.

It is possible to pebble u_i in such a way that all intermediate configurations are proper.

The following observations can be made for an arbitrary pebbling strategy:

(a) Since we do not allow the repebbling of inputs in the pebbling of u_i, a configuration must occur in which the last input gets pebbled before u_i gets pebbled ; if this configuration is not proper, then it is impossible to pebble u_i.

(b) Before any u_i can be pebbled the properness condition must be disturbed.

(c) Once the properness condition is established and it gets disturbed some time later, a situation will arise in which all outputs except possibly one have a pebble-free path to some input.

The above observations together imply proposition G : in order to pebble u_i the properness condition is established at the time the last input gets pebbled; at a later stage the properness gets disturbed, and from that stage onwards the pebble-free paths from outputs to inputs remain pebble-free since no input gets repebbled. The proofs of the observations are tedious but straightforward (see [13]) □

Proof of theorem D.

Choose $X_n = C_n$ and $Y_n = E_{n,n^4}$. The reader easily verifies that the dags H_n constructed by (3.3) have size $\Theta(n^4)$. Now $T'_1(H_n) = \Theta(n^4)$ whereas $T'_0(H_n) \geq n!$ by lemma F, thus yielding the required exponential blow-up. □

Theorem D shows that the explosion of time in minimizing register use, first reported by Paul and Tarjan [7] in case some constant fraction of the registers gets saved, can occur already if just one register is saved. We note that Lingas [5], independently, found a construction which yields a sequence of binary dags $\{G_n\}$ satisfying $S'(G_n) = 2n$, $T'_0(G_n) \geq 2^n$ and $T'_2(G_n) = \text{size}(G_n) = \Theta(n^3)$. The resulting trade-off is more extreme (because the dags are "smaller"), but one had to trade 2 pebbles to get it. An interesting problem might be to find a family of dags $\{G_n\}$

with $S'(G_n) = \Theta(n)$, such that the saving of some constant number of pebbles gives a jump from linear to exponential in pebbling time whereas size (G_n) is only $o(n^3)$.

5 References

[1] Aho, A.V. and J.D. Ullman, Principles of Compiler Design, Addison-Wesley Publ. Comp., Reading, Mass., 1977.

[2] Cook, S.A., An Observation on Time-Storage Trade Off, Journal Computer Systems Sciences 9 (1974) 308-316.

[3] Gilbert, J.R. and R.E. Tarjan, Variations of a pebble game on graphs. Rep. Stanford STAN-CS-78-661 (Sept. 1978).

[4] Hopcroft, J., W. Paul and L. Valiant, On Time versus Space, J.ACM 24 (1977) 332-337.

[5] Lingas, A., A PSPACE-complete Problem related to a Pebble Game, in: G. Aussiello and C. Böhm (eds.), Automata, Languages and Programming (Fifth Colloquium, Udine, 1978), Springer Lecture Notes in Computer Science 62, 1978, pp. 300-321.

[6] Paterson, M.S. and C.E. Hewitt, Comparative Schematology, Record of Project MAC Conference on Concurrent Systems and Parallel Computations (June 1970) 119-128, ACM, New Jersey, Dec. 1970.

[7] Paul, W. and R.E. Tarjan, Time-Space Trade-offs in a Pebble Game, in: A. Salomaa and M. Steinby (eds.), Automata, Languages and Programming (Fourth Colloquium, Turku, 1977), Springer Lecture Notes in Computer Science 52, 1977, pp. 365-369.

[8] Paul, W., R.E. Tarjan and J.R. Celoni, Space Bounds for a Game on Graphs, Math. Syst. Th. 10 (1976) 239-251.

[9] Pippenger, N, A Time-Space Trade-off, Computer Science Res. Rep. RC 6550 (#28265) IBM, Yorktown Heights, 1977 (also" J.ACM 25 (1978) 509-515).

[10] Reischuk, R., Improved bounds on the Problem of Time-Space Trade-off in the Pebble Game (Preliminary version), Conf. Record 19th Annual IEEE Symp. on Foundations of Computer Science, Ann Arbor, 1978, pp. 84-91.

[11] Savage, J.E. and S. Swamy, Space-Time Trade-offs in the FFT Algorithm, Techn. Rep. CS-31 (August 1977), Div. of Engineering, Brown University, Providence, 1977.

[12] Sethi, R., Complete Register Allocation Problems, SIAM J. Comput. 4 (1975) 226-248.

[13] van Emde Boas, P. and J. van Leeuwen, Move-rules and trade-offs in the pebble game, Techn. Rep. RUU-CS-78-4, Dept. of Computer Science, University of Utrecht, Utrecht, April/August 1978.

[14] Walker, S.A., Some Graph Games related to Efficient Calculation of Expressions, Res. Rep. RC-3633, IBM, 1971.

[15] Walker, S.A. and H.R. Strong, Characterizations of Flow-chartable Recursions, Journ. Computer System Sciences 7 (1973) 404-447.

TRANSITION DIAGRAMS AND STRICT DETERMINISTIC GRAMMARS

Dietmar Friede

1. Introduction

This paper is the first part of an approach to extend the class of languages parsable by the method of recursive descent (without backup) to all deterministic context-free languages. The main goal was to find a simple extension of LL(k) grammars characterizing all deterministic context-free languages. On the way to this class of grammars it is shown that the strict deterministic grammars [HarrisonHavel73] are parsable in a top-down manner by transition diagramms similar to those defined by Lomet [Lomet73].

Recursive descent is a quick top-down parsing method requiring little space. The parsers are clearly constructed. Error recovery in case of a syntactical error is very easy in contrast to bottom up methods. Semantics (i.e. predicates and action) can easily be inserted. The recursive descent is formally described by syntax and transition diagrams, being flow diagrams for the parsers. In the literature most authors assume the LL grammars to characterise the recursive descent (without backup).

As far as I know there is no intensive investigation on recursive descent despite (or because) of its simplicity. I only know the following investigations:

- Transition diagrams were introduced 1963 by Conway [Conway63] to describe a COBOL compiler. Tixier [Tixier67] formalized them. He has done the work only for single-exit diagrams, but Conway's transition diagrams specifically include multiple-exit diagrams. With single-exit diagrams one only gets parsers for LL(1) languages which are a proper subset of the deterministic context-free languages ([AhoUllmanI72,II73]).

- The papers by Lomet and Král/Demner ([Lomet73],[KrálDemner73], [Král74]) show, that multiple-exit transition diagrams describe all deterministic context-free languages. It follows that there are recursive descent parsers (without backup) for all deterministic context-free languages, if one extends the recursive descent slightly, but keeping it deterministic. Both papers show how to construct transition or syntax diagrams for LR(1) grammars (or SLR(1) grammars). Král was not interested in the class of grammars to which he converted the SLR(1) grammars. In [Lomet74] a grammatical characterization of multiple-exit diagrams is given, called LLP(k) ("left-local-precedence") grammars.

Pittl [Pittl77] made further investigations on this class of grammars, finding among others a connection to strict deterministic context-free grammars. But the definition of LLP(k) grammars is rather complicated.

In this paper I show how to construct transition diagrams for strict deterministic context-free grammars [HarrisonHavel73] and vice versa, if one defines the transition diagrams a little bit more restricted than Lomet. By this follows that strict deterministic context-free grammars are parsable by a slightly extended deterministic recursive descent and therefore in a top-down manner. Based on strict deterministic context-free grammars and LL(k) grammars a new class of grammars - the partitioned LL(k) ("PLL(k)") grammars - are defined. The PLL(k) grammars characterize the deterministic context-free languages. But this definition, in contrast to the other (for example LR), only depends on the rules of the grammar. To parse PLL(k) grammars transition diagrams are extended by a lookahead.

The grammars are always assumed to be reduced. The empty word is denoted by e. All automata are assumed to accept only by empty input and - if they have - by empty stack. The notations and definitions not given in this paper are that of Aho and Ullman [AhoUllmanI72,II73].

2. Transition diagrams

To define transition diagrams, I define at first a special deterministic pushdown automaton. This is a method similar to Lomet [Lomet73]. I define this automaton a little bit more restricted than Lomet. His strictly nested pushdown automaton is defined here as "extended" strictly nested pushdown automaton:

Definition 1:

An extended strictly nested deterministic pushdown automaton $M = (Z,T,P,f,z_0,F)$ is a deterministic pushdown automaton (Z states, T alphabet, P pushdown alphabet, f maps $Z \times (T \cup e) \times (P \cup e)$ into elements of $Z \times (P \cup e)$ such that no state has both an e-move and non-e-moves with respect to the pushdown or with respect to the input, z_0 is the initial state, F is a subset of Z called the final states); such that the moves of f are of only three forms:

1. $f(z,a,e) = (z',e)$ $\quad a \in T$.
2. $f(z,e,e) = (z',p)$ $\quad p \in P$; z is an invoking state and z' an entry state.
3. $f(z,e,p) = (z',e)$ $\quad p \in P$; z is an exit state and z' a return state.

And for all $w \in L(M)$, $(z_0,w,e) \vdash^* (z,e,e)$ for $z \in F$.

I.e. if there is a state z with one or more transitions of form 1, there will be acception only from this state, as M is a deterministic pushdown automaton, beside transitions of form 1 there can be no other transitions of the form $f(z,e,p) \neq \emptyset$. Correspondingly, if there is a transition of form 2 from a state z there are no other transitions, and if there is a transition of form 3 then all other transitions have to be of form 3.

Transitions of form 2 "call" a "subautomaton". Transitions of form 3 "terminate the calculation of a subautomaton", are "returns".

In the following a definition of the strictly nested deterministic pushdown automaton is given. This definition is more adequat to the structure of strict deterministic grammars.

Definition 2 :

A strictly nested deterministic pushdown automata $M = (Z,T,P,f,z_0,F)$ is an extended strictly nested deterministic pushdown automata, where for all final states $z \in F$ there are only transitions of the form:

$f(z,e,p) = (z',e)$

Example: $M = (\{1,\ldots,16\},\{a,b,c\},\{2,10\},f,1,\{5,6,7,8\})$

with f: 1. the "accepting transitions":

$f(1,a,e) = (2,e)$	$f(9,b,e) = (11,e)$	$f(3,b,e) = (7,e)$
$f(9,c,e) = (12,e)$	$f(4,c,e) = (8,e)$	$f(13,b,e) = (15,e)$
$f(9,a,e) = (10,e)$	$f(14,c,e) = (16,e)$	

2. the "call transitions":

$f(2,e,e) = (9,2)$	$f(10,e,e) = (9,10)$

3. the "return transitions":

$f(11,e,2) = (5,e)$	$f(15,e,2) = (3,e)$	$f(11,e,10) = (15,e)$
$f(15,e,10) = (13,e)$	$f(12,e,2) = (6,e)$	$f(16,e,2) = (4,e)$
$f(12,e,10) = (16,e)$	$f(16,e,10) = (14,e)$	

The automaton M is represented by the following graph, where ——a⟶ means accepting, ·······↓p····› call and – – – ↑p – – –› return.

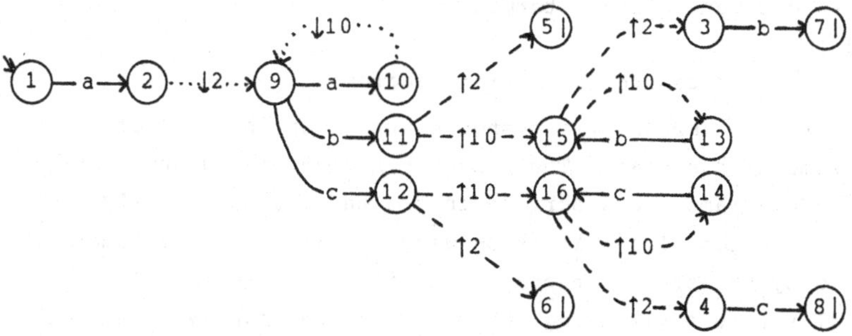

The language accepted by M is $L(M) = \{a^n b^n, a^n c^n : n \geq 1\}$.

To define transition diagrams we need the following definition:

Definition 3 :

Let M be an extended strictly nested deterministic pushdown automaton, as in defintion 1.

State z is connected to state z' if and only if:

1. $f(z,a,e) = (z',e)$. In this case, z is input connected to z'.
2. There are states z_1, z_1' and $p \in P$ such that $f(z,e,e) = (z_1,p)$ and $f(z_1',e,p) = (z',e)$ and z_1 is connected to z_1'. In this case, z is machine connected to z'.
3. There is a sequence of states (z_i), $i \in \{1,\ldots,n\}$, such that $z = z_1$, $z' = z_n$ and z_i is machine or input connected to z_{i+1} for $1 \leq i < n$.

In general z is not connected to z.

We call the model of a transition diagram a submachine. The alphabet of a submachine consists of the input alphabet of the strictly nested deterministic pushdown automaton and symbols for the other submachines, "called" by N.

Definition 4 :

A submachine of a strictly nested deterministic pushdown automaton $M = (Z,T,P,f,z_0,F)$ is a finite automaton $N = (Z_N,T_N,f_N,z_{0N},F_N)$ where

1. $z_{0N} = z_0$, or z_{0N} is an entry state in M.
2. $Z_N := \{z_{0N}\} \cup \{z \in Z : z_{0N}$ is connected to $z\}$.
3. $T_N := T \cup \{[z_1,z_1'] : z_1$ is an entry state and z_1' is an exit state of M, z_1 is connected to z_1', and there are states $z,z' \in Z_N$ such that $f(z,e,e) = (z_1,p)$ and $f(z_1',e,p) = (z',e)$ for some $p \in P\}$.
4. $F_N := \{z \in Z_N : z$ is an exit state or $z \in F\}$.
5. f_N is defined as:
   1. $f_N(z,a) = z'$ if $f(z,a,e) = (z',e)$ and $z, z' \in Z_N$.
   2. $f_N(z,[z_1,z_1']) = z'$ if $f(z,e,e) = (z_1,p)$, z_1 is connected to z_1' and $f(z_1',e,p)=(z',e)$ for some $z_1' \in Z$ and $p \in P$.

Remark: The defined automata are deterministic.

Definition 5 :

A submachine is also called transition diagram.

A strictly nested deterministic pushdown automaton is a set of transition diagrams with a stack. The pushdown mechanism and the control of the transition diagrams are described in the underlying strictly nested pushdown automaton. The transition diagrams are finite automata being represented by transition graphs. These finite automata call themselves mutually recursivly using the stack in the underlying strictly nested deterministic pushdown automaton.

(Initial, final) configuration, move, language, accepting etc. are defined for transition diagrams as they are defined for finite automata.

Example: From the above example we get two transition diagrams.

N1 = ({1,...,8},{a,b,c,[9,15],[9,16],[9,11],[9,12]},f_{N1},1,F)

with f_{N1} :

f(1,a) = 2, f(2,[9,15]) = 3, f(2,[9,16]) = 4, f(2,[9,11]) = 5,

f(2,[9,12]) = 6, f(3,b) = 7, f(4,c) = 8

N2 = ({9,...,16},{a,b,c,[9,15],[9,16],[9,11],[9,12]},f_{N2},9,{11,12,15,16})

with f_{N2} :

f(9,a) = 10, f(9,b) = 11, f(9,c) = 12, f(10,[9,11]) = 15,

f(10,[9,15]) = 13, f(10,[9,16]) = 14, f(10,[9,12]) = 16,

f(13,b) = 15, f(14,c) = 16

The transition graphs of these two automata are:

N1:

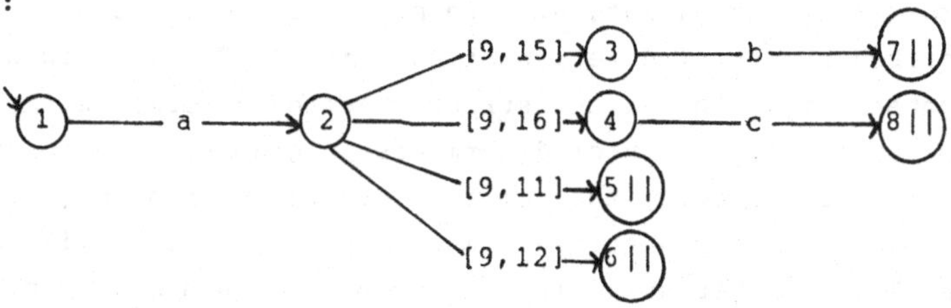

N2:

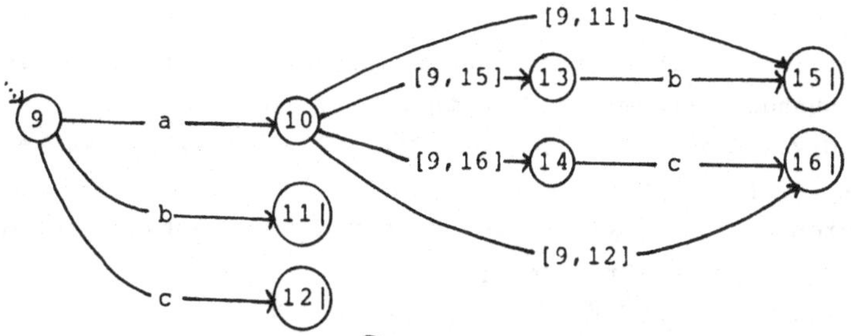

Final states are marked by (||) if they are in F, otherwise they are marked by (|) if they are in some F_N.

The class of grammars, being studied in their relation to transition diagrams are the strict deterministic grammars, defined by Harrison and Havel [HarrisonHavel73]. This is a class of grammars having until now no importance in the field of compilerwriting and language description. They seemed to be only interesting from a theoretical point of view.

Definition 6 :

A context-free grammar G = (N,T,R,S) (N nonterminals, T terminals, R rules, S startsymbol in N, all sets finite and nonempty, N and T disjoint, V = N ∪ T) is a strict deterministic grammar iff there is an equivalence relation ≡ with:

1. T ∈ V/≡ , i.e. T is equivalence class under ≡.
2. For any A,B ∈ N und a,b,c ∈ V^*, if A->ab, B->ac, A ≡ B

then either

$b \neq e$ and $c \neq e$ and ${}^{(1)}b \equiv {}^{(1)}c$

or $b = c = e$ and $A = B$.

Notation: ${}^{(n)}w$ is the prefix of w with the length min(lg(w),n).

Harrison and Havel showed a number of interesting properties of this class of grammars. They proofed for instance that they charaterize the prefix-free context-free languages.

3. The relations between transition diagram and strict deterministic grammars.

In this part will be shown, that the classes of languages of strictly nested deterministic pushdown automata are equal to the class of languages described by strict deterministic grammars. First it is shown that one can construct an equivalent strictly nested deterministic pushdown automaton for every strict deterministic grammar. The construction belonging to the following theorem is a general method to construct a parser for a strict deterministic grammar. The method is "semi" top-down [KrålDemner73] in contrast to that given by Harrison and Havel [HarrisonHavel72,73,74] basing on the shift-reduce algorithm.

Theorem 1:

To every strict deterministic grammar G there is a strictly nested deterministic pushdown automaton MG with L(G) = L(MG).

Construction: Given G = (N,T,R,S) with $V/\equiv = \{T, V_0, \ldots, V_n\}$, $V_0 := [S]$, $V_i := \{A_{i0}, \ldots, A_{im}\}$, $A_{ij} \in N$.

For this grammar a strictly nested deterministic pushdown automaton $MG = (Z,T,P,f,V_0,F)$ is constructed by

$Z := \{aV_i : A \to ab \in R,\ a,b \in V^*,\ A \in V_i \text{ and } V_i \in N/\equiv\}$

$P := \{aV_i : A \to aBb \in R,\ a,b \in V^*,\ A \in V_i,\ B \in N \text{ and } V_i \in N/\equiv\}$

$F := \{aV_0 : S \to a\}$

and the transition function f:

1. $f(aV_i,x,e) = (axV_i,e)$ for every $a,b \in V^*$, $x \in T$, $A \in V_i$ with $A \to axb \in R$.
2. $f(aV_i,e,e) = (V_j,aV_i)$ for every $a,b \in V^*$, $A \in V_i$, $B \in V_j$ with $A \to aBb \in R$.
3. $f(aV_i,e,bV_j) = (bAV_j,e)$ for every $a,b,c \in V^*$, $A \in V_i$, $B \in V_j$ with $A \to a$, $B \to bAc \in R$.

Attention, in case 2. and 3. i = j is possible.

The main idea of the construction is to construct a (finite) subautomaton for every equivalence class of the vocabulary of the grammar. A state of a subautomaton V_i is denoted by the symbol V_i and a prefix.

The prefix describes the "way" from the initial state V_i to the considered state. It is constructed from the terminals and nonterminals on the way, describing acception of terminals or already finished calls of subautomata.

The proof is not given here (in full length it is found in [Friede78]). It is based on induction on the length of the derivation of words in the grammar.

Theorem 2:

For every strictly nested deterministic pushdown automaton in standard form [Lomet73] $M = (Z,T,P,f,z_0,F)$ there is a strict deterministic grammar $GM = (N,T,R,S)$ with $L(M) = L(GM)$.

Construction: Suppose M has the subautomata N_i $(i=1,\ldots,n)$, $Z \cap T = \emptyset$, S is neither in $(Z \times Z)$ nor in T.

$N := \{(z,z') : z \in Z_{Ni},\ z' \in F_{Ni},\ i = 1,\ldots,n\ ,\ z \text{ connected to } z'\}$
$\quad \cup \{(z,z) : z = z_{0Ni} \text{ and } z \in F_{Ni}\} \cup S.$

R is conctructed as follows:

1. $(z,z')\text{->}a(z_1,z')$ for every $(z,z'),(z_1,z') \in N$ such that $f(z,a,e) = (z_1,e)$
2. $(z,z')\text{->}a$ for every $(z,z') \in N$ such that $f(z,a,e) = (z',e)$.
3. $(z,z')\text{->}(z_1,z'')(z_2,z')$ for every (z_1,z''), $(z,z'),(z_2,z') \in N$ with z machine connected to z_2 and there is a $p \in P$ such that $f(z,e,e) = (z_1,p)$, and $f(z'',e,p) = (z_2,e)$.
4. $(z,z')\text{->}(z_1,z'')$ for every $(z,z'),(z_1,z'') \in N$ such that there is a $p \in P$ with $f(z,e,e) = (z_1,p)$ and $f(z'',e,p) = (z',e)$.
5. $(z,z)\text{->}\ e$ for every $(z,z) \in N$
6. $S\text{->}(z_0,z)$ for every $z \in F$ and $(z_0,z) \in N$.

The partition $V/\equiv$ is:

$V_z := \{(z,z') \in N\}$ i.e. $(z,z') \equiv (z'',z''') \Leftrightarrow z = z''$

$N/\equiv\ := \{\{S\}\}$ unioned with the union of all $\{V_z\}$ over $z \in Z$.

$V/\equiv\ := \{T\} \cup N/\equiv$.

This proof is not given in it's length, too. It is found in [Friede78].

By this the equivalence of the transition diagrams as defined in this paper and the strict deterministic grammars is shown. As the transition diagrams are flow diagrams for recursive descent parsers one is now able to parse strict deterministic grammars by a slightly extended recursive descent (without backup) in a top-down like manner.

4. PLL(k) grammars.

In general it is difficult to construct a strict deterministic grammar G for an arbitrary prefix-free deterministic context-free language. To generate deterministic context-free languages which are not prefix-ree one must extend the strict deterministic grammars by a lookahead, like that of LL(k) and LR(k) grammars. On the other hand, the main property of LL(k) grammars is to know always exactly (with k symbols lookahead) the rule by which the leftmost nonterminal in a leftderivation of a given word is to be expanded.

The PLL(k) grammars are a synthesis of both classes of grammars. When producing the left derivation of a given word with a PLL(k) grammar, only a set (an equivalence class) containing the leftmost nonterminal to be expanded with k-lookahead is determined. The equivalence class of the leftmost nonterminal defines a set of rules to continue the derivation.

The fundamental idea of partitioning the vocabulary of a grammar aims to restrict to a minimum the "sub-grammar" with which the derivation of a given word has to continue.

A similar, but more complicated way is given by [Lomet74] and [Pittl77] with the "left local precedence grammars". The advantage of PLL(k) grammars is that the analyser is only a set of finite automata and not a set of precedence analysers.

Definition 7:

A context-free grammar $G = (N,T,R,S)$ $(V = N \cup T)$ is a partitioned LL(k) (in short PLL(k)) grammar iff there is an equivalence relation $\equiv$ such that:

1. $T \in V/\equiv$, i.e. T is an equivalence class under $\equiv$.
2. For any $A,B \in N$ and $a,b,c \in V^*$ with $A \to ab$, $B \to ac$, $A \equiv B$ holds:
   If $first_k(b\ follow_k(A)) \cap first_k(c\ follow_k(B)) \neq \emptyset$
   then either
   $b \neq e$ and $c \neq e$ and ${}^{(1)}b \equiv {}^{(1)}c$
   or $b = c = e$ and $A = B$.

Elsewhere [Friede78] it is shown:

- For any PLL(k) grammar there is an e-free PLL(k) grammar generating the same language (without e).
- The given definition of PLL(k) grammars refers only to the rules and not to a generally infinite set of derivations.
- It is easy to test wether a grammar is PLL(k) or not for a given k.
- The PLL(0) grammars are exactly the strict deterministic grammars.
- The PLL(k) languages form no proper hierarchy, i.e. the class of

PLL(k) languages is equal to the class of PLL(1) languages (for $k > 0$);. But the PLL(0) languages are a proper subset of the PLL(1) languages.

Especially for the PLL(1) grammars we have:

- They include the LL(1) grammars.
- They characterize the deterministic context-free languages.

5. Parsing PLL(k) grammars with k-transition diagrams

The transition diagrams as defined above have no lookahead on the input when deciding if they have to go into some subautomaton or have to accept or to jump back or stop. To parse PLL(k) grammars the transition diagrams are extended by a k-lookahead. At first a deterministic pushdown with k lookahaed is defined.

Definition 8 :

A k-deterministic pushdown automaton is a 6-tupel $M = (Z,T,P,f,z_0,F)$, Z,T,P,z_0,F are similar to the equal named sets above, f is a partiell map $f: Z \times T_e \times T_e^k \times P_e \rightarrow Z \times P_e$ with

1.) If $f(z,a,u,p) \neq \emptyset$ and $a \neq e$ or $p \neq e$ then $f(z,e,u,e) = \emptyset$ and if $a \neq e$ then $f(z,e,u,p) = \emptyset$.

2.) If $k > 0$ and $f(z,a,u,p) \neq \emptyset$ then $a = {}^{(1)}u$.

$(z,w,v) \in Z \times T^* \times P^*$ is called configuration of M.

$\vdash$ is a relation on $(Z \times T^* \times P^*)$, defined by $l \vdash l' :\Leftrightarrow$ $l = (z,xw,pv)$, $l' = (z',w,p'v)$ and $f(z,x,{}^{(k)}xw,p) = (z',p')$.

(Initial, final) configuration, language, accepting etc. are defined for k-deterministic pushdown automata similar as they are defined for deterministic pushdown automata.

Theorem 3 :

To every k-deterministic pushdown automaton M there is a deterministic pushdown automaton M' accepting the same language.

The idea of the proof is very simple, one has to get the finit lookahead into the finit control of the deterministic pushdown automaton.

Definition 9 :

A k-strictly nested deterministic pushdown automaton $M = (Z,T,P,f,z_0,F)$ is a k-deterministic pushdown automaton such that the moves of f are of only three forms:

1. $f(z,a,u,e) = (z',e)$ $a \in T$.
2. $f(z,e,u,e) = (z',p)$ $p \in P$.
3. $f(z,e,u,p) = (z',e)$ $p \in P$.

and if $z \in F$ and $u = e$ then there are only transitions of the form:

$$f(z,e,e,p) = (z',e).$$

I.e. if the lookahead is empty only "return" is possible.

Invoking, entry, exit and return state, subautomatons and transition diagrams etc. are defined for k-strictly nested deterministic pushdown automata similar as they are defined for strictly nested deterministic pushdown automata.

Theorem 4:

For every PLL(k)-grammar G there is a k-strictly nested deterministic pushdown automaton MG with L(G) = L(MG).

Only the construction is given here, the proof may be found in [Friede78].

Construction: $G = (N,T,R,S)$ with $V/\equiv\ = \{T, V_0, \ldots, V_n\}$,
$V_0 := [S]$, $V_i := \{A_{i0}, \ldots, A_{im}\}$ $A_{ij} \in N$.
$MG = (Z,T,P,f,V_0,F)$ is contructed by:
$Z := \{aV_i : A \rightarrow ab \in R,\ a,b \in V^*,\ A \in V_i,\ V_i \in N/\equiv\}$
$P := \{aV_i : A \rightarrow aBb \in R,\ a,b \in V^*,\ A \in V_i,\ B \in N,\ V_i \in N/\equiv\}$
$F := \{aV_0 : S \rightarrow a\}$
and the transition function f:

1. $f(aV_i,x,u,e) = (axV_i,e)$ for every $a,b \in V^*$, $x \in T$, $A \in V_i$, $u \in \mathrm{first}_k(xb\ \mathrm{follow}_k(A))$ such that $A \rightarrow axb \in R$.
2. $f(aV_i,e,u,e) = (V_j,aV_i)$ for every $a,b \in V^*$, $A \in V_i$, $B \in V_j$, $u \in \mathrm{first}_k(Bb\ \mathrm{follow}_k(A))$ such that $A \rightarrow aBb \in R$.
3. $f(aV_i,e,u,bV_j) = (bAV_j,e)$ for every $a,b,c \in V^*$, $A \in V_i$, $B \in V_j$, $u \in \mathrm{first}_k(c\ \mathrm{follow}_k(B))$ such that $A \rightarrow a$ and $B \rightarrow bAc \in R$.

6. Acknowledgment

I am very greatful to Mr.'s W. Brauer, M. Jantzen and F. Schwenkel who supervised my diploma thesis. This paper is based on the 1. and the main parts of the 2. chapter of this thesis [Friede78]. I am also very grateful to Gerd Friesland, Manuel Mall, Manfred Kudlek, Angelika Rudolph and Ingrid Westphal for their hints, remarks and help.

7. References

[AhoUllmanI72]: Aho, A.V., Ullman, J.D., The Theory of Parsing, Translation, and Compiling, Vol. 1: Parsing, Prentice Hall, Englewood Cliffs, New York, 1972.

[AhoUllmanII73]: Aho, A.V., Ullman, J.D., The Theory of Parsing, Translation, and Compiling, Vol. 2: Compiling, Prentice Hall, Englewood Cliffs, New York, 1973.

[Conway63]: Conway, M.E., Design of a seperable transition diagram compiler, Communication of the ACM Vol. 6, Nr.7, S. 396 - 400, New York, 1963.

[Friede78]: Friede, D., Über determistisch kontextfreie Sprachen und rekursiven Abstieg, Bericht Nr. 49 des Fachbereich Informatik der Universität Hamburg, 1978.

[GellerHarrison73]: Geller, M.M, Harrison, M.A., Strict Deterministic versus LR(0) Parsing, Conference Record of ACM Symposium on Principles of Programming Languages, 1973.

[HarrisonHavel72]: Harrison, M.A., Havel, I.M., Real-Time Strict Deterministic Languages, SIAM J. Computing, Vol.7 Nr.4, 1974

[HarrisonHavel73]: Harrison, M.A., Havel, I.M., Strict Deterministic Grammars, Journal of Computer and System Sciences, Vol. 7, Nr. 3, 1973.

[HarrisonHavel74]: Harrison, M.A., Havel, I.M., On the Parsing of Deterministic Languages, Journal of the ACM, Vol.21 Nr.4, 1974.

[KrálDemner73]: Král, J., Demner, J., Semi-Top-Down Syntactic Analysis, Technical Report 6/73, Techniqual University of Prague, 1973.

[Král74]: Král,J.,Bottum-up versus top-down syntax analysis revised. Technical Report 10/74, Techniqual University of Prague, 1974. Král,J., Semi-top-down transition diagrams driven syntactic analysis: Part 2. Techniqual Report 11/74, Techniqual University of Prague, 1974.

[Lomet73]: Lomet, D.B., A Formalisation of Transition Diagram Systems, Journal of the ACM, Vol. 20 Nr 2, 1973.

[Lomet74]: Lomet, D.B., Automatic generation of multiple-exit parsing subroutines. Proc. of the 2nd Colloquium on Automata , Languages and Programming. Springer-Verlag, Lecture Notes in Computer Science 14, New York, 1974, 214-231.

[Pittl77]: Pittl, Jan, Exponential Optimization for the LLP(k) Parsing Method, Lecture Notes in Computer Science 53: Mathematical Foundations of Computer Science, 1977.

[Tixier67]: Tixier, Recursive Functions of Regular Expressions in Language Analysis, Ph.D.Thesis Stanford, 1967.

EXACT EXPRESSIONS FOR SOME RANDOMNESS TESTS

Péter Gács

Abstract For a computable probability distribution P over the set of infinite binary sequences Martin-Löf defined a test $d(x|P)$ measuring the degree of nonrandomness of the sequence x with respect of P. We give some expressions in terms of Kolmogorov's and other complexities of the initial segments of x whose difference from $d(x|P)$ is bounded by a constant.

0. Introduction

For a statistician nothing seems to be more interesting than the question about randomness. Given an element ω of the event space Ω as the outcome of an experiment, and a distribution P he wants to find out how justified it is to suppose that the underlying distribution to the experiment was P; i.e. that ω is random w.r.t. P. However, his model is slightly different because in the typical cases he has an access to a large number of independently repeated experiments $P^n = P \times P \times \ldots \times P$ and what he wishes to decide on the basis of $\omega = (\omega_1, \ldots, \omega_n)$ is only the question about P, the product structure taken for granted. The decisions can then be made on the basis of central limit theorems, and it is, roughly speaking, the investigation of the conditions of such decisions to which most of mathematical statistics is devoted.

There are some highly interesting statistical situations where the product-space framework is not applicable: e.g. prediction problems or testing of pseudo-random sequences. After its revival in the sixties by the work of Kolmogorov and Martin-Löf (continued by Levin, Chaitin, Schnorr) the modern theory of randomness approaches now to a satisfiable form and its solutions to these problems are of convincing simplicity and generality. Unfortunately, after taking the efforts to understand them and later trying to apply them one notes with some disappointment the large gap between theoretical and practical computability.

The present paper does not bridge this gap, either. It gives some more exact relations between complexity and randomness and one can only hope that when the theory using general computability will be more perfect then the chances to find its practical extension increase. Our new results are presented in Section 5. The previous sections help to understand their general context. The unabridged variant of this lecture will appear in the Zeitschrift für Mathematische Logik, 26/1 (1980). It contains one additional section on uniform tests (see [11]).

1. Basic definitions

<u>Notations</u> All logarithms are to the base 2. N is the set of natural numbers, $N_k = \{0,1,..,k-1\}$. Q is the set of rational numbers, R the set of real numbers, $R_+ = R \cap (0,\infty)$, $\bar{R} = R \cup \{\infty\}$, $\bar{R}_+ = R_+ \cup \{\infty\}$. $N_2^* = \bigcup_n N_2^n \cup \{\Lambda\}$, where Λ is the so-called empty word. We fix a recursive one-to-one correspondence $\kappa : N_2^* \to N$ with $\kappa(x) \geq l(x)$, where $l(x)$ is the length of the word x. $\Omega = N_2^\infty$ = the set of infinite binary sequences. For $x,y \in N_2^*$, xy is the concatenation of x and y, $x \subset y$ iff $\exists z.\ xz = y$. For $\omega \in N_2^\infty, \omega = \omega_1\omega_2\ldots (\omega_i \in N_2)$ and $\omega^n = \omega_1\ldots\omega_n$.

For two nonnegative functions f,g let $f \leqslant g$ mean that a $c > 0$ exists with $cf \leq g$. $f \approx g$ iff $f \leqslant g$ and $g \leqslant f$, $f \precsim g$ iff $\exp(f) \leqslant \exp(g)$, $f \asymp g$ iff $f \precsim g$ and $g \precsim f$. We consider N_2^∞ with its usual topology determined by the basis $\{xN_2^\infty | x \in N_2^*\}$, R with the (usual) topology determined by $\{(r_1,r_2) | r_1,r_2 \in Q,\ r_1 < r_2\}$.

Let $\mathcal{M}$ be the set of all probability measures over Ω, with its (weak) topology determined by the subbasis of sets of the form $\{\mu \in \mathcal{M} | r_1 < \mu(x) < r_2\}$. Here for $x \in N_2^*, \mu(x) = \mu(xN_2^\infty)$, and $r_1,r_2 \in Q$.

Sometimes N, N_2^* will also be considered as discrete topological spaces (essentially equivalent by the correspondence κ). In any of these (locally compact) top. spaces X a basis $\{U_i | i \in N\}$ is given <u>with a fixed enumeration.</u> New spaces can be constructed by products.

<u>Definition</u> An element x of the space X will be called <u>computable</u> if $\{i | x \in U_i\}$ is enumerable. An open set $G \subset X$ is called <u>constructively open</u> if $\{i | \bar{U}_i \subset G\}$ is enumerable. $F \subset X$ is called <u>constructively closed</u> if F^c, the complement of F, is constructively open.

A function $f:X \to R$ is called semicomputable (from below) if $\{(r,x) \mid r \in R,\ x \in X,\ f(x)>r\}$ is constructively open. f is called computable if f and -f are semicomputable.

Especially: a measure is called computable iff it is computable as an element of $\mathcal{M}$. It is easy to see that this is equivalent to the condition that $\mu: N_2^* \to R$ be computable as a function.

2. Martin-Löf's tests

Martin-Löf declared for nonrandom those elements ω of Ω which belong to some constructively definable set of measure 0. Since rather different approaches to randomness lead to an equivalent definition, there is a wide agreement that Martin-Löf's random elements are convenient to be considered as "the" random ones. Every element of positive probability (in discrete spaces typically every element) is random, and one can only speak of their deficiency of randomness. Different "tests" assign different deficiencies of randomness. It is hard to vote for one test as the most natural but most proposed tests are asymptotically equal to Martin-Löf's (in the case of computable measures).

Definition [1] Let μ be a computable measure. A Martin-Löf-test is a semicomputable function $d: N_2^\infty \to R$ with $\forall k.\ \mu\{d(\omega)>k\} \le 2^{-k}$.

Theorem 2.1 (Martin-Löf) Among the Martin-Löf-tests there is a maximal one in the sense of the ordering $\preccurlyeq$.

Definition We fix a maximal ML-test once for all for each μ and call it $d_M(\omega|\mu)$, a universal ML-test. A sequence ω will be called random iff $d_M(\omega|\mu)<\infty$. The notion of a random sequence is more invariant than Martin-Löf's tests. One can imagine rather different reasonable ways of measuring the deficiency of randomness but the question which sequences are random at all will be answered equivalently by most of them. We generalize now the notion of a test.

Definition Given a computable measure μ a semicomputable function $d:\Omega \to R$ is a test if

$$\lim_m \mu\{\omega \mid d(\omega) \ge m\} = 0 \text{ recursively:}$$

i.e. a recursive function m(k) exists with

$$\mu\{\omega \mid d(\omega) > m(k)\} < 2^{-k}.$$

For a test d we have

$$\{\omega \mid d(\omega) = \infty\} \subset \{\omega \mid d_M(\omega) = \infty\}.$$

In case of equality the test is called universal. (Every universal test d we give in the following is asymptotically equal to d_M, i.e. $\lim_{d\to\infty} d_M(\omega)/d(\omega) = 1$ holds.)

3. Apriori probability

In the mathematical statistics one is often confronted with the need to use certain "apriori probability". Until now the principles have been missing which would allow a general definition of this distribution. The most important property required of apriori probability seems to be that all elements ω of the space be random w.r. to it. One sees immediately that the apriori probability cannot be a computable measure. We can find, however, a "semicomputable semimeasure" with this property.

Definition [2] A semimeasure over Ω is a function $\varphi: N_2^* \to R_+$ with $\varphi(x) \geq \varphi(x0) + \varphi(x1)$, $\varphi(\Lambda) \leq 1$. It is easy to prove that for any semimeasure φ, $\varphi(x) = \inf\{\mu(x) \mid \mu \geq \varphi, \mu \in \mathcal{M}\}$, and that the lower bound of any set of measures is a semimeasure.
A semimeasure is called semicomputable if it is semicomputable as a function from N_2^* to R_+. It is not hard to see that φ is semicomputable iff the set $\{\mu \in \mathcal{M} \mid \mu \geq \varphi\}$ is constructively closed in $\mathcal{M}$. Semimeasures over the discrete spaces N, N_2^* will also be considered. (A semimeasure over N is given by a function $\varphi: N \to R_+$; φ must satisfy the condition $\Sigma_x \varphi(x) \leq 1$.) Semimeasures over N_2^* correspond to those over N by κ.

Theorem 3.1 [Levin, 2] In the set of all semicomputable semimeasures there is a maximal element with respect to the relation $\preccurlyeq$.
Let us call a fixed maximal semimeasure $M = M_\Omega$ the apriori probability over Ω. The apriori probabilities over N, N_2^* will be denoted by M_N, (writing freely $M_N(x)$ for $M_N(\kappa(x))$. We do not write out the subscript if no misunderstanding may arise). Levin's following theorem establishes the role of apriori probability in determining randomness.

Theorem 3.2 [Levin 3], see also Schnorr [4]
$d_S(\omega \mid \mu) = \sup_n \log M_\Omega(\omega^n) - \log \mu(\omega^n)$ is a universal test for any computable measure μ.

Remarks 1. $\log (M_\Omega(\omega^n)/\mu(\omega^n))$ is bounded from below for every fixed computable , so ω is random w.r.t. to μ iff

$$\mu(\omega^n) \asymp M_\Omega(\omega^n).$$

2. d_S is defined also for noncomputable μ and for all $\mu \geq M_\Omega$ one has $d_S(\omega|\mu) \leq 0$.
In other words, if we measure nonrandomness by d_S, we find that "all sequences are random with respect to the apriori probability".

4. Complexity

The numbers

$$H_N(x) = -\log M_N(x), \; H_\Omega(x) = -\log M_\Omega(x)$$

can by many reasons be considered as a measure of the complexity of the finite sequence x.

Definition Kolmogorov's complexity of the sequence x given y with respect to a partial recursive function $A: N_2^* \times N_2^* \to N_2^*$ is defined as $K_A(x|y) = \min\{l(p)|A(p,y) = x\}$, $K_A(x) = K_A(x|\Lambda)$. Kolmogorov proved the existence of a p.r. function U with $K_U \preccurlyeq K_A$ for any other p.r. A. Fixing such a U, we define K as K_U.

A slight modification in Kolmogorov's definition of complexity proved very useful in the applications [6-8, 12]. A set $E \subset N_2^*$ is said to be prefix-free if $x,y \in E \Rightarrow x \not\subset y$.

If we confine us to the set of p.r. functions $\mathcal{F} = \{A| \forall y. \{p|A(p,y)$ is defined$\}$ is prefix-free$\}$ then in this class a function T can be found with $K_T \preccurlyeq K_A$ for all $A \in \mathcal{F}$. Let us fix such a T and take K_T for the new complexity. It turns out to be characterizable in terms of the apriori probability.

Theorem 4.1 [Levin, 6]

$$H_N(x) \asymp K_T(x).$$

We define here $M_\Omega(x|y)$ only for y as an element of the discrete space N_2^*. For this we take a maximal one (w.r.t. to $\preccurlyeq$) among the conditional semicomputable semimeasures, i.e. semicomputable functions $\varphi: N_2^* \times N_2^* \to R_+$, where $\varphi(x|y)$ is for each y a semimeasure over Ω.

The three kinds of complexity defined before are numerically close to each other. Indeed, it is easy to see (and well-known) that

Theorem 4.2 $K \lesssim H_N \lesssim K+2\cdot\log K$, $H_\Omega \lesssim H_N$, and for any prefix-free r.e. set $E \subset N_2^*$ $\exists c \forall x \in E, y \in N_2^*.\ H_N(x|y) \le H_\Omega(x|y) + c.$

5. Tests expressed by complexities

Let us start with a useful relation between K and H.

Theorem 5.1 (Levin)

$$K(x) \asymp \min\{i \mid H_N(x|i) \le i\},$$

$$K(x) \asymp H_N(x|K(x)). \qquad (5.1)$$

Remark $K(x|y)$ is similarly expressible.

Though by Theorem 3.2 we have a most satisfiable characterization of randomness by the behavior of the apriori probability (whose logarithm is a sort of complexity), two questions are of some technical interest:

a) to express Martin-Löf's test by some complexity

b) to see how the other complexities are suitable to express randomness.

For our characterization of Martin-Löf's test we introduce an auxiliary complexity.

Definition $\tilde{H}(x;k) = \min\{i \mid H(x|k-i) \le i\}$.

$\tilde{H}(x;k|y)$ can be defined similarly, with y everywhere in the condition. Then we have by Theorem 5.1:

$$\tilde{H}_N(x;k|k) \asymp K(x|k) \ . \qquad (5.2)$$

Thus H_N can be considered as a generalization of K.

Remarks 1. $\tilde{H}_\Omega \lesssim \tilde{H}_N$.

2. H is obviously semicomputable from above.

3. Similarly to (5.1) we have

$$\tilde{H}(x;k) \asymp H(x|k-\tilde{H}(x;k)). \qquad (5.3)$$

As we have seen in Theorem 3.2, the testing of the randomness of ω w.r.t. μ naturally involves a comparison of $-\log\ \mu(\omega^n)$ with some complexity of ω^n.

Notation $l_\mu(\omega^n) = [-\log \mu(\omega^n)]$.

<u>Theorem 5.2</u> For a fixed computable measure μ,
$d_M(\omega|\mu) \asymp \sup_n l_\mu(\omega^n) - \tilde{H}_\Omega(\omega^n; l_\mu(\omega^n)) \asymp$
$\asymp \sup_n l_\mu(\omega^n) - \tilde{H}_N(\omega^n; l_\mu(\omega^n))$.

We can deduce from this theorem the first known exact relation between tests and complexity established in [10]. Denote by π_n the equidistribution over N_2^n. A universal M-L-test $d_M(x|\pi_n)$ can be defined as a greatest (w.r. to $\preccurlyeq$) semicomputable (in (x,n)) function $d(x|\pi_n)$ with

$$\forall n,k. \quad \pi_n\{x|d(x|\pi_n) \geq k\} \leq 2^{-k}.$$

<u>Corollary 5.1</u> (see [10]) $d_M(x|\pi_n) \asymp n-K(x|n)$.

From the first part of Theorem 5.1 one can reprove Theorem 3.2. We have by definition $d_S(\omega|\mu) = \sup_n l_\mu(\omega^n) - H_\Omega(\omega^n)$.

<u>Corollary 5.2</u> d_S is asymptotically equal to d_M.

We have analogously
<u>Corollary 5.3</u> $d_C(\omega|\mu) = \sup_n l_\mu(\omega^n) - H_N(\omega^n)$
is a universal test, asymptotically equal to $d_M(\omega|\mu)$.
This test was proposed by Chaitin [7] for the case of the equidistribution, and proved to be a universal test by Schnorr. The test $d_C(\omega|\mu)$ has some other meaningful characterisations.

<u>Theorem 5.3</u> Put $t_C(\omega|\mu) = 2^{d_C(\omega|\mu)} = \sup_n \dfrac{M_N(\omega^n)}{\mu(\omega^n)}$.

For any fixed computable measure μ, $t_C(\omega|\mu)$ is $\leq$-maximal among the semicomputable functions $t(\omega)$ with the property $\int t(\omega)\mu(d\omega) \leq 1$.

We can use for the expression of the main term in Martin-Löf's tests Kolmogorov's complexity too, as shown by the following theorem.

<u>Theorem 5.4</u> Put

$$\Delta(\omega^n|\mu) = l_\mu(\omega^n) - K(\omega^n|n, l_\mu(\omega^n)).$$

Then

$$d_M(\omega|\mu) \asymp \sup_n \Delta(\omega^n|\mu) - \tilde{H}(n, l_\mu(\omega^n); \Delta(\omega^n|\mu))$$

As in the Corollary of Theorem 5.1, we get a simpler universal test expressed by K if we do not require it being a Martin-Löf-test.

<u>Corollary 5.4</u> $d_K(\omega|\mu) := \sup_n \Delta(\omega^n|\mu) - H(n, l_\mu(\omega^n))$

is a universal test, asymptotically equal to d_{ML}.

Especially for the Lebesgue measure λ we have the test:
$d_K(\omega|\lambda) = \sup_n n-K(\omega^n|n)-H(n)$.

References

[1] Martin-Löf, Per: The definition of random sequences. Information and Control 6 (1966) 602-619

[2] Zvonkin, A.K., Levin, L.A.: The complexity of finite objects and the development of the concepts of information and randomness by means of the theory of algorithms. Russ. Math. Surv.25/6 (1970) 83

[3] Levin, L.A.: On the notion of a random sequence. Soviet Math. Dokl. 14 (1973) 1413

[4] Schnorr, C.P.: Process complexity and effective random tests. J. Comput. Syst. Sci. 7 (1973) 376

[5] Kolmogorov, A.N.: Three approaches to the quantitative definition of information, Prob. Info. Transmission 1/1 (1965) 1

[6] Levin, L.A.: Some theorems on the algorithmic approach to Probability Theory and Information Theory (Ph.D.thesis, 1971)

[7] Chaitin, G.J.: A theory of program-size formally identical to Information Theory, J.A.C.M. 22 (1975) 329

[8] Chaitin, G.J.: Algorithmic Information Theory, IBM J. REs. Dev. (July 1977) 350-359

[9] Schnorr, C.P.: Unpublished manuscript

[10] Martin-Löf, P.: Algorithmen und zufällige Folgen. Lecture Notes, University of Erlangen, 1966

[11] Levin, L.A.: Uniform tests of randomness, Soviet Math. Doklady 17 (1976) 337

[12] Gács, P.: On the symmetry of algorithmic information. Soviet Math. Dokl. 15 (1974) 1477-1480, Corrections ibid. No. 6, V.

Acknowledgement: I want here to express my thanks to Professor C.P. Schnorr for inspiring discussions on the subject, and to L.A. Levin for having made accessible many of his unpublished ideas.

ON STORAGE OPTIMIZATION FOR AUTOMATICALLY GENERATED COMPILERS*

Harald Ganzinger

1. INTRODUCTION

The attribute grammars, as introduced in [Knu 68], form the basis of more than ten compiler generating systems which have been developed recently. (For an overview see e.g. [Räi 77].) One of the most important tasks of these systems is, therefore, the generation of efficient attribute evaluators from given attribute grammars. Several approaches to the generation of evaluators for specific subclasses of attribute grammars have been proposed in the literature, see [JaW 75], [Kas 76], [KeW 76], [Wat 77], [Kas 78] among others. The evaluators generated according to these methods are reasonably efficient with respect to the number of visits of attribute instances in syntax trees. The main disadvantage of these evaluators is, however, the excessive demand for space in order to store the attribute values. Every instance of an attribute in a tree usually occupies its own storage block. Even the more space-saving approaches (which use some stack mechanism for storing intermediate values) allocate different storage blocks for any of the attribute instances at the ancestors of a node when visiting this node. Such allocation mechanisms are acceptable if only primitive attributes, e.g. numbers, characters, etc., are to be evaluated. Thus, in most of the compiler-compilers there are additional possibilities to use global variables and/or pointers to attributes in order to avoid the use of non-primitive attributes, e.g. symbol tables, code sequences, etc. However, this leads to non-static compiler descriptions which depend on the specific evaluation strategy as implemented by the system.

The purpose of this paper is to investigate methods for reducing the consumption of storage for attribute evaluation. Special emphasis is laid on the recognition of global attributes, i.e. attributes which describe the administration of global information usually held in counters, tables, etc. The storage administration is represented by a storage allocation function which distinguishes these global attributes and maps them to, possibly common, storage blocks.

In section 4 we give some criteria for proving the "correctness" of a given allocation function. Section 5 sketches some aspects of the automatic determination of "good" allocation functions. Although the problem of storage allocation depends very much on the attribute evaluation method to be used, we shall not explicitly talk about such methods. Even the attribute grammars have not to be introduced formally. Instead we shall use a general graph-grammar approach. Its basic concepts are given in sections 2 and 3.

2. GRAPH-GRAMMARS FOR ATTRIBUTE DEPENDENCIES

Throughout this paper we assume X to be some fixed finite set, the set of *labels*. (Pairs, consisting of an attribute and a nonterminal which owns this attribute, are these labels.) The dependencies between attributes will be represented formally by A-graphs.

* This research was carried out within the Sonderforschungsbereich 49 - Programmiertechnik - at the Technical University of Munich.

DEFINITION. An *A-graph* F is a tupel $F=(V,\xi,P,\tau,\iota,\alpha)$, with the following properties: V is a non-empty finite set, the set of *nodes*. ξ is a mapping from V to X, called *labelling function*. ($\xi(v)$ is called the *label* of v.) $P=(p_i)_{1\le i\le n}$ is a partition of V into pairwise disjoint subsets p_i. (The p_i are called the *positions* of F.) None of these positions p contains two different nodes with the same label. τ determines the *type* $\tau(p)\in\{\underline{in},\underline{out},\underline{term}\}$ of any position. (A position p is called an *input, output* or *terminal position,* if $\tau(p)=\underline{in}$, $\underline{out}$ or $\underline{term}$, resp.) There is exactly one input position in F (denoted by p_I, subsequently). α and ι are binary relations on V, called the relations of *dependencies* and *identical dependencies*, resp. It is $\iota\subset\alpha$, i.e. any identical dependency is a dependency.

Attribute evaluation principles are formalized by strategy relations:

DEFINITION. A binary relation σ is called a *strategy* for F, iff $\alpha\subset\sigma$. (Informally: u may be evaluated before v, if $u\sigma v$ holds.)

EXAMPLE. We give some examples for A-graphs with strategies.

F_1:

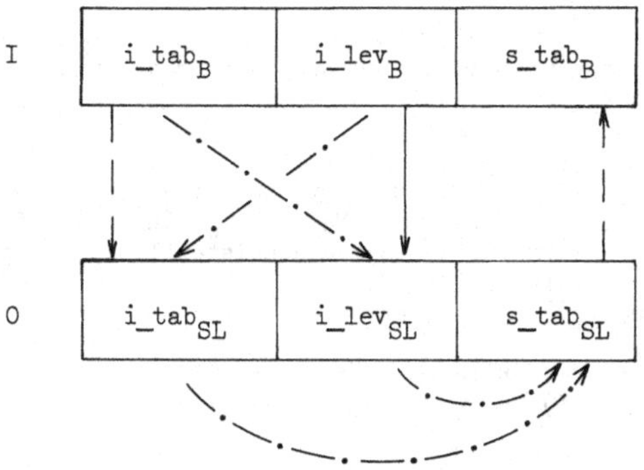

(The rectangles denote nodes and their labels. Nodes which contact each other belong to one position. The relations ι, $\alpha-\iota$, and $\sigma-\alpha$ are given by the edges ---> , ——> , and - • -> , resp. "I" specifies the input and "O" an output position.)

We can consider F_1 to be the dependency graph for an attribute grammar rule

B ::= <u>begin</u> SL <u>end</u>
i_tab(SL) := i_tab(B); i_lev(SL) := i_lev(B)+1; s_tab(B) := s_tab(SL)

representing the computation of symbol table attributes "i_tab" and "s_tab" and of a block level attribute "i_lev". The identities are distinguished. The strategy indicates left-to-right evaluation of attributes. In the rule for statement lists SL ::= S; SL one might define the dependency graph F_2 as depicted on the next page.

REMARKS AND NOTATIONS. A sequence $u_0,u_1,\ldots,u_n$, $n\ge 0$, of nodes is called a *ρ-path,* $\rho\in\{\iota,\alpha,\sigma\}$, if $u_i\,\rho\,u_{i+1}$, for $0\le i<n$. The restriction ξ_p of ξ to a position p is one-to-one. If ρ is a binary relation then ρ^+ denotes its transitive and ρ^* its transitive-reflexive closure.

F_2:

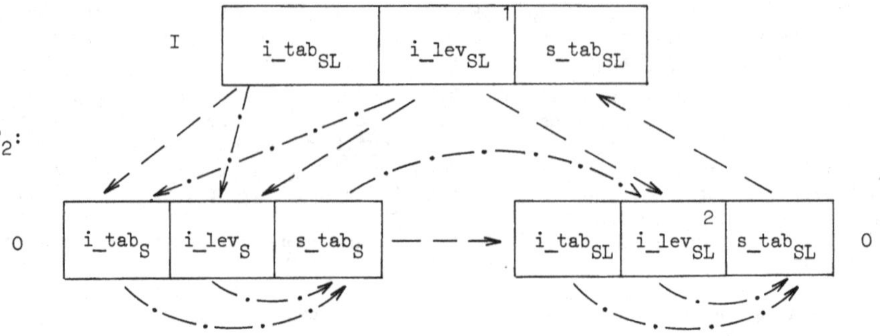

DEFINITION. Let F_1 and F_2 be two A-graphs, p_O an output position in F_1 and p_I the input position of F_2. F_2 is said to *match* F_1 at p_O, iff there is a bijective mapping $\varphi: p_O \to p_I$, such that $\xi_2(\varphi(v)) = \xi_1(v)$, for any $v \in p_O$.

EXAMPLE. F_2 matches F_1 at its only output position. F_1 doesn't match F_2.

Two A-graphs F_1 and F_2 may be melted into one another at an input-output position pair, if the matching property holds:

DEFINITION. Let F_1, F_2, p_O, and p_I be as above such that F_2 matches F_1 at p_O. The A-graph F_3 is the result of *inserting* F_2 at p_O in F_1, iff:
$V_3 = (V_1 \cup V_2) - p_I$, where V_2 is first renamed consistently such that $V_1 \cap V_2 = \emptyset$.
$\xi_3 = (\xi_1 \cup \xi_2) \cap (V_3 \times X)$, $P_3 = P_1 \cup P_2 - \{p_I\}$,
$\tau_3 = (\tau_1 \cup \tau_2 - \{(p_O,\underline{out}),(p_I,\underline{in})\}) \cup \{(p_O,\underline{term})\}$.

For $\rho \in \{\iota,\alpha\}$, if φ is the match function from p_O to p_I:
$\rho_3 = ((\rho_1 \cup \rho_2) \cap (V_3 \times V_3)) \cup \{(v,v') \mid v \in p_O \ \& \ (\varphi(v),v') \in \rho_2\} \cup$
$\cup \{(v,v') \mid v' \in p_O \ \& \ (v,\varphi(v')) \in \rho_2\}$

Additionally, if σ_1 and σ_2 are strategies for F_1 and F_2 then the strategy σ_3, as *induced* by σ_1 and σ_2, is given by the above equation for $\rho = \sigma$.

EXAMPLE. Inserting

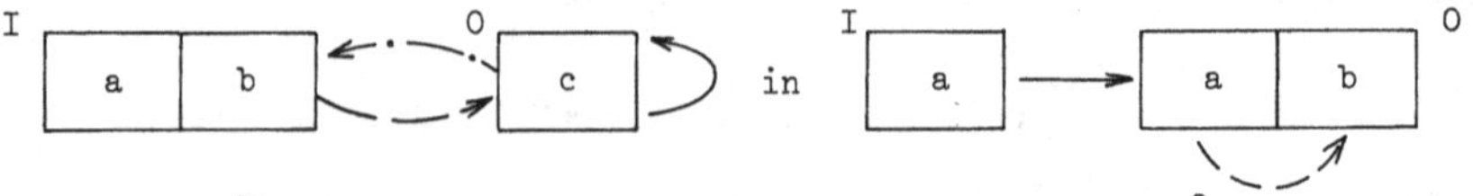

yields

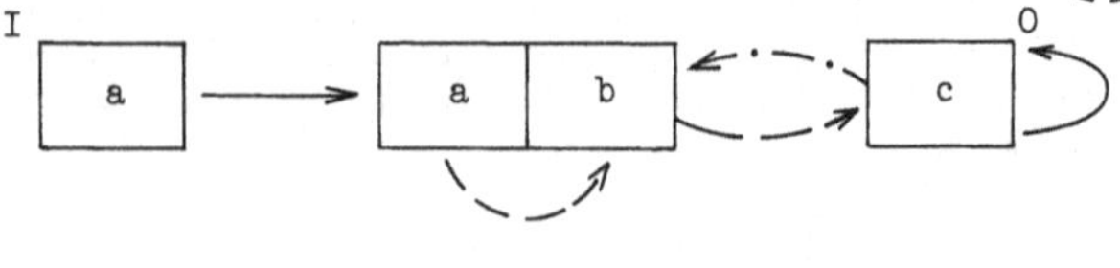

DEFINITION. A non-empty finite set $AG = \{F_1,\ldots,F_n\}$ of A-graphs is called a A-grammar. (The F_i are the *(production) rules* of AG.) An A-graph F is *produced* by AG, iff there exists a sequence $G_1,\ldots,G_k$ of A-graphs such that $G_1 = F_j$, for some $1 \le j \le n$, $G_k = F$, and G_{i+1} is obtained from G_i by inserting some rule F_{j_i} in

G_i, for $1 \leq i < k$. If strategies σ_i are associated with the F_i, then F is assumed to possess the induced strategy. The *language* L(AG) generated by AG is the set of *terminal* A-graphs, i.e. A-graphs without output positions, as produced by AG.

3. STORAGE ALLOCATION FUNCTIONS

First, we want to make some preliminary remarks about the informal meaning of the relation ι. The examples presented so far suggest that the *existence* of an ι-arc denotes identical transfer of attribute values. Later on this will not always be the case. Then, the *missing* of an ι-arc will indicate that an attribute value is *never* used to define another value identically. These situations are taken into account by the following definition:

DEFINITION. Let $u \neq v$ be nodes of an A-graph F. u is *identically transferred* to v ($u \Rrightarrow v$) in F, iff:

1. any α-path from u to v is an ι-path also. There is at least one ι-path from u to v, and
2. any α-path which ends in v touches u or is part of an α-path from u to v.

We will now start studying *storage allocation functions,* i.e. partial mappings S from the set X of labels into the natural numbers $\mathbb{N}$. The informal meaning of S for a given terminal A-graph G (e.g. the graph of attribute dependencies of a syntax tree) with strategy σ is the following: If a node v of G is visited for attribute evaluation according to σ then the value computed is stored into location x, if $x = S(\xi(v))$. (If $S(\xi(v))$ is undefined then we don't make assertions about the locations for the v-value.) Note, that the location x is then shared by all the attribute instances u in G, which have the same label $\xi(v)$. Then, of course, we are only interested in those functions S having the following property: If the value at v is used later on for the computation of the value at some u, i.e. $v \alpha u$, then the value of x at this time is (still or again) equal to the wanted parameter value. This will be called the usefulness property.

EXAMPLE. Assume $S(a) = S(b) = x$, S undefined elsewhere, in:

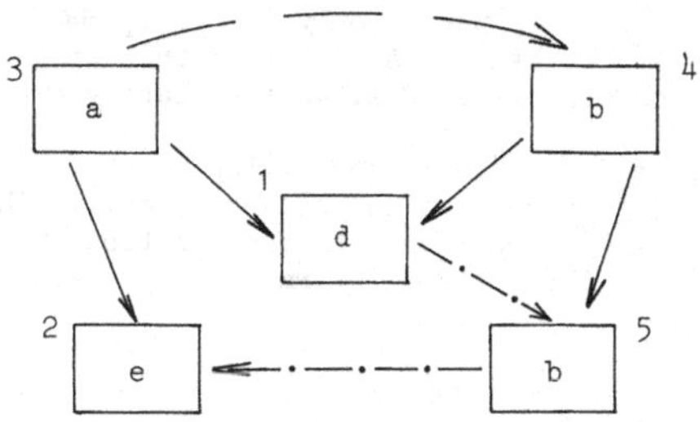

The value of $x = S(\xi(3))$ at the time when 1 is computed is the value at 4. Because of $3 \Rrightarrow 4$, S is useful in this case. S is not useful at 2, because of $3 \not\Rrightarrow 5$.

DEFINITION. Let F be an A-graph, u a node of F, σ a strategy and S as above such that $S(\xi(u)) = x$ is defined. Then the x-*cut* of u is defined by
$x\text{-cut}(u) = \{v \in V \mid \neg(u\sigma^+v) \;\&\; S(\xi(v)) = x \;\&\; (\forall u' \in V\colon v\sigma^+u'\sigma^+u \Longrightarrow S(\xi(u')) \neq x)\}$

The x-cut denotes the set of possible nodes the values at which may all be the content of x at the time when the value at u is computed. Now the usefulness property may be stated formally.

DEFINITION. S is *useful* for an A-grammar AG (with respect to the strategies associated with the rules), iff for any $G \in L(AG)$ and its induced strategy holds: If u,v are nodes in G such that $u \alpha v$ and $S(\xi(u)) = x$ then it is $u \Longrightarrow u'$, for all $u' \in x\text{-cut}(v)$.

4. PROVING THE USEFULNESS OF ALLOCATION FUNCTIONS

If a user of a compiler-compiler is allowed to provide an allocation function for the attributes of his grammar then the system should be able to prove the usefulness of the function in order to incorporate it safely into the evaluator to be generated.

At the moment we don't know whether the general usefulness property is decidable. However, the answer to this question is not important for practical applications.

THEOREM. If the general usefulness property is decidable then any decision algorithm is of at least exponential complexity (exponential in the size of the A-grammar).

Proof idea: Consider the A-graph

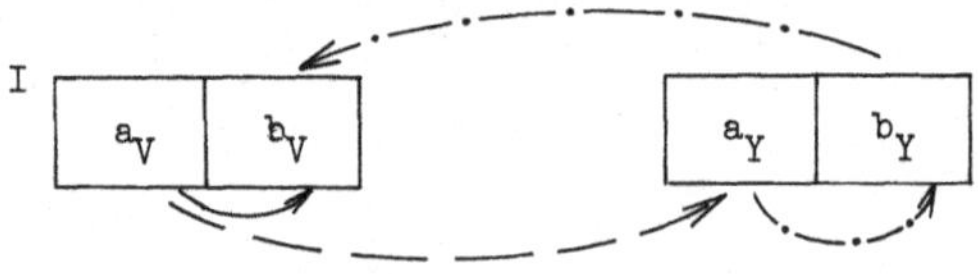

We assume the AG to contain, additionally, the rules obtained from the rules of an attribute grammar A with startsymbol Y (defining an inherited attribute a and a synthesized b at Y). Furthermore, we assume $S(a_Y) = S(b_Y) = S(a_V) = x$ and S undefined, elsewhere. Then S is useful only if $r \cdot a_Y \Longrightarrow r \cdot b_Y$ for the root r of any tree which is generated by A. A proof of this property is, however, of intrinsically exponential complexity, as follows immediately from [JOR 75].

The purpose of the rest of this section is to develop a sufficient criterion for proving the usefulness property which can be used practically. The criterion is based upon an association of context information with the positions of A-grammar rules. We first assert the properties of the context information.

DEFINITION. For any AG-rule G the *context information* consists of certain sets with properties as stated below. Thereby, $L(p,G)$ denotes for any position p in G some set of A-graphs which are produced by the AG. For the input position p of G $L(p,G)$ contains any A-graph which has exactly one output position p' which, additionally, matches p. For an output position p of G $L(p,G)$ contains any terminal A-graph the input position p' of which matches p. The sets are:

(1) $\text{NOT-INIT}(p,G) \subset X$, for any position p in G, such that
$x \in \text{NOT-INIT}(p,G) \Longrightarrow \forall F \in L(p,G)\ \forall u,v \in V : \xi(v) = x\ \&\ u\alpha^* v \Longrightarrow \exists w \in p' : w\alpha^* u.$
"x depends outside of p always from a p-node, and is, therefore, not initialized outside of p."

(2) For $x \in X$ and positions p in G : $\text{INPUTS}_x(p,G) \subset X$, such that:
$\forall F \in L(p,G)\ \forall u \in V : \xi(u) = x\ \&\ \text{INPUTS}_x(p,G) \neq \emptyset \Longrightarrow$
$(\forall v \in p' : (v\alpha^+ u \Longrightarrow \xi(v) \in \text{INPUTS}_x(p,G)\ \&\ v\iota^+ u))$

"If $INPUTS_x \neq \emptyset$ and if an x-node outside of p depends from some node v at p then this is an identical dependency and v belongs to $INPUTS_x$."

(3) $TRANS(p,G) \subset X \times X$, for any G-position p, such that $(x,y) \in TRANS(p,G) \Longrightarrow$ $\forall F \in L(p,G)\ \forall u \in p' : \xi(u) = y \Longrightarrow \exists v \in p' : \xi(v) = x \ \&\ v \Rrightarrow u$
"The y-node of p depends identically from its x-node."

(4) Let p_0 be the input, $p_1, \ldots, p_n$ the output positions of G. For nodes u,v of G and for $U \subset X$:
$LAST_U(u,v,G) \subset V_G \cup (P_G \times U)$ such that
$w \notin LAST_U(u,v,G) \Longrightarrow$
Let $\tilde{F}$ be any terminal A-graph which is obtained by first inserting G into some F_0 and then inserting terminal F_i at the output positions p_i, $1 \le i \le n$. Then it is:

a) $w \in V_G \ \&\ \xi_G(w) \in U \ \&\ \neg(v\tilde{\sigma}^+w) \ \&\ \neg(w\tilde{\sigma}^+u) \Longrightarrow$

$\exists w' \in \tilde{V} : w \neq w' \ \&\ \tilde{\xi}(w') \in U \ \&\ w\tilde{\sigma}^+w' \ \&\ w'\tilde{\sigma}^+v$

b) $w = (p_i, x) \Longrightarrow$

$\forall \tilde{w} \in V_i - p_i : (\neg(v\tilde{\sigma}^+\tilde{w}) \ \&\ \xi_i(\tilde{w}) = x \ \&\ \neg(\tilde{w}\tilde{\sigma}^+u) \Longrightarrow$

$\exists w' \in \tilde{V} : \tilde{\xi}(w') \in U \ \&\ (\tilde{\xi}(w') \neq x \lor w' \notin V_i - p_i) \ \&\ \tilde{w}\tilde{\sigma}^+w' \ \&\ w'\tilde{\sigma}^+v)$

"The nodes w of V_G or the nodes outside p_i with label x may be the last U-nodes which are visited between the visits of u and v."

EXAMPLE. Take $G = F_2$, p the S-output position and consider i_lev_{SL}, referring to the inherited attribute i_level at statement lists SL. Then:

(1) $i\_lev_{SL} \in$ NOT-INIT because any i_level depends on the level of the enclosing block.

(2) $INPUTS_{i\_lev_{SL}} = \emptyset$, because the dependencies are non-identical in the case when a new inner block is opened.

(3) $TRANS = \emptyset$, because there is no identical transfer between inherited and synthesized attributes.

(4) $(p, i\_lev_{SL}) \in LAST_{\{i\_lev_{SL}\}}(1,2,F_2)$, because it cannot be excluded that there is another i_lev_{SL} - attribute to be evaluated below p between the evaluations of i_lev_{SL} at the input and at the second output position.

The context information can be inserted into the AG-rules, yielding the extended AG-rules:

DEFINITION. Assume some context information to be given with properties as stated above. If F is an AG-rule then the *extended* rule F' is given by: Let $v_{x,p}$, for positions p in F and for $x \in X$, be new nodes not contained in V. Then:
$V' = V \cup \{v_{x,p} \mid x,p \text{ as above}\}$, P' and τ' may be fixed arbitrarily,
$\xi' = \xi \cup \{(v_{x,p}, x) \mid x,p \text{ as above}\}$,
$u\iota' v \Longleftrightarrow u \iota v$ or $\exists p \in P : (\exists (x,y) \in TRANS(p,F) : u = \xi_p^{-1}(x) \ \&\ v = \xi_p^{-1}(y))$ or
$(\exists y \in \text{NOT-INIT}(p,F)\ \exists x \in INPUTS_y(p,F) : \xi_p^{-1}(x) = u \ \&\ (v = \xi_p^{-1}(y) \text{ or } v = v_{y,p})))$,
$\alpha' = \alpha \cup \iota'$.

EXAMPLE. In F_2' now it is $\neg(1 \Rrightarrow' v_{p,i\_lev_{SL}})$, with p as in the last example, which indicates that there may be an instance of i_lev_{SL} below p which possesses a value different from the value of i_lev_{SL} at the input position of F_2.

THEOREM. An allocation function S is useful, if for any of the extended AG-rules F' holds: If u and v are nodes of F (and thus of F') such that $u\alpha v$ and that $S(\xi(u)) = a$ is defined, then it is $u \Rrightarrow' u'$ for any $u' \in LAST_{S^{-1}(a)}(u,v,F) \cap V$ and it is $u \Rrightarrow' v_{x,p}$ for any $(p,x) \in LAST_{S^{-1}(a)}(u,v,F)$. In this case we call S *admissible* for AG (with respect to the given strategy and context information).

EXAMPLE. A defined $S(i\_lev_{SL})$, would violate this criterion. This follows from the last two examples. $S(i\_tab_{SL}) = S(s\_tab_S)$, both defined, would be possible with respect to the criterion.

The proof of the theorem follows immediately from the properties of a context information.

Let us now apply this theorem to the attribute grammars. We see that after having once computed a certain context information the usefulness test according to the above theorem can be implemented easily and efficiently. The main problem is, therefore, the collection of the context information.

One part of the information, the sets NOT-INIT, INPUTS and TRANS, reveal certain types of possible attribute dependencies in the various contexts of a rule. One possibility is then to analyze all the paths in context graphs. These graphs are some kind of union of all the attribute grammar rules which may be applied below or above some position of the rule to be considered currently. Simple considerations, like those in [Bar 76], show that a good analysis may already be obtained in $O(n^{\log 7})$, if n is the size of the grammar.

The strategy to be used for attribute evaluation determines the LAST-sets of a context information. Obviously, our usefulness criterion becomes the sharper, the fewer elements these sets contain. Fortunately, it is very easy to compute minimal LAST-sets for three of the most common subclasses of attribute grammars and their corresponding evaluation strategies. These classes are the left-to-right well-formed grammars [Kos 71], the multipass-wellformed grammars [JaW 75, Boc 76, GRW 77], and the ordered attribute grammars [Kas 78] - we cannot go into details. We didn't yet investigate the problem of computing minimal LAST-sets for the general class of attribute grammars. We believe that methods similar to those in [Saa 78] should be applied when considering noncircular or absolutely noncircular [KeW 76] attribute grammars.

5. AUTOMATIC DETERMINATION OF STORAGE ALLOCATION FUNCTIONS

This section deals with the complexity of the automatic determination of allocation functions. It is necessary to define first some concept of quality for allocation functions, because it is not difficult to compute an arbitrary allocation function (such as e.g. the completely undefined function).

Throughout this section we assume a fixed A-grammar AG and a corresponding strategy to be given.

DEFINITION. Let γ be a class of allocation functions which are useful for the AG and its strategy. A $S \in \gamma$ is called *good* among the functions in γ, if for any $S' \in \gamma$ $|S'^{-1}(\mathbb{N})| < |S^{-1}(\mathbb{N})|$ or $|S'^{-1}(\mathbb{N})| = |S^{-1}(\mathbb{N})|$ & $|S'(X)| \leq |S(X)|$ holds. (Informally: There is no S' which has a greater number of elements in its domain. In the case of equality, S' must not have a greater number of elements in its range than S has.) A $x \in X$ is called *global* with respect to γ, if there is $S \in \gamma'$ such that S is defined for x.

As one might expect we shall not consider the set of all useful allocation functions but restrict ourselves to a certain subset. The reason is that we want to compute allocation functions by applying our admissability criterion of the last section. (On the other hand we don't know whether the problem of computing a good allocation function among all useful functions is decidable. But again, an answer to this question could only be of theoretical interest.) So we assume, additionally, some fixed context information for the given AG.

DEFINITION. A storage allocation function S is *simple*, iff
(1) S is admissible, and

(2) If S is defined for two (not necessarily different) labels $x_1, x_2 \in X$ and if $S(x_1) = S(x_2)$ then there is an admissible allocation function S' such that $S'(x_1) = S'(x_2)$ and S' is only defined for x_1 and x_2. (In this case we say x_1 may *overlap* x_2 ($x_1 \diamond x_2$).)

OBSERVATION. $\diamond$ is a reflexive and commutative relation on the set of all labels which are global with respect to simple allocation functions. A $x \in X$ is global in this sense, iff the function S, given by $S(y) = \underline{\text{if}}\ y = x\ \underline{\text{then}}\ 1\ \underline{\text{else}}\ \underline{\text{undefined}}$, is an admissible allocation function.

It follows that the recognition of global labels may be accomplished efficiently. Remember the meaning of the labels in the case of attribute grammars. There the globality of a pair (attribute a, nonterminal Y) indicates, that one storage block (the size of which depends only on the size of a) is sufficient for coping with the values of all instances of a at any Y. But it happens frequently that several such pairs are needed for defining the handling of one table (cf. the symbol table handling with the "tab"-attributes of our sample grammar). These situations are represented by the above relation of overlapping:

THEOREM. We assume $\mathrm{LAST}_U(u,v,G) \subset \bigcup_{x \in U} \mathrm{LAST}_{\{x\}}(u,v,G)$ to hold for the LAST-sets of the given context information[1]. For $x_1, \ldots, x_n \in X$ there exists a simple allocation function S such that $S(x_1) = \ldots = S(x_n) \in \mathbb{N}$, if and only if $x_i \diamond x_j$ holds for any of the pairs (x_i, x_j), $1 \le i,j \le n$.

Proof. Straightforward from the definitions of simplicity and admissibility.

In other words, consider the undirected, loop-free graph Γ, consisting of the nodes $x \in X$ such that $x \diamond x$ and of the undirected edges (x,y) such that $x \diamond y$ and $x \neq y$. Then, any good allocation function S among the simple allocation functions is characterized by

(1) $S(x)$ defined $\Leftrightarrow$ x is node in Γ.

(2) There is a partition of Γ into cliques $\Gamma_1, \ldots, \Gamma_n$ (i.e. subgraphs with the complete set of edges) such that n is minimal and that $S(x) = S(y)$ for x,y of Γ, iff x and y belong to the same clique.

EXAMPLE. For our sample attributes we might obtain for Γ :

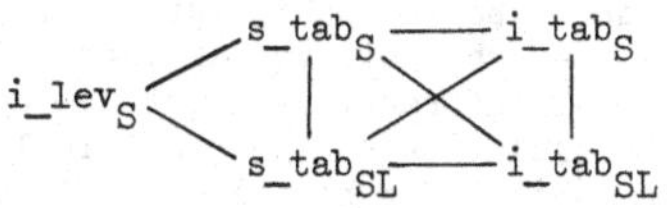

($\mathrm{i\_lev}_{SL}$ does not occurr because it is not global.) The two possible partitions into a minimal number of cliques are $\{\mathrm{i\_lev}_S\}$, $\{\mathrm{s\_tab}_S, \mathrm{i\_tab}_S, \mathrm{s\_tab}_{SL}, \mathrm{i\_tab}_{SL}\}$ and $\{\mathrm{i\_lev}_S, \mathrm{s\_tab}_S, \mathrm{s\_tab}_{SL}\}, \{\mathrm{i\_tab}_S, \mathrm{i\_tab}_{SL}\}$. (Note: Only the first of these partitions would lead to a practical allocation function, because the second partition would require copying between different instances of a symbol table.)

Now we can state a complexity property which is not surprising because of the NP-completeness of the clique-problem (see e.g. [AHU 74]).

[1] This precondition excludes LAST-sets which are unnecessarily redundant.

THEOREM. The problem of computing a simple allocation function S which is defined at exactly all global $x \in X$ and whose range contains exactly $k \geq 0$ elements is NP-complete. This holds even under the following modifications or restrictions:

(1) The class of A-grammars to be considered is the class obtained from left-to-right wellformed attribute grammars.

(2) The context information for the A-grammars is always computed (deterministically) with polynomial complexity.

(3) The class of allocation functions to be considered may lie arbitrarily between the class of simple and the class of useful functions.

Proof. see [Gan 78].

Thus it can be assumed, that the problem of computing a good (i.e. with k being minimal) allocation function is computationally intractable, even in the case when we restrict ourselves to practically computable types of context information.

6. CONCLUSIONS

We proposed a formal framework for the investigation of problems arising with storage allocation functions for attribute evaluators. The treatment was independent of specific attribute evaluation methods. This was established by introducing a simple general notion of an evaluation strategy for attribute dependency graphs.

We pointed out that there are possibilities for proving the usefulness of allocation functions. The proofs depend on information about all the attribute dependencies and evaluation sequences in the various contexts. They may be implemented efficiently and there are efficient methods for obtaining context information which convey properties sufficiently powerful for practical applications. (We remark that there are additional applications in the area of procedure optimization. The globality of a parameter of a function indicates that it may be implemented by a global variable. This kind of analysis is also required in order to prepare for more sophisticated program transformations.)

The problem of automatic determination of good allocation functions was shown to be too complex, although our quality criterion was not very sophisticated. (The last example in section 5 suggests that situations arise frequently where one has to select from several good allocation functions the one which is practical.)

Finally we want to make some remarks about the impacts of our results on the design of attribute definition languages and the corresponding evaluator generators. We remember that the set of global pairs (attribute, nonterminal) could be obtained automatically with reasonable efficiency. The system should, therefore, compute this set and return it to the user, together with the relations of possible overlappings. The user now can check whether all the pairs which describe the manipulation of certain tables or counters, etc. constitute cliques in the graph of overlappings. If this is not the case, the system can provide additional informations about the components of the attribute definitions which cause the violation of the admissibility criterion. Finally, the user indicates those cliques which must be allocated to one same storage block (e.g. symbol table) to exclude excessive inefficiencies. The system starts from this basic decisions and tries to improve them according to the possible overlappings. Thus, the definition language has to offer features for formulating hints concerning the allocation of attributes. Additionally, the correspondencies between the "calling" of a function in an attribute definition and the definition of the function should allow for implementation of parameters and/or results by the global variables which have been introduced by the allocation function.

In this paper we always assumed some arbitrary, but fixed, evaluation strategy to be given, when making assertions about allocation functions. Although the skeleton of a strategy is mainly implied by the subclass of attribute grammars to be implemented, there are usually many situations where the evaluation order may be fixed arbitrarily. It would be interesting to study attribute evaluators which allow their evaluation strategy to be influenced by considerations concerning storage optimization.

ACKNOWLEDGMENTS. Prof. J. Eickel, R. Giegerich, and W. Lahner suggested many improvements to this and to earlier versions of this paper.

REFERENCES

[AHU 74] Aho, A.V., Hopcroft, J.E., Ullman, J.D.: Design and analysis of computer algorighms, Addison-Wesley, Reading, Mass., 1974.

[Bar 77] Barth, J.M.: An interprocedural data flow analysis algorithm. Fourth ACM Symp. on Princ. of Prog. Languages, Los Angeles, 1977, 119-131.

[Boc 76] Bochmann, G.V.: Semantic evaluation from left to right. Comm. ACM, 19 (1976).

[Gan 78] Ganzinger, H.: Optimierende Erzeugung von Übersetzerteilen aus implementierungsorientierten Sprachbeschreibungen. TUM-INFO-7809, TU München, Inst. f. Informatik, 1978.

[GRW 77] Ganzinger, H., Ripken, K., Wilhelm, R.: Automatic generation of optimizing multipass compilers. In: Gilchrist, B. (ed.), Information Processing 77, North-Holland Publ. Co., Amsterdam, New York, Oxford, 1977, 535-540.

[JOR 75] Jazayeri, M., Ogden, W.F., Rounds, W.C.: The intrinsically exponential complexity of the circularity problem for attribute grammars. Comm. ACM 18 (1975) 679-706.

[JaW 75] Jazayeri, M., Walter, K.G.: Alternating semantic evaluator, Proc. ACM 1975 Ann. Conf., 230-234, 1975.

[Kas 76] Kastens, U.: Ein Übersetzer-erzeugendes System auf der Basis attributierter Grammatiken. Interner Bericht 10, Fak. für Informatik, Universität Karlsruhe, 1976.

[Kas 78] Kastens, U.: Ordered attributed grammars. Bericht 7/78, Inst. für Informatik II, Universität Karlsruhe, 1978.

[KeW 76] Kennedy, K., Warren, S.K.: Automatic generation of efficient evaluators for attribute grammars. Third ACM Symp. on Princ. of Programming Languages, Atlanta, 1976, 72-85.

[Knu 68] Knuth, D.E.: Semantics of context-free languages. Math. Systems Theory 2 (1968) 127-145.

[Kos 71] Koster, C.H.A.: Affix grammars. In: Peck, J.E.L. (ed.), Algol68 Implementation, North-Holland, Amsterdam, New York, Oxford, 1971.

[Räi 77] Räihä, K.-J.: On attribute grammars and their use in a compiler writing system. Report A-1977-4, Dep. of Comp. Science, Univ. of Helsinki, Helsinki, 1977.

[Saa 78] Saarinen, M.: On constructing efficient evaluators for attribute grammars. Proc. of the 5th ICALP, Udine, 1978, 382-397.

[Wat 77] Watt, D.A.: The parsing problem for affix grammars. Acta Informatica 8, (1977), 1-20.

ON CONTINUOUS COMPLETIONS

Irène Guessarian

Abstract - This paper is devoted to the study of various completions of posets which preserve the algebraic or ordering structure of the given poset.

1 - INTRODUCTION

It is now generally acknowledged that algebraic methods (/1,7,9/) provide the mathematically most satisfying programming language semantics. These semantics construct the solution of a program as the least upper bound of all its finite approximations: hence the values computed by programs belong to a "complete" set generated by a set of "finite" elements (i.e. the finite approximations to the computed values). Usually, one is given a canonical partially ordered set P of finite elements (e.g. the free F-magma, the finite subsets of ℕ) and has to construct its completion , that is to say the smallest complete set P_1 containing P and satisfying additional conditions according to the problem considered (e.g. the free complete F-magma, $P\omega$). Consider for instance the program scheme $G(v) = f(v,G(h(v)))$; its finite approximations are the:

t_n =

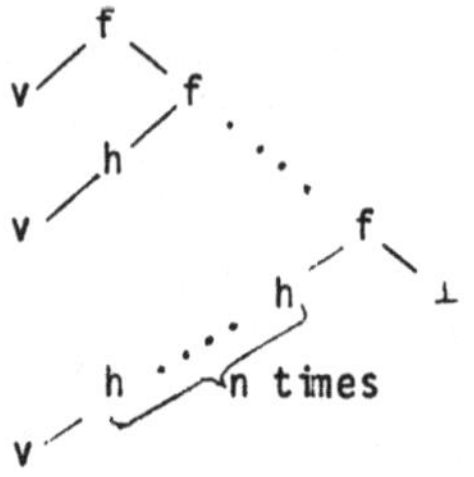

belonging to the free F-magma $M(F,\{v\})$; its solution is characterized by the infinite tree:

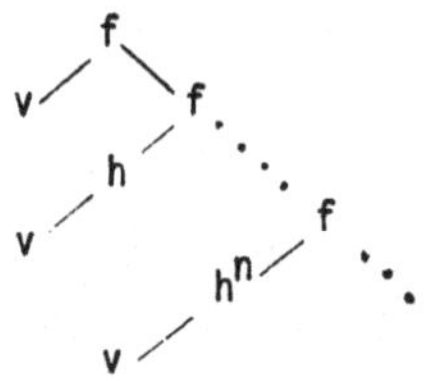

belonging to the completion $M^{\infty}(F,\{v\})$ of $M(F,\{v\})$ with respect to directed sets.

The completion of posets with respect to general sets (e.g. directed, chains, ...) is studied in /1/. In this paper, we study generalizations of this process ; namely, we look for completion processes which preserve some of the existing structures of the given poset: e.g. some of the least upper bounds which might exist, or its algebraic structure.

This preservation need arises very quickly in posets used to give the semantics of programming languages. First the completion of an F-algebra (or F-magma) must also be an F-algebra to be of any interest. Then, in algebraic semantics, the most interesting semantic domains are obtained as quotients of $M^\infty(F,V)$, corresponding to conditions imposed upon base function symbols (which are often interpreted as conditionals /6/ , or associative functions, etc...). These quotients are usually not complete, but might have some lub's which ought to be preserved in any further completion. Consider for instance the poset:

M(F) =

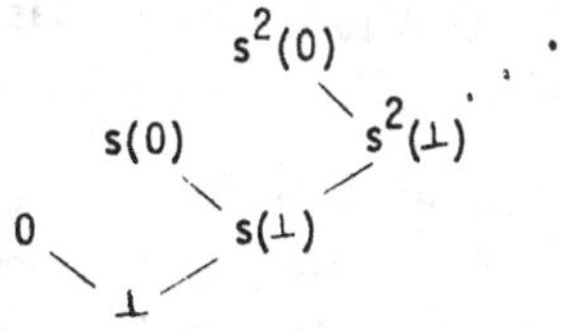

Then:

$M^\infty(F)$ =

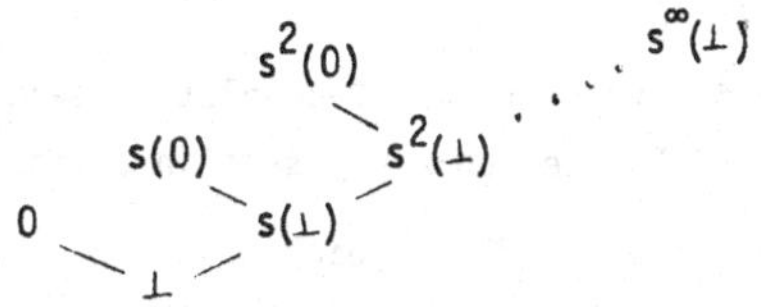

Let R be the relation $x \sqsubseteq s(x)$ for every x in $M^\infty(F)$; then $M^\infty(F)/R$ is not complete since the chain $\{ 0, s(0) , s^2(0) , \ldots \}$ has no upper bound ; but clearly, any completion process should preserve the lub $s^\infty(\perp)$ of the chain $\{\perp , s(\perp) , s^2(\perp) , \ldots \}$.

This paper is divided in 4 sections. In section 2 we recall the terminology (from /1/) and state some basic facts. In section 3 we study completions of posets which are continuous in the sense that they preserve some of the existing lub 's. In section 4 we study completions of algebras (or magmas) which are continuous and preserve the underlying algebraic structure.

2 - NOTATIONS AND PRELIMINARY RESULTS

We take here the same notations as in /1/. A *poset* is a set P together with a partial order $\sqsubseteq$ on P . The least upper bound of a subset S of P is denoted by $\sqcup S$. A subset I of P is an *ideal* iff: $p \sqsubseteq p' \in I$ implies $p \in I$. Let <u>Po</u> be the category of posets with monotonic (i.e. order-preserving) functions as morphisms. A *subset system* on Po is a function Z which assigns to each poset P a set Z(P) of subsets of P such that: 1) there exists a poset P such that Z(P) contains some non-empty set . 2) if $f: P \to P'$ is monotonic and $S \in Z(P)$ then $f(S) = \{f(s) \ / \ s \in S\}$ is in $Z(P')$.

The elements of Z(P) are called the *Z-sets* of P . A *Z-ideal* is an ideal generated by a Z-set.

Examples: An ω-set is a chain of order type $< \omega$; a Δ-set S is a directed set (non-empty and every pair from S has an upper bound in S); a PC-set S (pairwise compatible) is a non-empty set such that every pair from S has an upper bound in P; an n-set is a nonempty set with less than n elements; a ⊔-set is any non-empty set. Note that a singleton {p} is always a Z-set, for any Z.

In these 5 examples (all taken from /1/) the first two are the most usual in programming languages semantics (/ 3,4,8,10 /); the last three are of interest in building counter-examples.

A poset P is *Z-complete* if every Z-set of P has a least upper bound in P . A monotonic $f: P \to P'$ is *Z-continuous* if it preserves those least upper bounds of Z-sets which exist in P, i.e.: for any Z-set S of P having a lub in P $f(\sqcup S) = \sqcup\{f(s) \ / \ s \in S\}$.

For instance, an upper semi-lattice is a 2-complete poset; 2-continuous morphisms preserve lub's of finite non-empty sets in 2-complete posets.

An element p in P is *Z-compact* if for each Z-set S such that $\sqcup S$ exists, $p \sqsubseteq \sqcup S$ implies $p \sqsubseteq s$ for some s in S. The set of Z-compact elements is called the *Z-core* of P and is denoted by Z-core(P). A poset P is *Z-inductive* if every p in P is the lub of some Z-set in Z-core(P). Δ-compact elements are also called isolated or finite (because they are in some sense "finitely computable") and Δ-inductive posets are called algebraic.

The following results can be proved easily from the definitions.

Lemma 2.1 : For every poset P:

$$Z \cup Z' \text{ - core}(P) = Z\text{-core}(P) \cap Z'\text{-core}(P)$$
$$Z \cap Z' \text{ - core}(P) \supset Z\text{-core}(P) \cup Z'\text{-core}(P)$$

Proposition 2.2 : Let $i: P \to P'$ be a Z'-continuous injection such that $p \sqsubseteq p' \iff i(p) \sqsubseteq i(p')$ then, for any Z :

$$Z\text{-core}(P') \cap i(P) \subset i(Z \cap Z' \text{ - core } (P))$$

We need an equivalence relation between subsets of a poset P. This equivalence is of great use in programming theory (/1 , 5, 10 /) and is defined by:

$$S \precsim S' \quad \text{if} \quad \forall s \in S \quad \exists s' \in S' \quad \text{with} \quad s \sqsubseteq s'$$

S' is then said, following Wright et al. /1/, *cofinal* in S. $S \sim S'$ (S and S' are *mutually cofinal*) if $S \underset{\sim}{\sqsubseteq} S'$ and $S' \underset{\sim}{\sqsubseteq} S$.

3 - INDUCTIVE POSETS AND CONTINUOUS COMPLETIONS

3.1 - *Inductive posets and extension basis*

We now come to generalizing the results of /1/. Until now, we have been considering the category Po whose morphisms were monotonic; from now on we will mostly consider the category $\mathrm{Po}_{Z'}$, whose morphisms are Z'-continuous; clearly Po is the special case corresponding to $Z' = Z_2 = \omega \sqcap 2$; when restricted to that case, our results will fit in nicely and coïncide with those of /1/ .

A subset B of a poset P is a *Z'-continuous Z-extension basis* (abbreviated *Z'&Z-extension basis*) if, for every Z-complete poset Q and Z'-continuous map $f: B \to Q$, there exists a unique $Z' \cup Z$-continuous $\overline{f}: P \to Q$ extending f (note that we do not assume P Z-complete).

In the category Po , Z-core(P) is a Z-extension basis for any Z-inductive poset P (cf. /1/). Clearly, we cannot expect in the general case Z-core(P) to be a Z'&Z-extension basis of P without any additional conditions on Z and Z' , as shown by the following example.

Example 3.1 : Let $Z = \omega$ $Z' = \sqcup$ $P = \{a_i, a'_i, b_i, b'_i, c_i \ / \ i \in \mathbb{N}\} \cup \{a_\infty, a'_\infty, c_\infty\}$ with the order as indicated in figure 1.

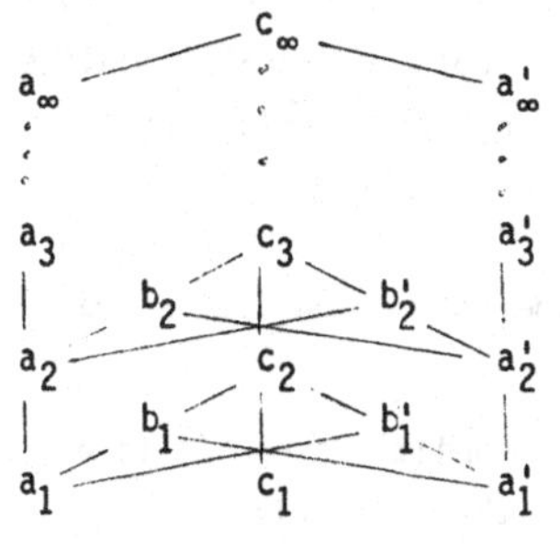

Figure 1

Then Z-core(P) $= \{a_i, a'_i, c_i, b_i, b'_i \ / \ i \in \mathbb{N}\}$. Let now Q be the $\sqcup$-complete lattice of all ideals of P , and f be the canonical injection associating to p in Z-core(P) the principal ideal f(p) generated by p; then f cannot have any $\sqcup$-continuous extension $\overline{f}: P \to Q$ since continuity implies on one hand: $\mathrm{lub}(\overline{f}(a_\infty), \overline{f}(a'_\infty)) = \{a_i, a'_i \ / \ i \in \mathbb{N}\}$ and on the other hand: $\overline{f}(c_\infty) = $ Z-core(P); hence $\overline{f}(\mathrm{lub}(a_\infty, a'_\infty)) = \overline{f}(c_\infty) \neq \mathrm{lub}(\overline{f}(a_\infty), \overline{f}(a'_\infty))$. Note that P is not Z'-inductive.

The results of /1/ can however be nicely generalized. We need first some more notations. Let σ be the support function from P to the subsets of Z-core(P), ordered by inclusion, defined by: $\sigma(p) = \{d \ / \ d \varepsilon Z\text{-core}(P) \text{ and } d \sqsubseteq p\}$. Its extension to the subsets of P is also denoted by σ; namely: $\sigma(S) = \{ d \ / \ d \ \varepsilon \ \sigma(s) \ \text{ for some } \ s \ \text{ in } \ S \ \}$. The reader can check that if P is Z-inductive, then σ is Z-continuous. Moreover, P is Z-inductive iff for every p in P, $\sigma(p)$ is a Z-ideal in Z-core(P) and $p = \sqcup\sigma(p)$ (cf./1/ Prop. 2.5).

If A is a subset of Z-core(P), let $\bar{c}_{Z'}(A)$ be the smallest Z'-closed ideal of Z-core(P) containing A - i.e. containing all the lub's (in Z-core(P)) of the Z'-sets contained in $\bar{c}_{Z'}(A)$. Let i(A) be the ideal generated by A in Z-core(P) and $c_{Z'}(A)$ be the closure of A, obtained by adjoining to A all lub's of Z'-sets in A. For any ordinal α define $A_\alpha = ic_{Z'}(\bigcup_{\lambda<\alpha} A_\lambda)$, where $ic_{Z'}$ is obtained by composing i with $c_{Z'}$. Then: $\bar{c}_{Z'}(A) = \bigcup_\alpha A_\alpha = A_\beta$ for some ordinal β.

Definition 3.2 : Z' is said to be P-*smaller* than Z iff for every Z'-set S' in P such that there exists a Z-set S in Z-core(P) with: $\sqcup S = \sqcup S'$, then $\sigma(\sqcup S') \underset{\sim}{\sqsubseteq} \bar{c}_{Z'}(\sigma(S'))$.

Theorem 3.3 : If P is Z-inductive and Z' is P-smaller than Z, then Z-core(P) is a Z'&Z-extension basis for P.

Proof: Let f: Z-core(P) $\to$ Q be Z'-continuous and $\bar{f}$ be its unique Z-continuous extension $\bar{f}$: P $\to$ Q (which is given by the fact that Z-core(P) is a Z-extension basis). Let S' be a Z'-set in P such that $\sqcup S' = p$. Since $\bar{f}$ is monotonic, $\bar{f}(p) = \bar{f}(\sqcup S') \sqsupseteq \sqcup\bar{f}(S')$. P being Z-inductive, $p = \sqcup\sigma(p)$ and $\sigma(p)$ is a Z-ideal in Z-core(P); $\bar{f}$ being Z-continuous, $\bar{f}(p) = \sqcup\bar{f}(\sigma(p))$. Similarly, $\sqcup\bar{f}(S') = \sqcup\bar{f}(\sigma(S')) = \sqcup\bar{f}(\bar{c}_{Z'}(\sigma(S')))$ since $\bar{f}$ restricted to Z-core(P) is equal to f which is Z'-continuous. Now, $\sigma(p) \underset{\sim}{\sqsubseteq} \bar{c}_{Z'}(\sigma(S'))$ implies $\bar{f}(\sigma(p)) \underset{\sim}{\sqsubseteq} \bar{f}(\bar{c}_{Z'}(\sigma(S')))$ whence $\sqcup\bar{f}(\sigma(p)) \sqsubseteq \sqcup\bar{f}(\bar{c}_{Z'}(\sigma(S')))$ and $\bar{f}(\sqcup S') \sqsubseteq \sqcup\bar{f}(S')$.

Q.E.D.

Remark : Example 3.1 shows that the assumption that Z' be P-smaller than Z is optimal.

Let us now give sufficient conditions for Z' to be P-smaller than Z which will be easier to check than the definition.

Proposition 3.4 : Let P be Z-inductive; the following 3 conditions are equivalent:

(i) Z-core(P) $\subset$ Z'-core(P)

(ii) For every Z'-set S' of P and every Z-set S of P included in Z-core(P) : $\sqcup S' = \sqcup S$ implies $S' \underset{\sim}{\sqsupseteq} S$

(iii) Every Z-continuous map P $\to$ Q is Z'-continuous

When they are satisfied, Z' is P-smaller than Z.

Proof: (i) $\Rightarrow$ (ii) : Let $\sqcup S = \sqcup S'$ and S be included in Z-core(P). Let d be in S; then $d \sqsubseteq \sqcup S'$ and $d \ \varepsilon$ Z-core(P); hence by (i) $d \sqsubseteq s'$ for some s' in S' and $S \underset{\sim}{\sqsubseteq} S'$.

(ii) ⇒ (iii) : Let $f: P \to Q$ be Z-continuous and S' be a Z'-set in P such that $\sqcup S'$ exists in P. Since f is monotonic, $f(\sqcup S') \sqsupseteq \sqcup f(S')$. P being Z-inductive, there exists a Z-set S in Z-core(P) such that $\sqcup S' = \sqcup S$; by (ii) $S \underset{\sim}{\sqsubseteq} S'$, hence $f(S) \underset{\sim}{\sqsubseteq} f(S')$ and $\sqcup f(S) \sqsubseteq \sqcup f(S')$; but f being Z-continuous, $f(\sqcup S) = \sqcup f(S)$ hence $f(\sqcup S') = f(\sqcup S) = \sqcup f(S) \sqsubseteq \sqcup f(S')$.

(iii) ⇒ (i) : P being Z-inductive, σ is Z-continuous; hence σ is Z'-continuous by (iii) and $\sigma(\sqcup S') = \sqcup\{ \sigma(s') \ / \ s' \in S' \}$ for any Z'-set S' in P. Now: $d \in$ Z-core(P) and $d \sqsubseteq \sqcup S'$ iff $d \in \sigma(\sqcup S')$ iff $d \in \sigma(s')$ for some s' in S' .

Now it is clear that if (ii) is satisfied, then Z' is P-smaller than Z : let $p = \sqcup S'$; P being Z-inductive, $\sigma(p)$ is generated by a Z-set S such that $\sqcup S = p$; by (ii) $S \underset{\sim}{\sqsubseteq} S'$ hence ā fortiori $\sigma(p) \underset{\sim}{\sqsubseteq} S'$.

Q.E.D.

Corollary 3.5 : Let P be Z-inductive and such that Z'-core(Z-core(P))=Z-core(P); then Z-core(P) is a Z'&Z-extension basis for P iff P,Z,Z' satisfy the conditions of proposition 3.4 .

Proof: If Z'-core(Z-core(P)) = Z-core(P) , every monotonic map Z-core(P) $\to$ Q is Z'-continuous. It remains to consider the natural injection of Z-core(P) in the set of all ideals of P (associating to p in P the principal ideal generated by p) and its unique $(Z \cup Z')$-continuous extension to conclude.

Proposition 3.6 : If $Z' \subset Z$ then Z' is P-smaller than Z for any P .

Let us note that this will be the most usual case, and is indeed the straightforward generalization of the case studied in /1/, where Z'-continuous functions are simply monotonic and $Z' = \omega \cap 2 \subset Z$ for every Z .

3.2 - *Continuous completions*

We are now considering the problem, stated in /1/, of finding Z'-continuous Z-completions, that is to say Z-completions which preserve the existing lub's of Z'-sets. Such a completion is of great interest when dealing with quotient spaces, and particular examples corresponding to $Z = Z' = \Delta$ or $Z = Z' = \omega$ can be found in / 4, 8 / . More precisely, we will show how to construct, for a suitable poset P, a poset P_1 together with a Z'-continuous injection $i: P \to P_1$ verifying : $p \sqsubseteq p'$ iff $i(p) \sqsubseteq i(p')$, and such that P_1 is Z-complete, Z-inductive, Z-core$(P_1) \subset i(P)$ and for every Z'-continuous map $f: P \to Q$ in a Z-complete poset Q there exists a unique $Z \cup Z'$-continuous map $\bar{f}: P_1 \to Q$ which extends f. Such a P_1 is called a Z'-*continuous* Z-*completion* of P . In the sequel, we shall identify P with its image i(P) in P_1

We know from /1/ that two equivalent approaches are possible, the first one considering a quotient of a set of subsets of P (cf./3/), the second one considering a set of Z-ideals of P ordered by inclusion (cf. /8, 10/); we choose here this second approach.

Notation: In the remainder of this section, we shall abbreviate $Z \cap Z'$ in Z''.

Lemma 3.7 : If P_1 is a Z'-continuous Z-completion of P, then:

$$Z\text{-core}(P_1) \subset i(Z''\text{-core}(P))$$

Proof: Let S be a Z"-set of P , p in P with i(p) in Z-core(P_1) , and suppose $p \sqsubseteq \sqcup S$. i being Z'-continuous, $i(p) \sqsubseteq \sqcup i(S)$. i(p) being in Z-core(P_1) , $i(p) \sqsubseteq i(s)$ for some s in S hence $p \sqsubseteq s$. Q.E.D.

Proposition 3.8 : Let Q be the set of all ideals of P and $P_1 \subset Q$ a Z'-continuous Z-completion of P. Then, Z-core(P_1) = Z"-core(P) iff the following condition holds:

For any Z-set S of P_1 having a lub $\sqcup S$ in P_1: $(\sqcup S) \cap Z''\text{-core}(P) = (\cup S) \cap Z''\text{-core}(P)$

Z is then said to be Z'-*unionized in* P_1.

Proof: Suppose Z-core(P_1) = Z"-core(P). Let S be a Z-set in P_1 and p in Z"-core(P) such that $p \in \sqcup S$; then $p \sqsubseteq \sqcup S$ hence $p \sqsubseteq s$ for some s in S and thus $p \in \cup S = \{s \ / \ s \in S\}$. Conversely, assume Z is Z'-unionized in P_1, and let p be in Z"-core(P) with $p \sqsubseteq \sqcup S$ for some Z-set S in P_1; then $p \in \sqcup S$, and, Z being Z'-unionized, $p \in \cup S$; thus, $p \sqsubseteq s$ for some s in S , and $p \in$ Z-core(P_1); the reverse inclusion results from lemma 3.7 . Q.E.D.

Remark : Proposition 3.8 remains true if Q is replaced by the set of ideals of Z"-core(P).

From now on, Z shall be supposed Z'-unionized in P_1 whichever P_1 we work with. Since we are looking for a Z-inductive P_1 such that Z-core(P_1) $\subset$ Z"-core(P), P_1 must be a subset of the set of ideals of Z"-core(P). Since $i: P \to P_1$ must be Z'-continuous, the elements of P_1 should be Z'-closed (i.e. contain the lub's of their Z'-sets); finally, since we are looking for a Z-inductive P_1 , its elements must be generated by Z-sets. However, we have two possibilities. The first one is to define P_1 as the set $I_{Z'}(P)$ of Z'-closed ideals in Z"-core(P) - namely, ideals generated by Z-sets in Z"-core(P) and which contain all the lub's of their Z'-sets which exist in Z"-core(P). The second one is to define $P_1' = \{ \bar{c}_{Z'}(I) \ / \ I$ is a Z-ideal of Z"-core(P) $\}$. Recall that $\bar{c}_{Z'}(I)$ is the Z'-closure of I in Z"-core(P). We shall see that these two approaches are equivalent.

Let i: Z"-core(P) $\to I_{Z'}(P)$ be defined by: for p in Z"-core(P) $i(p) = \{ u \in Z''\text{-core}(P) \ / \ u \sqsubseteq p \}$.

Lemma 3.9 : If $I_{Z'}(P)$ is Z-inductive and there exists a monotonic $i': P \to I_{Z'}(P)$ extending i and verifying $p \sqsubseteq p' \iff i'(p) \sqsubseteq i'(p')$ then for any p in P, $i'(p) = i(p) = \{ u \in Z''\text{-core}(P) \ / \ u \sqsubseteq p \}$ is a Z'-closed Z-ideal in Z"-core(P).

Proof: Let p be in P. $I_{Z'}(P)$ being Z-inductive, $i'(p) = \sqcup\{i(u) \in Z''\text{-core}(P) \ /$ $i(u) \sqsubseteq i'(p) \}$ and $i'(p)$ is a Z-ideal of Z"-core(P); but $i(u) \sqsubseteq i'(p) \iff u \sqsubseteq p$, hence $i'(p) = i(p) = \{ u \in Z''\text{-core}(P) \ / \ u \sqsubseteq p \}$ is a Z-ideal in Z"-core(P). It is Z'-closed, for suppose S' is a Z'-set contained in i(p) , then $\sqcup S' \sqsubseteq p$ hence if $\sqcup S' \in Z''\text{-core}(P)$, $\sqcup S' \in i(p)$. Q.E.D.

From now on let us suppose:

$$\left\{\begin{array}{l}\text{For any } p \text{ in } P,\quad i(p) = \{\, u \in Z''\text{-core}(P) \;/\; u \sqsubseteq p \,\} \text{ is a } Z'\text{-closed } Z\text{-ideal in} \\ Z''\text{-core}(P) \text{ and } \quad p = \sqcup i(p) \quad \text{in } P.\end{array}\right\} \quad (1)$$

(the last assumption is made in order to make sure that $i: P \to P_1$ is injective)

Recall that a poset P is Z-*core complete* iff every Z-set in Z-core(P) has a lub in P.

Proposition 3.10 : $I_{Z'}(P)$ is Z-core complete iff :

Any Z-ideal in Z"-core(P) is Z'-closed (2)

Proof: The "if" part is clear. "only if" part: let S be any Z-ideal in Z"-core(P); since Z is Z'-unionized in $I_{Z'}(P)$, Z"-core(P) = Z-core($I_{Z'}(P)$). Since $I_{Z'}(P)$ is Z-core complete, $\sqcup S$ exists in $I_{Z'}(P)$ and satisfies: $(\sqcup S) \cap Z''$-core(P) = $(\cup S) \cap Z''$-core(P) ; but $\sqcup S$ and $\cup S$ are both included in Z"-core(P) whence $\sqcup S = \cup S$ and S is Z'-closed. Q.E.D.

If we want to consider P_1' instead of $I_{Z'}(P)$, the same argument would be valid; hence our construction is forced and we have:

Proposition 3.11 : If (2) is satisfied $P_1' = I_{Z'}(P)$

Definition 3.12 : Z is said to be Z'-*union complete in a set* P_1 of ideals of P (or Z"-core(P)) iff for any Z-set S in P_1 , $\sqcup S$ exists in P_1 and $(\sqcup S) \cap Z''$-core(P) = $(\cup S) \cap Z''$-core(P) .

Proposition 3.13 : If Z is Z'-union complete in $I_{Z'}(P)$, then $I_{Z'}(P)$ is Z-complete.

Proposition 3.14 : Let P,Z,Z' be such that: Z and Z' satisfy (1) and (2) , Z is Z'-unionized in $I_{Z'}(P)$ and Z' is $I_{Z'}(P)$-smaller than Z; then:

1) Z-core($I_{Z'}(P)$) = Z"-core(P) where $Z'' = Z \cap Z'$

2) $i: P \to I_{Z'}(P)$ defined by $i(p) = \{\, u \in Z''\text{-core}(P) \;/\; u \sqsubseteq p \,\}$ is a Z'-continuous injection $P \to I_{Z'}(P)$ such that $i(p) \sqsubseteq i(p') \iff p \sqsubseteq p'$

3) $I_{Z'}(P)$ is Z-core complete, Z-inductive and is a Z'-continuous Z-completion of P .

Proof: Only point 2 remains to be verified. Let p in P be such that $p = \sqcup S'$ where S' is a Z'-set in P. Since i is monotonic, $i(p) \sqsupseteq \sqcup i(S')$. Z' being $I_Z'(P)$-smaller than Z, $i(p) \precsim \bar{c}_{Z'}(i(S'))$; hence $\sqcup i(S')$, which is the smallest Z'-closed ideal containing i(S') , must contain i(p), whence $i(p) = \sqcup i(S')$. Q.E.D.

In the most usual case where $Z' \subset Z$, all the hypothesis needed for our construction collapse into the following two conditions:

1) a "unionization" condition (as in definition 3.12 or proposition 3.8)

2) for every p in P, $i(p) = \{\, u \in Z'\text{-core}(P) \;/\; u \sqsubseteq p \,\}$ is a Z-ideal.

In the case where Z'-core(P) = P (as in /1/), this second condition also vanishes.

Now, clearly, Z'-continuous Z-completions are unique (up to an isomorphism) . Hence one can prove, exactly as in /1/ :

Proposition 3.15 : If B is a Z'&Z-extension basis for a Z-complete poset P and Z,Z',B satisfy the hypothesis of proposition 3.13 and 3.14, then B = Z-core(P)= = $Z \cap Z'$ - core(P) and there is a $Z \cup Z'$ -continuous isomorphism h: $P \to I_{Z'}(B)$.

Remark 3.16 : The completion here obtained is halfway between the completions by cuts and by ideals (/2/). The completion by ideals does not solve our problem (because it does not preserve lub's of Z'-sets), neither does the completion by cuts, which has not the extension property for Z'-continuous morphisms. In the case, considered in /4/, where Z = $\bigsqcup$, all the hypothesis needed for our construction are satisfied; if moreover, as in /2/, Z'=Z , any union of Z'-sets is again a Z'-set and Z'-closed ideals are obtained in a single iteration step by $\bar{c}_{Z'}(A) = ic_{Z'}(A)$. In this case our construction is very similar to the completion by cuts, of which it is a slight refinement.

4 - COMPLETE ALGEBRAS (MAGMAS)

Let F = { F_n / n=0,1,... } be a set of operator symbols; each f in F_n has *rank* n . An *ordered* F-*algebra* (or F-*magma* /9/) M consists of a non-empty poset D_M , together with a partial order $\sqsubseteq_M$, and, for each f in F_n a monotonic function f_M: $D_M^n \to D_M$ (D_M^n is ordered coordinatewise). An ordered F-algebra is *Z-continuous* iff the f_M's are Z-continuous.

Definition 4.1 (/1/) : Let Z be a subset system. Z is *crossed-up* if for all posets P_1 and P_2 and Z-sets S_i in $Z(P_i)$, i=1,2 , there exists a Z-set S in $Z(P_1 \times P_2)$ such that $S \sim S_1 \times S_2$. Z is *crossed-down* if for each S in $Z(P_1 \times P_2)$, $S \sim \pi_1(S) \times \pi_2(S)$, where $\pi_i(S)$ is the projection of S on P_i , i=1,2 .

The most usual Z's are crossed both ways; e.g. Δ and ω are crossed up and down.

Proposition 4.2 : Let f: $P_1 \times P_2 \to P$ be monotonic and $f_i = \lambda p_i . f(p_1,p_2)$, i=1,2, then f is Z-continuous iff f_1 and f_2 are Z-continuous.

Proposition 4.3 : For any posets P_1, P_2:

(i) Z-core($P_1 \times P_2$) $\subset$ Z-core(P_1)$\times$Z-core(P_2)

(ii) If Z is crossed-down, the reverse inclusion holds.

If moreover Z-core($P_1 \times P_2$) = Z-core(P_1)$\times$Z-core(P_2) , then for any S in $Z(P_1 \times P_2)$ which is included in Z-core($P_1 \times P_2$) , $S \sim \pi_1(S) \times \pi_2(S)$.

Proposition 4.4 : For any posets P_1, P_2:

(i) $P_1 \times P_2$ Z-inductive implies P_1 and P_2 Z-inductive

(ii) If Z is crossed-up, the reverse implication holds.

Proposition 4.5 : For any posets P_1, P_2 :

$P_1 \times P_2$ Z-complete $\Longleftrightarrow$ P_1 and P_2 Z-complete

The proofs of these 4 propositions are similar and rely on the following facts:

$\sqcup(x_i,y_i) = (\sqcup x_i, \sqcup y_i)$

If S is a Z-set in $P_1 \times P_2$, $\pi_i(S)$ is a Z-set in P_i, $i=1,2$

If $a \in P_1$ and S is a Z-set in P_2, $a \times S$ is a Z-set in $P_1 \times P_2$

We now come to the problem considered in section 3 in the case where P has an algebraic structure and we want the completion process to preserve this structure. We shall need the following lemma the proof of which is left to the reader:

Lemma 4.6 : If Z is crossed-down, Z' is crossed-up and Z' is P_i-smaller than Z for i=1,2 , then Z' is $P_1 \times P_2$ -smaller than Z.

Theorem 4.7 : Let Z be crossed-up and down, Z' be crossed-up and P_1 be a Z'-continuous Z-completion of a poset P with Z' P_1-smaller than Z. If P is a Z'-continuous algebra, then P_1 is a $Z \cup Z'$-continuous algebra; moreover, for any Z'-continuous homomorphism $h: P \to Q$ in a Z-complete algebra Q, there exists a unique $Z \cup Z'$-continuous homomorphism $\bar{h}: P_1 \to Q$ extending h.

Sketch of proof: This is an easy consequence of lemma 4.6 and theorem 3.3 by some "diagram chasing".

Note that the existence of completions of algebras proved in /3,4, 8/ can be deduced from this theorem.

When the hypothesis of theorem 4.7 are satisfied, our completion indeed provides us with an initial object in the category of Z'-continuous Z-complete algebras. And it clearly solves the completion problem for factor algebras stated in the introduction. Let us take a notation which will be of some mnemonic help in emphasizing these facts.

Notation 4.8 : Let P_c^∞ denote the Z'-continuous Z-completion of a poset P (the subscript c indicates the continuity - with respect to what will hopefully be clear by the context).

Corollary 4.9 : Let M be an F-algebra, R a congruence relation on M; suppose Z,Z', M/R satisfy the hypothesis of proposition 3.14 and theorem 4.7; then M/R can be embedded in the Z-complete algebra $(M/R)_c^\infty$ and this embedding preserves lub's of Z'-sets.

Let us go back now to the introduction and give a hint on how the preceding results can be applied to program schemes semantics. Let C be a class of interpretations and R be the congruence on $M^\infty(F,V)$ defined by: $T \mathrel{R} T'$ iff $\forall I \in C \quad T_I = T'_I$ (/5/). From now on, Z=Z' is either ω or Δ . We state 2 corollaries the proof of which is left to the reader.

Corollary 4.10 : Suppose $M^\infty(F,V)/R$ is Z-inductive, then $(M^\infty(F,V)/R)_c^\infty$ is the free initial interpretation in the class of interpretations compatible with R; namely, for every interpretation $I: M(F,V) \to A$ (A is a Z-complete continuous F-algebra) which is compatible with R, there exists a unique Z-continuous morphism $\bar{I}$ making the following diagram commutative:

$$\begin{array}{ccc} M(F,V) & \xrightarrow{\pi} & (M^{\infty}(F,V)/R)_C^{\infty} \\ & \searrow^{I} & \downarrow \bar{I} \\ & & A \end{array}$$

(where $\pi(t)$ denotes the class of t modulo R).

<u>Corollary 4.11</u> : If C is algebraic (or nice in the terminology of /5/), then $(M^{\infty}(F,V)/R)_C^{\infty}$ is isomorphic to $(M^{\infty}(F,V)/R)^{\infty}$.

ACKNOWLEDGMENTS : I wish to thank J. Meseguer for helpful comments on a first draft of this paper and for pointing out the connection with /8b/ which deals with closely related topics by more categorical methods.

REFERENCES

/1/ ADJ, A *uniform approach to inductive posets and inductive closure*, MFCS 77, Lect. Notes Comp. Sc. n° 53, Springer-Verlag (1977), 192-212

/2/ G. BIRKHOFF, *Lattice theory*, 3rd ed., New York (1967)

/3/ S. BLOOM, *Varieties of ordered algebras*, JCSS <u>13</u> (1976), 200-212

/4/ B. COURCELLE, J.C. RAOULT, *Complétions de magmas ordonnés*, to appear

/5/ I. GUESSARIAN, *Semantic equivalence of program schemes and its syntactic characterization*, Proc. 3rd ICALP, Edinburgh (1976), 189-200

/6/ I. GUESSARIAN, *Les tests et leur caractérisation syntaxique*, RAIRO <u>11</u> (1977), 133-156

/7/ K. INDERMARK, *Schemes with recursion on higher types*, MFCS 76, Lect. Notes Comp. Sc. n°45, Springer-Verlag (1976), 352-358

/8/ J. MESEGUER, *Factorizations, completions and colimits for ω-posets*, extended abstract (1978), to appear

/8b/ J. MESEGUER, *Ideal monads and Z-posets*, Not. Am. Math. Soc. <u>25</u> n°6(1978), 579-580

/9/ M. NIVAT, *On the interpretation of recursive polyadic program schemes*, Symposia Mathematica <u>15</u> , Rome (1975), 256-281

/10/ M. NIVAT, *Interprétation universelle d'un schéma de programme récursif*, Rivista di informatica <u>7</u> (1977), 9-16

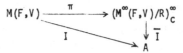

A NEW METHOD TO SHOW LOWER BOUNDS FOR POLYNOMIALS WHICH ARE HARD TO COMPUTE

Joos Heintz

This is a report of a joint work of the author with Malte Sieveking, Frankfurt/Main, [1] (to appear), about polynomials with algebraic coefficients over $\mathbb{Q}$, which are hard to compute.

The main results are as follows:
Let L_{nsc}, L_{sc}, L_+ be the nonscalar, the scalar and the additive complexity to compute polynomials in the indeterminate X over $\mathbb{C}$.

Let $L := \min (L_{nsc}^2, L_{sc}, L_+)$.

Then we have

(1) $$L\left(\sum_{j=1}^{d} e^{2\pi i/j} X^j\right) \gtrsim \frac{d}{\log d}$$

and

(2) $$L\left(\sum_{j=1}^{d} e^{2\pi i/p_j} X^j\right) \gtrsim d$$

where p_j is the j-th prime number.

(We write $\gtrsim$ for the corresponding inequality of order of magnitude, dropping thus constants.)

(1) and (2) are the consequences of the following more general result:

Let $k_1,\dots,k_d$ be a sequence of natural numbers $\neq 0$. Then

(3) $$L\left(\sum_{j=1}^{d} e^{2\pi i/k_j} X^j\right) \gtrsim \frac{\log \text{l.c.m.}(k_1,\dots,k_d)}{\log d \cdot \max(k_1,\dots,k_d)}$$

(We write short l.c.m. for "least common multiple".)

The method to prove (3) implies also the following well-known result of Strassen [2] improved by Schnorr [3]:

(4) $$L\left(\sum_{j=1}^{d} e^{2\pi i/2^{j}} X^{j} \geqslant \frac{d}{\log d}\right.$$

(5) $$L\left(\sum_{j=1}^{d} e^{2\pi i/2^{j^{k}}} X^{j}\right) \geqslant d \quad \text{for } k > 1,$$

while (1) and (2) are new results.

By the same method we obtain also a lower bound for the scalar operations needed to compute some systems of linear polynomials with algebraic coefficients over $\mathbb{Q}$.

Let $X_1,\dots,X_d$ be indeterminates over $\mathbb{Q}$. The following systems of linear polynomials need at least $\frac{d^2}{\log d}$ nonscalar steps to be computed

(6) $$\sum_{j=1}^{d} e^{2\pi i/j+(k-1)d} X_j \quad , \quad k = 1,\dots,d$$

(7) $$\sum_{j=1}^{d} e^{2\pi i/2^{j+(k-1)d}} X_j \quad , \quad k = 1,\dots,d$$

(8) $$\sum_{j=1}^{d} e^{2\pi i/2^{jk}} X_j \quad , \quad k = 1,\dots,d \; .$$

We want to give some ideas about the method how to obtain the announced results.

Let $Y_1,\dots,Y_d$ be indeterminates over $\mathbb{C}$.

A variety (over $\mathbb{C}$) is a subset of some $\mathbb{C}^d$, which is definable as the set of zeroes of some ideal of $\mathbb{C}[Y_1,\dots,Y_d]$. If this defining ideal can be chosen prime, then the corresponding variety is called irreducible. If the ideal can be chosen as being generated by a single polynomial, the corresponding variety is called a hypersurface. Each variety B is a finite union of irreducible varieties. Such a representation of B as a finite union of irreducible varieties is unique, if it is not redundant. Therefore the irreducible varieties appearing in it are called the components of B.

$\mathbb{C}^d$ with the varieties contained in it as closed sets is a topological space. Its topology is called the Zariskitopology of $\mathbb{C}^d$. $\mathbb{C}^d$ as topological space with the Zariskitopology is called the d-dimensional affine space and usually denoted by $\mathbb{A}^d$. A variety $B \subset \mathbb{A}^d$ is called $\mathbb{Q}$-definable if it is definable as set of zeroes of an ideal generated by polynomials of $\mathbb{Q}[Y_1,\ldots,Y_d]$.

Let $B \subset \mathbb{A}^d$ be $\mathbb{Q}$-definable and $y = (y_1,\ldots,y_d) \in B$ with $y_1,\ldots,y_d$ algebraic over $\mathbb{Q}$. Then for each automorphism σ of $\mathbb{C}$ leaving $\mathbb{Q}$ fixed we have $\sigma(y) = (\sigma(y_1),\ldots,\sigma(y_d)) \in B$, i.e. all conjugates of y are in B.

For all this material we refer to Lang [4].

We use the notion of degree of an irreducible variety $V \subset \mathbb{A}^d$, denoted by $\deg_{\mathbb{A}^d} V$. The degree of V is the maximal number of points which can arise intersecting V with dim V hypersurfaces of $\mathbb{A}^d$ such that the intersection has finite cardinality. For a hypersurface $W \subset \mathbb{A}^d$ defined by an irreducible polynomial $F \in \mathbb{C}[Y_1,\ldots,Y_d]$ we have $\deg_{\mathbb{A}^d} W = \deg F$.

We extend the notion of degree to arbitrary varieties. Let $B, D \subset \mathbb{A}^d$ be varieties.

We define $\deg_{\mathbb{A}^d} B := \sum_{C \text{ component of } B} \deg_{\mathbb{A}^d} C.$

We have the following fundamental "Bezout inequality" :

$$\deg_{\mathbb{A}^d} B \cap D \leq \deg_{\mathbb{A}^d} B \cdot \deg_{\mathbb{A}^d} D$$

This material can be found with direct proofs in Heintz [5]. It can also be easily deduced from Bezout's Theorem which holds for projective varieties. Instead of $\deg_{\mathbb{A}^d} V$ we shall only write degV.

For simplicity let us restrict to the case where only nonscalar operations are counted in the computation.
Also for simplicity, we only consider the case of the polynomial

$$\sum_{j=1}^{d} e^{2\pi i/j} X^j .$$

Without loss of generality we may assume that there exists an optimal computation $\beta = (r_1,\ldots,r_v)$, $r_1,\ldots,r_v \in \mathbb{C}(X)$ such that none of the $r_1,\ldots,r_v$ vanishes at $X = 0$.

Let $Z_1,\ldots,Z_m$, $m = (v+1)^2$ be indeterminates over $\mathbb{Q}$.

By Schnorr [3] there exist polynomials $P_1,..,P_d \in \mathbb{Q}[Z_1,..,Z_m]$ with $\deg P_j \leq j(2v-1)+2$, $j=1,..,d$, such that there are $\gamma_1,..,\gamma_m \in \mathbb{C}$ with

$$e^{2\pi i/j} = P_j(\gamma_1,..,\gamma_m).$$

We consider the morphism

$$\mathbb{A}^m \xrightarrow{P = (P_1,..,P_d)} \mathbb{A}^d.$$

Let W be the Zariskiclosure of the image of P in $\mathbb{A}^d$. W is $\mathbb{Q}$-definable.

We have the following Lemma:

(9) $$\dim W \leqslant v^2 \ , \ \frac{\log \deg W}{\log d} \leqslant v^2$$

(The second assertion uses the Bezout inequality).

The problem is now to find lower bounds for log deg W.

From the fact that W is $\mathbb{Q}$-definable and contains $x = (e^{2\pi i/1},..,e^{2\pi i/d})$, hence all conjugates of x, we obtain information about log deg W.

Let $Y_1,..,Y_d$ be the coordinate variables of $\mathbb{A}^d$.

Let $D = \{Y_1 - 1 = 0,..,Y_d^{\,d} - 1 = 0\}$ be the set of zeroes of $Y_1 - 1,..,Y_d^{\,d} - 1$.

D is $\mathbb{Q}$-definable and contains x. Furthermore it is finite, since all its components are 0-dimensional.

We intersect W with $1 + \dim W \leqslant v^2$ hypersurfaces defined as sets of zeroes of suitable chosen linear combinations of $Y_1 - 1,..,Y_d^{\,d} - 1$ such that we obtain as final result $D \cap W$. Thus by the Bezout inequality

(10) $$\deg D \cap W \leqslant d^{v^2} \cdot \deg W.$$

(The intersecting hypersurfaces have all degree $\leq d$).
$D \cap W$ is finite, $\mathbb{Q}$-definable and contains x.
Therefore

(11) $$\text{number of conjugates of } x \leq \# D \cap W = \deg D \cap W.$$

We proceed to estimate

log number of conjugates of x.

We have

(12) $$\text{number of conjugates of } x = \#\mathrm{Gal}\,(\mathbb{Q}(e^{2\pi i/1},\ldots,e^{2\pi i/d})/\mathbb{Q})$$

$$= [\mathbb{Q}(e^{2\pi i/1},\ldots,e^{2\pi i/d}) : \mathbb{Q}]$$

$$= \varphi\ \mathrm{l.c.m.}\ (1,\ldots,d)$$

where φ denotes the Eulerfunction.
It follows

$$\log \text{number of conjugates of } x \geqslant \log \mathrm{l.c.m.}\ (1,\ldots,d) \geqslant d.$$

From (9) - (12) we obtain

$$v^2 \geqslant \frac{\log \deg W}{\log d} \geqslant \frac{\log \deg D \cap W}{\log d} - v^2 \geqslant \frac{d}{\log d} - v^2.$$

It follows

$$v^2 \geqslant \frac{d}{\log d}, \text{ i.e.}$$

$$L^2_{nsc}\left(\sum_{j=1}^{d} e^{2\pi i/j} x^j\right) \geqslant \frac{d}{\log d}.$$

Literature

[1] J. Heintz, M. Sieveking — to appear in Theoretical Computer Science

[2] V. Strassen — Polynomials with rational coefficients which are hard to compute. Siam J. Comput. Vol.3 No.2 June 1974

[3] C.P. Schnorr — Improved lower bounds on the number of multiplications/divisions which are necessary to evaluate polynomials. in: Proceedings of the 6th International MFCS Symposium, High Tatras 1977. Springer: Lecture Notes in Computer Science 53

[4] S. Lang — Introduction to algebraic geometry 1964

[5] J. Heintz — Definability bounds in algebraically closed fields and a note on degree in affine algebraic geometry. 1977 unpublished

ON ZEROTESTING-BOUNDED MULTICOUNTER MACHINES

Matthias Jantzen

Introduction

Unrestricted multicounter machines accept all recursively enumerable sets. So various types of restricted multicounter machines have been considered to define proper subclasses (cf. [2], [8], [9], [10], [13]). One interesting class of languages has been defined by reversal-bounded multicounter machines in [2]. This class equals the least intersection-closed full semi-AFL containing the language $\{a^n b^n \mid n \geq 1\}$ and has a number of nice properties (cf. [2], [13], [16]).

We consider nondeterministic one-way multicounter machines which operate in such a way that for each accepting computation no counter is tested for zero more than a constant number of times.

Obviously each reversal-bounded machine can test its counters for zero only a bounded number of times. On the other hand a zerotesting-bounded multicounter machine need not be reversal-bounded. Thus zerotesting-bounded multicounter machines may define a larger class of languages.

In connection with Petri nets multicounter machines have been defined (cf. [9], [10], [11]) which differ from our model in that they cannot test their counters for zero but accept by final state and empty counter. All these types of automata define the same classes of Petri net languages.

It is a very well known method to characterize a family of languages as the least class containing a (hopefully simple) set of languages which is closed under a (hopefully small) set of operations. Within this framework the notion of a trio, semi-AFL, AFL, and cylinder in each case means a certain class of closure operations.

We introduce the notion duo($\mathcal{L}$) to denote the smallest class of languages containig $\mathcal{L}$ and closed under length-preserving homomorphism and inverse homomorphism.

As it turns out, the family of languages defined by zerotesting-bounded multicounter machines operating in realtime can be characterized either as a trio, as a duo, or by some infinite set ot hardest languages.

Most of the open problems are strongly connected with the difficult reachability problem for Petri nets (cf. [10], [14], [15], [18], [9]) .

Notation

It is assumed that the reader is familiar with the basic concepts from automata theory and formal languages. Throughout the paper we use the notion of Ginsburg [4], except that we denote the empty word by λ. In addition we use the following notation for each family of languages $\mathcal{L}$.

$$\mathcal{H}^{\alpha}(\mathcal{L}) := \left\{ L \;\middle|\; \begin{array}{l} L = h(L'),\ L' \in \mathcal{L},\ h \text{ some} \\ \text{length-decreasing homomorphism.} \end{array} \right\}$$

$$\mathcal{H}^{cod}(\mathcal{L}) := \left\{ L \;\middle|\; \begin{array}{l} L = h(L'),\ L' \in \mathcal{L},\ h \text{ some} \\ \text{length-preserving homomorphism.} \end{array} \right\}$$

If $\mathcal{L}$ contains at least one language $L \neq \{\lambda\}$, then we write $\mathcal{L}^{\blacktriangle} := \{ L - \{\lambda\} \mid L \in \mathcal{L} \}$.

Let $\mathbb{N}$ be the set of nonnegative integers and let $\mathbb{Z}$ be the set of integers.

Zerotesting-Bounded Multicounter Machines and Petri Nets

Definition

A k-counter machine M is defined by a tuple $M = (Z, X, I, z_0, F)$, where Z is a finite set of states, $z_0 \in Z$ is the initial state, F is the subset of final states, X is the finite input alphabet, and $I \subseteq Z \times (X \cup \{\lambda\}) \times Z \times \{0,1\}^k \times \mathbb{Z}^k$ is a finite set of instructions. An instantaneous description (ID) of M is a member $(w,z,n_1,n_2,\ldots,n_k)$ of $X^* \times Z \times \mathbb{N}^k$, where w is the input left on the input tape, z is the current state of the finite control unit, and n_i, $1 \leqslant i \leqslant k$, is the content of the i-th counter. The instruction $(z,x,z',t_1,\ldots,t_k,m_1,\ldots,m_k)$ is applicable to the ID $(xw,z,n_1,\ldots,n_k)$ iff $t_i = 0$ implies $n_i = 0$ and $n_i+m_i \geqslant 0$ for all $i \in \{1,\ldots,k\}$. If $t_i = 0$ then the counter machine performs a zerotest on the i-th counter. If the above instruction applies to the ID we write $(xw,z,n_1,\ldots,n_k) \Longrightarrow (w,z',n_1+m_1, \ldots ,n_k+m_k)$. As usual let $\overset{*}{\Longrightarrow}$ denote the reflexive transitive closure of the one-step relation $\Longrightarrow$.

The language defined by M is

$$L(M) := \left\{ w \in X^* \;\middle|\; \begin{array}{l} (w,z_0,0,\ldots,0) \overset{*}{\Longrightarrow} (\lambda,z,n_1,\ldots,n_k) \text{ for some} \\ z \in F,\ n_i \in \mathbb{N},\ 1 \leqslant i \leqslant k. \end{array} \right\}$$

Note that the multicounter machines as defined above are nondeterministic and accept by final state only.

Definition

A k-counter machine M accepts L(M) in realtime if for every word $w \in L(M)$ there exists an accepting computation with exactly $|w|$ steps.

A k-counter machine M accepts L(M) with m-bounded zerotesting, $m \in \mathbb{N}$, if for every $w \in L(M)$ there exists an accepting computation which performs at most m zerotests on each counter.

Definition

$$\mathcal{Z}_{(k,m)} := \left\{ L \;\middle|\; \text{There exists a k-counter machine accepting L in realtime and with m-bounded zerotesting.} \right\}$$

$$\mathcal{Z}^{\lambda}_{(k,m)} := \left\{ L \;\middle|\; \text{There is a k-counter machine accepting L with m-bounded zerotesting.} \right\}$$

$$\mathcal{Z} := \bigcup_{\substack{k \geq 1 \\ m \geq 0}} \mathcal{Z}_{(k,m)}$$ is the class of zerotesting-bounded multicounter languages accepted in realtime.

$$\mathcal{Z}^{\lambda} := \bigcup_{\substack{k \geq 1 \\ m \geq 0}} \mathcal{Z}^{\lambda}_{(k,m)}$$ is the class of zerotesting-bounded multicounter languages.

Theorem 1

For each language $L \in \mathcal{Z}_{(k,m)}$ there exists a k(m+1)-counter machine which accepts L in realtime and in such a way that each counter is tested for zero only once in the very last step of the computation. Thus $\mathcal{Z}_{(k,m)} \subseteq \mathcal{Z}_{(k(m+1),1)}$.

Sketch of proof

Suppose $L = L(M)$ for some k-counter machine M with m-bounded zerotesting. The equivalent k(m+1)-counter machine $\overline{M}$ is constructed as follows: For each counter count(i), $1 \leq i \leq k$, of M the new machine $\overline{M}$ has (m+1) counters, refered to as count(i,j), $1 \leq j \leq m+1$. These counters are devided into three classes classA, classB, and classC.

At the beginning of each computation of $\overline{M}$ all its counters belong to classC. $\overline{M}$ simulates a computation of M which accepts $w \in L$ in the following way:

In the first step $\overline{M}$ guesses how often M performs a zerotest on the counter count(i) during the computation of w and puts just as many of the counters count(i,j), $1 \leq j \leq m+1$, into classB.

If an instruction of M performs a zerotest on count(i), then first of all $\overline{M}$ transfers exactly one of the counters count(i,j), $1 \leq j \leq m+1$, from classB into classA.

If the same instruction changes the number stored in count(i) by adding the integer $n_i \in \mathbb{Z}$, then $\overline{M}$ adds the same number n_i to all the counters count(i,j), $1 \leq j \leq m+1$, which currently belong to classB. All the counters count(i,j) which belong to classC are changed by the same number m_i, where $0 \leq m_i \leq n_i$ or $m_i = n_i \leq 0$ must hold.
All the counters of $\overline{M}$ which belong to classA are left unchanged.
The change of the current state of M as well as the bookkeeping about the assignment of classA, classB, and classC to the counters is made in the finite state unit of $\overline{M}$.
If M finishes its computation, no counter of $\overline{M}$ belongs to classB and all the counters store zero if the simulation was proper. This can then be tested by $\overline{M}$ in the very last step.
Of course the formal proof of theorem 1 would involve a lot of technical details, so it is not presented here. The reader is refered to [15].

We are now in the position to compare zerotesting-bounded multicounter languages with Petri net languages.
Let $\mathcal{CSS}$ be the family of computation sequence sets as defined by Peterson [17] and let $\mathcal{L}_0^\lambda$ be the family of arbitrary Petri net languages as defined by Hack [10].

Theorem 2

(a) $\mathcal{Z} = \mathcal{CSS}$ (b) $\mathcal{Z}^\lambda = \mathcal{L}_0^\lambda$

Proof
By definition we have $\mathcal{L}_0^\lambda = \mathcal{H}^\alpha(\mathcal{CSS})$ so (b) follows from (a).
The inclusion $\mathcal{CSS} \subseteq \mathcal{Z}$ follows, since Hack [10, Theorem 5.8] has shown that each language $L \in \mathcal{CSS}^\blacktriangle$ can be defined by some Petri net which doesn't have selfloops. If one regards each place of such a Petri net as a counter then each transition corresponds to an instruction of some multicounter machine with one-bounded zerotesting.
The reverse inclusion follows from theorem 1, since each multicounter machine which performs a zerotest on all its counters exactly once at the end of every computation, can be written directly as a Petri net.

We are now able to use the known closure properties of Petri net languages (cf. [10], [17]) to obtain algebraic characterizations for the families of zerotesting-bounded multicounter languages.

Definition

For every symbol a let $\mathbb{D}(a)$ denote the semi-Dyck language over the pair of brackets $a\bar{a}$. The language $\mathbb{D}_k$, $k \geq 1$, is recursively defined by $\mathbb{D}_1 := \mathbb{D}(a_1)$, $\mathbb{D}_k := \mathrm{Shuf}(\mathbb{D}_{k-1}, \mathbb{D}(a_k))$.

Using the shuffle-iteration as defined in [12], [15] one may write
$\mathbb{D}_k = \{a_1\bar{a}_1, a_2\bar{a}_2, \ldots, a_k\bar{a}_k\}^{\text{⧢}}$.

Theorem 3

(a) $\mathcal{Z} = \mathcal{M}_\cap(\mathbb{D}_1) = \mathcal{M}(\{\mathbb{D}_k \mid k \geq 1\})$

(b) $\mathcal{Z}^\lambda = \hat{\mathcal{M}}_\cap(\mathbb{D}_1) = \hat{\mathcal{M}}(\{\mathbb{D}_k \mid k \geq 1\})$

Proof

By definition (b) follows directly from (a). The equation $\mathcal{M}_\cap(\mathbb{D}_1) = \mathcal{M}(\{\mathbb{D}_k \mid k \geq 1\})$ can be shown easily by AFL-theoretic considerations (see [4] or [14]). The inclusion $\mathcal{M}_\cap(\mathbb{D}_1) \subseteq \mathcal{CSS}$ follows from the closure properties shown in [10] and [17]. The reverse containment follows from the fact that each Petri net language which is generated by a Petri net with different labels at the transitions, is the finite intersection of deterministic one-counter languages from the family $\mathcal{M}(\mathbb{D}_1)$. For a proof of this result compare the ideas in [10 ,page 61] and [3 ,Theorem 3.5] or consult [14], [15], [19] . Since $\mathcal{Z} = \mathcal{CSS}$ by theorem 2, the proof is finished.

A Sufficient Condition for Trios to Have a Hardest Language

Possibly the simplest characterization of a family of languages is given by some hardest language (see [7]). A language K is called a hardest language for $\mathcal{L}$ iff $\mathcal{L} = \mathcal{H}^{-1}(\{K, K^\blacktriangle\})$. In reference [5] $\mathcal{L}$ is then called a principal ray.

We consider the closure of a family of languages under length-preserving homomorphism and inverse homomorphism.

Definition

Let $\mathrm{Duo}(\mathcal{L})$ be the smallest family of languages containing $\mathcal{L}$ and closed under length-preserving homomorphism and inverse homomorphism. The family $\mathrm{Duo}(\mathcal{L})$ is called the duo generated by $\mathcal{L}$ and is principal if $\mathcal{L}$ contains exactly one language.

The following result is as easy to show as the closure of rational transductions under composition. We omitt the proof.

Lemma 1

For every family of languages $\mathcal{L}$, $\mathrm{Duo}(\mathcal{L}) = \mathcal{H}^{cod}(\mathcal{H}^{-1}(\mathcal{L}))$.

The ideas which have been used by Greibach [7] to show that the family of context-free languages forms a principal ray can be used to prove the following:

Theorem 4

Let L be a language containing at least one nonempty word.
If $\mathrm{Duo}(\{L,L^{\blacktriangle}\}) = \mathcal{M}(L)$, then there is a hardest language $K \in \mathcal{M}(L)$, such that $\mathcal{M}(L) = \mathcal{H}^{-1}(\{K,K^{\blacktriangle}\})$. Moreover $K = K^{\blacktriangle}$ iff $L = L^{\blacktriangle}$.

Sketch of proof

Since $\mathcal{M}(L^{\blacktriangle}) = \mathcal{M}(L)^{\blacktriangle} = \{L' \in \mathcal{M}(L) \mid \lambda \notin L'\}$ (see [4]), we only need to consider the case where $L = L^{\blacktriangle}$. Otherwise suppose $\mathcal{M}(L^{\blacktriangle}) = \mathcal{H}^{-1}(K^{\blacktriangle})$ has already been shown and $L \neq L^{\blacktriangle}$ holds true. Then $\mathcal{M}(L) = \mathcal{M}(L^{\blacktriangle}) \cup \{L' \cup \{\lambda\} \mid L' \in \mathcal{M}(L^{\blacktriangle})\} = \mathcal{H}^{-1}(L^{\blacktriangle}) \cup \mathcal{H}^{-1}(L) = \mathcal{H}^{-1}(\{L,L^{\blacktriangle}\})$.

Let $L \subseteq X^{+}$, $L^{\blacktriangle} = L$, $\bar{X} := \{\bar{x} \mid x \in X\}$ and c, d be new symbols.
Define the length-decreasing homomorphism h_1 by

$$h_1(x) := \begin{cases} x , & \text{if } x \in X \\ \lambda , & \text{if } x \in \bar{X} \cup \{c,d\} \\ \text{undefined, else.} \end{cases}$$

Define the regular set $R := ((c\cdot\bar{X}^{*})^{*}\cdot c\cdot X^{*}\cdot(c\cdot\bar{X}^{*})^{*}\cdot d)^{*}$.
Finally define the length-preserving homomorphism h_2 by
$h_2(x) := h_2(\bar{x}) := x$ for each $x \in X$, $h_2(c) := c$, $h_2(d) := d$.

Then for $K := h_2(h_1^{-1}(L) \cap R) \in \mathcal{M}(L)$ one can prove the containment $\mathrm{Duo}(L) \subseteq \mathcal{H}^{-1}(K)$.

To do this, let $M \in \mathrm{Duo}(L)$ be arbitrary. Then $M = h_c(h^{-1}(L)) \subseteq Y^{*}$ for some length-preserving homomorphism h_c and some nonerasing homomorphism h .
Now for every $a \in X$ let $\{v_1^a, \ldots , v_{k(a)}^a\} = h(h_c^{-1}(a))$, $k(a) \geq 1$, be the nonempty finite set of words which under h^{-1} followed by h_c are all mapped onto the symbol a.
Define the nonerasing homomorphism $h_3 : X^{*} \longrightarrow Y^{*}$ by
$h_3(a) := cv_1^a cv_2^a c \ldots cv_{k(a)}^a d$ for each symbol $a \in X$.

With these definitions it is possible to show $h_3^{-1}(K) = h_c(h^{-1}(L)) = M$. As the proof is technical the reader is refered to [15]. This last equation shows $\mathcal{M}(L) = \mathrm{Duo}(L) \subseteq \mathcal{H}^{-1}(K) \subseteq \mathcal{M}(K) \subseteq \mathcal{M}(L)$ and thus the theorem.

For families of automata defined by a data store, Goldstine [5] has stated that such a family is a principal ray iff the finite state unit of these automata can be encoded into the data store in some way. So theorem 4 appears to be the algebraic counterpart of this statement.

A Class of Hardest Languages for the Family $\mathcal{Z}$

Definition

Let $a_0, \bar{a}_0$ be new symbols, then $\mathbb{L}_k := \mathrm{Shuf}(\mathbb{D}_k, \{a_0\bar{a}_0\}) \cup \{\lambda\}$

Theorem 5

The duo generated by the language $\mathbb{L}_2^{\blacktriangle}$ contains all the λ-free regular sets.

Proof

Suppose $A = (Z,X,f,z_0,F)$ is a completely defined deterministic finite automaton accepting the set $R \subseteq X^+$. $Z = \{z_0, z_1, \ldots, z_n\}$ is the finite set of states, z_0 is the initial state, $F \subset Z$ is the set of final states, and $f: Z \times X \longrightarrow Z$ is the transition function.

We now define the new alphabet $\tilde{X}$ by

$$\begin{aligned} \tilde{X} := & \{ [z_i,x] \mid x \in X, z_i \in Z, 0 \leqslant i \leqslant n \} \cup \\ & \{ [e_i,x] \mid x \in X, 0 \leqslant i \leqslant n, e_i \text{ special symbols} \} \cup \\ & \{ [s,x] \mid x \in X, s \text{ a special symbol} \} \cup \\ & \{ [x] \mid x \in X \} \end{aligned}$$

We define the homomorphism $h: \tilde{X}^* \longrightarrow \{a_0, \bar{a}_0, a_1, \bar{a}_1, a_2, \bar{a}_2\}^*$ for every $x \in X$ and $0 \leqslant i \leqslant n$ by

$$h([z_i,x]) := \bar{a}_1^{\,i}\, \bar{a}_2^{\,n-i}\, a_2^{\,n-j}\, a_1^{\,j} \qquad \text{iff} \quad f(z_i,x) = z_j$$

$$h([s,x]) := a_0 a_2^{\,n-j}\, a_1^{\,j} \qquad \text{iff} \quad f(z_0,x) = z_j$$

$$h([e_i,x]) := \bar{a}_1^{\,i}\, \bar{a}_2^{\,n-i}\, \bar{a}_0 \qquad \text{iff} \quad f(z_i,x) \in F$$

$$h([x]) := a_0\bar{a}_0 \qquad \text{iff} \quad f(z_0,x) \in F$$

Since f is a function h is indeed a homomorphism.

It is now possible to show the equation $h^{-1}(\mathbb{L}_2^{\blacktriangle}) = \tilde{L}$, where the set $\tilde{L}$ is defined by

$$\tilde{L} := \{ w \mid w = [x],\ x \in R \} \cup$$

$$\left\{ w \;\middle|\; \begin{array}{l} w = [s,x_1][e_j,x_2],\ x_1x_2 \in R,\ f(z_0,x_1) = z_j, \\ f(z_j,x_2) \in F \end{array} \right\} \cup$$

$$\left\{ w \;\middle|\; \begin{array}{l} w = [s,x_1][z_{i_1},x_2] \ldots [z_{i_{m-1}},x_m][e_{i_m},x_{m+1}] \quad , m \geqslant 2, \\ f(z_0,x_1) = z_{i_1},\ f(z_{i_{j-1}},x_j) = z_{i_j} \quad \text{for} \quad 2 \leqslant j \leqslant m, \\ f(z_{i_m},x_{m+1}) \in F,\ x_1x_2 \ldots x_{m+1} \in R \end{array} \right\}$$

When this equation has been verified one deduces immediately that R is a member of $\text{Duo}(\mathbb{L}_2^{\blacktriangle})$, since it is easy to find the appropriate length-preserving homomorphism h_c such that $h_c(h^{-1}(\mathbb{L}_2^{\blacktriangle})) = R$ holds.

For the proof of the following simple lemma one may use the above theorem.

Lemma 2

The family $\text{Duo}(\{\mathbb{L}_k^{\blacktriangle} \mid k \geqslant 1\})$ is closed under shuffle.

Using the preceding results we can find a set of hardest languages to characterize the family of zerotesting-bounded multicounter languages.

Theorem 6

There is a family $\mathcal{K} \subsetneq \mathcal{Z}$ such that the following equation is valid:

$$\mathcal{Z} = \text{Duo}(\{\mathbb{L}_k, \mathbb{L}_k^{\blacktriangle} \mid k \geqslant 1\}) = \mathcal{H}^{-1}(\mathcal{K}) .$$

Proof

By theorem 3 we have $\mathcal{Z} = \mathcal{M}(\{\mathbb{L}_k \mid k \geqslant 1\})$. Using the well known characterization of trios (cf. [4]) we get $\mathcal{Z} = \mathcal{H}^{cod}(\mathcal{H}^{-1}(\{\mathbb{L}_k \mid k \geqslant 1\}) \wedge \mathcal{R})$, where $\mathcal{R}$ denotes the family of regular sets. Since each shuffle-closed duo is also closed under intersection we can use theorem 5 and lemma 2 to obtain $\mathcal{Z} = \text{Duo}(\{\mathbb{L}_k, \mathbb{L}_k^{\blacktriangle} \mid k \geqslant 1\})$. As in the proof of theorem 4 we construct for every $k \geqslant 1$ a language $K_k \in \mathcal{M}(\mathbb{L}_k^{\blacktriangle})$ such that $\text{Duo}(\mathbb{L}_k^{\blacktriangle}) \subseteq \mathcal{H}^{-1}(K_k)$ holds. If we define $\mathcal{K} := \{K_k, K_k \cup \{\lambda\} \mid k \geqslant 1\}$ then $\mathcal{Z} = \text{Duo}(\{\mathbb{L}_k, \mathbb{L}_k^{\blacktriangle} \mid k \geqslant 1\}) \subseteq \mathcal{H}^{-1}(\mathcal{K}) \subseteq \mathcal{M}(\{\mathbb{L}_k \mid k \geqslant 1\}) \subseteq \mathcal{Z}$.

Some Hierarchy Results

The following result is not new and can be proved by counting the number of reachable configurations of a multicounter machine operating in real-time.

Lemma 3
For every $k \geqslant 1$, $m \geqslant 0$, $n \geqslant 0$ the following proper inclusions hold:

$$\mathcal{M}(\mathbb{D}_k) \subsetneq \mathcal{M}(\mathbb{D}_{k+1}) \quad \text{and} \quad \mathcal{Z}_{(k,m)} \subsetneq \mathcal{Z}_{(k+1,n)} .$$

Proof
The reader is refered to [6] or [4, Example 4.5.2] .

Lemma 3 shows that the family $\mathcal{K}$ from theorem 6 can never be chosen to be finite, since then $\mathcal{Z}$ would be a principal trio (and semi-AFL) which would contradict theorem 5.1.2 in [4] .

In reference [16] it has been shown that the language $\mathbb{D}_1$ is not a member of $\hat{\mathcal{M}}(\{a^n b^n \mid n \geqslant 1\})$ so that there really exist zerotesting-bounded multicounter languages which cannot be accepted by reversal-bounded multicounter machines.

In reference [21] the class RUD of rudimentary languages is characterized as the least family of languages containing $\{a^n b^n \mid n \geqslant 1\}$ and closed under the Boolean operations, inverse homomorphism, and non-erasing homomorphism. Since RUD contains every context-free language and Peterson [17] has shown that $\mathcal{CSS}$ does not contain the language $\{ww^R \mid w \in \{0,1\}^*\}$ we see that $\mathcal{Z}$ is not closed under complementation (cf.[3],[9]). Moreover we obtain

Lemma 4
The family $\mathcal{Z}$ is a proper subclass of the family RUD .

The next result has been proved in [9] and independently in [14],[15].

Theorem 7
The family $\mathcal{Z}$ is a proper subclass of the family $\mathcal{Z}^\lambda$.

In fact it has been shown that the language BIN := $\{wa^k \mid w \in \{0,1\}^*,\ 0 \leqslant k \leqslant n(w)\}$, where $n(w)$ denotes the integer represented by w as a binary number, is not a member of $\mathcal{Z}$.

On the other hand BIN can be accepted in lineartime by a two-counter machine without any zerotesting.

Some Open Problems

Of course there are a lot of questions which have not been considered yet. For instance nothing is known about the class of deterministic zerotesting-bounded multicounter machines, or about those machines which may perform $f(|w|)$ zerotests on input w, where f is not the constant function.
We believe that zerotesting-bounded multicounter machines are the natural generalization of reversal-bounded multicounter machines and the following problems are worthwhile to be solved:

Problem 1
Is there a hardest language for every trio $\mathcal{M}(\mathbb{D}_k)$, $k \geqslant 1$?

We already know from [1] that $\mathcal{M}(\mathbb{D}_1)$ is not a principal ray.

Problem 2
Is there a language $L \in \mathcal{Z}^\lambda$ which cannot be accepted in lineartime by any zerotesting-bounded multicounter machine?

Problem 3
Is it true that $\mathcal{Z}_{(k,m)} \subsetneq \mathcal{Z}_{(k,m+1)}$ holds for all $k \geqslant 1, m > 0$?

Problem 4
Is the question: " $h^{-1}(\mathbb{L}_k^\blacktriangle) = \emptyset$? " decidable for every homomorphism h and each $k \geqslant 1$?

Since $\mathbb{L}_1^\blacktriangle$ is context-free, the answer is "yes" for $k = 1$. Problem 4 is an equivalent formulation of the famous reachability problem for Petri nets which has been announced to be decidable in [18]. Unfortunately the proof given there has still some gaps, so we pose it as an open problem.

Problem 5
Is the family $\mathcal{Z}$ closed with respect to Kleene star?

The answer is "no" if the reachability problem is decidable. Unfortunately the same answer given by Hack [10, Theorem 9.8] is based on an incorrect proof as has been observed by Valk [20].

Problem 6

Does $\hat{\mathcal{M}}(\mathbb{D}_k) \subsetneqq \hat{\mathcal{M}}(\mathbb{D}_{k+1})$ hold for each $k \geq 1$?

If the answer to this question is "yes", then $\mathcal{Z}$ cannot be star-closed. Of course proper inclusion holds for $k = 1$, since $\hat{\mathcal{M}}(\mathbb{D}_2)$ contains languages which are not one-counter languages.

Problem 7

Is it decidable whether the Parikh image of a language $L \in \mathcal{Z}$ is a semilinear set?

This is probably the hardest question, since a positive answer would make the reachability problem decidable. We do not know whether problem 7 and problem 4 are equivalent.

Literature

[1] J.M.AUTEBERT, Non principalité du Cylindre des Langes a Compteur, Math. Syst. Theory, vol. 11, (1977), p. 157-167.

[2] B.S.BAKER and R.V.BOOK, Reversal-Bounded Multipushdown Machines, J. Comp. Syst. Sc., vol. 8, (1974), p. 315-332.

[3] S.CRESPI-REGHIZZI and D.MANDRIOLI, Petri Nets and Szilard Languages, Information and Control, vol. 33, (1977), p. 177-192.

[4] S.GINSBURG, Algebraic and Automata-Theoretic Properties of Formal Languages, North-Holland Publ. Comp., (1975).

[5] J.GOLDSTINE, Automata with Data Storage, Proc. 10th annual ACM Symp. on Theory of Computing, (1978),

[6] S.A.GREIBACH, An Infinite Hierarchy of Context-Free Languages, J. Assoc. Computing Machinery, vol. 16, (1969), p. 91-106.

[7] S.A.GREIBACH, The Hardest Context-Free Language, SIAM J. of Comp., vol. 2, (1973), p. 304-310.

[8] S.A.GREIBACH, Remarks on the Complexity of Nondeterministic Counter Languages, Theoretical Computer Science, vol. 1, (1976), p. 269-288.

[9] S.A.GREIBACH, Remarks on Blind and Partially Blind One-Way Multicounter Machines, Theoretical Computer Science, to appear.

[10] M.HACK, Petri Net Languages, Computation Structures Group Memo 124, Project MAC, MIT, (1975).

[11] M.HÖPNER, Über den Zusammenhang von Szilardsprachen und Matrixgrammatiken, Technical report, Univ. Hamburg, IFI-HH-B-12/74, (1974).

[12] M.HÖPNER and M.OPP, About Three Equational Classes of Languages Built up by Shuffle Operations, Lecture Notes in Comp. Sc., Springer, vol. 45, (1976), p. 337-344.

[13] O.H.IBARRA, Reversal-Bounded Multicounter Machines and Their Decision Problems, J. Assoc. Computing Machinery, vol. 25, (1978), p. 116-133.

[14] M.JANTZEN, On the Hierarchy of Petri Net Languages, R.A.I.R.O. Informatique théorique, to appear.

[15] M.JANTZEN, Eigenschaften von Petrinetzsprachen, Research report, Univ. Hamburg, (1978).

[16] M.LATTEUX, Cônes Rationelles Commutativement Clos, R.A.I.R.O. Informatique théorique, vol. 11, (1977), p. 29-51.

[17] J.L.PETERSON, Computation Sequence Sets, J. Comp. Syst. Sc., vol. 13, (1976), p. 1-24.

[18] G.S.SACERDOTE and R.L.TENNEY, The Decidability of the Reachability Problem for Vector-Addition Systems, Proc. 9th annual ACM Symp. on Theory of Computing, (1977), p. 61-76.

[19] P.H.STARKE, Free Petri Net Languages, Lecture Notes in Comp. Sc., Springer, vol. 64, (1978), p. 506-515.

[20] R.VALK, Self-Modifying Nets, a Natural Extension of Petri Nets, Lecture Notes in Comp. Sc., Springer, vol. 62, (1978), p. 464-476.

[21] C.WRATHALL, Rudimentary Predicates and Relative Computation, SIAM J. Computing, vol. 7, (1978), p. 194-209.

WHEN ARE TWO EFFECTIVELY GIVEN DOMAINS IDENTICAL? (Extended Abstract)

Akira Kanda
David Park

ABSTRACT

In this paper, we will observe that the notion of computability in an effectively given domain is dependent on the indexing of its basis. This indicates that we cannot identify two effectively given domains just because they are order isomorphic. We propose a suitable notion of effective isomorphism to compensate for this deficiency. Also we show that, for every recursion domain equation, there is an effectively given domain which is an initial solution to within effective isomorphism.

1. Effectively Given Domains

The fundamental idea of effectively given domains is to assume effectiveness of finite join operations on a basis of each counably based cpo and to define computable elements as the least upper bounds (lub) of r.e. chains of basis elements. For details of results based on this idea see Scott [7], Tang [6], Egli-Constable [1], Markowsky-Rosen [3] and Smyth [8].

In this theory it is tempting to avoid questions of indexing. In fact, initially it is not clear whether an effectively given domain is to be a domain which can be effectively given in some unspecified manner or is a domain where this is specified. One could ask if it makes any difference. One of the main purposes of this paper is to show it does. This calls for rather "tedious" definition of effectively given domains (See definition 1.1).

A poset is directed complete iff every directed subset has a lub. A directed complete poset with a least element (called bottom) is called a complete partial ordering (cpo). An element x of a poset D is compact iff for every directed subset $S \subseteq D$, s.t. $\sqcup S \in D$, $x \sqsubseteq \sqcup S \Rightarrow x \sqsubseteq s$ for some $s \in S$. A directed complete poset D is countably algebraic iff the set E_D of all compact elements of D is countable and for every $x \in D$, the set $J_x = \{e \mid e \in E_D, e \sqsubseteq x\}$ is directed and $x = \sqcup J_x$. In this case E_D is called the basis of D. The following extension property of the bases is well-known : Let D be countably algebraic, then for any cpo Q, every monotone

$m : E_D \to Q$ has a unique continuous extension $\bar{m} : D \to Q$ given by $\bar{m}(x) = \sqcup\{m(e) | e \in E_D, e \sqsubseteq x\}$. A poset is said to <u>have bounded joins</u> iff every bounded finits subset has a lub. If every bounded subset has a lub, we say that the poset is <u>bounded complete</u>. It can readily be seen that a countably algebraic cpo D has bounded joins iff E_D has bounded joins iff D is bounded complete.

<u>Definition 1.1</u> (1) Let D be a countably algebraic bounded complete cpo (<u>countably algebraic domain</u>) with the basis E_D. A (total) indexing $\varepsilon : N \to E_D$ is <u>effective</u> (or is an <u>effective basis</u> of D) iff the following relations are recursive in indices :

1. $\{\varepsilon(i_1), \ldots, \varepsilon(i_n)\}$ is bounded in E_D
2. $\varepsilon(k) = \sqcup\{\varepsilon(i_1), \ldots, \varepsilon(i_n)\}$ $\qquad n \geq 0$

Notice that $\sqsubseteq$ and $\perp$ are effective according to this definition.

(2) An <u>indexed domain</u> is an ordered pair $\langle D, \varepsilon \rangle$ when D is a countably algebraic domain and $\varepsilon : N \to E_D$ is a total indexing of E_D. An indexed domain $\langle D, \varepsilon \rangle$ is <u>effectively given</u> iff ε is an effective basis of D. We will write D^ε for $\langle D, \varepsilon \rangle$.

(3) Given an effectively given domain D^ε, $x \in D$ is <u>computable w.r.t.</u> ε (or is <u>computable in</u> D^ε) iff there exists a recursive function $\rho : N \to N$ s.t. $\varepsilon \circ \rho : N \to E_D$ is an ω-chain and $x = \sqcup\, \varepsilon \circ \rho(n)$. The set of all computable elements of D^ε will be denoted by Comp (D^ε).

(4) Given effectively given domains D^ε and $D'^{\varepsilon'}$, a function $f : D \to D'$ is <u>computable w.r.t.</u> $\langle \varepsilon, \varepsilon' \rangle$ iff the graph of f, which is $\{\langle n,m \rangle | \varepsilon'(m) \sqsubseteq f \circ \varepsilon(n)\}$, is an r.e. set.

Notice that an indexed domain D^ε is effectively given iff there exists a pair of recursive predicatis $\langle b, \ell \rangle$, which will be called the <u>characteristic pair of</u> D^ε s.t. :

$b(x) \Leftrightarrow \{\varepsilon(i_1), \ldots, \varepsilon(i_n)\}$ is bounded in E_D and

$\ell(k,x) \Leftrightarrow \varepsilon(k) = \sqcup\{\varepsilon(i_1), \ldots, \varepsilon(i_n)\}$

where f_s is the standard enumeration of finite subsets of N and $f_s(x) = \{i_1, \ldots, i_n\}$. Notice that if D^ε and $D'^{\varepsilon'}$ have the same characteristic pair, then D^ε is merely a "remaming" of $D'^{\varepsilon'}$. More formally, there exists an order isomorphism $f : D \to D'$ s.t. $f \circ \varepsilon = \varepsilon'$. We will denote this retation by $D^\varepsilon \overset{r}{\cong} D'^{\varepsilon'}$. Thus if $D^\varepsilon \overset{r}{\cong} D'^{\varepsilon'}$ then they are the same.

To within $\overset{r}{\cong}$ we can introduce the following partial indexing of the set of all effectively given domains. Let $\langle \phi_i \rangle$ and $\langle W_i \rangle$ to fixed (throughout this paper) acceptable indexings [5] of partial recursion functions and r.e. sets respectively s.t. range $(\phi_i) = W_i$. We say that an effectively given domain D^ε has an <u>acceptable index</u> $\langle i,j \rangle$ iff $\langle \phi_i, \phi_j \rangle$ is a characteristic pair of D^ε. We will denote this partial indexing of effectively given domains by $\bar{\xi}$. We will write $\xi(i)$ to denote the effective basis of $\bar{\xi}(i)$. Notice that for a partial indexing τ, we write $\tau(i)$ iff i is a τ-index, i.e. $\tau(i)$ is defined.

Given an effectively given domain D^{ε}, an r.e. set W is <u>ε-directed</u> iff $\varepsilon(W)$ is directed in E_D. In this case we say that $\varepsilon(W)$ is <u>effectively directed via</u> ε. It can readily be seen that $x \in \mathrm{Comp}(D^{\varepsilon})$ iff $x = \bigsqcup\varepsilon(W)$ for some ε-directed r.e. set W. Furthermore we can effectively "ε-direct" every r.e. set. More formally :

<u>Lemma 1.2</u> For every effectively given domain D^{ε}, there is a recursive function of $d_{\varepsilon}: N \to N$ s.t. for every $j \in N$, $W_{d_{\varepsilon}(j)}$ is ε-directed, and s.t. in case W_j is ε-directed, $\bigsqcup\varepsilon(W_j) = \bigsqcup\varepsilon(W_{d_{\varepsilon}(j)})$. This lemma gives us the following total indexing δ_{ε} of $\mathrm{Comp}(D^{\varepsilon})$. If $x = \bigsqcup\varepsilon(W_{d_{\varepsilon}(j)})$ then we say that x has a <u>directed index</u> j and denote it by $x = \delta_{\varepsilon}(j)$. ∎

Since we took the view that an effectively given domain is a domain with a specified effective basis, domain constructors must relate not only po structure but also effective structure.

Thus we have to be explicit about constructed effective bases.

<u>Definition 1.3</u> Given indexed domains D^{ε} and $D'^{\varepsilon'}$, define $D^{\varepsilon}\times D'^{\varepsilon'}$, $D^{\varepsilon}+D'^{\varepsilon'}$, and $[D^{\varepsilon}\to D'^{\varepsilon'}]$ to be the following indexed domains :

(1) $D^{\varepsilon}\times D'^{\varepsilon'} \overset{\text{def}}{=\!=} \langle D\times D', (\varepsilon\times\varepsilon')\rangle$ when $(\varepsilon\times\varepsilon')(n) = \langle\varepsilon.\pi_1(n), \varepsilon.\pi_2(n)\rangle$.

(2) $D^{\varepsilon}\times D'^{\varepsilon'} \overset{\text{def}}{=\!=} \langle D+D', (\varepsilon+\varepsilon')\rangle$ where $(\varepsilon+\varepsilon')(n) =$ <u>if</u> $n = 0$ <u>then</u> $\bot$ <u>else</u> <u>if</u> $n = 2m+1$ <u>then</u> $\langle 0, \varepsilon(m)\rangle$ <u>else</u> <u>if</u> $n=2m$ <u>then</u> $\langle 1, \varepsilon'(m)\rangle$

(3) $[D^{\varepsilon}\to D'^{\varepsilon'}] \overset{\text{def}}{=\!=} \langle [D\to D'], [\varepsilon\to\varepsilon']\rangle$ where $[\varepsilon\to\varepsilon'](n) =$ <u>if</u> $\sigma(n)$ has a lub <u>then</u> $\bigsqcup\sigma(n)$ <u>else</u> $\bot$, and $\sigma(n) = \{[\varepsilon(i), \varepsilon(j)] \mid \langle i,j\rangle \in P(n)\}$ where P is the standard enumeration of finite subsets of N×N, and $[e,e'](x) =$ <u>if</u> $x \sqsupseteq e$ <u>then</u> e' <u>else</u> $\bot$. □

It is well known that if D^{ε} and $D'^{\varepsilon'}$ are effectively given domains then so are $D^{\varepsilon}\times D'^{\varepsilon'}$, $D^{\varepsilon}+D'^{\varepsilon'}$, and $[D^{\varepsilon}\to D'^{\varepsilon'}]$. The following theorem says that $\times, +, \to$ are "effective" constructors :

<u>Theorem 1.4</u> There are recursin functions Prod, Sum, Func: $N\times N\to N$ s.t. if i, and j are acceptable indices of D^{ε} and $D'^{\varepsilon'}$, then Prod (i,j), Sum (i,j), and Func (i,j) are acceptable indices of $D^{\varepsilon}\times D'^{\varepsilon'}$, $D^{\varepsilon}+D'^{\varepsilon'}$, and $[D^{\varepsilon}\to D'^{\varepsilon'}]$ respectively. ∎

Smyth [7] showed that a function $f : D\to D'$ is computable w.r.t. $\langle\varepsilon,\varepsilon'\rangle$ iff $f \in \mathrm{Comp}([D^{\varepsilon}\to D'^{\varepsilon'}])$. We can show that this equivalence is "effective". Let $f: D\to D'$ to computable w.r.t. $\langle\varepsilon,\varepsilon'\rangle$. If W_j is the graph of f, then we say that j is a ($\langle\varepsilon,\varepsilon'\rangle$-) <u>graph index</u> of f.

<u>Lemma 1.5</u> There are recursive functions d_g, $g_d: N\times N\to N$ s.t.,

(1) If k is a graph index of f which is computable w.r.t. $\langle\xi(i), \xi(j)\rangle$ then $f = \delta_{[\xi(i)\to\xi(j)]}(d_g(k,\langle i,j\rangle))$

(2) If $f = \delta_{[\xi(i)\to\xi(j)]}(k)$ then f has a graph index $g_d(k,\langle i,j\rangle)$ ∎

In addition to 1.5, we have further evidence to convince us that our notion of computability is really satisfactory.

Lemma 1.6 (1) A function from an effectively given domain to another is computable w.r.t. their effective bases iff it maps computable elements to computable elements recursively in directed indices.

(2) The composition of computable functions is recursive in directed indices. More formally there exists a recursive function d-Compose : $N\times N\times N\times N\times N\to N$ s.t. :

$$\delta_{[\xi(k)\to\xi(\ell)]}(i) \cdot \delta_{[\xi(\ell)\to\xi(m)]}(j) = \delta_{[\xi(k)\to\xi(m)]}(\text{d-Compose}(i,j,k,\ell,m)).$$

∎

2. Effective Embeddings

In this section, we will observe why the indexing of a basis of an effectively given domain must be specified.

Theorem 2.1

(1) There is a countably algebraic domain D with two different effective bases ε and ε' s.t. Comp (D^{ε}) = Comp $(D^{\varepsilon'})$ but s.t. Comp$([D^{\varepsilon}\to \mathbb{O}^{\pi}])$ is not isomorphic to Comp$([D^{\varepsilon'}\to \mathbb{O}^{\pi}])$, when $\mathbb{O}$ is the two point lattice and π is an arbitary effective basis of $\mathbb{O}$.

(2) There is a countably algebraic domain D with two different effective bases ε and ε' s.t. Comp $(D^{\varepsilon}) \not\cong$ Comp $(D^{\varepsilon'})$.

proof (outline) (1) Let $(D,\sqsubseteq)$ be the following countably algebraic domain:

Note that D has only one limit point $\odot$. Thus the basis E_D of D is the poset obtained from D by removing $\odot$. Think of the following poset $(N\cup(N\times N),\sqsubseteq)$ where $i\sqsubseteq j$ iff $i\leq j$, $i\sqsubseteq\langle m,n\rangle$ iff $\phi_m(n)$ takes at least i steps, and $\langle m,n\rangle\sqsubseteq\langle m',n'\rangle$ iff m=m' and n=n'. Evidently the partial ordering $\sqsubseteq$ is decidable in terms of the Gödel numbering of $N\cup(N\times N)$. Thus this Gödel numbering provides an effective indexing ε' of E_D. Now think of the following poset $(N\cup(N\times N)\cup(\{w\}\times N),\sqsubseteq)$ s.t. $i\sqsubseteq j$ iff $i\leq j$, $i\sqsubseteq\langle m,n\rangle$ iff $i\leq m$, and $\langle m,n\rangle\sqsubseteq\langle m',n'\rangle$ iff m=m' and n=n'. It is also easy to observe that the Gödel numbering of $N\cup(N\times N)\cup(\{w\}\times N)$ provides an effective indexing ε of E_D. Obviously Comp (D^{ε}) = Comp $(D^{\varepsilon'})$ = D. Now let $f : D\to\mathbb{O}$ for a continuous function s.t. $f(x)$ = if $x\sqsupseteq\odot$ then $\top$ else $\bot$. Then f is computable w.r.t. $\langle\varepsilon,\pi\rangle$ but not so w.r.t. $\langle\varepsilon',\pi\rangle$. Now let $M = \{h\in[D\to O] \mid \{g\in[D\to O] \mid g\sqsupseteq h\}$ is finite$\}$. Then $M = \{h_X \mid X$ is a finite set of leaves above compact elements of D$\}$ where $h_X(x)$ = if $x\sqsubseteq y\in X$, then $\bot$ else $\top$. It can be readily seen that $M\subseteq$Comp$([D^{\varepsilon}\to D^{\pi}])$ and $M\subseteq$Comp$([D^{\varepsilon'}\to D^{\pi}])$. Let Φ: Comp$([D^{\varepsilon}\to D^{\pi}])\to$ Comp $([D^{\varepsilon'}\to D^{\pi}])$ be a monotone isomorphism. Then $\Phi(M) = M$. Notice that $f=\sqcap M$. Therefore $\sqcap M\in$Comp

$([D^{\varepsilon}\to D^{\pi}])$. Since Φ is an isomorphism, $\Phi(\sqcap M) = \sqcap' M \in Comp([D^{\varepsilon'}\to D^{\pi}])$. But it is easy to see that M has no greatest lower bound in $Comp([D^{\varepsilon'}\to O^{\pi}])$. For suppose g is a lower bound of M in $Comp([D^{\varepsilon'}\to O^{\pi}])$. Then $g(x) = \bot$ for some $x \supseteq 0$, since $g \sqsubseteq f$. But then $h(y) =$ if $y=x$ then $\top$ else $g(y)$ is also a lower bound of M in $Comp([D^{\varepsilon'}\to O^{\pi}])$ and above g. ☐

Notice that 2.1 is more than a counter-example to a careless definition of effectively given domains. In fact (1)-2.1 indicates that Comp (D^{ε}) = Comp $(D^{\varepsilon'})$ is not sufficient to identify ε and ε'. Remember that in domain theory, domain constructors must preserve equality of domains, more technically, they must be functors. But if we assume that D^{ε} and $D^{\varepsilon'}$ are equivelant iff Comp (D^{ε}) = Comp $(D^{\varepsilon'})$, then "$\to$" does not preserve this equality as shown in (1)-2.1. We claim that the following equivalence of effectively given domains is appropriate :

<u>Definition 2.2</u> Let D^{ε} and $D^{\varepsilon'}$ be indexed domains. We say that ε and ε' are <u>effectively equivalent</u> (in symbols, $\varepsilon \overset{e}{=} \varepsilon'$) iff there are recursive functions r,s, : $N\to N$ s.t. $\varepsilon' = \varepsilon \circ s$ and $\varepsilon = \varepsilon' \circ r$. ☐

It can readily be seen that if either ε or ε' is effective then $\varepsilon \overset{e}{=} \varepsilon'$ implies both ε and ε' are effective and $Comp(D^{\varepsilon}) = Comp(D^{\varepsilon'})$.

Notice that D^{ε} and $D^{\varepsilon'}$ of (1)-2.1 are not effectively equivelent. In fact, if ε and ε' were effectively equivelent then there could exist a recursive function r : $N\to N$ s.t. $\phi_m(n)$ terminates iff $r(\langle m,n\rangle) = \langle m',n'\rangle$ with $m' \neq \infty$, and we could solve the Halting problem.

We can easily extend the notion of effective equivalence to isomorphism.

<u>Definition 2.3</u> Let D^{ε} and $D'^{\varepsilon'}$ be indexed domains. A function $f:E_D\to E_{D'}$ is an <u>effective imbedding from ε to ε'</u> (in symbol $f:\varepsilon\to\varepsilon'$) iff

1. f is injective
2. there exists a recursion function $r_f:N\to N$ s.t. $f\circ\varepsilon=\varepsilon'\circ r_f$.
3. $\{\varepsilon(i_1), \ldots, \varepsilon(i_n)\}$ is bounded iff $\{t\circ\varepsilon(i_1), \ldots, f\circ\varepsilon(i_n)\}$ is bounded.
4. $f(\sqcup\{\varepsilon i_1), \ldots, \varepsilon(i_n)\}) = \sqcup\{f\circ\varepsilon(i_n), \ldots, f\circ\varepsilon(i_n)\}$, $n\geq 0$. ☐

In case both D^{ε} and $D'^{\varepsilon'}$ are effectively given domains, then we have : $\bar{f}(Comp(D'^{\varepsilon'})) \subseteq Comp(D'^{\varepsilon'})$, when $\bar{f}$ is the continuous extension of f.

Remember that a continuous function f : $D\to D'$ is an <u>embedding</u> iff there exists a continuous function $g:D'\to D$ s.t. $f\circ g \sqsubseteq id_{D'}$ and $g\circ f = id_D$. Every embedding f uniquely determines such g, which will be called the <u>adjoint of</u> f. Also every embedding is strict. In case D and D' are algebraic cpo's, we have $f(E_D) \subseteq E_{D'}$ and $g(E_{D'}) \subseteq E_D$.

<u>Theorem 2.4</u> (1) Let $D^{\varepsilon}, D'^{\varepsilon}$ be indexed domains and f be an effective imbedding from ε to ε', then $f:D\to D'$ is an embedding with

the adjoint $g:D'\to D$ given by $g(y) = \sqcup\{e\in E_D | f(e) \sqsubseteq y\}$. Furthermore $g\restriction f(E_D) = f^{-1}$.

(2) In case D^{ε} and $D'^{\varepsilon'}$ are effectively given domains, $\bar{f}$ is computable w.r.t. $<\varepsilon,\varepsilon'>$ and g is computable w.r.t. $<\varepsilon',\varepsilon>$. ∎

We will call $\bar{f}$ an <u>effective embedding</u> when f is an effective imbedding. A <u>pair-wise computable embedding</u> (<u>p-computable embedding</u>) is an embedding which is computable as well as its adjoint. Thus by (2)-2.4, an effective embedding from an effectively given domain to an effectively given domain is a p-computable embedding. The converse of this also is true.

<u>Theorem 2.5</u> Let D^{ε} and $D'^{\varepsilon'}$ be effectively given domains s.t. $\bar{f}:D\to D'$ be a p-computable embedding, then $\bar{f}$ is an effective embedding.

<u>proof</u> Let $\bar{g}$: $D'\to D$ be the adjoint of $\bar{f}$. Then both $\varepsilon'(n) \sqsubseteq f\cdot\varepsilon(m)$ and $\varepsilon(n) \sqsubseteq g\cdot\varepsilon'(m)$ are r.e. in indices. We will show the existence of a recursive function $r:N\to N$ s.t. $f\cdot\varepsilon=\varepsilon'\cdot r$. We claim that the following terminating program computes such $r(m)$ for each $m\in N$:

- enumerate n s.t. $\varepsilon'(n) \sqsubseteq f\cdot\varepsilon(m)$.
- for each enumerated n, enumerate k s.t. $\varepsilon(k) \sqsubseteq g\cdot\varepsilon'(n)$.
- continue this process until we obtain a k s.t. $\varepsilon(k) = \varepsilon(m)$.

The n for which this k is produced is r(m).

By a "dove-tailing" technique [5], we can compute the above process. We can check that such r is actually the one desired. Assume k, n are the values when the above process terminates. Then $\varepsilon(k) \sqsubseteq g\cdot\varepsilon'(m)$ $\sqsubseteq g\cdot f(\varepsilon(m)) = \varepsilon(m)$. Since $\varepsilon(k)=\varepsilon(m)$, we have $g.\varepsilon'(n)=\varepsilon(m)$. But $\varepsilon'(n) \sqsupseteq$ $f\cdot g\cdot\varepsilon'(n)=f\cdot\varepsilon(m)$. Therefore $\varepsilon'(n)=f\cdot\varepsilon(m)$. ∎

In fact, we can observe that the equivalence of effective embeddings and p-computable embeddings is "effective". Given an effective imbedding $f : \varepsilon\to\varepsilon'$, if $r_t = \phi_j$ we say that f has a <u>recursive index</u> j. In this case we say that the effective embedding $\bar{f}$ has a <u>recursive index</u> j.

<u>Theorem 2.6</u> (1) There is a recursive function $\xi_d : N\times N\times N\to N$ s.t. if i and j are directed indices of a p-computable embedding $\bar{f} \in$ Comp $([\bar{\xi}(k) \to \bar{\xi}(\ell)])$ and its adjoint $\bar{g} \in$ Comp $([\bar{\xi}(k)\to\bar{\xi}(\ell)])$ respectively, then $\xi_d(i,j,<k,\ell>)$ is a recursive index of $\bar{f}$.

(2) There are recursive functions d_p, d_a : $N\times N\to N$ s.t. if i is a recursive index of an effective embedding $\bar{f}\in$Comp$([\bar{\xi}(j) \to \bar{\xi}(k)])$ then d_p $(i,<j,k>)$ is a directed index of $\bar{f}$ and $d_a(i,<j,k>)$ is a directed index of the adjoint $\bar{g}\in$ Comp$([\bar{\xi}(k) \to \bar{\xi}(j)])$ of $\bar{f}$. ∎

Now we can define what an effective isomorphism is about.

<u>Definition 2.7</u> Let D^{ε} and $D'^{\varepsilon'}$ be indexed domains. We say ε and ε' are <u>effectively isomorphic</u> iff there exists an effective imbedding

$f : \varepsilon \to \varepsilon'$ s.t. f^{-1} is also an effective imbedding from ε' to ε. We will denote this by $\varepsilon \overset{e}{\cong} \varepsilon'$. In this case we also say that D^{ε} and $D'^{\varepsilon'}$ are effectively isomorphic and denote it by $D^{\varepsilon} \overset{e}{\cong} D'^{\varepsilon'}$. Evidently $(\bar{f}, \bar{f}^{-1})$ is a continuous isomorphic pair. We will call $\bar{f}$ (or $\bar{f}^{-1}$) an effective isomorphism.

If $D^{\varepsilon} \overset{e}{\cong} D'^{\varepsilon'}$ and either of them is an effectively given domain, then both of them are effectively given and $\mathrm{Comp}(D^{\varepsilon}) \cong \mathrm{Comp}(D'^{\varepsilon'})$. Also an isomorphism between two effectively given domains is an effective isomorphism iff both itself and its adjoint are computable.

Remember that we have claimed that the notion of effective isomorphism gives an appropriate criterion for identifying two effectively given domains. We can provide quite convincing evidence to this claim. First, evidently $\overset{e}{\cong}$ is an equivalence relation. Furthermore we can show that $\overset{e}{\cong}$ is invariant under the domain constructions $\times$, $+$, and $\to$. More formally:

Theorem 2.8 Let A^{α}, B^{β}, C^{γ}, and D^{δ} be indexed domains s.t. $A^{\alpha} \overset{e}{\cong} C^{\gamma}$ and $B^{\beta} \overset{e}{\cong} D^{\delta}$. Then we have:

(1) $A^{\alpha} \times B^{\beta} \overset{e}{\cong} C^{\gamma} \times D^{\delta}$ (2) $A^{\alpha} + B^{\beta} \overset{e}{\cong} C^{\gamma} + D^{\delta}$

(3) $[A^{\alpha} \to B^{\beta}] \overset{e}{\cong} [C^{\gamma} \to D^{\delta}]$.

Note that if $A^{\alpha}, B^{\beta}, C^{\gamma}, D^{\delta}$ are effectively given domains, then the invariance of $\overset{e}{\cong}$ immediately follows from 1.6.

3. Algebraic Completion

Smyth showed (in [8]) that for continuous cpo's, we cannot introduce effectiveness as we did for algebraic cases in 1.1. He characterized an effectively given continuous domain as a continuous domain which is "isomorphic" to the completion of an effective R-structure but this characterization ignores the precise indexing of the effectively given domain. We will provide an algebraic version of Smyth's characterization, taking care of effective isomorphisms. In fact we will observe that this characterization is an alternation characterization to 1.1.

By the (algebraic) completion of a poset $(E, \sqsubseteq)$, we mean a poset $(\bar{E}, \subseteq)$ when $\bar{E}$ is the set of all directed subsets of X which are down-ward closed i.e. $x \in X$ & $y \sqsubseteq x$ implies $y \in X$. In case $(E, \sqsubseteq)$ is a countable poset with a bottom and bounded joins, then there exists an embedding $\tau : E \to \bar{E}$ s.t. $(\bar{E}, \subseteq)$ is a countably algebraic domain with the basis $(\tau(E), \subseteq)$. In fact $\tau(x) = \{e \in E \mid e \sqsubseteq x\}$. Conversely if D is a countably algebraic domain then the basis E_D is a countable poset with a bottom and bounded joins, and $D \cong \bar{E}_D$.

Definition 3.1 Let $(E, \sqsubseteq)$ be a countable poset with a bottom and bounded joins and $\varepsilon : N \to E$ be a total indexing. We call $\langle E, \varepsilon \rangle$ indexed poset. In case ε is effective, which means ε satisfies (1)-1.1, we call $\langle E, \varepsilon \rangle$ an effective poset. The (algebraic) completion of an indexed poset $<E,\varepsilon>$ is an indexed domain $<\bar{E},\bar{\varepsilon}>$ where $\bar{\varepsilon}:N\to\tau(E)$ is given by $\bar{\varepsilon}(n)=\tau\cdot\varepsilon(n)$. □

Theorem 3.2 (1) Let $<E,\varepsilon>$ be an effective poset. Then the completion of it is an effectively given domain.

(2) Given an effectively given domain D^{ε}, E^{ε}_{D} is an effective poset and $<\bar{E}_D,\bar{\varepsilon}>=<D,\varepsilon>$.

(3) An indexed domain is an effectively given domain iff it is effectively isomorphic to the completion of some effective poset. ☒

4. Inverse Limits

Given an ω-sequence $<D_m,f_m>$ of embeddings of countably algebraic domains, the inverse limit of the sequence, in symbols $\varprojlim<D_m,f_m>$, is the poset $\{<x_m>|x_m=g_m(x_{m+1})\}$ with the coordinate-wisw ordering, where g_m is the adjoint of f_m. It is well-known that $\varprojlim<D_m,f_m>$ is again a countably algebraic domain (see Plotkin [4]). We will write D_∞ for $\varprojlim <D_m,f_m>$. Define $f_{n\infty}:D_n\to D_\infty$ and $g_{\infty n}:D_\infty\to D_n$ by:

$$f_{n\infty}(x)=<g_o\cdot g_1\cdot\ldots\cdot g_{n-1}(x),\ldots,g_{n-1}(x),x,f_n(x),f_{n+1}\cdot f_n(x),\ldots\ ,>$$

$$g_{\infty n}(<x_o,x_1,\ldots>) = x_n.$$

We call $<f_{n\infty}>$ the universal cone of $<D_m,f_m>$. Evidently $f_{n\infty}$ is an embedding with the adjoint $g_{\infty n}$.

As an obvious extension of this notion, we have the inverse limit of ω-sequences of embeddings of indexed domains. Let $<D^{\varepsilon}_{m}m,f_m>$ be an ω-sequence of embeddings of indexed domains. By the inverse limit of this sequence , in symbols $\varprojlim< D^{\varepsilon}_{m}m,f_m>$, we mean an indexed domain $<D_\infty,\varepsilon_\infty>$ where $\varepsilon_\infty:N\to E_{D_\infty}$ is given by :

$$\varepsilon_\infty(0) = f_{0\infty}(\varepsilon_0(0)) \qquad \varepsilon_\infty(1) = f_{0\infty}(\varepsilon_0(1))$$
$$\varepsilon_\infty(2) = f_{1\infty}(\varepsilon_1(0)) \qquad \varepsilon_\infty(3) = f_{0\infty}(\varepsilon_0(2))$$
$$\varepsilon_\infty(4) = f_{1\infty}(\varepsilon_1(0)) \qquad \varepsilon_\infty(5) = f_{2\infty}(\varepsilon_2(0))$$

In case $D^{\varepsilon}_{m}m$ are effectively given domains, $\varprojlim<D^{\varepsilon}_{m}m,f_m>$ need not be an effectively given domain. Smyth [8] showed that if $<D^{\varepsilon}_{m}m,f_m>$ is "effective" then $\varprojlim<D^{\varepsilon}_{m}m,f_m>$ is effectively given. We observe that Smyth's effectiveness of ω-sequences is essentially equivalent to the constraint that the sequence of approximate domains can be obtained in a uniform way.

Definition 4.1 Let $<D^{\varepsilon}_{m}m,f_m>$ be an ω-sequence of effective embeddings of effectively given domains. In case three exists a recursive function q: N→N s.t. $\pi_1.q(m)$ is a recursive index of $f_m\in\mathrm{Comp}([D^{\varepsilon}_{m}m\to D^{\varepsilon}_{m+1}m+1])$ and $\pi_2.q(m)$ is an acceptable index of $D^{\varepsilon}_{m}m$, we say that this sequence is effective. □

From 2.6 and 4.1, we immediately have the following alternative characterization of effective sequences of effective embeddings.

Lemma 4.2 An ω-sequence $<D_m^{\varepsilon}m, f_m>$ of effective embeddings is effective iff there exists a recursive function $q:N\to N$ s.t. $\pi_1 \bullet \pi_1 \bullet q(m)$ is a directed index of $f_m \in Comp([D_m^{\varepsilon}m \to D_{m+1}^{\varepsilon}m+1])$, $\pi_2 \bullet \pi_1 \bullet q(m)$ is a directed index of the adjoint g_m, and $\pi_2 \bullet q(m)$ is an acceptable index of $D_m^{\varepsilon}m$. ☒

Theorem 4.3 (The Inverse Limit Theorem)

Let $<D_m^{\varepsilon}m, f_m>$ be an effective sequence of effective embeddings of effectively given domains. Then $<D_\infty, \varepsilon_\infty>$ is an effectively given domain. Also $f_{m\infty}:D_m \to D_\infty$ is an effective embedding from ε_m to ε_∞. Therefore $f_{m\infty} \in Comp([D_m^{\varepsilon}m \to D_\infty^{\varepsilon}\infty])$ and $g_{\infty m} \in Comp([D_\infty^{\varepsilon}\infty \to D_m^{\varepsilon}m])$. Furthermore there exist recursive functions $\lambda_d, \delta_d:N\to N$ s.t. $\lambda_d(m)$ and $\delta_d(m)$ are directed indices of $f_{m\infty}$ and $g_{\infty m}$ respectively. ☒

To obtain further affirmitive evidence for the notion of effective isomorphisms, let us examine if it is invariant under the inverse limit construction. Notice that unlike previously studied domain constructors the inverse limit constructor works not only on domains but also on embeddings among them. Thus we need the following notion to be preserved under the inverse limit construction.

Definition 4.4 Given two effective sequences $<D_m^{\varepsilon}m, f_m>$ and $<D_m'^{\varepsilon'}m, f_m'>$ of effective embeddings, we say that they are effectively isomorphic (in symbols $<D_m^{\varepsilon}m, f_m> \overset{e}{\cong} <D_m'^{\varepsilon'}m, f_m'>$) iff there exist recursive functions $u,v:N\to N$ s.t. $u(m)$ is a recursive index of an effective isomorphism $i_m \in Comp([D_m^{\varepsilon}m \to D_m'^{\varepsilon'}m])$ and $v(m)$ is a recursive index of the adjoint $j_m \in Comp([D_m'^{\varepsilon'}m \to D_m^{\varepsilon}m])$; and $f_m' \bullet i_m = i_{m+1} \bullet f_m$, $g_m \bullet j_{m+1} = j_m \bullet g_m'$ where g_m and g_m' are the adjoints of f_m and f_m' respectively.

Theorem 4.5 Let $<D_m^{\varepsilon}m, f_m> \overset{e}{\cong} <D_m'^{\varepsilon'}m, f_m'>$ then $\varprojlim <D_m^{\varepsilon}m, f_m> \overset{e}{\cong} \varprojlim <D_m'^{\varepsilon'}m, f_m'>$. ☒

5. Effective Categories and Effective Functors

Smyth-Plotkin [9] proposed a theory of ω-catrgories and ω-functors which admits an initial solution to each recursive object equation $X = F(X)$ where F is an ω-functor, but without consideration of effectiveness. By showing that the category of cpo's and continuous embeddings is an ω-category where $\times, +, \to$ are ω-categories, they guranteed initial solution to each recrsive domain equation which involves these domain constructors. We will play an effective version of this game.

Definition 5.1 An E-category is a category $\underline{K}$ together with (possibly partial) object indexing κ, and a morphism indexing $\partial(K,K'):N\to Hom(K,K')$ for each pair (K,K') of objects, s.t. the composition of morphisms is effective, i.e. there is a recursive function ∂-compose s.t.:

$\partial(\kappa(i),\kappa(k))(\partial\text{-compose}(i,j,k,\ell,m)) = \partial(\kappa(j),\kappa(k))(m) \bullet \partial(\kappa(i),\kappa(j))(\ell)$.

Definition 5.2 (1) $\underline{\omega}$ is the category of non-negative integers and $\leq$, pictorially: $0 \leq 1 \leq 2 \leq$ ....

(2) An effective diagram in an E-category $(\underline{K}, \kappa, \partial)$ is a functor $G:\underline{\omega}\to\underline{K}$

s.t. $G(n)=\kappa(\pi_1 \bullet q(n))$ and $G(n \leq n+1)=\partial(G(n),G(n+1))(\pi_2 \bullet q(n))$ for some recursive function $q:N \to N$.

(3) Given an effective diagram G in an E-category $(\underline{K},\kappa,\partial)$, an <u>effective cone</u> of G is a cone $\langle\lambda_n : G(n) \to K\rangle$ of G s.t. $\lambda_n=\partial(G(n),K)(c(n))$ for some recursive function c.

(4) An effective diagram G in an E-category $(\underline{K},\kappa,\partial)$ has an <u>effective colimit</u>, in symbols ef-colim G, iff there exists an effective cone $\langle\delta_n : G(n) \to \text{ef-colim } G\rangle$ of G s.t. for every effective cone $\langle\lambda_n : G(n) \to K\rangle$ of G, there exists a unique morphism σ:ef-colim G→K s.t. the following diagram commutes:

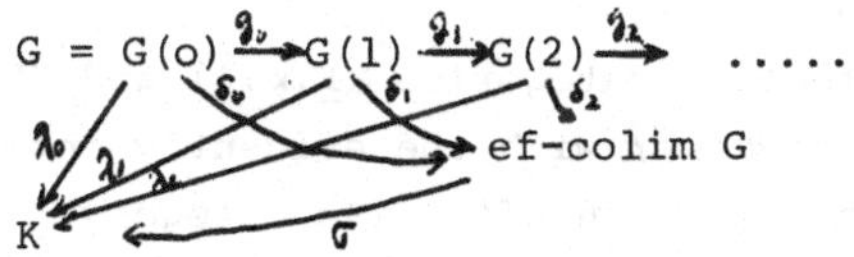

where $g_n=G(n \leq n+1)$.

$\langle\delta_n\rangle$ will be called an <u>effective colimiting cone</u>.

(5) An E-category is an <u>effective category</u> iff every effective diagram has an effective colimit.

<u>Definition 5.3</u> Given effective categories $(\underline{K},\kappa,\partial)$ and $(\underline{K}',\kappa',\partial')$ a functor $F:\underline{K} \to \underline{K}'$ is an effective functor iff it maps effectively on both objects and morphisms, and it preserves effective colimits and effective colimiting cones. More formally, iff there are recursive functions f_o and f_m s.t. $F(\kappa(n))=\kappa'(f_o(n))$ and $F(\partial(\kappa(i),\kappa(j))(n)=\partial(\kappa(\pi_1 \bullet \pi_1 \bullet f_m(n)), \kappa(\pi_2 \bullet \pi_1 \bullet f_m(n)))(\pi_2 \bullet f_m(n))$ and F preserves effective colimits and effective colimiting cones.

Let $(\underline{K},\kappa,\partial)$ be an effective category and $F:\underline{K} \to \underline{K}$ be an effective functor. For every $K \in \underline{K}$ and $\theta:K \to FK$, define an ω-diagram $\Delta_{(F,K,\theta)}:\underline{\omega} \to \underline{K}$ by $\Delta_{(F,K,\theta)}(n)=F^n(K)$ and $\Delta_{(F,K,\theta)}(n \leq n+1)=F^n(\theta)$. Evidently $\Delta=\Delta_{(F,K,\theta)}$ is an effective diagram. Let $\langle\delta_n : \Delta(n) \to \text{ef-colim}\Delta\rangle$ be an effective colimiting cone. Then by the effectiveness of F, $\langle F(\delta_n) : F(\Delta(n)) \to F(\text{ef-colim}\Delta)\rangle$ is an effective colimiling cone of $F \bullet \Delta$. Since $\langle\delta_n\rangle_{n \geq 1}$ is an effective cone of $F \bullet \Delta$, there exists a unique morphism $\rho:F(\text{ef-colim}\Delta) \to \text{ef-colim}\Delta$. Now define $\langle\lambda_n\rangle$ by $\lambda_n=F(\delta_{n+1})$ for $n \geq 1$ and $\lambda_o=F(\delta_o) \bullet \theta$. Then $\langle\lambda_n\rangle$ is an effective cone of Δ. Thus there is a unique morphism η:ef-colimΔ →F(ef-colimΔ). Therefore (ρ,η) is an isomorphism pair. In summary we have observed $F(\text{ef-colim}\Delta) \cong \text{ef-colim}\Delta$.

Given an effective category $(\underline{K},\kappa,\partial)$ and an effective functor $F:\underline{K} \to \underline{K}$ an <u>F_θ-algebra</u> is a triple (α,x,γ) s.t.:

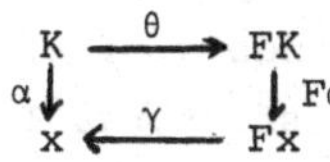

commutes.

An <u>F_θ-homomorphism</u> from an F_θ-algebra (α,x,γ) to an F_θ-algebra (α',x',γ') is an K-morphism $\pi:x \to x'$ s.t. the following diagram commutes:

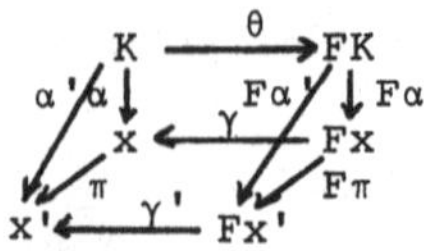

It can readily be seen that the class of all F_θ-algebras and the class of all F_θ-homomorphisms form a category, which we will denote by AF_θ.

Theorem 5.4 Let $(\underline{K},\kappa,\partial)$ be an effective category and $F:\underline{K}\to\underline{K}$ be an effective functor. Let $\theta\in Hom(K,FK)$ and $<\delta_n>$ be the effective colimiting cone of $\Delta_{(F,K,\theta)}$. Then $(\delta_o, \text{ef-colim}\Delta, \rho)$ is an initial object in the category AF_θ, where ρ is as above. ∅

Lemma 5.5 Given two effective categories $(\underline{K},\kappa,\partial)$ and $(\underline{K}',\kappa',\partial')$, the product category $\underline{K}\times\underline{K}'$ together with the evidently induced objects indexing and morphism indexing is an effective category. ∅

Lemma 5.6 Let $(\underline{K},\kappa,\partial)$, (K',κ',∂'), $(K'',\kappa'',\partial'')$ be effective categories. A bi-functor $F:\underline{K}\times\underline{K}'\to\underline{K}''$ is effective iff it is effective in both $\underline{K}$ and $\underline{K}'$.

Lemma 5.7 The composition of two effective functors is an effective functor. ∅

Theorem 5.8 The category of effectively given domains and effective embeddings together with $\overline{\xi}$ as an object indexing and the recursive (or deirected) indexing as a morphism indexing is an effective category. The effective diagrams are effective sequences and effective colimits are the inverse limits of effective sequences. We will denote this category by ED^E without explicitly mentioning the indexings. ∅

Definition 5.9 The arrow functor $\to:ED^E \times ED^E \to ED^E$ is defined on objects by $\to(D^\varepsilon, D'^{\varepsilon'})=[D^\varepsilon\to D'^{\varepsilon'}]$, and on morphisms by $\to(p:D_1\to D_2, q:D_1'\to D_2')=\lambda f.q\bullet f\bullet p'$ where p' is the adjoint of p. We can similarly define product functor and sum functor from the domain constructors × and +. □

Theorem 5.1o The arrow functor , product functor , and sum functor are effective functors. ∅

Notice that 1.6 coincides with 5.1o. In fact 1.6 is a part of a proof of this theorem.

In summary we have guranteed initial solutions, which are effectively given domains, to recursive domain equations. In fact these solutions are up to effective isomorphisms. This is very satisfactory for we have observed that we should identify two effectively given domains iff they are effectively isomorphic.

Notice that a theory of effective categories developed here is not unconditionally satisfactory. In fact the abstract notion of effective categories does not include effectiveness (or acceptability) constraint to the object indexing. There seems to be no easy way to axiomatize this effectiveness. A fundamentally different approach for defining more appropriate notion of effective categories which does not have this problem is currently being developed by Smyth.

There are more examples of effective categories (in our sense).

Theorem 5.11 (1) Let D^{ε} be an effectively given domain. Comp(D^{ε}) together withthe directed indexing as an object indexing and the evident mor morphism indexing is an effective category.

(2) Let D^{ε} and $D'^{\varepsilon'}$ be effectively given domains. Every computable function $f \in$ Comp$([D^{\varepsilon} \to D'^{\varepsilon'}])$ restricted to Comp(D^{ε}) is an effective functor.

This indicate that Comp(D^{ε}) is more substeitial than D^{ε}, and suggests a theory of effective domains (see Kanda [2]). Furthermore we can show that the category of effectively given SFP objects (and effective embeddings), the category of effective domains, and the category of effective SFP are effective categories where $\times, +, \to$ are effective functors. Thus we can solve recursive domain equations within these categories up to effective isomorphisms. Details of these results will appear elsewhere.

ACKNOWLEDGEMENT We are very grateful to M.B.Smyth and M.Paterson for helpful suggestions and discussions. Especially M.B.Smyth indicated to us that the effectiveness of object functions is missing in Kanda's preliminary report [2] on effective categories. This point is amended in this paper. The first auther was supported by the SRC grant GR/A66 772 under the direction of M.B.Smyth.

REFERENCES

[1] Egli-Constable, Computability concepts for programming language semantics, Theoritical Computer Science, Vol.2 (1976).

[2] Kanda. A, Data types as effective objects, Theory of Computation Report No.22, Warwick University, (1977).

[3] Markowsky-Rosen, Bases for chain complete posets, IBM Journal of Research and Development, Vol.2o, No.2, (1979).

[4] Plotkin. G, A power domain construction, SIAM Journal on Computing, Vol.5, (1976).

[5] Rogers. H, Theory of recursive functions and effective computability, McGraw Hill, New York, (1967).

[6] Tang. A, Recrusion theory and descriptive set theory in effectively given T_o-spaces, Ph.D. theesis, Princeton Univ. (1974).

[7] Scott. D, Outline of the mathematical theory of computation, Proc. of the 4th Princeton Conference on Information Science,(197o).

[8] Smyth. M, Effectively given domains, Theoretical Computer Science, Vol. 5 (1977).

[9] Smyth-Plotkin, The categorical solution of recursive domain equations, Proc. of the 18th IEEE FOCS Conference, (1977).

SUR DEUX LANGAGES LINÉAIRES

M. Latteux

Abstract.

First, we prove that if the language Sym = $\{w\bar{w}^R / w \in \{a,b\}^*\}$ *belongs to* $F_\sigma(L)$, *the smallest substitution closed full AFL generated by the family* L, *then there exists a language* $L \in L$ *such that* $Sym \in C(L)$. *We prove that this property does not hold for* $C_1 = \{a^n b^n / n \geq 0\}$, *by characterizing the languages* $L \subseteq C_1$ *such that* $C_1 \in C(L)$.

INTRODUCTION

Un des travaux, dans la théorie des familles agréables de langages (FAL), est de comparer différentes familles de langages. En particulier, on rencontre souvent le problème de la non-appartenance d'un langage L à une famille L. Ce problème est rarement simple. Dans le cas où L est égal à $F(L') = \text{Rat} \,\square\, L'$ (resp. $F_\sigma(L')$), la plus petite FAL (resp. FAL close par substitution) engendrée par un cône rationnel L' strictement inclus dans L, on peut décomposer le problème en montrant d'abord que L n'appartient pas à L', mais il reste ensuite à passer de L' à L. Ainsi, il est relativement simple de montrer que $\bar{D}_1^*$, le complémentaire du langage de Dyck sur une lettre, n'appartient pas à Lin, la famille des langages algébriques linéaires, par contre, il semble beaucoup plus difficile d'écrire la preuve que $\bar{D}_1^* \notin F_\sigma(\text{Lin})$, la famille des langages quasi-rationnels. On peut, aussi, raisonner, dans l'ordre inverse et commencer par déduire de l'appartenance supposée de L à L, l'existence, dans L', d'un langage "assez proche" de L. Un tel exemple est donné dans [12] où il est montré que pour tout cône rationnel L clos par union, $D_1^* \in F(L)$ si et seulement si il existe un langage $L \in L$ tel que $D'^*_1 \subseteq L \subseteq D_1^*$, où D'^*_1 désigne le langage de semi-Dyck sur une lettre. De ce point de vue certains langages ont des propriétés intéressantes. Ainsi, pour tout cône rationnel clos par union L, un CIL-langage $L \in F(L)$ implique $L \in L$ (cf.[11]) et un langage sans insertion $L' \in F_\sigma(L)$ implique $L' \in L$ (cf [13]). Dans [9], Greibach a montré que pour tout cône rationnel L et tout générateur L d'un cône rationnel clos par substitution, $L \in F_\sigma(L)$ implique, aussi, $L \in L$.

Dans la première section, nous allons montrer que cette propriété est vérifiée pour les générateurs de la famille, notée Lin, des langages algébriques linéaires.

Dans la section 2, pour établir que $C_1 = \{a^n b^n / n \in 0\}$ ne vérifie pas cette propriété, nous caractérisons les langages inclus dans C_1 qui dominent rationnellement C_1 : $C_1 \in C(L)$ avec $L = \{a^n b^n / n \in A\}$ si et seulement si il existe un ensemble fini $F \subseteq \mathbb{N}$ tel que $\mathbb{N} = FA + F = \{in+j \ / \ i, j \in F, n \in A\}$.

Enfin, dans la dernière section, nous établissons un résultat qui fait intervenir les complémentaires et les transductions rationnelles (proposition 11). Nous en déduisons une caractérisation des langages $L \subseteq C_1$ tels que $L' = a^*b^* \backslash L$ domine rationnellement $L_{\neq} = \{a^n b^p / n \neq p\}$: $L_{\neq} \in C(L')$ si et seulement si L contient un langage algébrique infini. Nous terminons en tirant d'autres conséquences de la proposition 11. En particulier, tout langage algébrique borné appartenant à $C(L)$ avec $L \subseteq a^*$ est rationnel (corollaire 13).

PRÉLIMINAIRES

Notons $\mathbb{N}$, l'ensemble des entiers naturels et posons $\mathbb{N}_+ = \mathbb{N} \setminus \{0\}$. Si A et B sont des parties de $\mathbb{N}$, posons $A + B = \{a+b / a \in A, b \in B\}$ et $AB = \{ab / a \in A, b \in B\}$. Pour $k \in \mathbb{N}_+$, une partie S de $\mathbb{N}^k$ est un ensemble *linéaire* s'il existe $x_o, x_1, \ldots, x_n \in \mathbb{N}$ tels que $S = \{x_o + \sum_{i=1}^{n} \lambda_i x_i \ / \ \lambda_i \in \mathbb{N}\}$. Une partie S de $\mathbb{N}^k$ est un *semi-linéaire* si S est une union finie d'ensembles linéaires inclus dans $\mathbb{N}^k$.

A tout alphabet ordonné $T = \{a_1, \ldots, a_k\}$, on peut faire correspondre une *fonction de Parikh*, notée Ψ_T ou Ψ s'il n'y a pas d'ambiguité, définie sur T^* par : $\forall w \in T^*$, $\Psi(w) = (\ell_{a_1}(w), \ldots, \ell_{a_k}(w)) \in \mathbb{N}^k$ où $\ell_{a_i}(w)$ désigne le nombre d'occurrences de la lettre a_i dans le mot w.

Un langage $L \subseteq T^*$ est un *PSL-langage* si $\Psi(L)$ est un semi-linéaire.

Pour tout ce qui concerne les traductions rationnelles, nous renvoyons le lecteur au livre de Berstel [3]. Précisons, cependant, quelques notations :

pour toute famille de langage $\mathcal{L}$, notons $C(\mathcal{L})$ (resp. $C_U(\mathcal{L})$), le plus petit cône rationnel (resp. le plus petit cône rationnel clos par union) contenant $\mathcal{L}$. Nous dirons qu'un langage L_1 *domine rationnellement* un langage L_2 si $L_2 \in C(L_1)$ (nous convenons d'écrire $C(L_1)$ à la place de $C(\{L_1\})$). Les langages L_1 et L_2 sont *rationnellement équivalents* si $C(L_1) = C(L_2)$. Une substitution s définie sur un alphabet T est une *$\mathcal{L}$-substitution* si $\forall a \in T$, s(a) est un langage de la famille $\mathcal{L}$. Nous poserons :

$$\mathcal{L}_1 \square \mathcal{L}_2 = \{s(L) \ / \ L \in \mathcal{L}_1, \text{ s est une } \mathcal{L}_2\text{-substitution}\}.$$

Si $\mathcal{L}_1$ est un cône rationnel, $F(\mathcal{L}_1) = \text{Rat} \square \mathcal{L}_1$ désigne la plus petite FAL contenant $\mathcal{L}_1$, c'est à dire le plus petit cône rationnel clos par union, produit et étoile. De même $F_\sigma(\mathcal{L}_1) = \bigcup_{i \geq 1} \mathcal{L}_i$, avec $\forall i \in \mathbb{N}_+$, $\mathcal{L}_{i+1} = \mathcal{L}_i \square \mathcal{L}_1$, désignera le plus petit cône rationnel clos par substitution contenant $\mathcal{L}_1$.

I - LE LANGAGE $Sym = \{w\bar{w}^R \,/\, w \in \{a,b\}^*\}$

Le but de cette section est d'établir pour la famille des langages algébriques linéaires, notée Lin, une propriété vérifiée par tout cône rationnel principal clos par substitution (cf. [9]), à savoir le résultat suivant :

<u>*Proposition 1*</u>. *Pour toute famille de langages $\mathcal{L}$ telle que Lin $\subseteq F_\sigma(\mathcal{L})$, il existe un langage $L \in \mathcal{L}$ vérifiant Lin $\subseteq C(L)$.*

La démonstration de cette proposition repose sur deux lemmes. Dans [10], Greibach montre que si L_1 et L_2 sont des langages algébriques linéaires vérifiant $L_1 \cup L_2 = L = \{w c \tilde{w}^R \,/\, w \in \{a,b\}^*\}$, alors L appartient à $C(L_1)$. En fait, l'hypothèse de linéarité des langages L_1 et L_2 n'est pas utile. Plus généralement, on peut montrer :

<u>*Lemme 2*</u> : *Soient L_1 et L_2 deux langages tels que $C(L_1 \cup L_2)$ contienne Lin la famille des langages algébriques linéaires. Alors, soit Lin $\subseteq C(L_1)$, soit Lin $\subseteq C(L_2)$.*

Le lemme suivant étend un résultat de Beauquier qui établit dans [2] que si L_1 et L_2 sont des langages algébriques qui ne dominent pas rationnellement Sym, alors Sym n'appartient pas à $C(L_1) \square C(L_2)$. En utilisant une démonstration tout à fait différente, nous montrons que l'hypothèse d'algébricité est inutile :

<u>*Lemme 3*</u> : *Soient $\mathcal{L}_1$ et $\mathcal{L}_2$ deux cônes rationnels clos par union tels que $\mathcal{L}_1 \square \mathcal{L}_2$ contienne la famille Lin. Alors, soit Lin $\subseteq \mathcal{L}_1$, soit Lin $\subseteq \mathcal{L}_2$.*

Considérons, maintenant, une famille de langages $\mathcal{L}$ telle que $\mathcal{L}in \subseteq F_\sigma(\mathcal{L})$, posons $\mathcal{L}'_1 = C_\cup(\mathcal{L}) = \mathcal{L}'$ et définissons pour tout $i \in \mathbb{N}_+$, $\mathcal{L}'_i$ par la relation $\mathcal{L}'_{i+1} = \mathcal{L}'_i \square \mathcal{L}'$. Pour tout $i \in \mathbb{N}_+$, $\mathcal{L}'_i$ est un cône rationnel clos par union et comme $Sym \in F_\sigma(\mathcal{L}) = \bigcup_{i \geq 1} \mathcal{L}'_i$, il existe i tel que $Sym \in \mathcal{L}'_i$ et $\mathcal{L}in \subseteq \mathcal{L}'_i$. Le lemme précédent entraine, alors, par induction $\mathcal{L}in \subseteq \mathcal{L}'$.

Alors $Sym \in \mathcal{L}' = C_\cup(\mathcal{L})$ et il existe des langages $L_1,\dots,L_n \in \mathcal{L}$ tels que $Sym \in C_\cup(\{L_1,\dots,L_n\})$, donc $\mathcal{L}in \subseteq C(\bar{L}_1 \cup \dots \cup \bar{L}_n)$ où pour tout $i \in \{1,\dots,n\}$, $\bar{L}_i$ est une recopie de L_i sur un alphabet disjoint des autres. Alors, le lemme 2 permet de montrer par induction qu'il existe $i \in \{1,\dots,n\}$ tel que Lin $\subseteq C(\bar{L}_i) = C(L_i)$ avec $L_i \in \mathcal{L}$ ce qui achève la démonstration de la proposition 1.□

Cette proposition peut s'écrire autrement :

<u>*Corollaire 4*</u> : *La famille Ext(Lin) = $\{L \,/\, \text{Lin} \not\subseteq C(L)\}$ est une FAL close par substitution.*

Si nous nous restreignons aux langages appartenant à $\mathcal{L}in$ nous retrouvons une propriété que l'on peut aussi montrer pour tout cône rationnel principal clos par produit :

Corollaire 5 [10] : *La famille* Ng *(Lin)* = *Lin* ∩ *Ext(Lin) est un cône rationnel clos par union.*

II - LE LANGAGE $C_1 = \{a^n b^n \ / \ n \geq 0\}$

Ginsburg et Spanier ont montré dans [6] que le langage C_1 n'était pas premier, c'est à dire que le lemme 2 n'était plus valable si l'on remplaçait Sym par C_1. Nous allons, maintenant, caractériser les langages inclus dans C_1 qui dominent rationnellement C_1. Cette caractérisation va nous permettre de retrouver immédiatement le résultat de Ginsburg et Spanier et d'établir que le lemme 3 n'est pas non plus vérifié si l'on remplace Sym par C_1.

Proposition 6. Soient A *une partie de* $\mathbb{N}$ *et* L_A, *le langage* $\{a^n b^n / n \in A\}$. *Alors*, L_A *domine rationnellement* C_1 *si et seulement s'il existe une partie finie* F *de* $\mathbb{N}$ *telle que* $FA + F = \mathbb{N}$.

Pour tout $i,j \in \mathbb{N}$, il est clair que L_A domine rationnellement $L = \{a^n b^n / n = ip+j, p \in A\}$. Donc s'il existe un ensemble fini F tel que $\mathbb{N} = \{ip+j / i,j \in F, p \in A\}$, $C_1 \in C(L_A)$.

Pour démontrer la réciproque, nous utilisons la décomposition des transductions rationnelles en bimorphismes alphabétiques (cf. [14]), ainsi que le lemme 7 qui nécessite quelques définitions :

soient $q \in \mathbb{N}_+$ et $p \in \mathbb{N}$. Le résultat de la division entière de p par q sera noté $[p/q]$ et pour tout $A \subseteq \mathbb{N}$, $[A/q] = \{[p/q] \ / \ p \in A\}$. Nous dirons que A est *proche* de B, s'il existe $k \in \mathbb{N}$ tel que $\forall x \in A, \exists y \in B, |x-y| \leq k$ et que A est *dense* si $\mathbb{N}$ est proche de A.

Prenons $q \in \mathbb{N}_+$, $A \subseteq \mathbb{N}$. Il est facile de vérifier :

Propriété A : si A est dense et $0 \in A$, il existe un ensemble fini $G \subseteq \mathbb{N}$ tel que $A+G = \mathbb{N}$.

Propriété B : $[A/q]$ dense implique A dense.

Propriété C : si $G \subseteq \mathbb{N}$ est fini, $[A/q]\,G$ est proche de $[AG/q]$.

Propriété D : pour $q, q' \in \mathbb{N}_+$ et $p \in \mathbb{N}$, $[A/q]\,p$ est proche de $[A/qq']\,pq'$.

Nous pouvons, alors, établir :

Lemme 7 : Si $\mathbb{N}$ *est union finie d'ensembles de la forme* $\{r'+jr/j \in \mathbb{N}, k'+jk \in A\}$ *avec* $k \in \mathbb{N}_+$, $r', k', r \in \mathbb{N}$, *il existe un ensemble fini* $F \subseteq \mathbb{N}$ *tel que* $\mathbb{N} = AF+F$.

Pour $A \subseteq \mathbb{N}$ et $n \in \mathbb{N}_+$, notons A_n l'ensemble $\{i \in A \;/\; i \leq n\}$ et $d_n(A) = |A_n| \;/\; n$. De la proposition 6, on peut déduire :

Corollaire 8 : Si $L_A = \{a^n b^n / n \in A\}$ *domine rationnellement* C_1, *il existe* $k \in \mathbb{N}_+$ *tel que* $k\, d_n(A) \geq 1$, $\forall n \geq k$.

En particulier, si $\lim_{n\to\infty} d_n(A) = 0$, le langage L_A ne domine pas rationnellement C_1. C'est le cas pour le langage Car $= \{a^{n^2} b^{n^2} / n \geq 0\}$. Remarquons, d'autre part, que $\lim_{n\to\infty} d_n(A) = 1$ n'implique pas que L_A domine rationnellement C_1. Considérons, en effet, l'ensemble $B = \{j \in \mathbb{N} \;/\; \exists k \in \mathbb{N}_+,\ \exists i \in \{1,\ldots,k\},\ k! \leq i\, j < k! + k\}$. Alors, le langage L_A avec $A = \mathbb{N}\setminus B$ vérifie : $\lim_{n\to\infty} d_n(A) = 1$ et pour tout $t \in \mathbb{N}_+$, $\{0,\ldots,t\}\, A + \{0,\ldots,t\} \neq \mathbb{N}$, ce qui entraine, d'après la proposition 6, que L_1 ne domine pas rationnellement C_1.

Considérons, maintenant, les ensembles $A = \{n / (2m)! \leq n < (2m+1)!,\ m \in \mathbb{N}_+\}$, $B = \{n/(2m+1)! \leq n < (2m+2)!,\ m \in \mathbb{N}\}$ (cf. [6]). Pour tout $m \in \mathbb{N}_+$, $|A_{(2m)!}| \leq (2m-1)!$, donc $\lim_{m\to\infty} d_{(2m)!}(A) = 0$ et le corollaire 8 entraine que C_1 n'appartient pas à $\mathcal{C}(L_A)$. De même L_B ne domine pas rationnellement C_1 et le cône rationnel $\mathcal{L} = \mathcal{C}(\{L_A, L_B\})$ ne contient pas C_1. Par contre $C_1 = L_A \cup L_B \in \mathcal{C}_\cup(\mathcal{L})$ et nous retrouvons :

Corollaire 9 [6] : *Il existe un cône rationnel* $\mathcal{L}$ *tel que* $C_1 \notin \mathcal{L}$ *et* $C_1 \in \mathcal{C}_\cup(\mathcal{L})$.

Comme C_1 est un CIL-langage, pour tout langage L, $C_1 \in \mathcal{F}(L)$ si et seulement si $C_1 \in \mathcal{C}(L)$ (cf. [11]). Par contre, ce résultat n'est plus vérifié si nous remplaçons $\mathcal{F}(L)$ par $\mathcal{F}_\sigma(\mathcal{L})$. En effet d'après le corollaire 8, le langage Car $= \{a^{n^2} b^{n^2} / n \geq 0\}$ ne domine pas rationnellement le langage C_1. Par contre, comme tout élément de $\mathbb{N}$ est la somme de quatre carrés, il est facile de vérifier que l'on peut passer de Car à C_1 par insertions et $C_1 \in \mathcal{F}_\sigma(\text{Car})$, donc :

Proposition 10. Il existe un langage L *tel que* $C_1 \notin \mathcal{F}(L)$ *et* $C_1 \in \mathcal{F}_\sigma(L)$.

III - TRANSDUCTION RATIONNELLE ET COMPLÉMENTAIRE

Soient un langage L inclus dans C_1 et $L_{\neq} = a^*b^* \setminus C_1$. On peut se poser la question de savoir quelle est la relation entre les deux propriétés, $C_1 \in \mathcal{C}(L)$ et $L_{\neq} \in \mathcal{C}(a^*b^* \setminus L)$. Pour y répondre, nous allons établir un résultat dont nous montrerons ensuite d'autres utilités.

Prenons un langage $L \subseteq X^*$ et une transduction rationnelle τ de X^* dans Y^*. Posons $L' = \tau(L)$, $\bar{L} = X^* \setminus L$ et $\bar{L}' = Y^* \setminus L'$. Considérons le langage $L'' = \tau^{-1}(\bar{L}')$ où τ^{-1} est la transduction inverse de τ (définie par : $\forall y \in Y^*$, $\tau^{-1}(y) = \{x \in X^* \;/\; y \in \tau(x)\}$). On peut vérifier que L" est inclus dans $\bar{L}$ et que $L' = \tau(X^* \setminus L'')$. Comme, pour tout langage rationnel R contenant L, $L_1 = L \cup (X^* \setminus R)$ est rationnellement équivalent à L et que

$\bar{L}_1 = R \setminus L$, on obtient :

Proposition 11. Soient R *un langage rationnel et* L, L' *deux langages tels que* $L \subseteq R$ *et* $L' \in C(L)$. *Alors, il existe* $L'' \subseteq R \setminus L$ *vérifiant :* $L'' \in C(\bar{L}')$ *et* $L' \in C(\bar{L}'')$.

Prenons alors, un langage $L_A \subseteq C_1$ et posons $L = a^*b^* \setminus L_A$. Si $L_{\neq} \in C(L)$, la proposition précédente implique que $L_A = a^*b^* \setminus L$ contient un langage infini appartenant à $C(\bar{L}_{\neq}) = C(C_1) \subseteq \mathrm{Alg}$, la famille des langages algébriques (context-free). Réciproquement si L_A contient un langage algébrique infini L_B, il existe $p \in \mathbb{N}$, $q \in \mathbb{N}_+$ tels que $p+q\,\mathbb{N} \subseteq A$. Donc $L \cap a^p(a^q)^*\, b^p(b^q)^*$ est égal à $L_{\neq} \cap a^p(a^q)^*\, b^p(b^q)^*$ qui est, clairement rationnellement équivalent à $L_{\neq}$, ce qui entraine $L_{\neq} \in C(L)$ et nous pouvons énoncer :

Proposition 12. Soit L_A *un langage inclus dans* C_1. *Le langage* $a^*b^* \setminus L_A$ *domine rationnellement* $L_{\neq} = a^*b^* \setminus C_1$ *si et seulement si* L_A *contient un langage algébrique infini.*

Il est donc clair d'après les propositions 6 et 12 que, pour tout langage $L_A \subseteq C_1$, $L_{\neq} \in C(a^*b^* \setminus L_A)$ implique $L_A \in C(C_1)$. Par contre, la réciproque est fausse. Prenons, en effet, $A = \{n \ / \ 2^{2p+1} \leq n \leq 2^{2p+2},\ p \in \mathbb{N}\}$. Comme $\mathbb{N} = FA + F$ avec $F = \{0,1,2\}$, la proposition 6 entraine que $C_1 \in C(L_A)$. Il est facile de vérifier que L_A ne contient aucun langage algébrique infini puisque $\{a^n \ / \ n \in A\}$ ne contient aucun facteur itérant. La proposition précédente implique, alors, que $L_{\neq}$ n'appartient pas à $C(a^*b^* \setminus L_A)$.

Terminons, en montrant que la proposition 11 permet d'obtenir d'autres résultats. Dans [5], Duriéux démontre que tout langage algébrique inclus dans a^*b^* dominé rationnellement par un langage $L \subseteq a^*$ est rationnel. Montrons que cette propriété reste vérifiée pour tout langage algébrique borné. Supposons, en effet, que $C(L)$ contienne un langage non rationnel $L' \subseteq w_1^* \dots w_p^*$. Alors $C(\bar{L}') = C(w_1^* \dots w_p^* \setminus L')$ est un PSL-cône rationnel, c'est à dire ne contient que des PSL-langages et donc ne peut pas contenir de langages non rationnels inclus dans a^*, ce qui contredit la proposition 11 et nous obtenons :

Corollaire 13 : Tout langage algébrique borné appartenant au cône rationnel engendré par un langage inclus dans a^* *est rationnel.*

Comme la famille des langages algébriques déterministes est close par complémentation, le même raisonnement permet d'établir :

Corollaire 14 : Tout langage algébrique déterministe appartenant au cône rationnel engendré par un langage inclus dans a^* *est rationnel.*

Malheureusement, la proposition 11 ne semble pas assez puissante pour se passer, dans les corollaires précédents, de l'hypothèse borné ou déterministe, en établissant :

Conjecture : *Tout langage algébrique* $L' \in C(L)$ *avec* $L \subseteq a^*$ *est rationnel.*

Considérons, maintenant, le langage de Goldstine, $L_G = \{a^{j_0}ca^{j_1}\ldots ca^{j_t}/t\geq 0,\ \exists i\neq j_i\}$. L'intérêt de l'étude de ce langage algébrique provient de la possible minimalité de son cône (cf. [1]). Le langage $\bar{L}_G = \{caca^2c \ldots ca^k \ /\ k \geq 0\}$ est rationnellement équivalent à Init $(\bar{L}_G) = \{x\ /\ \exists y,\ xy \in \bar{L}_G\}$. Pour tout langage infini L inclus dans $\bar{L}_G$, Init (L) = Init $(\bar{L}_G)$ et donc $\bar{L}_G \in C(L)$. La proposition 11 entraine, alors :

Corollaire 15 : Si L_G *domine rationnellement un langage non rationnel* L, $\bar{L}_G$ *appartient à* $C(\bar{L})$.

Remarquons que ce résultat reste vrai si on remplace L_G par le complémentaire du langage d'un mot infini (cf. [13]).

Supposons, maintenant, que L_G domine rationnellement un langage borné L. Comme L_G est un langage algébrique, $C(\bar{L})$ est un PSL-cône rationnel et ne peut donc pas contenir $\bar{L}_G$ et la proposition 11 permet de retrouver une propriété démontrée, en premier lieu, par Goldstine :

Corollaire 16 [7] : *Tout langage borné appartenant à* $C(L_G)$ *est rationnel.*

Enfin, considérons les langages $L_{\neq}^{(k)} = \{a_1^{n_1} \ldots a_k^{n_k}\ /\ \exists i < k,\ n_i \neq n_{i+1}\}$ pour $k \geq 2$. Si $L_{\neq}^{(k)}$ domine rationnellement un langage non rationnel $L \subseteq a_1^* \ldots a_{k-1}^*$, il existe, d'après la proposition 11, un langage infini inclus dans $E_k = \{a_1^n \ldots a_k^n/n \geq 0\}$ appartenant à $C(\bar{L})$, ce qui est impossible (cf. [8], [13]). Il est, alors, facile d'en déduire :

Corollaire 17 : Tout langage inclus dans $a_1^* \ldots a_{k-1}^*$ *appartenant à* $F_\sigma(L_{\neq}^{(k)})$ *est rationnel.*

En particulier, nous retrouvons un résultat de Berstel et Boasson [4] qui ont montré que les FAL $F(L_{\neq}^{(k)})$ formaient une hiérarchie infinie décroissante.

*

* *

RÉFÉRENCES

1. J.M. Autebert, J. Beauquier et L. Boasson, "Contribution à l'étude des cônes minimaux", C.R. Acad. Sc. 287 (1978), 353-355.

2. J. Beauquier, "Substitutions de langages linéaires et à compteur", 1978, soumis à J. Comp. Syst. Sc. .

3. J. Berstel, "Transductions and Context-free languages", Teubner Verlag, 1979.

4. J. Berstel et L. Boasson, "Une suite décroissante de cônes rationnels", in Loeckx (Ed.), Automata, languages and programming, 2nd Colloquium, Saarbrücken, Springer Verlag (1974), 383-397.

5. J.L. Durieux, "Sur l'image, par une transduction rationnelle, des mots sur une lettre", RAIRO Informatique Théorique (1975), 25-37.

6. S. Ginsburg et E.H. Spanier, "On incomparable abstract families of languages (AFL)", J. Comp. Syst. Sc. 9 (1974), 88-108.

7. J. Goldstine, "Substitution and bounded languages", J. Comp. Syst. Sc. 6 (1972), 9-29.

8. J. Goldstine, "Bounded AFL's", J. Comp. Syst. Sc. 12 (1976), 399-419.

9. S. Greibach, "Chains of full AFL's", Math. Syst. Theory 4 (1970), 231-242.

10. S. Greibach, "Simple Syntactic Operators on full semi-AFL's", J. Comp. Syst. Sc. 6 (1972), 30-76.

11. M. Latteux, "Cônes rationnels commutativement clos", RAIRO Informatique Théorique 11 (1977), 29-51.

12. M. Latteux, "Cônes rationnels commutatifs", 1977, à paraître dans J. Comp. Syst. Sc.

13. M. Latteux, "Langages commutatifs", Thèse de Doctorat d'Etat, Université de Lille I, 1978.

14. M. Nivat, "Transductions des langages de Chomsky", Annales de l'Institut Fourier 18 (1968), 339-456.

AN EFFICIENT ON-LINE POSITION TREE CONSTRUCTION ALGORITHM

M. Majster
A. Reiser

0. INTRODUCTION

Text-editing systems, symbol manipulation problems as well as a number of other computer applications often require a search function which locates instances of a given string within a larger main string (P1). In some applications all positions, in others the leftmost position have to be found. Other pattern matching problems are to search consecutively or simultaneously for pattern strings $p_1, \dots p_k$ within a given main string s (P2), to find the longest repeated substring of the main string s (P3), the internal matching problem, i.e. to find for each position i in $s = s_1 \dots s_n$ another position j in s such that the common prefix of $s_i s_{i+1} \dots s_n$ and $s_j s_{j+1} \dots s_n$ is not shorter than the longest common prefix of $s_i \dots s_n$ and $s_k \dots s_n$, $k \neq i$, $k \neq j$ (P4). For the external matching problem (P5) we consider two strings $s = s_1 \dots s_n$ and $s' = s'_1 \dots s'_m$ and a position i in s and search for a position j in s' such that the longest common prefix of $s_i \dots s_n$ and $s'_j \dots s'_m$ is not shorter than the longest common prefix of $s_i \dots s_n$ and $s'_k \dots s'_m$, $k \neq j$. Another problem is concerned with finding the longest common substring of two strings s and s' (P6).

A naive algorithm for the solution of problem P1, where all possible alignments are tried successively takes $O(n \cdot m)$ steps, where n is the length of the main string and m the length of the pattern. In 1970 [KPM] showed how to solve P1 in time proportional to $(n+m)$. If we consider the problem to search for the patterns $p_1, \dots p_k$ consecutively in the same string s the above algorithm would take

$O(k\cdot|s| + |p_1| + \ldots |p_k|)$. The wish to give a better solution of this problem and to solve the problems P3, P4, P5, P6 efficiently led in [W] to the development of an auxiliary data structure, the prefix tree, storing information about the main string. The prefix tree is called position tree in [AHU] . For space considerations one usually constructs a compacted version of the tree which can be done in $O(|s|)$ steps. Given the position tree, a single search for a pattern e.g. costs time linear in the length of the pattern.

At this point it is now important to note that the position tree construction algorithm processes the main string s from right to left. This feature presupposes that the whole text must be known before we can start to build the position tree. Similarly, another solution for the pattern matching problems P1, P2 [CC] presupposes that at least the length of the main string and the set of patterns are known in advance.

If we have to wait with the construction of the position tree until the whole main string is known we must face some considerable drawbacks: D1) It is not possible to answer pattern matching problems and perform corrections, if necessary, for that part of the main string which has been already read in. This is particularly annoying if we consider for example a text editing system where pattern matching is used to find those positions in the text which have to be corrected. Here, one should like to process that part of the string which is already known. In a typical text editing system with a usually small computer dedicated to the text editing job we must face further considerable drawbacks, namely D2) the processing unit keeps waiting until the input device has scanned the last symbol of the input, D3) as the main store will be usually too small a considerable part of the text has to be transported onto secondary storage until it is going to be processed. The position tree construction algorithm of [W] constructs the position tree for $s_i \ldots s_n$ from the position tree for $s_{i+1} \ldots s_n$. As this position tree will be too large to be kept in main store we have to transfer it onto secondary storage. For the construction of the tree for $s_i \ldots s_n$ we have to process the tree for $s_{i+1} \ldots s_n$ from the root downwards in a part of the tree which cannot be predicted before the letter s_i is known. Hence, we have the problem D4) of transferring considerable amounts of data between secondary and main storage for each letter of the main string.

Hence, we are looking for a possibility to construct the position tree, respectively the compacted position tree in an on-line way. Moreover, we are interested in answering pattern matching questions and in the possibility of "updating" or "correction" of that part of the string which has been already read. And at last, we want to get rid of problem D4).

I. PRELIMINARIES

In this paper we will use the following notations. An *alphabet* Σ is a finite set of symbols. A *string* over an alphabet Σ is a finite-length sequence of symbols from Σ. The empty string denoted by ϵ, is the string with no symbols. If x and y are strings, then the *concatenation* of x and y is the string xy. If xyz is a string, then x is a *prefix*, y a *substring* and z is a *suffix* of xyz. The *length* of a string x, denoted by $|x|$ is the number of symbols in x.

A *position* in a string of length n is an integer between 1 and n. The symbol $a \in \Sigma$ *occurs* in position i of string x if $x = yaz$ with $|y| = i-1$. Let $\$ \notin \Sigma$.

A *position identifier* for position i in $x\$$ is the shortest substring u of $x\$$ such that

i) $x\$ = yuz$ $\quad |y| = i-1$
ii) if $x\$ = y'uz'$ then $y = y'$, $z = z'$

A Σ-tree is a labeled tree T such that for each node n in T the edges leaving n have distinct labels in Σ. If the edge (n,m) in T is labeled by a, we call m the a-son of n.

A *position tree* for a string $x\$ = a_1 \ldots a_{n+1}$ where $a_i \in \Sigma$, $1 \le i \le n$, is a $(\Sigma \cup \{\$\})$ - tree such that

i) T has $n+1$ leaves labeled $1, \ldots, n+1$. The leaves of T are in one-to-one correspondance with the positions in $x\$$.

ii) The sequence of labels of edges on the path from the root to the leaf labeled i is the position identifier for position i.

Example.
The position tree for the string abba$ is given by

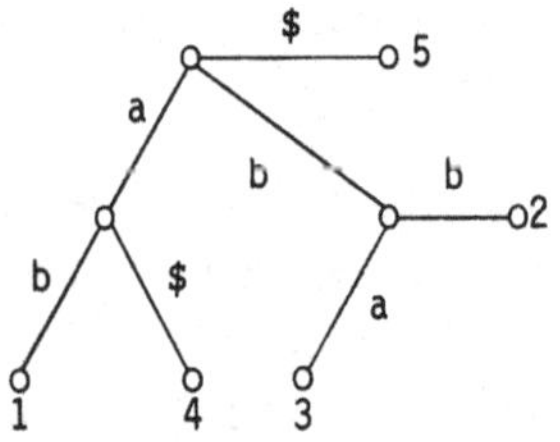

It is well-known that a position tree for a string of length n can contain $O(n^2)$ nodes. This can be seen e.g. in the case of the string $a^m b^m a^m b^m \$$. Hence, compacted position trees are considered which consist of $O(n)$ nodes [W]. Here, compacted means that successive edges corresponding to single sons are contracted into one edge named by a string, e.g.

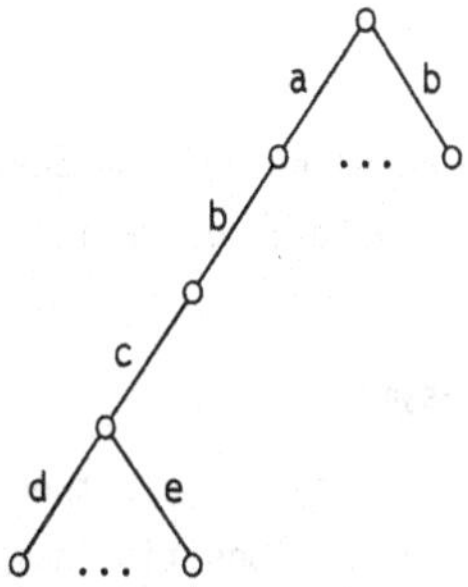

is compacted into

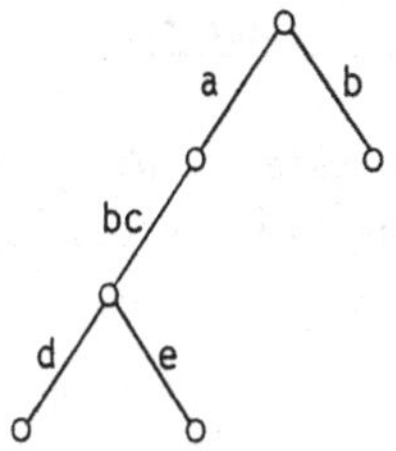

II. ON-LINE CONSTRUCTION OF POSITION TREES

The problem which we want to solve in the following is: Let a string $x = x_1 x_2 \cdots$ be read from left to right without knowing the whole string in advance and construct after the reading of each letter the position tree, respectively the compacted tree for the actual prefix. For simplicity we shall consider here only the construction of the non-compacted position tree. The construction of the compacted tree is basically the same but a little more complicated as compactification has to be taken into account.

The problem with the construction of the position tree when reading the text from left to right is based on the fact that we need an endmarker $ for each string in order to guarantee that there exists a position identifier for each position in the string. This has the consequence that reading from left to right means the transition from

$$x_1 x_2 \cdots x_i \$ \quad \text{to} \quad x_1 \cdots x_i x_{i+1} \$$$

The efficiency of Weiner's algorithm stems from the fact that the changes which are caused by updating the tree reading the text from right to left are "local". If we work from left to right changes are no more "local". In particular we have to solve the following two problems

i) a position identifier may become invalid by reading a new symbol, as e.g. the position identifier for position 1 in

   abcb$ → abcba$

ii) all position identifiers which contain the endmarker have to be changed whenever a new symbol is read in, e.g. the position identifier for position 4 in

   abcb$ → abcba$

In the following we describe how to construct the position tree for a string xa$ from the position tree for x$, where $x \in \Sigma^*$, $a \in \Sigma$.

Algorithm: Position tree on-line

1) For *each* node n which has a $-son n' the following steps have to be performed. The order in which the nodes with $-sons have to be processed is given in Lemma 1 below.

   a) If n does not have an a-son then substitute the $-symbol by a

   b) If n has an a-son n" which is not a leaf then remove the edge between n and n' and make n' the $-son of n" (together with the position number of n')

   c) If n has an a-son n" which is a leaf then remove the edge between n and n' and make n' the $-son of n" together with the position number associated with n'. Moreover, attach a new son to n", transfer the position number j of n" to the new son; label the edge between n" and its new son by the (j+l)th letter in xa$, where l is the length of the position identifier for position j in x$.

2) Attach a $-son at the root and give it the next position number.

Example.
Consider the string x$ = abbab$. We construct the position tree for xa$ from that for x$. The position tree for x$ is

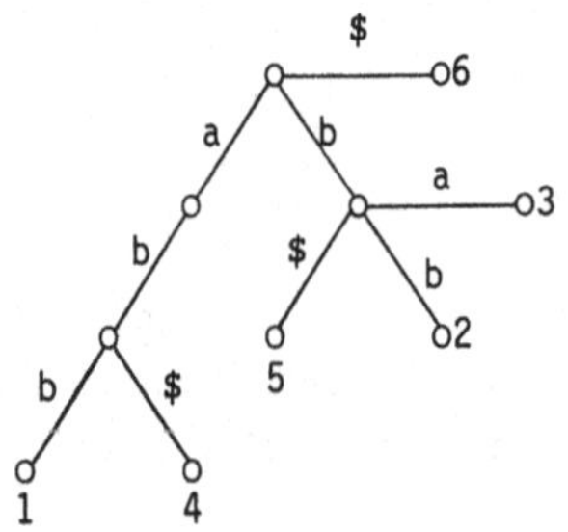

The father of leaf 4 falls into case a). The father of leaf 5 falls into case c), the father of leaf 6 falls into case b).
Performing the algorithm for the father of leaf 4, 5, 6 (in that order) yields

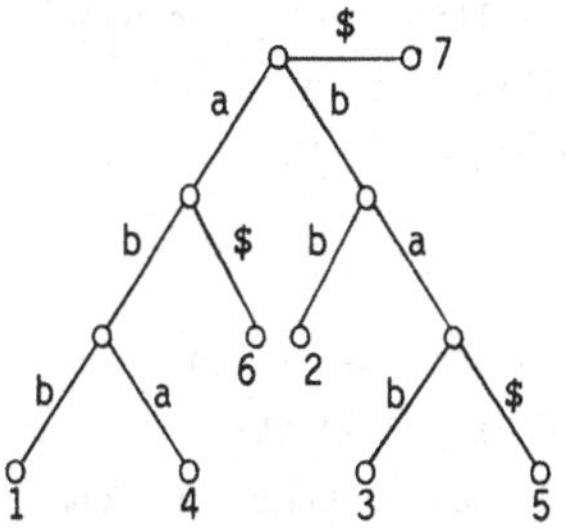

We now want to make sure that the algorithm works correctly.

LEMMA 1.

Assume that step 1 of the above algorithm is performed successively for all nodes n with a \$-son in such a way that if a node is processed then all his descendants have been processed previously. Then the algorithm constructs the position tree for xa\$ from the position tree for x\$.

Sketch of Proof.

1) The tree constructed by the algorithm is a uniquely determined $(\Sigma \cup \{\$\})$ - tree because of the postulated order of processing.

2) The next fact to be verified is that for each position identifier which is affected by the new letter a there is a change in the tree reflecting this change. There are three possibilities for a position identifier to be affected.

   a) For a position j with identifier $x_j \ldots x_{j+r-1}\, a$ there is a position i with identifier $x_i \ldots x_m \$$ such that $x_j \ldots x_{j+r-1} = x_i \ldots x_m$
      The position identifier for position j must be prolonged to $x_j \ldots x_{j+r+1}$ which is achieved by step 1c .

   b) The endmarker \$ is part of the position identifier. Similarly.

   c) The position identifier for a position i in xa\$ starts with the letter a . Then either a occurs only once in x\$ then the position identifier for i is obtained by step 1c , or a occurs more than once in x\$ then the position identifier for the new letter a is obtained by step 1a .

LEMMA 2.

If we organize all nodes n which have a \$-son in the position tree for x\$ in a list $L = n_1, \ldots n_k$ such that for all nodes n, m with \$-sons the following holds:

(*) (if n is descendant of m then $n = n_i$ and $m = n_j$ for some $i, j \in \{1, \ldots k\}$ and $i < j$)

then the updating of the List L resulting in L' caused by the algorithm processing the nodes in the order given by the list L can be performed sequentially, i.e. without searching through L . Furthermore L' fulfills (*) .

Proof: Straightforward.

The compacted position tree can be constructed in the same way as the non-compacted one. This can be seen from the fact that if we start with an already compacted tree for x$ and want to construct the compacted tree for xa$ then at most those nodes which are in the list L are candidates for compactification. The algorithm for the construction of compacted trees can be found in [MR].

III. COSTS OF THE ALGORITHM

In order to be able to analyse the costs of the algorithm we assume that

1) we hold the text which has been already read in an array

2) we represent the tree in the following form:
   Each node is represented by a natural number; in particular the root is given by 0 . Then we associate with each node three fields. The first contains the position number m , if the node is a leaf corresponding to position m . If the node is not a leaf then it contains a list of the sons, each given by its number and the name of the edge leading to it. The second field contains information about the depth of the node. The depth of the root is 0 . The third field serves for linking those nodes into a list which have a $-son. For example, the tree for aaa$ is

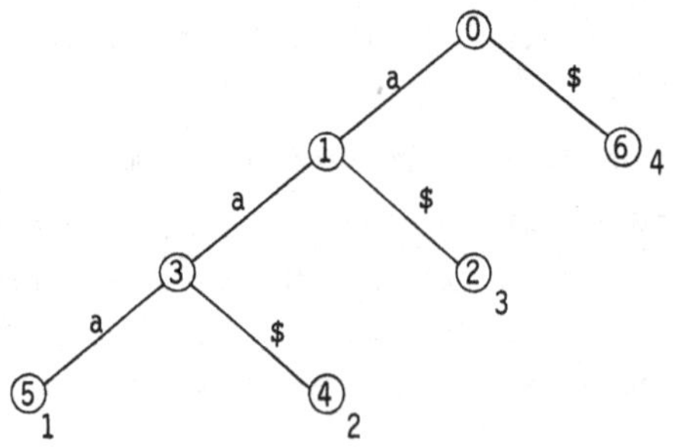

which is represented by

NR	sons or p.n.	depth
0	(1,a), (6,$)	0
1	(3,a), (2,$)	1
2	3	2
3	(5,a), (4,$)	2
4	2	3
5	1	3
6	4	1

Based on this representation the costs for step 1a, 1b, 1c for each node in the list is O(number of sons), as we first check if the node has an a-son. The test for leaf and the update can be done in constant time; in particular the search for the letter following the position identifier in the text for step 1c can be performed by selecting the (m+h)-th component of the array where m is the position number of the leaf and h its depth. Hence step 1 takes for each node $O(|\Sigma|)$ where Σ is the alphabet. Step 2 costs constant time. With this the cost of the on-line construction of the position tree for the string $x\$$, $x \in \Sigma^n$ can be bounded above by

$$O\left(\sum_{i=1}^{n} |p_i(x)| \cdot |\Sigma|\right) = O(l_x \cdot n \cdot |\Sigma|)$$

where $p_i(x)$ is the position identifier for the position i in x and

$$l_x = \sum_{i=1}^{n} |(p_i(x))| \Big/ n$$

the average length for a position identifier in $x\$$. This is based on the fact that - for each position i - the identifier $p_i(x)$ has to be updated as often as $|p_i(x)|$. Hence, the father of the leaf with position number i can occur at most as often as $|p_i(x)|$ in the disjoint union of all lists $\cup L_k$, where L_k is the list of nodes with $-sons in the k-th application of the algorithm.

In various applications, in particular in natural language processing it is a reasonable assumption that the average length l_x for a position identifier in $x\$$ is bounded above by $\log(|x|)$. Hence, in these cases the on-line construction takes $O(n \cdot \log n)$ steps.

IV. TRANSPORT COST

Let us now briefly consider the problem D4, i.e. given a small computer, we consider the question, how we can keep low the cost of main store and of transport between main and secondary store.

As the algorithm mainly processes the nodes in the list L, a first solution to this problem would be to store the list L in main store. Once can show, however, that this solution may cause up to 5 page transfers for a single invocation of the algorithm. Hence, in order to reduce this cost we suggest to modify slightly the representation of the position tree such that, I) we do not store the $-sons in the tree representation but keep them separately, II) for each $-son we store a reference to its father, III) instead of maintaining the list L in main store we maintain a list of $-sons in main store. One can show that this organisation will cost at most 2 page transfers for a single invocation of the algorithm [MR].

Let us finally remark that the correction problem, i.e. the problem to substitute a substring β by a substring γ, can be fruitfully discussed in terms of position trees [MR].

References:

[AHU] Aho, A., Hopcroft, B., Ullmann, J.: The design and analysis of computer algorithms. Addison-Wesley, Reading, Mass., 1975

[KMP] Knuth, D.E., Morris, J.H., Pratt, V.R.: Fast pattern matching in strings. Siam Journal of Computing, Vol. 6, No. 2, June 1977

[McC] McCreight, E.M.: A space-economical suffix tree construction algorithm. Journal of the ACM, Vol. 23, No. 2, April 1976

[W] Weiner, P.: Linear pattern matching algorithms. Conf. Record, IEEE 14th Annual Symposium on Switching and Automata Theory, 1973

[CC] Cohen, R., Cimet, M.: A scheme for constructing on-line linear time recognition algorithms. Conference on Theoretical Computer Science, Waterloo, 1977

[MR] Majster, M.E., Reiser, A.: Efficient on-line construction and correction of position trees. Submitted for publication.

SORTING PRESORTED FILES

Kurt Mehlhorn

Abstract: A new sorting algorithm is presented. Its running time is $O(n(1+\log(F/n))$ where $F = |\{(i,j);\ i < j \text{ and } x_i < x_j\}|$ is the total number of inversions in the input sequence $x_n\ x_{n-1}\ x_{n-2} \cdots x_2\ x_1$. In other words, presorted sequences are sorted quickly, and completely unsorted sequences are sorted in $O(n \log n)$ steps. Note that $F \leq n^2/2$ always. Furthermore, the constant of proportionality is fairly small and hence the sorting method is competitive with existing methods.

I. Introduction

In this paper we consider the problem of sorting presorted files. Consider the following two permutations of the number 1,2,3,...,7:

1 3 2 7 5 4 6 and

7 6 1 5 2 4 3

Intuitively speaking, the second permutation is more out of order than the first. A precise notion of this observation is to count the number of inversions; in our example the first permutation has 5 inversions (namely (3,2), (7,5), (7,4), (7,6) and (5,4)) and the second permutation has 15 inversions.

In general, let $x_n\ x_{n-1}\ x_{n-2} \cdots x_3\ x_2\ x_1$ be a sequence of elements x_p from an ordered universe. Define

$$F = |\{(i,j);\ x_i < x_j \text{ and } i < j\}|$$

as the number of inversions in this sequence. Then $0 \leq F \leq n(n-1)/2$. (Note that $F = n(n-1)/2$ if $x_n > x_{n-1} > \ldots > x_2 > x_1$). We take F as a measure of the "sortedness" of sequence $x_n\ x_{n-1} \cdots x_2\ x_1$.

We will sort sequence $x_n\ x_{n-1} \cdots x_2\ x_1$ by an insertion sort, i.e. we start with the sorted sequence consisting of only element x_1 and then insert $x_2, x_3 \ldots$ at the proper places. Let

$$f_j = \left| \{ i;\ x_i < x_j \text{ and } i < j \} \right| .$$

Then $\sum f_j = F$. Also f_j is the number of elements smaller than x_j and to the right of x_j in the input sequence. Hence x_j has to be inserted at the f_j-th position during the insertion sort. If the input sequence is presorted, i.e. F is small with respect to $n^2/2$, then f_j will tend to be small on the average. Hence most elements will have to be inserted near the front of the sorted sequence.

There is a well-known method for inserting an element into a ordered sequence $y_1 < y_2 < \ldots < y_m$ in time $O(\log t)$ where t is such that $y_t < y \leq y_{t+1}$. This method was used by Fredman and Bentley & Yao and was termed exponential and binary search in Mehlhorn 77. The basic idea is to compare y with y_{2i} for $i = 0,1,2,\ldots$ until $y \leq y_{2i}$ (exponential search) and then to perform a binary search on the interval $y_{2i-1},\ldots,y_{2i}$.

After having found the proper position by exponential + binary search we will have to insert y at the proper place. Note that it will not do to have numbers $y_1,\ldots,y_n$ is an array. The following data structure supports the search and the insertion process efficiently: A linear list L of AVL-trees $T_0, T_1, T_2, \ldots,$ where T_i has height i.

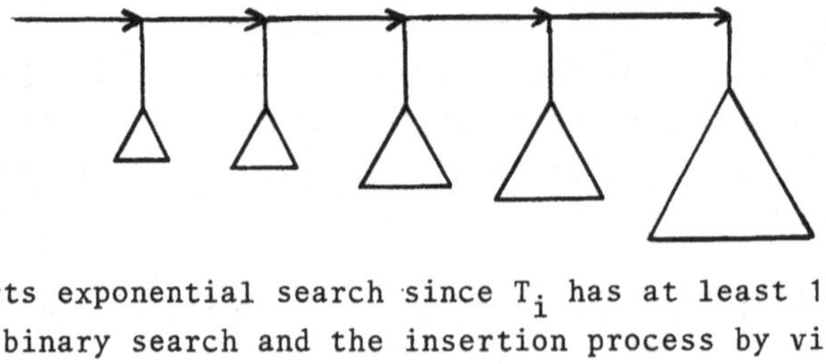

It supports exponential search since T_i has at least 1.65^i leaves. It supports binary search and the insertion process by virtue of AVL-trees. (The actual data structure will be slightly more complicated).

In the next section we introduce the data structure, describe the sorting algorithm and prove that its running time is $O(n(1 + \log(F/n)))$. This is optimal up to a constant factor.

Our algorithm solves a special case of a more general problem considered by Guibas et al. and Brown & Tarjan. They study finger trees which re- represent linear lists in a way, as to make insertion in the vicinity of certain points (called fingers) efficient. In their terminology we have just one finger which is always directed at the front end of the file. However, our data structure solves this special case more efficient. A sorting method arises which is competitive with (and maybe superior to) existing methods. Our data structure has storage requirement 3n vs. 6n for the structure due to Brown & Tarjan. Guibas et al's data structure is based on B-trees of degree at least 25 and hence seems suitable only for very large n. Also, though their algorithms have the same asymptotic behavior, the constant of proportionality for our algorithm is smaller.

II. The Algorithm

Our algorithm uses the following data structure:

1) Let L be a linear list $L_0, L_1, \dots, L_k$.

2) Each L_i, $0 \le i \le k$, is a linear list of AVL-trees $T_{i,0}, T_{i,1}, \dots, T_{i,\ell_i}$ with $\ell_i \ge 0$. The L_i are called sublists.

3) $T_{i,0}$ is an AVL-tree of height i-1, i or i+1 and $T_{i,j}$, $1 \le j \le \ell_i$, is an AVL-tree of height i-1 or i. Furthermore $\ell_0 = 0$ and $T_{0,0}$ has height 0 or 1.

A sublist L_i is either <u>clean</u> or <u>dirty</u> . If $\ell_i = 0$ then L_i is clean, if $\ell_i \ge 1$ then L_i is dirty. We use our data structure to store ordered sets S:

3') Let T be an AVL with m leaves and let S be an ordered set with m elements. We store the elements of S in increasing order from left to right in the leaves of T. In an interior node v of T we store the largest element in the left subtree of the tree with root v. Fig. 1 shows an AVL-tree of height 2 and 3 leaves. The set {7,9,13} is stored in it.

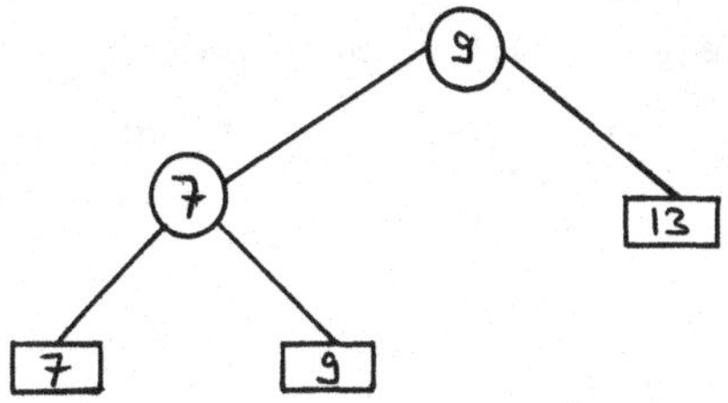

Fig. 1:

Fact 1 (Adel'son-Vel'skii + Landis)

Let T be an AVL-tree of height h and let m be the number of leaves of T. Then

$$F_{h+2} \leq m \leq 2^h$$

where $F_1 = F_2 = 1$ and $F_{i+2} = F_{i+1} + F_i$ are the Fibonaccinumbers.

Since $F_i = (\alpha^i - \beta^i)/\sqrt{5}$ with $\alpha = (1+\sqrt{5})/2 \approx 1.618$ and $\beta = (1-\sqrt{5})/2 \approx -0.618$ it follows that

$$(\alpha^{h+2} - \beta^{h+2})/\sqrt{5} \leq m$$

and hence

$$(\alpha^{h+2}-1)/\sqrt{5} \leq m$$

(2') Let L_i be a sublist, i.e. L_i is a linear list of AVL-trees $T_{i,0}, T_{i,1}, \ldots, T_{i,\ell_i}$ with $\ell_i \geq 0$. Let m_j be the number of leaves of tree $T_{i,j}$ and let S be a set with $\sum_{j=0}^{\ell_i} m_j$ elements.

We store the m_0 largest elements of S in $T_{i,0}$, the next m_1 largest elements in $T_{i,1}, \ldots$, and the m_{ℓ_i} smallest elements in T_{i,ℓ_i}. In the sublist L_i we store pointers to the roots of the trees $T_{i,j}$. Along with the pointer to tree $T_{i,j}$ we also store the largest element stored in Tree $T_{i,j}$, denoted $max_{i,j}$. Fig. 2 shows a list L_1 consisting of 3 trees $T_{1,0}$, $T_{1,1}$, $T_{1,2}$ of height 2,0,1 respectively. Set $S = \{2,4,6,7,9,13\}$ is stored in it. We have $m_{1,0}=13$, $m_{1,1}=6$, and $m_{1,2}=5$. Note that we draw the

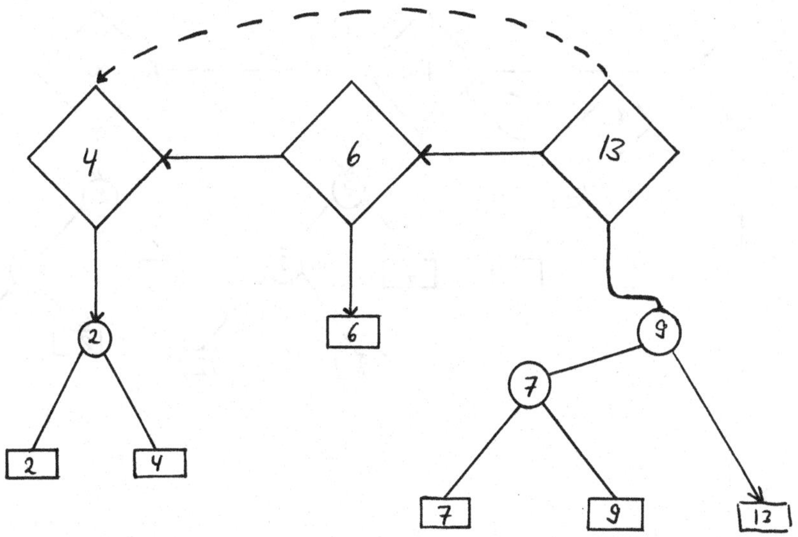

first element of the list at the right end. Also the first element always contains a pointer to the last element.

Fact 2: Let L_i be a sublist. Then the total number of leaves of the trees in sublist L_i is at least $(\alpha^{i+1}-1)/\sqrt{5}$.

Proof: Since tree $T_{i,o}$ has height at least i-1 this follows immediately from Fact 1.

(1') Let finally L be the linear list $L_0, L_1, \ldots, L_k$, let n_i be the total number of leaves of trees in sublist L_i, $0 \le i \le k$, and let S be a set with $n = \sum_{i=o}^{k} n_i$ elements. We store the n_0 smallest elements of S in L_0 as described in 2', the next n_1 smallest elements in $L_1, \ldots$. Fig. 3 shows a possible data structure for set $\{2,5,6,7,9,13,19,21,\infty\}$. We draw list L as consisting of the first elements of the sublists L_i. In our example sublists L_0 and L_2 are clean and L_1 is dirty.

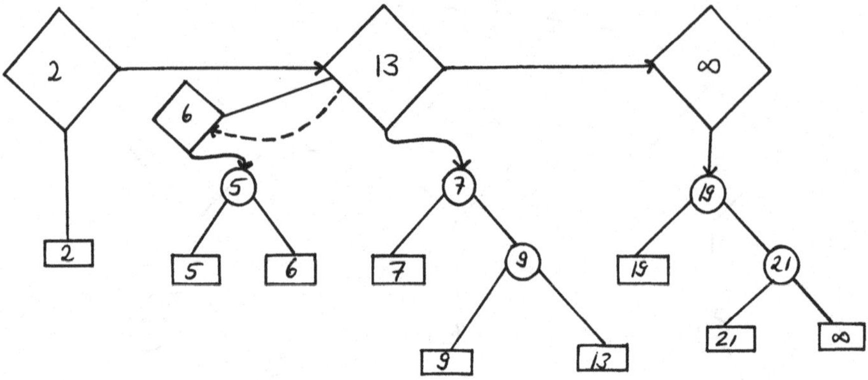

Fig. 3

We use our data structure to do an insertion sort. Let $x_n x_{n-1} x_{n-2} \cdots x_2 x_1 x_0$ be an unordered list of reals (to be specific). We assume that $x_0 = \infty$, i.e. x_0 is at least as large as all other elements in the list. This assumption will allow us to eliminate some special cases and is quite customary in sorting.

We start with our data structure for the singleton set x_0 , i.e. L consists of sublist L_0 only, L_0 consists of one tree of height 0 and the only leaf of that tree contains x_0. Next we insert $x_1, x_2, x_3, \ldots$ into the structure. Suppose we inserted $x_1, \ldots, x_{p-1}$ and obtained structure L. We want to insert x_p next.

First we locate the sublist L_i in which x_p is to be inserted.

$i \leftarrow 0$

<u>while</u> $x_p > max_{i,o}$ <u>do</u> $i \leftarrow i+1$

Remember that $max_{i,o}$ is the largest element of tree $T_{i,o}$ and hence the largest element stored in sublist i. Suppose L consists of sublists $L_0, L_1, \ldots, L_k$. Then $max_{k,o} = \infty$ and hence the while-loop terminates although we have not included a test for end of list. Let h be the final value of variable i. Then $x_p \leq max_{h,o}$ and either $h = 0$ or $x_p > max_{h-1,o}$. In our example we would have $h = 1$ if we try to insert 12 and we would have $h = 2$ if we try to insert 35.

Definition: Let $f_p := |\{q; q < p \text{ and } x_q < x_p\}|$ be the number of inversions caused by element x_p. f_p is the number of elements to the right of x_p yet smaller than x_p.

From now on, $\log f_p$ always denotes $\log \max(2, f_p)$.

Lemma 1: Let h be defined as above. Then

$$h = O(\log f_p)$$

Proof: If $h = 0$ then we have nothing to show. Suppose $h > 0$. Then $x_p > max_{h-1,o}$.

Furthermore, sublist L_{h-1} contains at least tree $T_{h-1,o}$ which has height at least h-2 and hence at least $F_h \geq (\alpha^h - 1)/\sqrt{5}$ leaves. These leaves contain elements x_q with $q < p$ and $x_q < x_p$. Hence $f_p \geq (\alpha^h - 1)/\sqrt{5}$.

□

At this point we have located sublist L_h and we want to insert x_p into one of the trees $T_{h,j}$, $0 \leq j \leq \ell_h$, on sublist L_h. We distinguish whether L_h is clean or dirty.

Case 1: L_h is clean, i.e. $\ell_h = 0$. We insert x_p into AVL-tree $T_{h,o}$ using the standard insertion algorithm for AVL-trees. Tree $T_{h,o}$ has height h-1, h or h+1. After the insertion $T_{h,o}$ has height h-1, h+1, h+2. If its height is $\leq$ h+1 then we are done and proceed to insert x_{p+1}. If its height is h+2, then let T' and T'' be its left and right subtree and let v be its root. Trees T' and T'' have height h or h+1, not necessarily the same. We let T' be the new $T_{h,o}$ and append T'' at the end of sublist L_{h+1}. If L_{h+1} did not exist, then we also have to create L_{h+1}. Note also that the maximal element in T' is stored in v and that the maximal element in T'' is the old $max_{h,o}$. Hence we are able to maintain our data structure.

Lemma 2: $O(\log f_p)$ time units suffice to insert x_p into $T_{h,o}$ and to update the data structure.

Proof: Tree $T_{h,o}$ has height at most h+1. Hence $h+1 = O(\log f_p)$ (by Lemma 1) time units suffice.

Case 2: L_h is dirty. We will first clean L_h by pairing the trees in it and moving some of the resulting trees to L_{h+1}. Let L_h consist of trees $T_{h,o}, T_{h,1}, \dots, T_{h,\ell_h}$ with $\ell_h \geq 1$. Remember that $T_{h,o}$ has height h-1, h or h+1 and that trees $T_{h,j}$, $1 \leq j$, have height h-1 or h.

if height of $T_{h,o}$ is h+1

then delete $T_{h,o}$ from L_h and append $T_{h,o}$ to the end of L_{h+1};

co all trees on L_h have height h-1 or h;

while L_h contains at least 3 trees

do delete the first two trees T' and T" from L_h; combine them into a new AVL-tree of height h or h+1;append this tree to the end of list L_{h+1}

co L_h now contains either one or two trees;

if L_h contains two trees T' and T"

then combine T' and T" into a single tree T, delete T' and T" from L_h and make t the only tree of list L_h;

At this point L_h is clean, but L_{h+1} may be dirty. Now we try again whether x_p has to be inserted into L_h, i. e. we execute $x_p > max_{h,o}$ again. If it has to be inserted into L_h then we proceed as in case 1. Otherwise we increase i by 1 to h+1 and try to insert x_p into L_{h+1}. If L_{h+1} is dirty, then we clean L_{h+1} first, ...

Cleaning L_h means to move at most one tree unchanged from L_h and L_{h+1} and to pair off the remaining trees. Since at least one tree is moved unchanged or at least one pair is formed, the time required to clean L_h is proportional to the number of trees moved unchanged (at most one) plus the number of pairs formed. We will use this fact when analysing the total time complexity of all cleaning processes.

This ends the description of the algorithm.

Example:

Fig. 5 shows the effect of inserting 12 into the structure of Fig. 3. We first determine h = 1. L_1 is dirty. Hence L_1 is cleaned and the structure in 5a is obtained. Next we find out that i has to be increased to h+1. L_2 is dirty and we clean L_2. The structure in 5b is obtained. Now i stays stable and L_2 is clean. Hence we insert 12 into $T_{2,0}$ and obtain 5c.

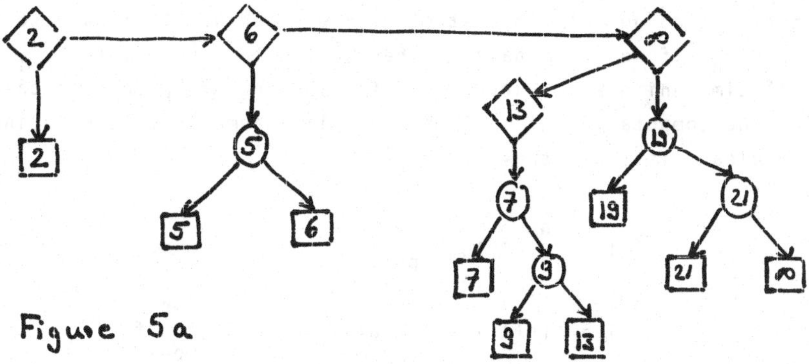

Figure 5a

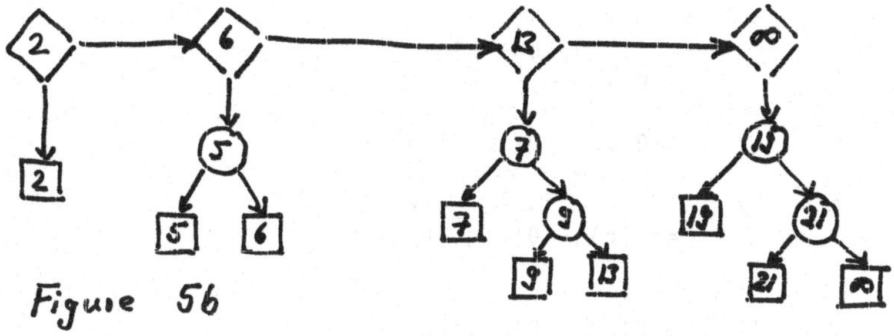

Figure 5b

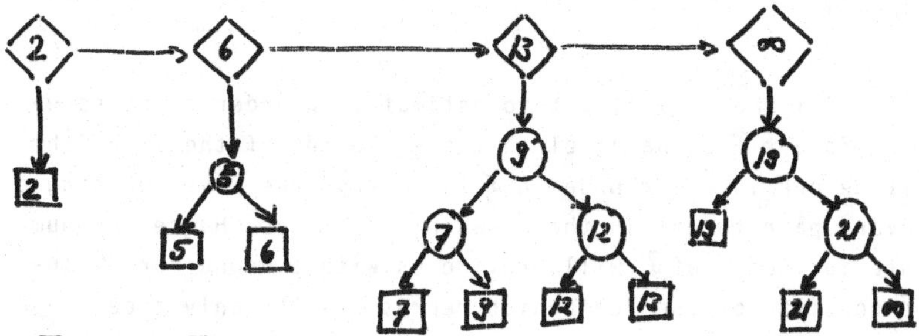

Figure 5c

It remains to estimate the running time of the algorithm. Suppose we used the algorithm to sort $x_n, x_{n-1}, \ldots, x_1, x_0$. Let S be the total time spent on cleaning and let T be the total time spent outside the cleaning processes.

Note that $T = \sum_{p=1}^{n} O(\log f_p)$ if we never try to insert into a dirty sublist. Suppose now that at some point we try to insert into a dirty sublist L_h. Then L_h is cleaned first. The cost of cleaning is allotted to S. Then we find out at the cost of O(1) whether we still have to insert into L_h. If we don't have to then we try to insert into L_{h+1}. Hence O(1) time units are charged to T for looking at L_h in this case. Hence for the computation of T we may as well assume that we only insert into clean lists and thus

$$T = \sum_{p=1}^{n} O(\log f_p).$$

Lemma 3: $T = O(n(1 + \log(F/n)))$ where $F = \sum_{p=1}^{n} f_p$

Proof: By the discussion above

$$\begin{aligned} T &= \sum_{p=1}^{n} O(\log f_p) \\ &= O(n) + O(\sum_{p=1}^{n} \log f_p) \\ &= O(n) + O(\log \prod_{i=1}^{n} f_i) \\ &= O(n) + O(n \log(F/n)) \end{aligned}$$

since $(\Pi f_i)^{1/n} \leq (\Sigma f_i)/n$ (the geometric mean is never larger than the arithmetic mean).

The quantity S is more difficult to estimate. In order to do so we construct a forest $\mathcal{F}$ in parallel to the execution of the algorithm. There will be one interior node in $\mathcal{F}$ for every tree moved unchanged and for every pair formed in the cleaning processes. Hence the number of interior nodes of $\mathcal{F}$ will provide us with a bound for S. Initially $\mathcal{F}$ consists of one leaf which represents the only tree $T_{0,0}$ in our structure.

a) The leaves of $\mathfrak{F}$: The leaves of $\mathfrak{F}$ will be constructed after inserting new elements into our data structure. Suppose we insert element x_p into clean list L_h, i. e. we insert x_p into AVL-tree $T_{h,o}$. After the insertion $T_{h,o}$ is either split or not.

a1) $T_{h,o}$ is not split. Then we create one new leaf which represents the tree $T_{h,o}$ on list L_h after the insertion took place.

a2) $T_{h,o}$ is split into T' and T". T' stays on list L_h and T" is moved to list L_{h+1}. We construct two new leaves of forest $\mathfrak{F}$ representing trees T' on list L_h and T" on list L_{h+1} respectively. Since at most two leaves are constructed after inserting an element into our data structure, forest $\mathfrak{F}$ has at most 2n+1 leaves.

b) The interior nodes of $\mathfrak{F}$: The interior nodes are constructed by the cleaning process. Suppose we clean list L_h. Then tree $T_{h,o}$ may be moved unchanged to list L_{h+1}. If this is the case then we construct one new node with a single son. This new node represents tree $T_{h,o}$ on list L_{h+1}. Its single son is the node which represented tree $T_{h,o}$ on list L_h. Also pairs of trees of L_h are formed. For every pair formed we construct a new node with two sons. The new node represents the newly formed tree on whatever list it is on (either L_h or L_{h+1}) and its two sons are the two nodes which represent the two constituent trees on list L_h.

From the construction of forest $\mathfrak{F}$ is it apparent that at every point during the execution of our algorithm every tree in the data structure will be represented by a node of $\mathfrak{F}$. Interior nodes of $\mathfrak{F}$ have either one or two sons.

Lemma 4: Let v be a node of $\mathfrak{F}$ having exactly one son w. Then w is either a leaf or has two sons.

Proof: Assume otherwise. Then w has a single son x. x represents some tree T on some list L_h. Hence T has height $\leq$ h+1. Node w represents the same tree on list L_{h+1}. Hence w represents a tree of height $\leq$ h+1 on list L_{h+1}. Such a tree is never moved unchanged during the cleaning. Hence there can be no node having w as its only son. Contradiction.

Forest F has at most 2n+1 leaves. Hence it has at most 2n nodes with two sons and hence at most 4n+1 nodes with one son. This shows that at most 8n+2 trees are handled during the whole of the cleaning processes. Hence $S = O(n)$.

We thus proved:

<u>Theorem:</u> Let $x_n\ x_{n-1} \ldots x_1$ be an unordered sequence and let

$$F = |\{(i,j);\ i > j \text{ and } x_i > x_j\}|$$

be the total number of inversions in that sequence. Then our algorithm sorts the sequence in

$$O(n(1 + \log(F/n)))$$

time units.

Guibas et al have shown that the logarithm of the number of permutations of $\{1,2,\ldots,n\}$ with at most F inversions is $\Omega(n(\log(1+F/n))$. Hence our algorithm is optimal up to a constant factor. This is also true for the algorithms due to Guibas et al and Brown & Tarjan. However, our constant of proportionality is smaller. A first analysis shows that the running time is about 24n log(F/n) + 40n on the machine defined in Mehlhorn 77. Comparing this with the running time of Quicksort which is about 9n log n on the average on that machine shows that

$$24n \log(F/n) + 40n \leq 9n \log n$$

if $$\log(2^{40/24}.F/n) \leq (9/24) \log n$$

if $$F \leq 1/2^{(40/24)} n^{33/24} \approx 0.314 n^{1.375}$$

and hence the algorithm is competitive with Quicksort for

$$F \leq 0.314 n^{1.375}.$$

Guibas et al base their data structure on B-trees (Bayer & McCreight) of order (degree of branching) at least 25. Hence it seems unsuitable for small or moderate size n. Brown & Tarjan base their data structure on 2 - 3 trees. The storage requirement of their structure is 6n. Our data structure requires only 4n storage, a 3n implementation is possible. An obvious implementation of AVL-trees is to use 3 storage cells per node and one storage cell per leaf. This makes 4m-3 storage cells for an AVL-tree with m leaves. In addition, we need for each AVL-tree an element in sublist L_i which points to it. Again three storage cells are required for such an element. Finally, we need two additional storage cells for each sublist L_i: a pointer to L_{i+1} and a pointer to the last element in L_i. Altogether, 4n+O(log n) storage cells suffice.

Also our algorithm is more time efficient than theirs. This is due to the fact that it uses AVL-trees instead of 2-3 trees and that list L above can be kept in an array.

III. Conclusion

We presented a new sorting algorithm. Several variations of the general theme are possible.

1) Usage of some other kind of balanced trees instead of AVL-trees, e. g. B-trees [Bayer-McCreight].

2) List L starts with sublist L_s, $s \geq 1$, instead of L_o. This might remove some overhead.

3) It is conceivable to use the same datastructure recursively to organize list L. After all, list L has length log n and inserting element x_p corresponds to finding the $(\log f_p)$-th position in this list.

4) Usage of random trees instead of balanced trees. This might result in a sorting algorithm with fast average running time.

5) We chose to delay cleaning list L_{i+1} after it became dirty by a split of $T_{i,0}$. It would be possible to clean list L_{i+1} (and L_{i+2}, L_{i+3}, ... as necessary) immediately after that split.

   The same analysis and time bound applies. It requires more study which solution is more efficient with respect to time and space requirements.

B i b l i o g r a p h y

Adelson-Velskii-Landis: "An algorithm for the organization of information", Soviet. Math. Dokl,3,1259-1262, 1962

Aho, Hopcroft & Ullman: "The Design and Analysis of Computer Algorithms", Addison Wesley, 1974

Bayer & McCreight: "Organization and Maintenance of Large Ordered Indizes", Acta Informatica, 1 (1972), 173-189

Bentley & Yao: "An almost Optimal Algorithm for Unbounded Searching", Information Processing Letters, Vol. 5, No. 3, p. 82-87, August 1976

Brown & Tarjan: "A Representation for Linear Lists with Movable Fingers", 10th ACM Symposium on Theory of Computing, p. 19-29, 1978

Fredman, M. L.: "Two applications of a Probabilistic Search Technique: Sorting X + Y and Building Balanced Search Trees", 7th ACM Symposium on Theory of Computing, 1975 240-244

Guibas, Creight, Plass, Roberts: "A new representation for linear lists, 9th ACM Symposium on Theory of Computing 1977, 49-60

Mehlhorn, K.: "Effiziente Algorithmen", Teubner Studienbücher Informatik, Stuttgart 1977

NODE-VISIT OPTIMAL 1 - 2 BROTHER TREES

Th. Ottmann
A.L. Rosenberg
H.W. Six
D. Wood

Abstract:

We characterize node-visit optimal 1-2 brother trees and present a linear time algorithm to construct them.

1. Introduction

In many data processing situations we are given a large set of keys as an initial configuration. Then the set is dynamically altered by inserting new keys and deleting unwanted keys. Furthermore, member operations and other queries which do not alter the set of keys are also posed. Queries of this latter type may far exceed the others. Data structures for which an arbitrary sequence of member, insert, and delete operations can be carried out efficiently are usually called dictionaries, see Aho, Hopcroft and Ullman [1974]. It is well known that dictionaries can be implemented in such a way that all three dictionary operations can be performed in time O(log N). Various balanced tree schemes are known which may be used for this task. Among them are the AVL trees of Adelson-Velskii and Landis [1962], the 2,3 trees of Hopcroft (see Aho, Hopcroft and Ullman [1974]), the brother (leaf search) trees of Ottmann and Six [1976] and Ottmann, Six and Wood [1978], and the 1-2 brother trees of Ottmann and Wood [1978]. The insertion procedure for a balanced tree scheme can also be used to handle the initialisation phase in the above mentioned data processing situation: By iteratively inserting the N keys of the given initial set, beginning with the empty tree, we obtain an initial tree in time O(N log N). However, this iterative insertion method does not utilize the often valid assumption that the initial set of N keys is given in lexicographic order. Therefore a natural question arises, namely, construct efficiently a balanced tree which is optimal in some sense, when given a set of keys in lexicographic order. This problem has been solved for the class of 2,3 trees in Miller, Pippenger, Rosenberg and Snyder [1977] and in Rosenberg and Snyder [1977]. The present paper addresses that question for 1-2 brother trees. We characterize those trees which are optimal with respect to the expected number of node-visits per access. A linear time algorithm to construct such a tree is designed.

2. Brother trees, 1-2 brother trees and their costs.

A brother tree is a rooted, oriented tree each of whose nonleaf nodes has either one or two sons. Each unary node must have a binary brother. All root-to-leaf paths have the same length.
Storing the keys at internal nodes in a manner which is analogous to the usual way of storing keys in 2,3 trees leads to the notion of a 1-2 brother tree.

In a 1-2 brother tree a binary node has one key and both unary nodes and leaves have no keys. All keys resident in a binary node's left subtree are strictly less than the key resident at the node; all keys resident in a binary node's right subtree are strictly greater than the key resident at the node.
We will make frequent use of some basic notions of trees. The depth of a node p in a tree is its distance from the root, i.e. the number of edges on the path from the root to p. The height of a node p is the largest distance from p to a leaf in the subtree of the tree with root p. The height of a tree is the height of its root.
The root of a tree is said to be at level 0; the sons of a node at level ℓ are said to be at level $\ell+1$.

Given a brother tree T of height h.
The profile $\Pi(T)$ is the integer sequence

$$\Pi(T) = \nu_0,\ldots,\nu_h$$

where ν_i is the number of nodes at level i in T. The detailed profile $\Delta(T)$ is the sequence of pairs

$$\Delta(T) = \langle\upsilon_0,\beta_0\rangle,\ldots,\langle\upsilon_h,\beta_h\rangle$$

where each υ_j (resp., β_j) denotes the number of unary (resp., binary) nodes at level j in T.
From these definitions we immediately obtain:

(2.1) $\nu_0 = 1$

(2.2) $\nu_h = 1 + \sum_{i=o}^{h-1} \beta_i$ = the number of leaves of T

(2.3) $\nu_i = \upsilon_i + \beta_i \quad , 0 \leq i < h$

(2.4) $\nu_{i+1} = \upsilon_i + 2 \cdot \beta_i \quad , 0 \leq i < h$

In analogy with the related cost measures for 2,3-trees, see Miller, Pippenger, Rosenberg and Snyder [1977], we define the node-visit cost NVCOST, of 1-2 brother trees:

Let T be a 1-2 brother tree of height h with

$\pi(T) = \nu_o, \ldots, \nu_h$ and $\Delta(T) = \langle\upsilon_o, \beta_o\rangle, \ldots, \langle\upsilon_h, \beta_h\rangle$.

(2.5) (a) $\text{NVCOST }(T) = \sum_{i=o}^{h-1} (i+1) \cdot \beta_i$

(b) $= h \cdot \nu_h - \sum_{i=o}^{h-1} \nu_i$ (by (2.3), (2.4)).

We say a tree T is node-visit optimal (NVO, for short), if for all trees T' with the same number of leaves (and keys) we have

$$\text{NVCOST}(T) \leq \text{NVCOST}(T')$$

3. Node visit optimal 1-2 brother trees

We will characterize the NVO 1-2 brother trees and design a linear time algorithm to construct them.
By definition, all 1-2 brother trees having the same detailed profile are equally costly.
(2.5) (b) shows that this can be strengthened

Lemma 3.1

1-2 brother trees having the same profile have the same NVCOST.

The following result gives a necessary condition for 1-2 brother trees to be NVO, namely, height-minimality.

Lemma 3.2

A 1-2 brother tree T of N+1 leaves is NVO only if T has minimal height $h = \lceil \log_2(N+1) \rceil$.

It is easy to give an example which shows that height minimality is not sufficient for NV-optimality of a 1-2 brother tree.

Roughly speaking our characterization theorem will reflect the following observation: Consider a 1-2 brother tree containing a pair of binary nodes in a configuration

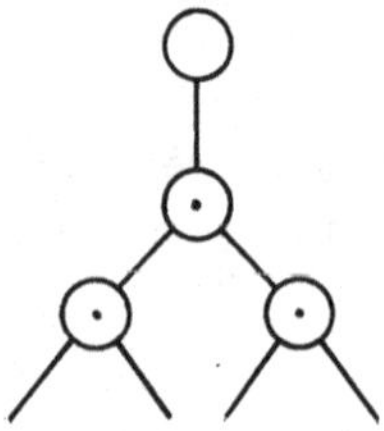

where the dots denote stored keys.
Then we can move one key upwards one level and thus reduce the NVCOST of the tree by replacing the above configuration by:

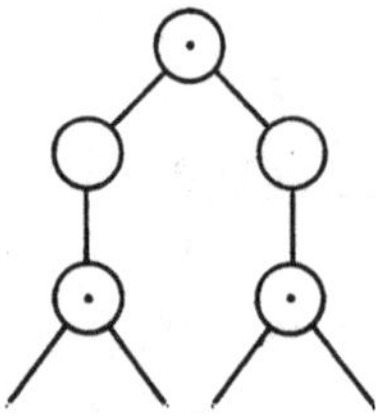

This replacement, of course, destroys the brother property of the resulting tree. However, if there is a binary node having a binary brother on the same level as the two unary brothers, then one obtains a NVCOST equivalent 1-2 brother tree by interchanging one unary node and its subtree with a binary node and its subtree (disregarding keys).

A node is said to be a <u>surplus node</u> if it is a binary node having a binary brother. The following Lemmas show that occurrences of surplus nodes in NVO 1-2 brother trees are subject to strong constraints.

<u>Lemma 3.3</u>

If a NVO 1-2 brother tree of height h has a unary node on level h-2, then it does not contain any surplus nodes on level h-1.

<u>Lemma 3.4</u>

If a NVO 1-2 brother tree of height h has a unary node on level h-3 then it does not contain any surplus nodes on level h-1.

Lemma 3.5

If a NVO 1-2 brother tree contains surplus nodes on level ℓ and $\ell+1$ then no level $\ell' \leq \ell-1$ contains a unary node.

The trees

$T_3=$

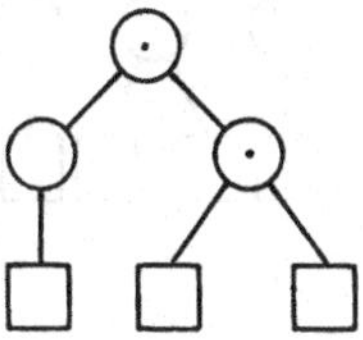

and $T_4=$

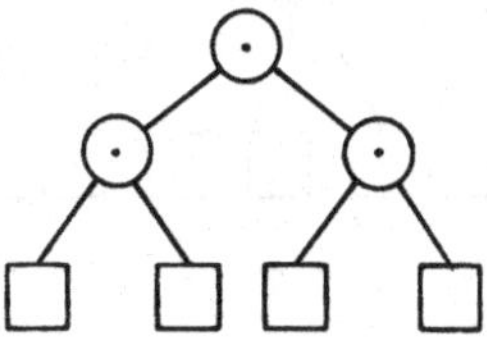

are used in the next theorem which constitutes one part of our result characterizing NVO 1-2 brother trees.

Theorem 3.6

Let T be a 1-2 brother tree with N keys and the minimal possible height $h = \lceil \log_2(N+1) \rceil$ where $3 \cdot 2^{h-2} \leq N+1 \leq 2^h$. Then T is NVO iff T is a complete binary tree up to level h-2 with $2^h-(N+1)$ subtrees T_3 and $(N+1)-3 \cdot 2^{h-2}$ subtrees T_4 dangling from its leaves.

The proof of this and the next theorem make frequent use of the previously stated Lemmas and also utilize quite involved counting arguments.

The following trees $T_8,\dots,T_{12}$ of height 4 are used for the second half of our characterization result.

$T_8=$

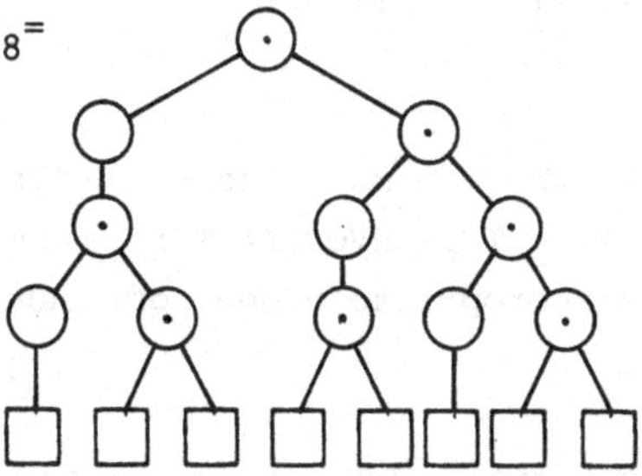

$T_9=$

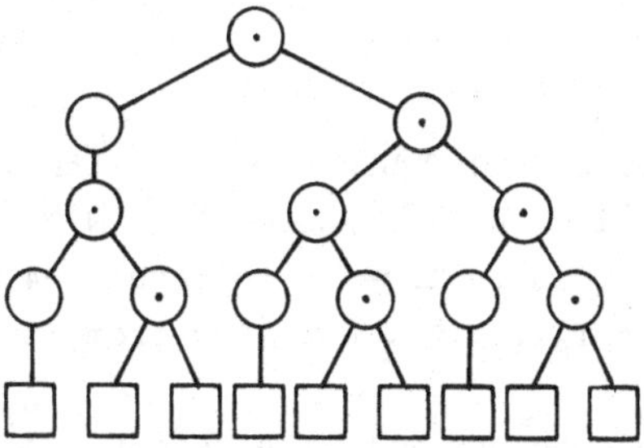

$T_{10}=$ $T_{11}=$

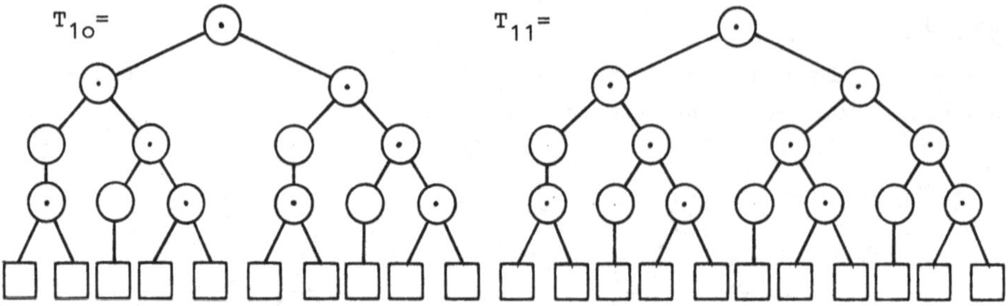

$T_{12}=$

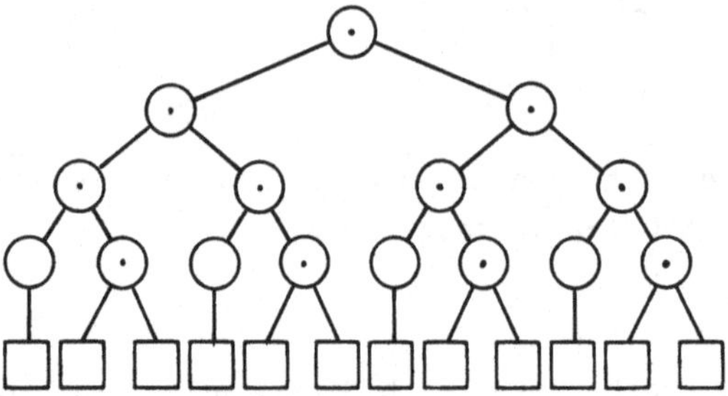

The trees $T_9,\ldots,T_{12}$ are NVO, but T_8 is not NVO.

For each desired number of leaves N+1 where $8\cdot 2^{h-4} < N+1 \leq 12\cdot 2^{h-4}$ a 1-2 brother tree of height h can be built as follows:
Construct a complete binary tree of height h-4 and append to its 2^{h-4} leaves an appropriate number of trees $T_8,\ldots,T_{12}$ such that N+1 leaves are generated.

It can be shown that all combinations of subtrees $T_8,\ldots,T_{12}$ which generate N+1 leaves yield 1-2 brother trees with the same NVCOST. In fact, for each tree T of this kind we obtain

$$\mathrm{NVCOST}(T) = (h-1)\cdot(N+1)-2^{h-2}+1.$$

<u>Theorem 3.7</u>
Let T be a 1-2 brother tree with N keys and the minimal possible height $h = \lceil \log_2(N+1) \rceil$, where $2^{h-1} < N+1 \leq 3\cdot 2^{h-2}$. Then T is NVO iff T is a complete binary tree up to level h-4 with (an appropriate number of) subtrees $T_8,\ldots,T_{12}$ dangling from its leaves.

When combined with the height condition of Lemma 3.2 Theorems 3.6 and 3.7 completely characterize the structure of NVO 1-2 brother trees.

Our characterization of NVO 1-2 brother trees directly leads to a linear time algorithm for constructing such a tree T for a given sorted list of N keys. In the first stage the "skeleton" of T is constructed by performing the procedure NVO-SKELETON. The skeleton is then filled by performing FILL. The construction is described in a very high level language . Choosing an appropriate implementation involves only standard techniques.

<u>Procedure</u> NVO-SKELETON

<u>Input</u>: Natural number N (of keys to be stored)

<u>Output</u>: The skeleton of a NVO 1-2 brother tree with N binary nodes and N+1 leaves

```
begin
    h: = ⌈log₂(N+1)⌉;
    if   N+1 = 2^h
         then  T:=complete binary tree of height h
    else if N+1 > 3·2^(h-2)
         then  T: = complete binary tree of height h-2;
               append to leaves of T (N+1-3·2^(h-2)) copies of T_4 and
                      2^h-(N+1) copies of T_3
    else
         T: = complete binary tree of height h-4;
         x_12: = ⌈(N+1-2^(h-1))/4⌉;
         i: = 8 + (N+1-2^(h-1))-4·x_12;
         append to leaves of T x_12 copies of T_12,
         one copy of T_i, and (2^(h-4)-x_12-1) copies of T_8
end;
```

<u>Procedure</u> FILL

<u>Input</u> The skeleton of a 1-2 brother tree T with N+1 leaves and a sorted list $K_1, \ldots, K_N$ of keys in ascending order.

<u>Output</u> 1-2 brother tree T with input list of nodes stored at its binary nodes.

<u>Method</u> Traverse T in postorder and deposit the next key whenever a binary node is visited.

We conclude our paper with a remark on the storage requirement of 1-2 brother trees. This cost measure is defined as follows:

$$\text{SPACECOST}(T) = \sum_{i=0}^{h-1} \nu_i = \text{number of internal nodes of } T.$$

For a given number N of keys all 1-2 brother trees storing N keys have the same number N of binary nodes. This means that a 1-2 brother tree has minimal SPACECOST, (is SCO, for short), iff it has the minimal number of unary nodes.

It can be shown that the structure of SCO 1-2 brother trees having N keys (and N+1 leaves) can be read off the binary expansion of the number $2^{\lceil \log_2(N+1) \rceil} - (N+1)$.

The two cost measures NVCOST and SPACECOST are distinct in the sense that there are N-key 1-2 brother trees which are NVO but not SCO and 1-2 brother trees which are SCO but not NVO. However, the cost measures are not totally unrelated. Both NVO and SCO 1-2 brother trees must have the minimal possible height. Moreover NVO and SCO 1-2 brother trees are in one sense dual to each other, since, for the given height, in NVO trees the number of nodes is maximal, while in SCO trees the number of nodes is minimized.

The complete binary tree of height h (storing $N = 2^h-1$ keys) is both NVO and SCO. Let $T_{NVO}(N)$ and $T_{SCO}(N)$, respectively, denote a NVO and SCO 1-2 brother tree storing N keys, where N is arbitrary. Then we can obtain the following bounds:

$$1 \leq \frac{\mathrm{SPACECOST}(T_{NVO}(N))}{\mathrm{SPACECOST}(T_{SCO}(N))} < \frac{3}{2}$$

and

$$1 \leq \frac{\mathrm{NVCOST}(T_{SCO}(N))}{\mathrm{NVCOST}(T_{NVO}(N))} < \frac{4}{3}$$

The proofs of this and the previously stated results are contained in Ottmann, Rosenberg, Six and Wood [1978].

References:

1. Adelson-Velskii, G.M, and Landis, Y.M.: An algorithm for the organization of information, Doklady Akademij Nauk SSSR 146, 1962,263-266.
2. Aho, A.V., Hopcroft, J.E., and Ullman, J.D.: The design and analysis of computer algorithms, Addison-Wesley, Reading Mass., 1974.
3. Miller, R., Pippenger, N., Rosenberg, A., and Snyder, L.: Optimal 2,3-trees. IBM Res.Rep. RC 65o5, 1977, to appear in SIAM J.Comp.
4. Ottmann, Th., and Six, H.W.: Eine neue Klasse von ausgeglichenen Binärbäumen. Angewandte Informatik 8, 1976, 395-4oo.
5. Ottmann, Th., Six, H.W., and Wood, D.: Right brother trees. Comm. ACM 21, 1978, 769-776.

6. Ottmann, Th., and Wood, D.: 1-2 brother trees or AVL trees revisited. To appear in The Computer Journal.

7. Ottmann, Th., Rosenberg, A.L., Six, H.W., and Wood, D.: Minimal-Cost Brother Trees, Institut für Angewandte Informatik und Formale Beschreibungsverfahren, Report 73, Karlsruhe, 1978.

8. Rosenberg, A., and Snyder, L.: Minimum comparison 2,3 trees, IBM Res.Rep. RC6551, 1977. To appear in SIAM J.Comp.

A GRAPH THEORETIC APPROACH TO DETERMINISM VERSUS NON-DETERMINISM

(short preliminary version)

W.J. Paul
R. Reischuk

Abstract: A graph theoretic conjecture which implies lower bounds for the difficulty of certain computational tasks is discussed. A graph theoretic result related to this conjecture is proven. Alternation is shown to increase the power of multitape Turing machines.

1.) By $DTIME_k(t(n))$ $[NTIME_k(t(n))]$ we denote the set of all languages which are accepted by some deterministic [nondeterministic] $O(t(n))$-time bounded k-tape Turing machine. Let

$$DTIME(t(n)) = \bigcup_k DTIME_k(t(n)) \text{ and}$$
$$NTIME(t(n)) = \bigcup_k NTIME_k(t(n)).$$

We call a function time constructible if there is a deterministic $O(t(n))$-time bounded 2-tape Turing machine which given any input of length n produces the binary representation of t(n).

Suppose $DTIME(t(n)) \subsetneq NTIME(t(n))$ for some contructible function t(n). By easy padding [RF] implies.

(1.1) $\qquad DTIME(n) \subsetneq NTIME(n)$

but it is not known, if (1.1) holds.

We use dag for a directed acylic graph and write n-dag for a dag with n edges. If(u,v) is an edge in a graph G, u is called father of v and v is called son of u. A source is a node without father and a sink is a node without son. The indegree of a node is the number of its fathers and the indegree of a graph is the maximum of the indegrees of its nodes. If there is a directed path from u to v, u is called predecessor of v. With Pred(v,G) we denote the set of all predecessors of v in G.

If $G=(V,E)$ is a dag and $S\subset E$, then $G(S)$ denotes $(V,E\setminus S)$. We call S a k-depth separator for G, if the depth (i.e. the maximum number of edges in a directed path) of $G(S)$ is at most k. With $D(k,n)$ we denote the smallest number s, such that every n-dag has a k-depth separator with s edges.

It is known [EGS] that

(2.1) $\Omega(n/\log n)\leq D(n/\log n,n)\leq O(n\log\log n/\log n)$.

Valiant has shown

Fact 1 [V77]: If $G=(V,E)$ is an n-dag of depth d and $s\leq\log d$, then there is $S\subset E$ such that $|S|\leq ns/\log d$ and $G(S)$ has depth at most $d/2^s$.
Also in [V77] Valiant proposes the problem to settle:

Depth separator conjecture (DSC):

$D(\log n,n)=o(n)$
Fact 1 and DSC imply that there exist functions ℓ_1,ℓ_2 such that (2.2), (2.3) and (2.4) hold:

(2.2) $\ell_1(n)=o(\log n)$, (2.3) $\ell_2(n)=o(n)$, (2.4) $D(\ell_1(n),n)\leq\ell_2(n)$.

Let $G=(V,E)$ be a dag and $S\subset E$. S is called a Pr-separator for G, if $|\mathrm{Pred}(v,G(S))|\leq|S|$ for all $v\in V$. Let $m_c(n)$ denote the smallest number s such that every n-dag with indegree c has a Pr-separator with s edges. Assume DSC, let $G=(V,E)$ be an n-dag with indegree c, let $S\subset E$ be an $\ell_1(n)$-depth separator for G with $\ell_2(n)$ edges and let $v\in V$. Then $|\mathrm{Pred}\,(v,G(S))|\leq c^{\ell_1(n)}=2^{0(\log n)}=o(n)$. Thus DSC implies

Predecessors separator conjecture (PSC):

(2.5) $m_c(n)=o(n)$. In the next section we prove

Theorem 1: PSC implies $\mathrm{DTIME}(n)\subsetneq\mathrm{NTIME}(n)$.

2.) For languages L let $A(L)$ be the smallest alphabet A such that $L\subset(A(L))^*$ and $\bar{L}=(A(L))^*\setminus L$. For classes of languages K let $CK=\{\bar{L}\mid L\in K\}$. Assume (1.1) is false, then (*) $\mathrm{DTIME}(n)=\mathrm{NTIME}(n)=\mathrm{CNTIME}(n)$.

In what follows we represent elements of sets as 0/1-strings, sets or lists as the list of their elements separated by #. A list represents a set, if no element occurs twice. Graphs G are represented by representing for each node the set of its fathers and then forming with these lists a list r_G. In what follows we often identify sets with their representation.

Lemma 1(*): The following languages are all in DTIME(n).

$L_1=\{S\mid S$ represents a set$\}$
$L_2=\{(S_1,S_2)\mid S_1$ represents a subset of $S_2\}$

$L_3 = \{(r,S) \mid r$ represents a graph $G = (V,E)$, $S \subset E$ is a path in $G\}$

$L_4 = \{(r,u,v) \mid r$ represents a graph $G = (V,E)$, $u,v \in V$ and there is no path from u to v$\}$

$L_5 = \{r \mid r$ represents a dag$\}$

$L_6 = \{(r,S,P,v) \mid r$ represents a dag $G = (V,E)$, $S \subset E$, $P \subset V$, $P = \mathrm{Pred}(v,G(S))\}$

$L_7 = \{(r,S) \mid r$ represents a dag G and S is a Pr-separator for G$\}$

Proof: Because we assume (*) it sufficies in any case to give nondeterministic linear time algorithms for the recognition of $\bar{L}_i$. Moreover for the construction of the recognition algorithm for $\bar{L}_i$ one can use deterministic linear time recognition algorithms for $L_1,\dots,L_{i-1}$ as subroutines. The details are an easy exercise. □

Fix some standard encoding of nondeterministic 2-tape Turing machines into $\{0,1\}^*$. For $u \in \{0,1\}^*$ let M_u denote a machine with encoding u. It is then easy to construct a universal 2-tape machine U which given input $u \# v$, $u,v \in \{0,1\}^*$ simulates M_u on input v such that if M_u given input v makes $t \geq |v|$ steps, then U given input $u \# v$ makes at most $c_1 |u|^2 t$ steps, where c_1 does not depend on u and v. For symbols s and natural numbers k s^k denotes the string s...s (k-times).

Lemma 2 (*): If T(n) is time constructible, then $\mathrm{NTIME}(T(n)) \subseteq \mathrm{DTIME}_c(T(n))$ for some c.

Proof: Let

$L_8 = \{u \# v \#^{|u|^2 T(|v|)} \mid$ there is an accepting computation of M_u given v with at most $T(|v|)$ steps$\}$.

Clearly $L_8 \in \mathrm{NTIME}(n)$, hence by (*) $L_8 \in \mathrm{DTIME}_c(n)$ for some c. Let $L \in \mathrm{NTIME}(T(n))$, then $L \in \mathrm{NTIME}_2(T(n))$ by [BGW]. But then L can be reduces by a deterministic T(n)-time bounded 2-tape Turing machine to L_8, hence $L \in \mathrm{DTIME}_c(T(n))$. □

Lemma 3 (*): If T(n) is time constructible and $\liminf t(n)/T(n) = 0$ then $\mathrm{DTIME}(T(n))/\mathrm{NTIME}(t(n)) \neq \emptyset$.

Proof: We describe a nondeterministic 3-tape Turing machine M. Given input $u \# v$, $u,v \in \{0,1\}^*$ M first generates the binary representation of $T(|u \# v|)$ and stores it on tape 3. Then M simulates on tapes 1 and 2 M_u on input $u \# v$; in parallel M counts on tape 3 from $T(|u \# v|)$ to 0. If M finds that M_u accepts before the number on tape 3 is zero, M accepts, otherwise M rejects.

It is easy to organize M such that M is O(T(n))-time bounded and such that given input $u \# v$ M simulates M_u for at least $c_2 T(|u \# v|)/|u|^2$ steps, where c_2 does not depend on u and v.

Let L denote the language accpeted by M: clearly $L \in \mathrm{NTIME}(T(n))$. Lemma 2 implies $\mathrm{NTIME}(T(n)) = \mathrm{DTIME}(T(n))$ which in turn implies $\bar{L} \in \mathrm{DTIME}(T(n))$. But [BGW] together with the usual diagonal argument shows $\bar{L} \notin \mathrm{NTIME}(t(n))$. □

Lemma 4(*): If T(n) is time constructible, then for all c:
$DTIME_c(T(n)) \subseteq NTIME(n+T^{1/2}(n)m_{2c+1}(T^{1/2}(n)))$.

Lemma 4 together with PSC yields the following contradiction. Choose c as in lemma 2 and T(n) large enough, then

$$NTIME(T^{1/2}(n)m_{2c+1}(T^{1/2}(n)) \subsetneq DTIME(T(n)) \quad \text{by lemma 3 and PSC}$$
$$\subseteq DTIME_c(T(n)) \quad \text{by lemma 2}$$
$$\subseteq NTIME(T^{1/2}(n)m_{2c+1})(T^{1/2}(n)) \quad \text{by lemma 4.}$$

Proof of Lemma 4: Let M be a $C\cdot T(n)$-time bounded deterministic c-tape Turing machine. Given input w for M with $|w| = n$ divide the tape of M in blocks of $\Delta(n) = C(2c+1)T^{1/2}(n)$ tape squares each and divide the time M spends into time intervals of $\Delta(n)$ steps each. A block b is called active in time interval i if at least one tape square of it is visited by a head during that time interval. There are at most $\tau = \Delta(n)/(2c+1)$ time intervals and in each time intervals at most 2c blocks are active. We define the computation graph $G = (V,E)$ of M given w:

$V = \{0,1,\dots,\tau\}$ = the set of time intervals $\cup\{0\}$:
For $u \neq 0$:
$(u,v) \in E$ if there is a block b which is active in time intervals v and u, $v > u$ and b is not active in time intervals $u+1,\dots,v-1$.
$(0,v) \in E$ if there is a block b which is active in time interval v, $v > 0$ and b is not active in time intervals $1,\dots,v-1$.
$(u,u+1) \in E$ for all $u < \tau$.

Clearly the indegree of G is bounded by 2c+1.

For $u \in \{1,\dots,\tau\}$ res(u) denotes a straight forward encoding of the inscriptions of the blocks which are active in time interval u, the headpositions and the state of M at the end of time interval u. res(0) = w = the input. The encoding can easily be choosen such that $|res(u)| = O(\Delta(n)) = O(T^{1/2}(n))$ for all $u > 0$. Also res(v) can be computed in $O(\Delta(n))$ steps from $\{res(u) \mid (u,v) \in E\}$ by simulation of M for exactly b steps where $b = O(\Delta(n)$ is the lenght of the block inscriptions in the res(u)'s. Note that in order to determine if M accpets w it sufficies to compute $res(\tau)$.

A fragment for w is a pair $(r_G,\{res(v) \mid v \in U\})$ where $G = (V,E)$ is the computation graph of M given w and $U \subseteq V$. If we encode a fragment in a straight forward way and identify the fragment with its encoding then

$$|r_G,\{res(v) \mid v \in U\}| \leq O(T^{1/2}(n)(\log T(n)+|U|)).$$

A potential fragment F is any string which has the format of a fragment, i.e. F is a pair $\{r_{G'},\{res'(v) \mid v \in U'\}$ where $G' = (V',E')$ is a graph, $U' \subset V'$ and the res'(v) have the format of strings res(v). If $v \in U'$ and if we can simulate M starting from w and $\{res'(u) \mid u \in Pred(v,G') \cap U\}$ in the obvious way and obtain res'(v), then the potential fragment F is called (v,w)-consistent. F is called w-consistent, if it is (v,w)-consistent for all $v \in U'$. Clearly a potential fragment is a fragment for w iff G' is acyclic and F is w- consistent.

We now describe a nondeterministic machine Q which simulates M. Given input w with $|w| = M$. Q guesses the representation of a graph $G = (V,E)$, $V = \{0,\ldots,\tau\}, \tau = \Delta(n)/(2c+1)$ and a subset $S \subset E$. If G is not a dag or S is not a Pr-separator for G, Q rejects. Otherwise let $V(S) = \{v \mid \exists u \in V: (u,v) \in S\} \cup \{\tau\}$. Q guesses $\{res'(v) \mid v \in V(S)\}$ and accepts iff the potential fragment $(r_G, \{res'(v) \mid v \in V(S)\})$ is w- consistent and $res'(\tau)$ contains the accepting state of M. Clearly Q simulates M.

It remains to show how to organize Q such that there is an accepting computation of Q given w of at most $O(T^{1/2}(n) m_{2c+1}(T^{1/2}(n)))$ steps if M accepts w. If Q guesses $G = (V,E)$ as the computation graph of M given w then $|E| \leq \Delta(n)$. If Q guesses S as a minimal Pr-separator for G, i.e. $|S| = m_{2c+1}(|E|)$, then

$$|(r_G, \{res'(v) \mid v \in U'\})| \leq O(\Delta(n)(\log \Delta(n) + m_{2c+1}(|E|)$$

$$= O(\Delta(n) m_{2c+1}(\Delta(n))) = O(T^{1/2}(n) m_{2c+1}(T^{1/2}(n))).$$

As by lemma 1 Q can test quickly if r_G represents a dag and if S is a Pr-separator it now suffices to show

Lemma 5(*): The following languages are all in DTIME(n)

$L_9 = \{(w,r,S,v,P,\{res'(n) \mid u \in U\}) \mid r$ represents a dag $G = (V,E)$, S is Pr-separator for G, $P = Pred\ (v,G(S))$, $U = V(S) \cup P$, $|res'(u)| = |res'(u')|$ for all $u,u' \in U$, $(r,\{res'(u) \mid u \in U\})$ is (v,w)-consistent$\}$

$L_{10} = \{(w,r,S, \{res'(u) \mid u \in U\}) \mid r$ represents a dag $G = (V,E)$, S is a Pr-separator for G, $U = V(S)$, $|res'(u)| = |res'(u')|$ for all u,u', $(r,\{res'(u) \mid u \in U\})$ is not (v,w)-consistent$\}$

$L_{11} = \{(w,r,S,\{res'(u) \mid u \in U\}) \mid r$ represents a dag $G = (V,E)$, S is a Pr-separator for G, $U = V(S)$, $|res'(u)| = |res'(u')|$ for all u,u', $(r,\{res'(u) \mid u \in U\})$ is w.consistent$\}$.

The proof of lemma 5 follows exactly the pattern of the proof of lemma 1. □

3.) We construct a family of graphs G_n with big depth separators.

In [PT] a bipartite graph with n inputs and n outputs, called <u>n-i/j-expander</u> is defined, which has the property, that for every subset of n/i inputs there exists a subset of n/j outputs, such that to each of these outputs there is an edge from the given n/i inputs. It exists $s \in \mathbb{N}$ such that for all $n \geq s$ n-8/2-expanders exist with outdegree of every input exactly 16. These 16 edges running from an input can be replaced by a complete binary tree. Let E_n be such a graph with $s \cdot 2^n$ inputs/outputs, outdegree ≤ 2 and path length from an input to an output exactly 4.

Let G_0 be the graph E_0. G_{n+1} consists of 3 copies of E_{n+1} called E^{ℓ}_{n+1}, $\ell = 1,2,3$, with input $I^{\ell}(i^1_1,\dots,i^{\ell}_{s2^{n+1}})$ and outputs $O^{\ell} = (o^{\ell}_1,\dots,o^{\ell}_{s2^{n+1}})$, and 2 copies of G_n called G^{ℓ}_n, $\ell = 1,2$, with inputs $J^{\ell} = (j^{\ell}_1,\dots,j^{\ell}_{s2^n})$ and outputs $Q^{\ell} = (q^{\ell}_1,\dots,q^{\ell}_{s2^n})$. The inputs of G_{n+1} are $J = I^1$ and the outputs $Q = O^2$. Identify I^1 with I^3 by $i^1_r = i^3_r$ and O^1 with O^3 by $o^1_r = o^3_r$ for $1 < r \leq s2^{n+1}$ and add the following edges:
(o^1_r, j^1_r), $(o^1_{s\cdot 2^n + r}, j^1_r)$, (q^1_r, j^2_r), (q^2_r, o^2_r), $(q^2_r, o^2_{s\cdot 2^n + r})$ for $1 \leq r \leq s2^n$.

We get $|V(G_n)| = O(n2^n)$ and the outdegree of G_n is bounded by 4. In the sequel $n \geq 8$ is fixed and we consider G_n and the 2^{n-m} copies of G_m for $0 \leq m \leq n$ in this graph. In G_n we remove nodes instead of edges to reduce depth, this makes no difference because the outdegree is bounded. Let $S \subset V(G_n)$ be a depth separator.

<u>Definition</u>: E_m is called <u>blocked</u>, if $|V(E_m) \cap S| \geq s2^{m-3}$. G_m is called blocked, if at least one of the graphs $E^{\ell}_m (\ell = 1,2,3)$ corresponding to G_m is blocked.

One can easily prove <u>Lemma 6</u>:
Let $E_m(G_m)$ not be blocked, then for every subset A of inputs of $E_m(G_m)$ with $|A| \geq 1/4\ s\ 2^m$ there exists a subset B of outputs of $E_m(G_m)$ with $|B| \geq 3/8\ s\ 2^m$, such that for all $b \in B$ there exists $a \in A$ and a path w from a to b in $E_m \setminus S$ $(G_m \setminus S)$ of length 4.

Let $S(n,k)$ be the minimal size of a k-depth separator of G_n and $N = |V(G_n)|$.

<u>Theorem 2</u>: There exist $c_1, c_2 > 0$, such that for all $8 \leq k \leq 2^n$

$$c_1\ N/\log k \leq S(n,k) \leq c_2\ N/\log k.$$

For $k = 2^n = O(N/\log N)$ we get the same lower bound up to a constant factor as in [EGS]. This family of graphs gives lower bounds for arbitrary little depth, especially $D(O(\log N), N) \leq \Omega(N/\log \log N)$.

<u>Proof of the lower bound</u>:
Choose k as above and suppose $S \subset V(G_n)$ is a k-depth separator. We can assume $k = 2^t$ with $t \in \mathbb{N}$. For $r = 1,2,\dots,\lfloor n/t \rfloor$ let be $j_r = n-(r-1)\,t$ and consider the 2^{n-j_r} disjoint subgraphs G_{j_r} of G_n.
In what follows we deal only with a fixed subgraph G_{j_r} and its subgraphs up to $G_{j_r - t}$.

<u>Definition</u>: For $0 \leq x \leq t$ let $m(x)$ be the number of graphs G_{j_r-x}, which are blocked and no supergraph G_{j_r-y} of G_{j_r-x} for $0 \leq y < x$ is blocked.
An <u>open</u> path is a path which uses only nodes of $V(G_n) \setminus S$.

By induction on x we construct an open path w in G_{j_r}, which touches only subgraphs G_{j_r-x} of G_{j_r} for $0 \leq x \leq t-1$.

<u>x = 0</u>

<u>Case i)</u>: G_{j_r} is blocked; then choose $w = \emptyset$.

<u>Stop</u>.

<u>Case ii)</u>: G_{j_r} is not blocked; then the following statements are trivially true for $x = 0$:

a) there exists $A \subset$ inputs of $G_{j_r-x} - S$, $|A| \geq 1/4\ s\ 2^{j_r-x}$, such that for all $a \in A$ there exists an open path w_1 from J_{j_r} = inputs of G_{j_r} to a

b) there exists $B \subset$ outputs of $G_{j_r-x} - S$, $|B| \geq 3/8\ s\ 2^{j_r-x}$, and for all B with this property holds: there is an open path w_2 from B to Q_{j_r} = outputs of G_{j_r}.

c) there exists an open path w from J_{j_r} to Q_{j_r}, which runs over the graph $E^3_{j_r-x}$ corresponding to G_{j_r-x}.

For $x = 0$ c) says that there exists an open path of length 4 from J_{j_r} to Q_{j_r} over $E^3_{j_r}$.

<u>Induction step $x \to x+1$:</u>
Let G_{j_r-x} be a subgraph of G_{j_r}, such that neither in this (G_{j_r-x}) nor in one of his supergraphs there has been a Stop, and let $G^1_{j_r-(x+1)}$ and $G^2_{j_r-(x+1)}$ be the two subgraphs of G_{j_r-x}. For G_{j_r-x} a) - c) holds.

<u>Case i)</u>: $G^1_{j_r-(x+1)}$ or $G^2_{j_r-(x+1)}$ is blocked or $x = t-1$.

<u>Stop</u>.

<u>Case ii)</u>: Otherwise we can choose according to a) a subset A of inputs of G_{j_r-x}. As G_{j_r-x} is not blocked, we can conclude from lemma 6 that there is $C_1 \subset$ outputs of $E^1_{j_r-x} - S$, $|C_1| \geq 3/8\ s\ 2^{j_r-x}$, such that for all $c \in C_1$ there exists an open path from A to c, call it w_3.

C_1 is connected to at least $3/8\ s\ 2^{j_r-x}/2 - s\ 2^{j_r-(x+1)-3} = 1/4\ s\ 2^{j_r-(x+1)}$ inputs of $G^1_{j_r-(x+1)} - S$, call this set of nodes A_1. It follows that there exists $B_1 \subset$ outputs of $G^1_{j_r-(x+1)} - S$,

$|B_1| \geq 3/8\ s\ 2^{j_r-(x+1)}$, such that for all $b_1 \in B_1$ there is an open path w_4 from A_1 to b_1 over $E^3_{j_r-(x+1)}$

For B_1 and for all $B_1' \subset$ outputs of $G^1_{j_r-(x+1)}-S$ with $|B_1'| \geq 3/8\ s\ 2^{j_r-(x+1)}$ we have:

it exists $A_2 \subset$ inputs of $G^2_{j_r-(x+1)}-S$, $|A_2| \geq 1/4\ s\ 2^{j_r-(x+1)}$, such that for all $a_2 \in A_2$ there is an open path (edge) w_5 from B_1 (B_1') to a_2, because $G^2_{j_r-(x+1)}$ is not blocked.

Now we can find $B_2 \subset$ outputs of $G^2_{j_r-(x+1)}-S$, $|B_2| \geq 3/8\ s\ 2^{j_r-(x+1)}$, such that for all $b_2 \in B_2$ there is an open path w_6 from A_2 to b_2 over $E^3_{j_r-(x+1)}$. Let C_2 be the set of inputs of $E^2_{j_r-x}-S$ connected with nodes of B_2 by an edge, then

$|C_2| \geq 2 \cdot 3/8\ s\ 2^{j_r-(x+1)} - s\ 2^{j_r-x-3} = 1/4\ s\ 2^{j_r-x}$.

The last statement is also true for all $B_2' \subset$ outputs of $G^2_{j_r-(x+1)}-S$ with $|B_2'| \geq 3/8\ s\ 2^{j_r-(x+1)}$

Finally there is $B \subset$ outputs of $E^2_{j_r-x}-S$ with $|B| \geq 3/8\ s\ 2^{j_r-x}$, such that for all $b \in B$ there exists an open path w_7 from C_2 to b.

One sees easily, that statement a)(b)) holds for $G^l_{j_r-(x+1)}$ ($l = 1,2$) with A_1 (B_1) and the path $w_1\ w_3$ edge between C_1 and A_1, resp. $w_1\ w_3$ edge between C_1 and $A_1\ w_4\ w_5$ ($w_5\ w_6$ edge between B_2 and $C_2 w_7 w_2$, resp. edge between B_2 and $C_2 w_7 w_2$).

The path $w_1\ w_3$ edge between C_1 and $A_1\ w_4\ w_5\ w_6$ edge between B_2 and $C_2\ w_7\ w_2$ satisfies c). The length of the path from J_{j_r} to Q_{j_r} has changed by:

$|w_3|+1+|w_4|+|w_5|+|w_6|+1+|w_7| - |\text{path in } E^3_{j_t-x}| = 4+1+4+1+4+1+4-4 = 15.$

Let p_{j_r} = number of removed nodes in the graphs $E_{j_r},\dots,E_{j_r-(t-1)}$ which are subgraphs of G_{j_r}. By definition of m(x) we have:

$$P_{j_r} \geq \sum_{x=0}^{t-2} m(x) s\ 2^{j_r-x-3};$$

on the other hand the maximal length L of a path satisfies: if we never stop in a graph G_{j_r-x} with $0 \leq x \leq t-2$ then

$$L = 4 + \sum_{x=1}^{t-1} 15\ 2^x/2 = \sum_{x=0}^{t-1} 15\ 2^x = (2^{t-1}-1)\ 15$$
$$\geq 4\ 2^t = 4k;$$

if we stop in a graph G_{j_r-x} with $x \neq t-1$, L decreases by

$$L(x) = \sum_{i=1}^{t-1-x} 15\ 2^i/2 = (2^{t-1-x}-1)\ 15 \leq 2^{t-x+3}$$

As we stop m(x) -times in a graph G_{j_r-x} we get for L

$$L \geq 4\ 2^t - \sum_{x=0}^{t-2} m(x)\ 2^{t-x+3}$$

By hypothesis S is a k-depth-separator, i.e. $L \leq k = 2^t$. Therefore

$$\sum_{x=0}^{t-2} m(x)\ 2^{t-x+3} \geq 4\ 2^t - L \geq 3\ 2^t$$

This gives: $p_{j_r} \geq \sum_{x=0}^{t-2} m(x)\ 2^{t-x+3}\ s\ 2^{j_r-t-6} \geq 3\ 2^t\ s\ 2^{j_r-t-6} = 3\ s\ 2^{j_r-6}$

This holds for all r and all subgraphs G_{j_r}, therefore we get for the size of S:

$$|S| \geq \sum_r \sum_{j_r} p_{j_r} \geq \sum_r 2^{n-j_r} p_{j_r} \geq \sum_r 3\ s\ 2^{n-6} \geq$$

$$3\ s\ \lfloor n/t \rfloor\ 2^{n-6} \geq c\ n\ 2^n/t \geq c_1\ N/\log k$$

for suitable $c, c_1 > 0$. □

Proof of the upper bound:

Let be $t = \log k - 4$ and r and j_r as defined before. Remove all inputs and outputs of G_{j_r} to get an depth separator S. The construction of G_n shows that every open path, which hits G_{j_r}, cannot hit nodes outside of G_{j_r} nor nodes in graphs G_{j_r-x} for $x \geq t$, because inputs and outputs of G_{j_r+1} are also removed. Therefore any open path can touch at most $3(2^0 + 2^1 + \ldots 2^{t-1}) = 3 \cdot 2^t$ expanders. This bounds the maximal length of paths by $5 \cdot 3 \cdot 2^t = 15\ 2^{\log k-4} < k$.

The size of S is:

$$|S| \leq \sum_{r=1}^{n/t} 2^{n-j_r}\ 2 \cdot s\ 2^{j_r} \leq n/t\ 2s\ 2^n$$

$$= 2\ s\ n\ 2^n/(\log k - 4) \leq 4\ s\ n\ 2^n/\log k \leq c_2\ N/\log k$$

for suitable $c_2 > 0$ because $\log k \geq 8$. □

4.) For definitions of alternating Turing machines and their complexity see [CS]. Let ATIME(t(n)) = {L|L is accepted by some alternating O(t(n))-time bounded Turing machine}.

Theorem 4: For all t(n)

$$\mathrm{DTIME}(t(n)) \subseteq \mathrm{ATIME}(n + t(n) \log\log t(n)/\log t(n)).$$

Standard diagonalization implies

Corollary 2: If $t_1(n)$ is time constructible and
$\liminf t_1(n)\log\log t_1(n)/t_2(n)\log t_1(n) = 0$ then $DTIME(t_1(n)) \subsetneq ATIME(t_2(n))$.

Proof of theorem 4: Let M be a $O(t(n))$-time bounded multitape Turing machine. We describe an alternating machine Q which simulates M. Given input w with $|w| = n$ Q guesses existentially (i.e. in existential states) a potential fragment

$$F = (r_G, \{res'(v) \mid v \in U \cup \{\tau\}\})$$

where $G = (V,E)$ is intended to be the computation graph of M given w for block size $\Delta(n) = t^{1/2}(n)$, τ the node corresponding to the last time interval and $U \subset E$. Q accepts iff F is w-consistent and $res'(\tau)$ contains the accepting state of M.

In order to check if F is w-consistent, Q chooses universally a node $u \in U \cup \{\tau\}$ and accepts iff F is (u,w)-consistent. In order to check the latter Q proceeds recursively

(7.1) guess existentially
$F' = \{res'(v) \mid v \text{ is father of } u\}$

(7.2) Simulate M for $\Delta(n)$ steps starting from the data in F'. If the outcome is not $res'(u)$ reject.

(7.3) Choose universally $v_0 \in F'$; if $v_0 \in U$ then accepts iff $res'(v_0)$ as guesses in (7.1) equals $res'(v_0) \in F$,
else check if $F' = (r_G, \{res'(v) \mid v \in U \cup \{\tau, v_0\}\})$ is (v_0,w)-consistent.

Q simulates M. Let $m = |E|$ and $k = m/\log m$. By (2.1) U can be chosen as a k-depth separator with $|U| = O(m \log\log m/\log m)$. If M accepts w, if F is guessed correctly and U is chosen as above, then $|E| = O(t^{1/2}(n))$ and one can easily verify that the computation tree of Q given w has an accepting subtree of depth
$O(t(n) \log\log t(n)/\log t(n))$. □

5. References

[CS] A. Chandra and L. Stockmeyer: Alternation
17th IEEE-FOCS, 98-108, 1976

[EGS] P. Erdös, R. Graham and E. Szemeredi: Sparse graphs with nse long paths
Stan-CS-75-504, Computer Science Dept., Stanford University, 1975

[HPV] J. Hopcroft, W. Paul and L. Valiant: On time versus space
J. ACM 24, 332-337, 1977

[LT] R. Lipton and R. Tarjan: Applications of a planar separator theorem
18th IEEE-FOCS, 162-170, 1977

[P] N. Pippenger: Superconcentrators
Preprint

[PF] N. Pippenger and M. Fischer: Relations among complexity measures
Preprint

[PT] W. Paul and R. Tarjan: Time-space trade-offs in a pebble game
To appear in Acta Informatica

[PTC] W. Paul, R. Tarjan and J. Celoni: Space bounds for a game on graphs
Math. Syst. Theory, 10, 239-251. 1977

[RF] Ruby and P. Fischer: Translational methods and computational complexity
IEEE-SWAT 1965, 173-178

[S] C.P. Schnorr: The network complexity and the Turing complexity of finite functions
Acta Informatica 7, 95-107, 1976

[V75] L. Valiant: On non-linear lower bounds in computational complexity
7th ACM-SOC, 45-53, 1975

[BGW] R.V. Book, S.A. Greibach and B. Wegbreit: Time and tape bounded Turing acceptors and AFL's.
J. CSS 4, 606-621, 1970

UNE CARACTERISATION DE TROIS VARIETES DE LANGAGES BIEN CONNUES

J.E. Pin

La théorie des variétés a été introduite par S. Eilenberg pour unifier la présentation de plusieurs résultats caractérisant certaines familles de langages rationnels. Parmi les plus connus des résultats de ce type citons le théorème de Schützenberger caractérisant les langages apériodiques (ou "star-free") [13], le théorème de Simon sur les langages J-triviaux [17], ou encore les travaux de Brzozowski - Simon [1], Mc Naughton [5], Zalcstein [18] sur les langages localement testables.

La théorie des codes, inaugurée par Schützenberger en 1956 [16] se proposait quant à elle d'étudier les sous-monoïdes libres d'un monoïde libre. Nous renvoyons le lecteur à l'article de synthèse de J-F. Perrot [6] pour un historique et une bibliographie plus complète sur cette théorie.

A priori, la théorie des variétés et la théorie des codes semblaient être totalement indépendantes l'une de l'autre. Mais l'introduction des codes à délai de synchronisation borné (Golomb et Gordon [3]) a mis en évidence le caractère syntactique de nombreuses propriétés des codes. Par la suite, les travaux de Schützenberger [12] Restivo [10] [11], Hashigushi-Honda [4] ont souligné le lien qui existait entre les codes purs (resp très purs) et les langages apériodiques (resp localement testables). Par ailleurs diverses tentatives ont été faites par Eilenberg [2B chap X] et par Schützenberger [15] visant à utiliser des codes pour décrire certaines variétés.

Le but de cet article est de compléter ces résultats en caractérisant 3 variétés bien connues (les rationnels, les apériodiques et les localement testables à l'aide des codes préfixes <u>finis</u> qu'elles contiennent. Avec les notations d'Eilenberg [2B], on a le

<u>Théorème principal</u>. La variété des langages rationnels (resp. apériodiques, localement testables) est la plus petite +-variété $\mathcal{V}$ telle que

(i) Pour tout alphabet X, $X^+\mathcal{V}$ contient les parties de X^2

(ii) Pour tout code préfixe fini (resp fini pur, fini très pur) $P \subset X^+$,

$P \in X^+$ entraîne $P^+ \in X^+$

Ce résultat appelle plusieurs commentaires. Nous commencerons par une précision d'ordre technique : les langages sont ici des parties de X^+ (et non de X^*) ce qui permet une formulation unique du résultat principal. On constate en effet que tous les théorèmes connus sur les $*$-variétés correspondent à des théorèmes sur les $+$-variétés, mais la réciproque n'est pas vraie : ainsi pourrions-nous formuler un résultat analogue en termes de $*$-variétés pour les rationnels et les apériodiques mais pas pour les localement testables.

En second lieu, on constate que les 3 variétés considérées sont caractérisées en utilisant la seule opération "plus inambigu". On peut d'ailleurs en déduire que les langages rationnels forment la plus petite $+$-variété littérale(1) fermée pour l'opération "plus" ce qui constitue le pendant des théorèmes de Perrot [8] sur les $*$-variétés fermées par étoile.

Notre troisième observation concerne les langages apériodiques : la caractérisation que nous en donnons est à notre connaissance la seule à ne pas faire appel à l'opération produit. On s'aperçoit d'ailleurs, et ce sera notre quatrième remarque, que le théorème général démontré par Eilenberg [2B chap 10. Th 4.1] pour caractériser les variétés à l'aide des semi-groupes libres qu'elles contiennent ne s'applique qu'à des variétés fermées par produit. Or la variété des langages localement testables n'est pas fermée par produit (ni même par produit inambigu) et notre résultat montre qu'elle admet cependant une caractérisation du même type.
On notera par ailleurs que les codes préfixes qui interviennent sont finis ce qui n'était pas le cas dans les théorèmes évoqués plus haut.

Enfin, la similitude d'énoncés obtenue pour ces 3 variétés est quelque peu surprenante si on se réfère aux résultats précédemment connus que nous rappelons plus loin.

1. Préliminaires

1) Soit X un ensemble fini et soit X^* et X^+ respectivement le monoïde et le semi-groupe libre engendrés par X. On appelle lettres les éléments de X, mots les éléments de X^+ et langages les sous-ensembles de X^+. On notera $|f|$ la longueur du mot $f \in X^+$.

Si $L \subset X^+$ est un langage, le semi-groupe syntactique Synt L de L est le quotient de X^+ par la congruence $\sigma(L)$ suivante. $u \equiv v \mod \sigma(L)$ ssi pour tout $f, g \in X^*$ $fug \in L \Leftrightarrow fvg \in L$. Rappelons que L est rationnel ssi Synt L est fini. Nous supposerons désormais que tous les langages considérés sont rationnels et que tous les semi-groupes sont finis.

Rappelons également que l'automate minimal d'un langage a pour ensemble d'états $Q = \{ u^{-1}L : u \in X^* \}$ (où $u^{-1}L = \{ v \in X^* : uv \in L \}$). L'action d'un mot v sur l'ensemble Q est donnée par la formule $(u^{-1}L).v = (uv)^{-1} L = v^{-1}(u^{-1}L)$.

(1) Une variété $\mathcal{V}$ est littérale ssi pour tout alphabet X, $X^+\mathcal{V}$ contient les lettres

On sait alors que le semi-groupe de transition de l'automate minimal d'un langage L est isomorphe à Synt L.
Si $A = (Q, X, \delta)$ est un automate, on dit qu'un état $q_0 \in Q$ est un <u>zéro</u> ("sink state") si pour toute lettre $x \in X$, $q_0 x = q_0$. Si l'automate A possède un zéro q_0, on dit qu'un mot m est une <u>constante</u> dans A s'il existe un état $q_1 \in Q$ tel que pour tout $q \in Q$ $qm = q_0$ ou q_1. Il est clair que l'ensemble des constantes dans A est un idéal bilatère de X^+.

2) Une variété de langages (ou +-variété cf [2 B]) associe à tout alphabet X une classe $X^+\mathcal{V}$ de langages rationnels de $X^+\mathcal{V}$ telle que

(i) Pour tout alphabet X, $X^+\mathcal{V}$ est fermée pour les opérations booléennes finies
(ii) Si X et Y sont deux alphabets et φ un morphisme de semi-groupe de X^+ vers Y^+, alors $L \in Y^+\mathcal{V}$ entraine $L\varphi^{-1} \in X^+\mathcal{V}$
(iii) Pour tout alphabet X, $x \in X$ et $L \in X^+\mathcal{V}$ entraine $X^+ \cap x^{-1}L$, $X^+ \cap Lx^{-1} \in X^+\mathcal{V}$

Toujours en suivant Eilenberg, mais en évitant le préfixe "pseudo", nous appelerons variété de semi-groupes finis une classe V de semi-groupes finis telle que
(i) Si S_1, S_2 sont dans V, $S_1 \times S_2$ est dans V
(ii) Si S est un sous-semi-groupe de T et si T est dans V, alors S est dans V
(iii) Si S est un quotient de T et si T est dans V, alors S est dans V.

Associons à toute variété de langages $\mathcal{V}$, la plus petite variété de semi-groupes finis V contenant tous les semi-groupes syntactiques des langages de $\mathcal{V}$. Réciproquement, associons à toute variété V de semi-groupes finis une variété de langages $\overline{\mathcal{V}}$ en choisissant, pour chaque alphabet X , $X^+\mathcal{V}$ égal à la classe des langages de X^+ dont le semi-groupe syntactique est dans V.

Le théorème des variétés d'Eilenberg [2B] affirme que $\mathcal{V} = \overline{\mathcal{V}}$
En d'autres termes, il existe une correspondance bijective entre variétés de langages et variétés de semi-groupes finis.

3) Un langage L de X^+ est un code ssi le sous-semi-groupe A^+ engendré par A est libre de base A ie si tout élément de A^+ admet une factorisation et une seule en produit d'éléments de A . Un code A est dit préfixe si pour tout $u, v \in X^+$ $uv \in X^+$ et $u \in A^+$ entrainent $v \in A^+$.
Il est bien connu qu'un code préfixe A est aussi caractérisé par la condition $A \cap A X^+ = \emptyset$ ce qui signifie qu'un mot de A ne peut être facteur gauche d'un autre mot de A.

Un code est <u>pur</u> si $u^n \in A^+$ pour un entier $n > 0$ entraine $u \in A^+$
Un code est <u>très pur</u> si pour tout $u,v \in X^+$, les conditions $uv \in A^+$ et $vu \in A^+$ entrainent $u,v \in A^+$.

Enfin, un code est à délai de synchronisation borné s'il existe une entier $d > 0$ tel que pour tout $u \in A^d$ et pour tout $m_1, m_2 \in X^+$ on ait $m_1 u m_2 \in A^+$ entraine $m_1 u \in A^+$ et $u m_2 \in A^+$.

Les deux résultats qui suivent seront utilisées constamment dans la suite. Le premier a été énoncé et prouvé par Perrot en [7] et repose sur un résultat de Schützenberger [12]. Le second est une synthèse de 3 résultats de Restivo [11] (conditions (i) (ii) (iii)) de Hashigushi-Honda [4] (conditions (iii) et (IV)) et de Schützenberger [14]

<u>Proposition 1</u> Soit A un code apériodique. Alors A est pur ssi A^+ est apériodique.

(Dans le cas A fini, ce résultat avait déjà été établi par Restivo [10])

<u>Proposition 2</u> Soit A un code fini. Les conditions suivantes sont équivalentes

(i) A est très pur

(ii) A est à délai de synchronisation borné

(iii) A^+ est strictement localement testable

(iv) A^+ est localement testable

(v) Il existe un entier n tel que tout mot de A^n soit une constante dans l'automate minimal de A^+

2. Langages rationnels, apériodiques et localement testables

Soient L_1 et L_2 deux langages. $L_1 \cup L_2$ et $L_1L_2 = \{u_1u_2 : u_1 \in L_1, u_2 \in L_2\}$ désignent respectivement l'union et le produit de L_1 et L_2. Si $L_1 \cap L_2 = \emptyset$, l'union est dite <u>inambiguë</u>. Si tout mot de L_1L_2 s'écrit d'une façon et d'une seule comme produit d'un mot de L_1 par un mot de L_2, le produit est inambigu. Enfin si A est un code, l'opération "plus" appliquée à A sera dite inambiguë puisque le sous-semi-groupe A^+ est libre par définition.(En règle générale, on notera L^+ le sous-semi-groupe de X^+ engendré par L dans X^+).

1) Rappelons qu'on langage est <u>rationnel</u> s'il peut être obtenu à partir des lettres de l'alphabet à l'aide des opérations union, produit et plus. D'après le théorème de Kleene, un langage est rationnel ssi son semi-groupe syntactique est fini. Les langages rationnels forment donc une variété, que nous noterons Rat et dont voici deux autres caractérisations.

Proposition 3 (Eilenberg 2A p 186). Les langages de X^{+}Rat s'obtiennent à partir des lettres de l'alphabet X à l'aide des opérations union inambiguë, produit inambigu et plus inambigu.

(En fait l'énoncé original est formulé en termes de $*$-variétés, mais l'adaptation est immédiate.)

Proposition 4 (adaptée de Perrot [8]). Rat est la plus petite variété littérale fermée pour l'opération plus.

Là aussi l'énoncé original est formulé sur les $*$-variétés, ce qui permet de supprimer l'hypothèse "littérale". En revanche, cette hypothèse est ici nécéssaire: en effet les variétés suivantes sont fermées pour l'opération plus: les deux variétés triviales, à savoir la variété vide et la variété définie par $X^{+}\mathcal{U} = \{\emptyset, X^{+}\}$ pour tout alphabet X, mais aussi la variété non triviale correspondant à la variété de semi-groupes finis engendrée par $\mathbb{Z}/2\mathbb{Z}$. On peut démontrer la proposition 4 en adaptant la preuve de Perrot. Nous la retrouverons également comme corollaire du résultat principal.

2) Un langage est dit apériodique s'il peut être obtenu à partir des lettres de l'alphabet X à l'aide des opérations booléennes et du produit. Précisons que les opérations booléennes sont l'union finie, l'intersection finie et le passage au complémentaire dans X^{+}. D'après le théorème de Schützenberger (13) un langage rationnel est apériodique ssi son semi-groupe syntactique est apériodique (i.e. si tout groupe dans Synt L est trivial). Les langages apériodiques forment donc une variété, que nous noterons Ap et dont voici deux autres caractérisations:

Proposition 5 (Schützenberger (14)) X^{+}Ap est la plus petite classe $\mathcal{C}$ de langages de X^{+}, contenant les lettres de X, fermée pour les opérations union et produit et satisfaisant la condition:

(i) Pour tout code préfixe P à délai de synchronisation borné, $P \in \mathcal{C}$ entraine $P^{+} \in \mathcal{C}$

Proposition 6 (Eilenberg (2B p278 et280)) X^{+}Ap est la plus petite classe $\mathcal{C}$ de langages de X^{+}, contenant les lettres et l'ensemble vide, fermée pour les opérations union et produit inambigus et satisfaisant la condition

(i) Pour tout code préfixe pur P, $P \in \mathcal{C}$ entraine $P^{+} \in \mathcal{C}$

3) Soit k un entier positif. Un langage L de X^+ est k-testable s'il est saturé modulo l'équivalence $\sim_k$ ainsi définie sur X^+: pour tout u,v dans X^+ $u \sim_k v$ ssi

(a) u et v ont les mêmes préfixes et suffixes de longueur inférieure ou égale à k-1

(b) Tout facteur de longueur k de u est aussi facteur de v et réciproquement.

L est localement testable ssi il est k-testable pour un certain entier k. Le résultat qui suit a été obtenu indépendamment par Brzozowski-Simon (1) et par Mc Naughton (5)

Proposition 7 Un langage L est localement ssi S = Synt L est fini et si pour tout idempotent e, le sous-semi-groupe eSe est idempotent et commutatif.

On en déduit alors que les langages localement testables forment une variété que nous noterons Lt. Une autre caractérisation de cette variété, que l'on trouve également dans Zalcstein (18) est la suivante:

Proposition 8 X^+Lt est la fermeture booléenne des langages wX^*, X^*wX^* et X^*w (où w varie dans X^+)

Il existe de nombreuses autres caractérisations de cette variété dont nous ne ferons pas usage ici.

3) Résultats et commentaires

Théorème 1 La variété Rat est la plus petite variété $\mathcal{V}$ telle que

(i) Pour tout alphabet X, $X^+\mathcal{V}$ contient les parties de X^2

(ii) Pour tout code préfixe fini $P \subset X^+$, $P \in X^+\mathcal{V}$ entraine $P^+ \in X^+\mathcal{V}$

On en déduit le

Corollaire 1 La variété Rat est la plus petite variété $\mathcal{V}$ telle que pour tout alphabet X, $X^+\mathcal{V}$ contienne les langages P^+ où P est un code préfixe fini

Ce corollaire peut se déduire également de [9].

Théorème 2 La variété Ap est la plus petite variété $\mathcal{V}$ telle que

(i) Pour tout alphabet X, $X^+\mathcal{V}$ contient les parties de X^2

(ii) Pour tout code préfixe, fini et pur $P \subset X^+$, $P \in X^+\mathcal{V}$ entraine $P^+ \in X^+\mathcal{V}$

Corollaire 2 La variété Ap est la plus petite variété $\mathcal{V}$ telle que pour tout alphabet X, $X^+\mathcal{V}$ contienne les langages P^+ où P est un code préfixe fini pur.

Ces deux énoncés semblent fournir une généralisation de la proposition 6. En fait il existe une différence fondamentale entre la proposition 6 et le théorème 2 ci-dessus. La proposition 6 permet en effet de décrire, pour tout alphabet X, la classe X^+ Ap . Ce n'est pas le cas pour le théorème 2 : la description de la variété obtenue est globale.

Théorème 3 La variété Lt est la plus petite variété $\mathcal{V}$ telle que

(i) Pour tout alphabet X , $X^+\mathcal{V}$ contient les parties de X^2

(ii) Pour tout code préfixe, fini et très pur $P \subset X^+$, $P \in X^+\mathcal{V}$ entraine $P^+ \in X^+\mathcal{V}$

Corollaire 3 La variété Lt est la plus petite variété $\mathcal{V}$ telle que pour tout alphabet X, $X^+\mathcal{V}$ contienne les langages P^+ où P est un code préfixe fini très pur.

Compte tenu de la propsotion 2, ces énoncés restent valables si on remplace "très pur" par "à délai de synchronisation borné".

4) Schéma de la preuve

La preuve est malheureusement trop longue pour figurer ici in extenso. Nous nous contenterons d'en indiquer les principales étapes.
Il résulte des propositions 1 et 2 (section 1) que la variété Rat (resp Ap, Lt) satisfait les conditions (i) et (ii) du théorème 1 (resp 2 et 3). Il s'agit donc de prouver la partie réciproque de ces théorèmes. On va déjà montrer qu'une variété vérifiant les conditions des théorèmes 1, 2 ou 3, contient tous les langages finis. Nous allons prouver en fait un résultat un plus fort :

Proposition 9 Soit $\mathcal{V}$ une variété de langages vérifiant les deux conditions suivantes :

(a) Pour tout alphabet X ayant au moins 2 lettres, on a $\{xy\} \in X^+$ pour toute paire de lettres $x \neq y$ de X.

(b) Pour tout code préfixe, fini, très pur $P \subset X^+$, on a $P \in X^+\mathcal{V}$ entraine $P^+ \in X^+\mathcal{V}$

La preuve de cette proposition s'inspire assez largement de la preuve du théorème de Perrot sur les variétés fermées par étoile [8]. Il apparait cependant en cours de démonstration des difficultés techniques dues au fait que les codes utilisés doivent toujours être très purs. On commence par prouver que $\mathcal{V}$ contient les langages locaux (i.e. 2-testables) en remarquant que $\{x, yx\}$ est un code préfixe très pur sur l'alphabet $X = \{x,y\}$ et que Synt $\{x,yx\}^+$ engendre précisément la variété des semi-groupes finis associée - via le théorème des variétés d'Eilenberg-aux langages locaux.

On sait en particulier qu'un mot multilinéaire w sur X (i.e. tel que chaque lettre de X ait au plus une occurrence dans w) constitue à lui seul un langage local. Donc $\{w\} \in X^+\mathcal{V}$ si w est multilinéaire. On démontre ensuite - et c'est la partie la plus difficile de la preuve - que si u est un mot primitif sur l'alphabet X (c'est-à-dire un mot qui n'est pas puissance d'un autre mot), alors $u^+ \in X^+\mathcal{V}$. Pour cela on exhibe un code préfixe fini très pur C formé de mots multilinéaires sur un alphabet Y et un morphisme φ de X^+ dans Y^+ tel que $u^+ = C^+\varphi^{-1}$. Comme C est formé de mots multilinéaires, C est dans Y^+ , ainsi que C^+ d'après la condition (b). On en déduit $u^+ \in X^+\mathcal{V}$ d'après la définition d'une variété.

On prouve enfin que pour tout $n \geqslant 1$, $X^n \in X^+\mathcal{V}$ de la façon suivante : on remarque que si $Y = \{x,y\}$, on a l'égalité $\{yx^{n-1}\} = (yx^{n-1})^+ - X^*xy\,X^*$. Comme les deux langages intervenant dans le membre droit de cette égalité sont dans $Y^+\mathcal{V}$ d'après ce qui précède, on a aussi $\{yx^{n-1}\} \in Y^+$ et donc $C_n = \{xy, yx^{n-1}\} \in Y^+\mathcal{V}$. Or pour $n \geqslant 3$, C_n est un code préfixe fini très pur tel que Synt X^n divise Synt C_n^+ . On conclut à l'aide du théorème des variétés.

La fin de la preuve est maintenant facile. Soit w un mot quelconque de X^+. On écrit $w = u^k$ avec u primitif et on remarque que $\{w\} = u^+ \cap X^{|w|}$. On en déduit $\{w\} \in X^+\mathcal{V}$. Comme une variété est fermée par union, $\mathcal{V}$ contient tous les langages finis comme annoncé.

La suite repose sur la proposition suivante

<u>Proposition 10</u> Soit $A = (Q,X)$ un automate fini ayant un zéro. On suppose en outre qu'il existe une lettre qui n'envoie pas tous les états sur le zéro. Alors il existe un code préfixe fini C_A tel que le semi-groupe de transition S de A divise

Synt C_A^+. Si S est apériodique, on peut choisir pour C_A un code pur. S'il existe un entier n tel que tout mot de X^n soit une constante dans A, on peut choisir pour C_A un code très pur.

La démonstration de cette proposition est longue et technique. Démontrons à présent le théorème 3. Soit $\mathcal{V}$ la plus petite variété satisfaisant les hypothèses du théorème 3. D'après la proposition 9, $\mathcal{V}$ contient les langages finis. D'après la condition (ii), $X^+\mathcal{V}$ contient P^+ pour tout code préfixe fini très pur. Pour montrer que Lt est contenue dans $\mathcal{V}$, il suffit, d'après la proposition 8 de démontrer que wX^*, X^*w et X^*wX^* sont dans $X^+\mathcal{V}$ pour tout alphabet X.

Soit $A = (Q,X)$ l'automate minimal de l'un des langages précédents et soit A_0 l'automate déduit de A par adjonction d'un zéro si A ne possédait pas déjà un zéro. On peut alors vérifier que tout mot de longueur supérieure ou égale à la longueur de w est une constante dans A_0. Nous sommes dans les conditions d'application de la proposition 10. On en déduit que le semi-groupe syntactique du langage considéré L divise le semi-groupe de transition de A_0, lequel divise Synt $C_{A_0}^+$ où C_{A_0} est un code préfixe fini très pur. D'après le théorème des variétés, on a donc $L \in X^+\mathcal{V}$ ce qui achève la preuve du théorème 3

<u>Preuve du corollaire 3</u> : Soit $\mathcal{V}$ la plus petite variété satisfaisant les conditions du corollaire 3. L'inclusion $\mathcal{V} \subset$ Lt a déjà été démontrée. En utilisant le théorème 3 et la proposition 9, la seule chose à démontrer est que $L = \{xy\} \in X^+\mathcal{V}$ pour tout alphabet X contenant au moins deux lettres. Or l'automate minimal du langage L satisfait les hypothèses de la proposition 10 : il existe donc un code préfixe fini très pur tel que Synt L divise Synt C^+. Comme C^+ est dans $\mathcal{V}$ par hypothèse L est dans $X^+\mathcal{V}$.

<u>Preuve des théorèmes 1 et 2 et des corollaires 1 et 2</u>

Si une variété $\mathcal{V}$ satisfait les conditions de l'un de ces 4 énoncés, elle satisfait aussi les conditions du théorème 3 ou du corollaire 3. Par conséquent $\mathcal{V}$ contient Lt et les conditions du théorème 1(resp 2) sont équivalentes à celle du corollaire 1 (resp. 2).

Soit L un langage rationnel de X^+ et soit A son automate minimal. Supposons tout d'abord que A ait un zéro et que toute lettre de X envoie n'importe quel état sur le zéro. Alors L est localement testable et est donc élément de $X^+\mathcal{V}$. Cette situation étant ainsi éliminée, on peut supposer que l'automate A_0 (obtenu à partir de A par adjonction d'un zéro si A n'en a pas déjà un) vérifie les hypothèses de la proposition 10. Il existe donc un code préfixe fini C tel que Synt L divise Synt C^+. En outre si L est apériodique on peut choisir pour C un code pur. Il en résulte, par le théorème des variétés, que Rat est la plus petite variété satisfaisant les hypothèses du théorème 1 et que Ap est la plus petite variété satisfaisant les hypothèses du théorème 2.

BIBLIOGRAPHIE

[1] J. BRZOZOWSKI et I. SIMON . Characterizations of locally testable events, Discrete Math. 4 (1973) 243-271.

[2] S. EILENBERG. Automata, Languages and Machines, Ac. Press. Vol A (1974) Vol B (1976.)

[3] S.W. GOLOMB et B. GORDON. Codes with bounded synchronization delay. Information and Control 8-p 355-372 (1965).

[4] K. Hashiguchi et N. Honda : Properties of Code events and homomorphisms over regular events, J. Comp. Syst. Sci. 12 (1976) p. 352-367.

[5] R. Mc NAUGHTON. Algebraic Decision Procedures for Local Testability. Math. Syst. Theory Vol 8 N°1.

[6] J-F. PERROT. Informatique et Algèbre : la théorie des codes à longueur variable. Proceedings of the 3rd GI Conference, Lecture Notes in Computer Science N°48,Springer (1977) p 27-44.

[7] J-F. PERROT. On the theory of syntactic monoids for rational languages, dans: Fundamentals of Computation Theory, Lecture Notes in Computer Science N°56 Springer (1977) 152-165.

[8] J-F. PERROT. Variétés de langages et opérations. Theoretical Computer Science 7 (1978) 198-210.

[9] J.E. PIN. Sur le monoïde syntactique de L^* lorsque L est un langage fini. Theoretical Computer Science 7 (1978) p 211-215.

[10] A. RESTIVO. Codes and aperiodic languages in 1. Fachtagung über Automatentheorie und formalle Sprachen, Lecture Notes in Computer Science N°2, Springer (1973) p 175-181.

[11] A. RESTIVO. On a question of Mc Naughton and Papert. Information and Control Vol 25, N°1 mai 1974 p 93-101.

[12] M.P. SCHÜTZENBERGER. Sur certaines pseudovariétés de monoïdes finis. IRIA-Laboria. Rapport de Recherche N°62, 1974.

[13] M.P. SCHÜTZENBERGER. On finite monoids having only trivial subgroups. Information and Control 8 (1965) 190-194.

[14] M.P. SCHÜTZENBERGER. Sur certaines opérations de fermeture dans les langages rationnels. Istituto Nazionale di Alta Mathematica. Symposia Mathematica Vol XV (1975).

[15] M.P. SCHÜTZENBERGER. Sur le produit de concaténation non ambigü. Semigroup Forum 13, p 47-75 (1975)

[16] M.P. SCHÜTZENBERGER. On an application of semigroup methods to some problems in coding, I.R.E. Trans. on Information theory, I.T.2, (1956) 47-60

[17] I. SIMON. Piece wise testable events. 2nd GI Conference Lecture Notes in Computer Science, Springer Verlag (1976) p 214-222

[18] Y. ZALCSTEIN. Locally testable languages, J. Comput System Sci 6 (1972), 151-167.

ÜBER EINE MINIMALE UNIVERSELLE TURING-MASCHINE

Lutz Priese

ÜBERBLICK

Die Frage, wie 'einfach' universelle Maschinen sein können, hat in der theoretischen Informatik ein großes Interesse gefunden. Um diese Frage präziser zu fassen, müssen die Begriffe 'universelle Maschine' und 'einfach' definiert werden. Während für den ersten der beiden Begriffe akzeptierte Definitionen existieren, ist es nicht unumstritten, was man unter der Einfachheit von Maschinen verstehen soll. Wir werden in dieser Arbeit einfache, universelle Turing-Maschinen untersuchen und beide Begriffe für Turing-Maschinen präzisieren. Dabei sollen keine Modifikationen von Turing-Maschinen für diese Fragestellung neu konstruiert werden (dies würde das Problem natürlich vereinfachen), sondern es werden zwei einfache, universelle Maschinen in den bereits bekannten und untersuchten Klassen von Turing-Maschinen vorgestellt.

UNIVERSELLE TURING-MASCHINEN

Die Suche nach einfachen, universellen Turing-Maschinen war vor ca 15 Jahren recht beliebt. Bekannt sind die Resultate von Watanabe [12], der eine universelle Turing-Maschine mit 8 Zuständen und 5 Buchstaben konstruierte, und von Minsky [7], der durch Simulation von TAG-Systemen eine universelle Turing-Maschine mit 7 Zuständen und 4 Buchstaben erhielt. Diese Fragestellung verlor dann an Interesse, da Minsky's Maschine nicht weiter vereinfacht werden konnte und es andererseits auch nicht gelang, die Lücke zwischen universellen und nicht-universellen Maschinen 'von unten' zu schließen, indem man zeigt, daß gewisse Klassen von Turing-Maschinen keine universelle Maschine enthalten können. Eines dieser Unmöglichkeitsresultate ist der Satz von Fischer [1] , daß Turing-Maschinen mit Quadrupel-Instruktionen (es darf pro Instruktion nur gedruckt oder der Kopf bewegt werden) und nur 2 Zuständen nicht universell sein können.

Einige Verallgemeinerungen von Turing-Maschinen zu Maschinen mit Mehrfach-Köpfen, mehreren Bändern oder mehrdimensionalen Bändern führte zu gewissen Verbesserungen der Resultate.

So konnte Hooper [3] zeigen, daß bereits universelle Mehrfach-Kopf Turing-Maschinen mit 2 Köpfen, 2 Zuständen und 3 Buchstaben, oder mit 4 Köpfen, 1 Zustand und 2 Buchstaben existieren. Hasenjäger [2] verschärfte Hooper's Resultat zu einer universellen Turing-Maschine mit 3 Köpfen, 2 Zuständen und 2 Buchstaben. Dabei arbeitet ein Kopf auf einem zyklischen Band, einer auf einem Band vom Wang-Typ und einer simuliert ein Register. Da Hooper's 4-Kopf-Maschine ebenfalls ein zyklisches Band besitzt, erhält man aus Hasenjäger's Maschine eine mit ebenfalls 4 Köpfen, 1 Zustand und 2 Buchstaben mittels einer einfachen Zustandsreduktion bei Hinzunahme eines weiteren Kopfes.

Wagner [11] zeigte die Existenz einer universellen Turing-Maschine mit 8 Zuständen und 4 Buchstaben, die auf einem 2-dimensionalen Band mit einem Kopf operiert. Diese 2-dimensionalen Maschinen konnten von Kleine Büning und Ottmann erheblich vereinfacht werden. Kleine Büning und Ottmann [5] wiesen universelle 2-dimensionale Turing-Maschinen mit 3 Zuständen und 6 Buchstaben nach, und Kleine Büning [4] fand eine universelle 2-dimensionale Turing-Maschine mit 2 Zuständen und 5 Buchstaben, bzw. mit 10 Zuständen und 2 Buchstaben.

Tabelle 1 gibt einen Überblick über die genannten Resultate. Dabei werden drei verschiedene Komplexitätsmaße verwendet, die Präzisierungen des Einfachheitsbegriffes sind:

Komplexitätsmaß 1 gibt als Komplexität einer Turing-Maschine den Vektor (z,b,d,k) aus der Zahl der Zustände (z), der Buchstaben (b), der

Author	Jahr	Zustände	Buchstaben	Band-Dim.	Köpfe	Komplexität 1	2	3
Watánabe	1961	8	5	1	1	(8,5,1,1)	30	10^{76}
Minsky	1962	7	4	1	1	(7,4,1,1)	28	10^{49}
Hooper	1963	2	3	1	2	(2,3,1,2)	18	10^{37}
Hooper	1963	1	2	1	4	(1,2,1,4)	16	10^{50}
Hasenjäger	1973	2	2	1	3	(2,2,1,2)	16	10^{42}
Wagner	1973	8	4	2	1	(8,4,2,1)	32	10^{67}
Kleine Büning - Ottmann	1977	3	6	2	1	(3,6,2,1)	18	10^{44}
Kleine Büning	1977	2	5	2	1	(2,5,2,1)	10	10^{16}
Kleine Büning	1977	10	2	2	1	(10,2,2,1)	20	10^{38}

Tabelle 1

Dimension des Bandes (d) und der Köpfe (k) an. Mit $[(z,b,d,k)]$ bezeichnen wir im folgenden die Klasse aller Turing-Maschinen mit der 1-Komplexität (z,b,d,k).

Komplexitätsmaß 2 ist eine Verallgemeinerung des Shannon'schen [10] Maßes $z \cdot b$ für Maschinen aus $[(z,b,1,1)]$: Die 2-Komplexität mißt die maximale Anzahl der Befehle, die eine Maschine in $[(z,b,d,k)]$ besitzen kann, das ist gerade $z \cdot b^k$.

Komplexitätsmaß 3 mißt die Zahl der Instruktionen, die einer Turing-Maschine aus $[(z,b,d,k)]$ - bei festem Zustands- und Buchstabenalphabet - zur Verfügung stehen. Diese Zahl berechnet sich als $(z \cdot b^k \cdot d' + r)^{z \cdot b^k}$, wobei $d' = 2d$ oder $d' = 2d+1$ und $r = 0$ oder $r = 1$ gilt, je nachdem ob man für die Maschineninstruktionen einen Haltebefehl und/oder eine Kopfbewegung fordert.

Wir werden zwei universelle 2-dimensionale Turing-Maschinen angeben, die bzgl. jedes der drei Komplexitätsmaße einfacher als die bekannten Maschinen sind. Die Frage nach minimalen Turing-Maschinen stellen wir bzgl des Maßes 3. Komplexitätsmaß 3 liefert einen Verband mit $\leq$ im Sinne der Vektorenordnung. Eine Turing-Maschine aus $[(z,b,d,k)]$ nennen wir minimal , falls sie universell ist und ein Vektor (z',b',d',k') mit (z',b',d',k') ≤ (z,b,d,k) existiert, so daß in [(z',b',d',k')] keine universelle Maschine existiert.

Offensichtlich sind in diesem Sinn bereits minimale Maschinen bekannt. So ist jede universelle 2-Zustands Turing-Maschine aus [(2,b,1,1)] minimal, da in [(1,b,1,1)] nur triviale Maschinen liegen. Für Mehrfach-Kopf Turing-Maschinen folgt hingegen sofort die Existenz einer minimalen 1-Zustands Turing-Maschine: Man geht etwa von einer bekannten universellen Maschine aus [(z,2,1,1)] aus, die man leicht in eine Maschine aus [(1,2,1,$\lceil \log_2(z)+1 \rceil$)] übersetzen kann, wobei alle Köpfe, bis auf einen, nur lesen und drucken und somit Zustände kodieren. Jede universelle Maschine aus [(1,2,1 k)] ist auch minimal, da in [(1,1,1,k)] nur triviale Maschinen liegen.

Wagner [11] zeigt weiterhin, daß keine universelle Turing-Maschine in [(2,2,d,1)] für beliebige d liegen kann. Damit ergibt sich eine Chance, nicht-triviale minimale Turing-Maschinen zu konstruieren, falls man das Resultat von Kleine Büning weiter verbessern kann. Dies ist in der Tat möglich.

Wir werden in dieser Arbeit zwei universelle 2-dimensionale Turing-Maschinen in [(2,4,2,1)], [(2,2,2,2)],und eine modifizierte Turing-Maschine der 1-Komplexität (8,2,2,1) vorgestellt.Tabelle 2 ergänzt Tabelle 1.

Maschine	Jahr	Zustände	Buchstaben	Band-Dim.	Köpfe	Komplexität 1	2	3
U_1	1978	2	4	2	1	(2,4,2,1)	8	10^{12}
U_2	1978	2	2	2	2	(2,2,2,2)	8	10^{12}
U_3^*	1978	8	2	2	1	(8,2,2,1)	16	10^{31}

Tabelle 2

Da in [(2,2,2,1)] nach Wagner keine universelle Turing-Maschine liegt, ist mit U_1 nur noch die Klasse [(2,3,2,1)] offen. Eine positive oder negative Antwort zur Existenz universeller Maschinen in dieser Klasse führt zu einer interessanten, nicht-trivialen minimalen Maschine.

Ebenfalls mit Wagner's Satz folgt, daß U_2 minimal ist. Es existiert keine universelle Maschine in [(2,1,2,2)]. Offen sind die Klassen [(1,2,2,2)] und [(2,2,1,2)] . Es ist zu vermuten, daß beide Klassen keine universelle Maschine enthalten. Trifft diese Vermutung zu, so haben wir eine minimale Maschine, U_2, gefunden, so daß eine Vereinfachung in irgendeinem Parameter zu nicht-universellen Maschinen führt. Figur 1 verdeutlicht die gegenwärtige Situation.

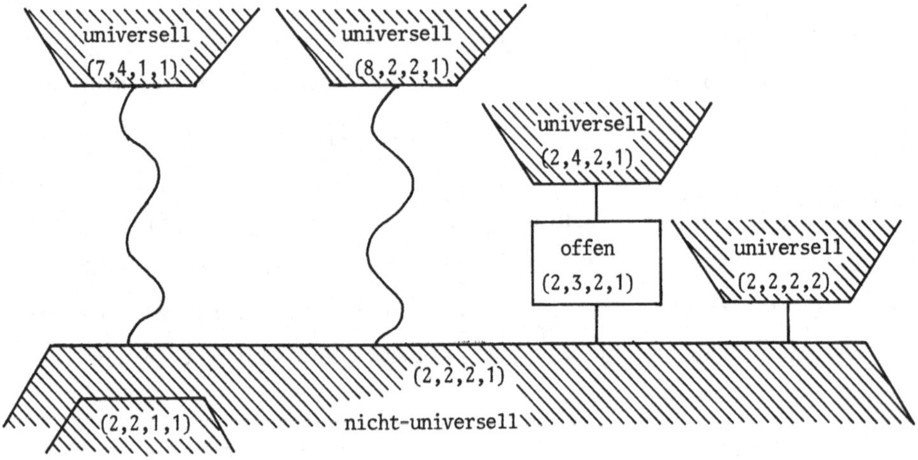

Figur 1

Die Technik zur Konstruktion von U_1 ist die gleiche wie in [4] und [5] . Diese Technik, Simulation von 'Normierten Netzen' durch 2-dimensionale Kalküle, wurde zuerst vom Author in [8] angewendet.

DIE MASCHINE U_1

Das Konzept der 2-dimensionalen Turing-Maschinen soll nun formal definiert werden:

<u>Definition 1</u>: Eine <u>2-dimensionale Turing-Maschine</u>, M, ist ein Tupel $M = (S,L,I)$ mit

a) S ist eine endliche Menge von Zuständen mit einem initialen Zustand s_0,

b) L ist eine endliche Menge von Buchstaben mit einem ausgezeichneten (Blank-)Symbol B,

c) I ist eine endliche Menge von Instruktionen: $I \subseteq (S\times L)\times(S\times L\times B)$, mit $B = \{r,l,u,d\}$, so daß für alle $((s,b),(s',b',x')),((s,b),(s^+,b^+,x^+))$ aus I folgt: $s' = s^+$, $b' = b^+$, $x' = x^+$.

Eine <u>Konfiguration</u> C von M ist eine Abbildung $C\colon F \to (S \cup \{¤\})\times L$ mit

a) $F = \mathbb{Z}^2$ oder $F = \mathbb{N}_0^2$,

b) $\#\{c \in F;\ C(c) \notin (S\cup\{¤\})\times\{B\}\} < \infty$,

c) $\#\{c \in F;\ C(c) \in S\times L\} = 1$.

$\mathbb{C}$ ist die Menge aller Konfigurationen von M.

Eine Konfiguration C heißt <u>initial</u> $:\Leftrightarrow$ $C((0,0)) \in \{s_o\}\times L$.

Eine Konfiguration C' heißt <u>Nachfolgekonfiguration</u> einer Konfiguration C $:\Leftrightarrow$ Gilt $C((x_0,y_0)) = (s,l)$ für ein s aus S, ein l aus L und ein (x_0,y_0) aus F, so existiert eine Instruktion $((s,l),(s',l',x))$ in I mit:

a) $C'((x_0,y_o)) = (¤,l')$,

b) $(\ C((x_0+d_1,y_0+d_2)) = (¤,l^+) > C'((x_0+d_1,y_0+d_2)) = (s',l^+)\ )$ gilt

für $d_1 = 1,\ d_2 = 0$, falls $x = r$
für $d_1 = -1,\ d_2 = 0$, falls $x = l$
für $d_1 = 0,\ d_2 = 1$, falls $x = u$
für $d_1 = 0,\ d_2 = -1$, falls $x = d$,

c) $C'(c) = C(c)$ gilt für alle restlichen c aus F .

Dabei steht r,l,u,d für einen Bewegungsbefehl des Kopfes nach rechts (r), links (l), oben (u : up), unten (d : down). Eine 2-dimensionale

Turing-Maschine liest also den Zustand des Arbeitsfeldes, druckt ein neues Symbol auf das Arbeitsfeld, bewegt den Kopf nach r,l,u oder d und geht in einen neuen Zustand über. Eine Konfiguration ist ein endliches 2-dimensionales Wort (fast alle Zellen c von F tragen das Blank-Symbol B), wobei das Zeichen ¤ andeutet, daß diese Zelle nicht das Arbeitsfeld ist, und ein Zustand das Arbeitsfeld mit dem Zustand der Turing-Maschine angibt. Wir werden Konfigurationen auch kanonisch als flächenhafte Muster von Zeichen wiedergeben, wobei auf das Zeichen ¤ stets verzichtet wird.

<u>Definition 2:</u> Eine <u>Berechnung</u> $\mathbb{B}$ einer 2-dimensionalen Turing-Maschine M ist eine endliche oder unendliche Folge $C_0, C_1, C_2, \ldots$ von Konfigurationen C_m von M mit:

a) C_0 ist eine initiale Konfiguration,

b) Für alle m gilt: Liegt C_{m+1} in $\mathbb{B}$, so ist C_{m+1} eine Nachfolgekonfiguration von C_m,

c) Die Folge darf nur mit einem C_m abbrechen, falls zu C_m keine Nachfolgekonfiguration existiert.

Damit haben wir gerade die intuitive Vorstellung der Arbeitsweise einer 2-dimensionalen Turing-Maschine erfaßt. In einer initialen Konfiguration liegt das Arbeitsfeld im Ursprung (0,0) von F und M ist im initialen Zustand s_0. Das flächenhafte 'Band' F ist die Zahlenebene $\mathbb{Z}^2$ oder nur deren erster Qudrant, $\mathbb{N}_0^2$. Falls M auf $\mathbb{N}_0^2$ arbeitet und ein Befehl den Kopf zum Verlassen von $\mathbb{N}_0^2$ zwingt, ist die Nachfolgekonfiguration nicht definiert und die Berechnung $\mathbb{B}$ stoppt (Stop by error). Ebenfalls kann man einen Stop erreichen, falls M im Zustand s einen Buchstaben l liest, wobei für das Paar (s,l) keine Instruktion in I existiert. Wir haben I als rechtseindeutige Relation definiert, d.h. wir betrachten nur determinierte Maschinen.

<u>Definition 3:</u> Eine 2-dimensionale Turing-Maschine M heißt <u>universell</u> $:\Leftrightarrow$ Es existieren zwei primitiv rekursive Wortfunktionen Φ und Ψ, $\Phi: F_R \times \mathbb{N}_0 \to \mathbb{C}$, $\Psi: \mathbb{C} \to \mathbb{N}_0 \times \{+\}$, mit:

a) F_R ist die Klasse aller partiellen rekursiven Funktionen,

b) Für alle f aus F_R , n aus $\mathbb{N}_0$, Berechnungen $\mathfrak{B} = C_0, C_1, C_2, \ldots$, die mit $C_0 = \Phi(f,n)$ beginnen, gilt:

i) f(n) ist undefiniert $\Leftrightarrow \Psi(C_m) = +$, für alle C_m in $\mathfrak{B}$,

ii) f(n) ist definiert $\Leftrightarrow$ Es existiert ein Index m_0 mit :

$\Psi(C_m) = +$ für alle C_m in $\mathfrak{B}$ mit $m_0 > m$, und

$\Psi(C_m) = f(n)$ für alle C_m in $\mathfrak{B}$ mit $m_0 \leq m$.

Anschaulich bedeutet $\Psi(C_m) = +$, daß in der Konfiguration C_m einer Berechnung $\mathfrak{B}$ von M noch kein Resultat f(n) gefunden wurde. Die Bedingungeni) und ii) stellen sicher, daß ein Resultat gefunden wird (falls f(n) definiert ist) und ein einmal gefundenes Resultat in allen erlaubten weiteren Nachfolgekonfigurationen in $\mathfrak{B}$ nicht verloren geht. Man beachte, daß damit M nicht stoppen muß , falls ein Resultat gefunden ist.

Da eine Konfiguration C ein endliches 2-dimensionales Wort ist, genügt es, C nur in irgendeinem Rechteck R von F zu betrachten (mit C besitzt den Wert (¤,B) außerhalb von R), wobei wir R bei Bedarf vergrössern dürfen. Damit können wir C leicht als ein lineares Wort $W_1|W_2|\ldots|W_n$ kodieren. | ist ein Trennungssymbol, die W_i sind lineare Wörter über dem Alphabet $(S \cup \{¤\}) \times L$. Da der Begriff 'primitiv-rekursive Wortfunktion' für Funktionen über linearen Wörtern wohlbekannt ist, vgl etwa[6],können wir mittels dieser kanonischen Goedelisierungvon Konfigurationen auf lineare Wörter die Begriffe 'primitiv-rekursive Wortfunkten Φ und Ψ ' verstehen.

Es gilt nun:

<u>Satz 1:</u> Die folgende 2-dimensionale Turing-Maschine, U_1, ist universell.

$U_1 = (\{1,2\}, \{B,C,D,U\}, I)$, mit den Instruktionen (dabei schreiben wir $s,l \rightarrow s',l',x$ statt $((s,l),(s',l',x))$) :

I :	1,B → 2,C,u	1,D → 2,D,d
	2,B → 2,B,d	2,D → 1,U,d
	1,C → 1,C,r	1,U → 2,U,u
	2,C → 2,C,l	2,U → 1,D,u

U_1 kann man etwa durch ein 'Buchstaben-Diagramm' wie in Figur 2 repräsentieren. Dabei wird 'right' und 'left' für die Zustände 1, bzw. 2, geschrieben. Dies wird durch die Arbeitsweise von U_1 motiviert.

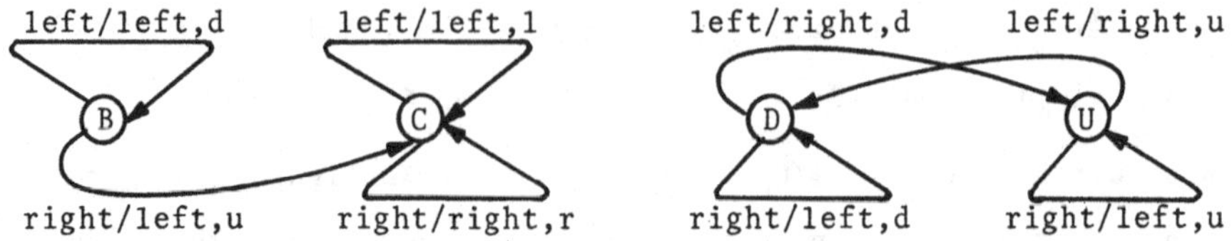

Figur 2

Wir wollen hier eine Beweisübersicht zu Satz 1 geben. Ein detaillierter Beweis findet sich in [9]. Dieser Übersicht kann man implizit die Gödelfunktionen Φ und Ψ entnehmen.

Wir benötigen einige Resultate aus der Theorie der Normierten Netze von D.Rödding. Gegeben sei eine rekursive Funktion f aus F_R. So existiert ein f berechnendes Programm P_f einer Register-Maschine R mit $n \geq 2$ Registern. R mit dem Programm P_f simulieren wir durch ein Automatennetz (Normiertes Netz), N_f, mit einem Input, START, einem Output, STOP, das aus genau n Kopien des unendlichen Automaten REG^+ und verschiedenen Kopien der Automaten K und P besteht. REG^+ ist ein Automat mit den Inputs {sub,test}, Outputs $\{0_1, 0_2\}$, den ganzen Zahlen $\mathbb{Z}$ als Zuständen und den folgenden Automatenübergängen:

$$\begin{aligned} &\text{sub},n \rightarrow 0_1, n-1 &&, \text{ für } n \in \mathbb{Z} \\ &\text{test},n \rightarrow 0_1, n+1 &&, \text{ für } n \in \mathbb{Z},\ n > 0 \\ &\text{test},n \rightarrow 0_2, n+1 &&, \text{ für } n \in \mathbb{Z},\ n \leq 0\ . \end{aligned}$$

K ist ein ODER-Element mit zwei Inputs '1,2' einem Output '3' einem Zustand 'a', und den beiden Übergängen: $1,a \rightarrow 3,a$ und $2,a \rightarrow 3,a$. P ist ein Flip-Flop mit zwei Inputs 't,s', vier Outputs 't^u, t^d, s^u, s^d', Zuständen 'up,down', und den Übergängen:

$$\begin{aligned} &t,\text{up} \rightarrow t^u,\text{up} &&, \quad s,\text{up} \rightarrow s^u,\text{down} \\ &t,\text{down} \rightarrow t^d,\text{down} &&, \quad s,\text{down} \rightarrow s^d,\text{up}\ . \end{aligned}$$

REG^+ testet beim Addieren und kann auch negative Zahlen speichern. Offensichtlich lassen sich mit derartigen Speichern beliebige Register-Maschinen aufbauen. Dabei genügen Automatennetze aus K- und P-Bausteinen zur Verschaltung der Programme. Ferner benötigt man noch Leitungen und Kreuzungen von Leitungen in diesen Normierten Netzen.

Derartige Normierte Netze werden wir in endliche 2-dimensionale Wörter über dem Alphabet {A,C,D,U} übersetzen. Der Verlauf eines Signals in einem Netz wird durch die Bewegung des Kopfes von U_1 simuliert. Die Initiierung eines Normierten Netzes mittels eines Signales auf dem einzigen Input START wird durch die Lage des Kopfes im Ursprung (0,0) von F im initialen Kodewort simuliert. Damit sind die Kodewörter gerade Konfigurationen von U_1. Eine Endkonfiguration soll erreicht sein, falls das Signal des Netzes den einzigen Output STOP erreicht, wobei wir (Ψ) die Inhalte der kodierten Register dieser Endkonfiguration ablesen.

U_1 arbeitet im wesentlichen wie folgt: Liest U_1 im Zustand 1 ein C, so bewegt es den Kopf nach rechts, im Zustand 2 hingegen nach links, ohne C zu verändern. Damit lassen sich waagerechte Leitungen darstellen. Liest U_1 im Zustand 1 ein U oder D, so bewegt es den Kopf nach oben (U für up), bzw. nach unten (D für down), ohne U oder D zu verändern. Im Zustand 2 wird der Kopf ebenso bewegt, allerdings werden die Buchstaben U (D) durch D (U) ersetzt. Damit gelingt eine Implementierung des Flip-Flop P und von verschiedenen Kurvenarten für Leitungen. Im Zustand 1 verwandelt der Kopf ein B in ein C. Damit werden wir eine Verlängerung von linearen, waagerechten C-Wörtern erhalten, in denen wir beliebige (ganze) Zahlen speichern können.

Man kann eine graphische Darstellung eines Normierten Netzes, N_f, mit den standardisierten topologischen Elementen aus Figur 3 erhalten. In Figur 3 ist zugleich die Implementation dieser Elemente durch 2-dimensionale Teilwörter angegeben. U/D in P bedeutet, daß in dieser Zelle von F der Buchstaben U (D) stehen soll, falls P im Zustand up (bzw. down) ist. Figur 4 zeigt, wie der Kopf ein Signal in l-u-r simu-

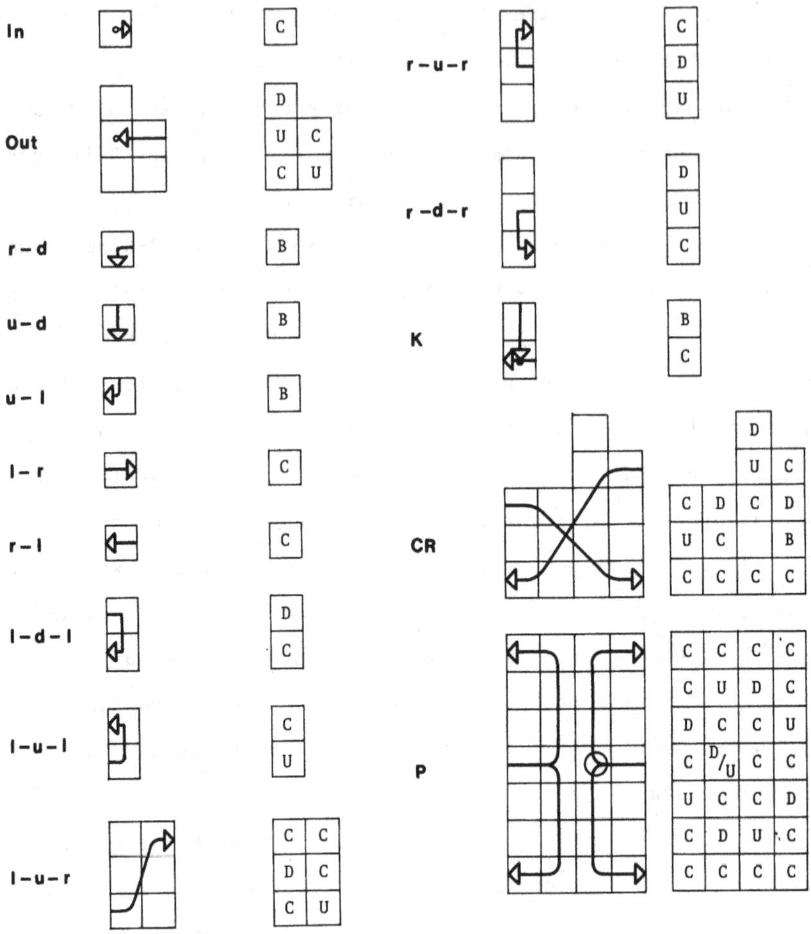

Figur 3

C	C		C	C		C	C		C	C		C	C		C	C	
D	C	→	D	C	→	D	2C	→	2D	C	→	U	C	→	U	C	→
1C	U		C	1U		C	U		C	U		1C	U		C	1U	

C	C		C	C		1C	C		C	1C
U	2C	→	2U	C	→	D	C	→	D	C
C	U		C	U		C	U		C	U

Figur 4

liert. Dabei erreicht der Kopf den Eingang im Zustand 1 (er bewegt sich nach rechts) und verläßt 1-u-r im korrekten Zustand 1 (er bewegt sich weiter nach rechts).

Wir speichern eine ganze Zahl durch zwei nebeneinanderliegende, waagerechte C-Wörter, siehe Figur 5.

...	B	B	B	B	B	...	B	B	B	B	...
...	C	C	C	C	C	...	C	C	B	B	B ...
...	C	C	C	C	C	...	C	C	C	C	B ...

Figur 5

Die Differenz d der Länge des unteren zu der des oberen C-Wortes kodiert den Inhalt m := d+1 eines Registers. Läuft der Kopf von U_1 auf dem unteren C-Wort im Zustand 1 nach rechts, so schaltet er das erste B in C (das C-Wort wird verlängert), geht in den Zustand 2 und bewegt den Kopf nach oben. Gilt $n \leq 0$, so befindet sich dort ein Buchstabe C des längeren oberen C-Wortes. Der Kopf läuft auf dem oberen C-Wort zurück. Gilt $n > 0$, so liest der Kopf einen Buchstaben B. Er bewegt sich wieder nach unten und läuft auf dem unteren C-Wort zurück. Damit kann man offensichtlich eine Testoperation des Registerbausteines REG^+ simulieren. Zur Subtraktion verlängert man einfach das obere C-Wort.

Implementieren wir auf diese angedeutete Art eine universelle Register-Maschine, so können wir U_1 als universell nachweisen.

DIE MASCHINEN U_2 UND U_3^*

Die 4-Buchstaben,1-Kopf Turing-Maschine U_1 kann man trivialerweise in eine 2-Buchstaben-2-Kopf Turing-Maschine, U_2, übersetzen. Mit den vorherigen Überlegungen ist U_2 minimal. Also gilt:

Satz 2: Es existiert eine (minimale) universelle Turing-Maschine in [(2,2,2,2)].

V.Claus verdanke ich die Idee, U_1 in eine 2-Buchstaben, 8-Zustands Turing-Maschine zu übersetzen. Dies geht in einem modifizierten Maschinenkonzept.

Wir verschlüsseln die Buchstaben von U_1 durch 2-buchstabige Wörter über dem Alphabet {B,X}. Auf ein 2-dimensionales Wort über {B,C,D,U} wenden wir die Koordinatentransformation $(x,y) \to (x,y+x)$ an und verschlüsseln anschließend die Buchstaben durch Wörter über {B,X}. Figur 6 gibt diese Verschlüsselung und ein Transformationsbeispiel an.

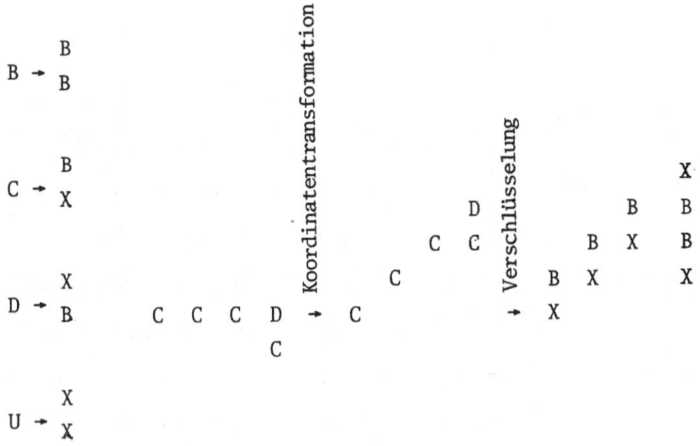

Figur 6

U_3 operiert nun auf B und X mit 8 Zuständen $1,2,1_B,2_B,1_X,2_X,1_s$ und 2_s und besitzt die folgenden Instruktionen:

$1,B \to 1_B,X,u$	$2,B \to 2_B,B,d$
$1,X \to 1_X,X,u$	$2,X \to 2_X,X,d$
$1_B,B \to 2,B,u^2$	$2_B,B \to 2,B,d$
$1_B,X \to 1_s,X,d$	$2_B,X \to 2,X,1$
$1_X,B \to 1,B,r$	$2_X,B \to 1,X,d^2$
$1_X,X \to 2,X,u^2$	$2_X,X \to 2_s,B,u$
$1_s,X \to 2,B,d$	$2_s,X \to 1,X,u$.

U_3^* ist eine modifizierte Turing-Maschine: Eine Bewegung u^2 (bzw. d^2) in der Instruktionsliste zwingt den Kopf zu einer Bewegung über <u>zwei</u> Zellen nach oben (bzw. unten). Figur 7 zeigt eine Ableitung in U_3^* des Beispiels aus Figur 6:

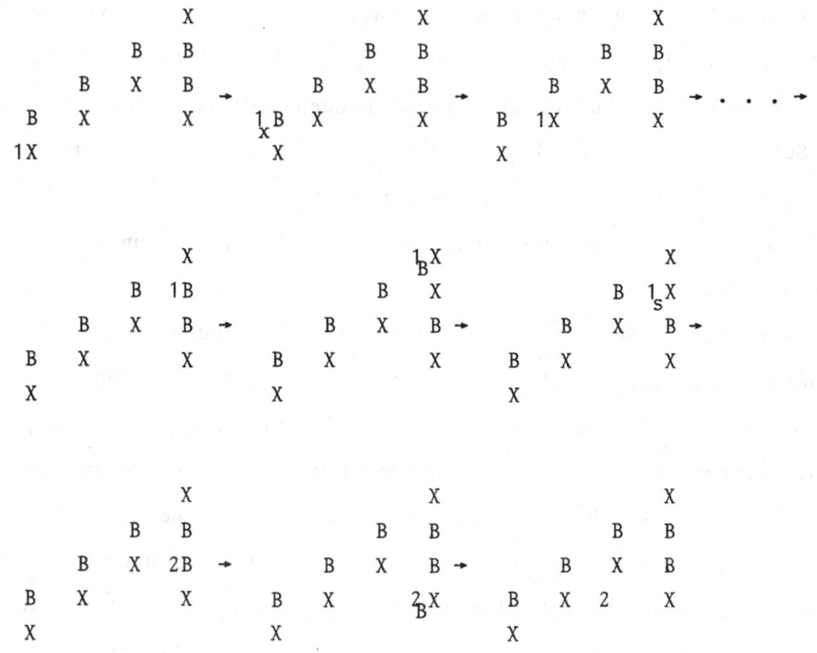

Figur 7

Man überprüft leicht, daß U_3^* auf den Verschlüsselungen von Konfigurationen von U_1 so arbeitet wie U_1. Damit gilt:

<u>Satz 3:</u> U_3^* ist universell.

EIN WEITERES KOMPLEXITÄTSKRITERIUM

Beide Maschinen U_1 und U_2 sind nach den vorgestellten Komplexitätsmaßen die kleinsten bisher bekannten universellen Maschinen. Als ein weiteres Maß interessiert eine Abschätzung der Schrittzahlfunktion. Wir wollen dies für U_1 durchführen. Diese Schrittzahlfunktion soll eine obere Schranke der benötigten Schritte von U_1 zur Berechnung einer Funktion f(n) darstellen. Eine solche Schranke hängt natürlich von der Form ab, in der f in U_1 eingegeben wird. Da U_1 gerade Register-Maschinen simuliert, gehen wir von einer f berechnenden Register-Maschine,M, aus mit einer Schrittzahlfunktion $Sz_M : \mathbb{N}_0 \to \mathbb{N}_0$ - $Sz_M(n)$ ist eine obere Schranke für die Schrittzahl, die M zur Berechnung von f(n) bei Input n benötigt - aus, und untersuchen die 'Verlangsamung ' von U_1 bei Simulation von M.

M besitze $\leq$ s Befehle und $\leq$ s Register. Wir finden dann ein M simulierendes Normiertes Netz,N_M, mit $c_1 \cdot s$ Kopien von K, $c_2 \cdot s$ Kopien von P, $\leq$ s Kopien von REG^+, und einer Schrittzahlfunktion $Sz_{N_M} = c' \cdot s \cdot Sz_M$, die die zur Berechnung notwendigen 'Signalbenutzungen' der K-,P- und REG^+-Bausteine beschränkt. Diese Konstanten c_1, c_2 und c' sind recht klein. Im nächsten Schritt wird N_M in ein 2-dimensionales Wort übersetzt. Die Zahl der dazu notwendigen Zellen hängt stark davon ab, wie 'geschickt' man N_M implementieren kann. Insbesondere ist es sinnvoll, nicht nur mit den standardisierten Elementen aus Figur 3 zu arbeiten - die im Prinzip zur Implementation ausreichen -, sondern weitere 'Teile' von Normierten Netzen direkt zu übersetzen. Unabhängig von derartigen technischen Tricks braucht man Leitungsverbindungen zwischen den $c_1 \cdot s$ K-, den $c_2 \cdot s$ P- und den $\leq$s REG^+-Bausteinen, deren maximale Länge proportional der Zahl der zu verbindenden Bausteine ist. Damit erhalten wir eine Schrittzahlfunktion $\bar{c} \cdot s \cdot Sz_M$ für das Durchlaufen des Kopfes von U_1 durch die Implementationen der K- und P-Bausteine sowie der Leitungen. Zusätzlich wird bei jeder REG^+-Benutzung ein C-Wort un eine Zelle verlängert, d.h. bei der nächsten Benutzung dieses Registers erhalten wir zwei zusätzliche Schritte in U_1. Insgesamt ergibt sich damit eine Schrittzahlfunktion $Sz_{U_1} = c \cdot (Sz_M)^2$ für U_1. D.h., U_1 erfordert eine quadratische Rechenzeit zu M.

[1] P.C.Fischer. On Formalisms for Turing Machines. J.ACM,12(65),pp.570-580.

[2] G.Hasenjäger. Unveröffentlicher Vortrag, WWU,Münster, 1973.

[3] Ph.K.Hooper. Some Small,Multitape Universal Turing Machines. Comp. Laboratory Harvard University, 1963.

[4] H.Kleine Büning. Über Probleme bei homogener Parkettierung von ℤxℤ durch Mealy-Automaten bei normierter Verwendung. Dissertation, WWU, Münster, 1977.

[5] H.Kleine Büning und Th.Ottmann. Kleine universelle mehrdimensionale Turingmaschinen. Elek.Inf.Kyb.,13(77),pp.179-201.

[6] F.K.Mahn. Über die Strukturunabhängigkeit des Begriffes der primitiv-rekursiven Funktion. Dissertation, WWU,Münster, 1965.

[7] M.L.Minsky. Size and Structure of Universal Turing Machines Using TAG Systems. Proc. 5th Symp. in Apl. Math.,(62),AMS,pp.229-238.

[8] L.Priese. Über einfache unentscheidbare Probleme: Computational und constructional universelle asynchrone Räume. Dissertation, WWU,Münster, 1974.

[9] L.Priese. Towards a Precise Characterization of the Complexity of Universal and Non-Universal Turing Machines. Erscheint in: SIAM J.on Computing.

[10] C.E.Shannon. A Universal Turing Machine With Two Internal States. In: Automata Studies, Princeton University Press, Princeton, 1956,pp.157-166.

[11] K.Wagner. Universelle Turing-Maschinen mit n-dimensionalem Band. Elek.Inf.Kyb.,9(73),pp.423-431.

[12] S.Watanabe. 5-Symbol 8-State and 5-Symbol 6-State Turing Machines. J.ACM,8(61),pp.476-584.

SUR LES VARIETES DE LANGAGES ET DE MONOÏDES

Christophe Reutenauer

1. Introduction

Ces dernières années, l'étude des liens profonds entre langages formels et monoïdes a connu un développement intense grâce à la théorie des variétés de langages et de monoïdes (cf. (1), (2), (3), (5), (6)) introduites par S. Eilenberg (voir aussi l'article de J.E. Pin dans le présent ouvrage). Nous caractérisons ici quelques propriétés de fermeture des variétés : M.P. Schützenberger a défini un produit de monoïdes, que nous notons $\diamond$, tel que si le monoïde M_i reconnait le langage L_i $(i = 1,2)$ alors $M_1 \diamond M_2$ reconnaît L_1L_2 ; nous prouvons une réciproque à ce résultat : tout langage reconnu par $M_1 \diamond M_2$ appartient à l'algèbre de Boole engendrée par les langages de la forme A, B ou Ax B (A est reconnu par M_1, B est reconnu par M_2, x est une lettre)
(théorème 1). Comme conséquence du th. 1 et du fait que toute variétés de langages fermée par produit contient les lettres (Perrot (3)) on obtient qu'une variété de langages est fermée par produit seulement si la variété correspondante de monoïdes est fermée par le produit $\diamond$: la réciproque avait déjà été établie dans (5).
Nous introduisons aussi la notion de variété de langages fermée par substitution inverse, par morphisme alphabétique, et montrons qu'elles sont caractérisée par le fait que la variété correspondante de monoïdes est fermée par passage au monoïde des parties.

2. Variétés

Une variété (pseudo-variété) de monoïdes est une famille V de monoïdes finis telle que

. $M \in V$ et M' divise M (i.e. M' est isomorphe à un quotient d'un sous-monoïde de M) $\Rightarrow M' \in V$.

. $M, M' \in V \Rightarrow M \diamond M' \in V$.

Nous dirons M-variété.

Une variété de langages est un opérateur $\mathcal{V}$ qui à chaque alphabet (fini) X associe une algèbre de Boole $X^*\mathcal{V}$ de langages rationnels sur X tel que :

. $L \in X^*$, $x \in X \Rightarrow x^{-1}L = \{w \in X^* | xw \in L\}$ et $Lx^{-1} = \{w \in X^* | wx \in L\}$ sont dans X^* .

. Si Y est un autre alphabet et φ un homomorphisme $Y^* \to X^*$, alors $L \in X^*\mathcal{V} \Rightarrow \varphi^{-1}(L) \in Y^*\mathcal{V}$.

Nous dirons L-variété.

Le résultat suivant, dû à S. Eilenberg (2), (chap. VI § 3) est fondamental.

Théorème. Il y a bijection entre M-variétés et L-variétés : à une M-variété V est associée la L-variété $\mathcal{V}$ des langages dont le monoïde syntactique est dans V ; à une L-variété $\mathcal{V}$ est associée la M-variété V engendrée par les monoïdes syntactiques des langages dans $\mathcal{V}$.

3. Résultats

Soient M,N deux monoïdes ; le produit de Schützenberger de M et N, noté $M \diamond N$, noté $M \diamond N$, est défini par : $V = \mathcal{P}(M \times N)$ est muni canoniquement d'une structure de M-module à gauche et N-module à droite ; le support ensembliste de $M \diamond N$ est $M \times V \times N$ et le produit est défini par : $(m,a,n)(m',a',n') = (mm',ma' + an',nn')$, où + désigne l'union dans V. De ceci se déduit aisément la formule

$(m_1,a_1,n_1)(m_2,a_2,n_2)\dots(m_r,a_r,n_r) = (m_1\dots m_r,a,n_1\dots n_r)$ avec

$a = m_1\dots m_{r-1}.a_r + m_1\dots m_{r-2}.a_{r-1}.n_r +\dots+m_1.a_2.n_3\dots n_r + a_1.n_2\dots n_r$

Soit X un alphabet et $\rho : X^* \to M \diamond N$ un homomorphisme ; ρ est déterminé par ses projections μ,ν et ξ sur M,V et N respectivement : $\rho = (\mu,\nu,\xi)$; μ et ξ sont clairement des homomorphismes et d'après la formule ci-dessus, on a : $\forall w \in X^*$

$$(1) \qquad \nu w = \sum_{\substack{u,v \in X^* \\ x \in X \\ w=uxv}} \mu u.\nu x.\xi v$$

Nous démontrons le

Théorème 1 Soient M et N deux monoïdes finis et $L \subset X^*$ un langage reconnu par $M \diamond N$. Alors L appartient à la fermeture booléenne des langages reconnus par M ou N et des langages de la forme A.x.B (A reconnu par M, $x \in X$, B reconnu par N).

La preuve s'appuie sur un lemme technique et s'inspire d'un résultat analogue pour les variétés de séries rationnelles (4) (où les calculs sont plus faciles).

Lemme 1. Soit ρ un homomorphisme $X^* \to M \diamond N$, $a \in V$ et $x \in X$. Alors $L_{a,x} = \{w \in X^* | \exists\, u,v \in X^*$ tels que $w = uxv$ et $\mu u.\nu x.\xi v = a\}$ est soit égal à $\emptyset$ ou à X^*, soit réunion finie de langages de la forme A.x.B ou $A = \mu^{-1}\mu(A)$ (resp. $B = \xi^{-1}\xi(B)$) est reconnu par M (resp. N).

Preuve. Rappelons que si P est un monoïde et $p,q \in P$, pq^{-1} désigne l'ensemble $\{r \in P | rq = p\}$ et $q^{-1}p = \{r \in P | qr = p\}$.

Si a ou νx est égal à $\emptyset$, on a $L_{a,x} = X^*$ ou $\emptyset$ (selon que $a = \nu x$ ou non). Supposons que a et νx soient tous deux distincts de $\emptyset$.

Posons $a = \{(m_1,n_1),\dots,(m_r,n_r)\}$

$\nu x = \{(m'_1,n'_1),\dots,(m'_s,n'_s)\}$

$\forall i,j \quad 1 \leqslant i \leqslant r, \quad 1 \leqslant j \leqslant s$

$A_{i,j} = \mu^{-1}(m_i m'^{-1}_j), \; B_{i,j} = \xi^{-1}(n'^{-1}_j n_i).$

Soient E l'ensemble des applications $\{1,\dots,r\} \to \{1,\dots,s\}$ et F l'ensemble des applications $\{1,\dots,s\} \to \{1,\dots,r\}$.

Alors

(2)

$$L_{a,x} = \bigcup_{\substack{\varphi \in E \\ \psi \in F}} \left(\bigcap_{\substack{1\leqslant i\leqslant r \\ 1\leqslant j\leqslant s}} A_{i,\varphi(i)} \cap A_{\psi(j),j}\right) \times \left(\bigcap_{\substack{1\leqslant i\leqslant r \\ 1\leqslant j\leqslant s}} B_{i,\varphi(i)} \cap B_{\psi(j),j}\right)$$

$L_{a,x}$ a donc bien la forme annoncée dans l'énoncé, puisque les A_{ij} (resp. les B_{ij}) sont tous de la forme $\mu^{-1}(M')$, $M' \subset M$ (resp. $\xi^{-1}(N')$, $N' \subset N$) donc une intersection d'un certain nombre d'entr'eux est encore de cette forme. Montrons (2).

(i) Soit $w \in L_{a,x}$: w s'écrit donc $u\,x\,v$ avec $\mu u\,\nu x\,\xi v = a$, i.e.
$\{(\mu u.m'_1, n'_1.\xi v),\dots,(\mu u.m'_s, n'_s.\xi v)\} = \{(m_1,n_1),\dots,(m_r,n_r)\}$

De l'égalité de ces deux ensembles découle l'existence d'applications $\varphi \in E$ et $\psi \in F$ telles que : $\forall i, (m_i,n_i) = (\mu u.m'_{\varphi(i)}, n'_{\varphi(i)}.\xi v)$ et

$\forall j, (\mu u.m'_j, n'_j.\xi v) = (m_{\varphi(j)}, n_{\varphi(j)})$. Par suite

$\forall i,j$, $u \in A_{i,\varphi(i)} \cap A_{\psi(j),j}$ et

$v \in B_{i,\varphi(i)} \quad B_{\psi(j),j}$ et w

est élément du membre droit de (2).

(ii) Soit w élément du nombre droit de (2). Il existe $\varphi \in E$, $\psi \in F$ et $u,v \in X^*$ tels que $w = uxv$ et

$\forall i,\; u \in A_{i,\varphi(i)}$ et $v \in B_{i,\varphi(i)}$ et

$\forall j,\; u \in A_{j,\psi(j)}$ et $v \in B_{j,\psi(j)}$.

Par suite, comme ci-dessus, on a : $a = \mu u.\nu x.\xi v$, donc $w \in L_{a,x}$. □

<u>Preuve du théorème 1.</u> Soit $\rho : X^* \to M \diamond N$ un homomorphisme, $P \subset M \diamond N$ tels que $L = \rho^{-1}(P)$. On est ramené à Card(P) = 1, $p = \{p\}$, $p \in M \diamond N$. Soit $p = (m,b,n)$; alors $L = \mu^{-1}(m) \cap \nu^{-1}(b) \cap \xi^{-1}(n)$. On est donc ramené à $L = \nu^{-1}(b)$. Soit $\mathfrak{F}$ l'ensemble fini des parties de V dont la somme (i.e. la réunion) des éléments est b :

$\mathfrak{F} = \{F \subset V \mid \sum_{a \in F} a = b\}$.

D'après la formule (1) on a donc : $\forall w \in X^*$, $w \in L \Leftrightarrow \nu w = b \Leftrightarrow \{\mu u.\nu x.\xi v \mid u,v \in X^*, x \in X, w = uxv\} \in \mathfrak{F}$.

Par suite, $L = \bigcup_{F \in \mathfrak{F}} K_F$ où K_F est le langage des $w \in X^*$ tels que $\{\mu u.\nu x.\xi v \mid u,v \in X^*, x \in X, w = uxv\} = F$.

On est donc ramené à $L = K_F$, $F \subset V$. Or $L = K_F = K_1 \cap K_2$ avec
$K_1 = \{w \in X^* | \forall u,x,v \text{ tels que } w = uxv,\ \mu u.\nu x.\xi v \in F\}$ et

$K_2 = \{w \in X^* | \forall a \in F,\ \exists\ u,x,v \text{ tels que } w = uxv \text{ et } \mu u.\nu x.\xi v = a\}$

or $X^* \backslash K_1 = \bigcup_{a \in V \backslash F,\ x \in X} L_{a,x}$ et $K_2 = \bigcap_{a \in F} \bigcup_{x \in X} L_{a,x}$

et l'on conclut avec le lemme 1.□

Rappelons qu'une L-variété $\mathcal{V}$ est dite <u>fermée par produit</u> si pour tout alphabet X et tous $A, B \in X^*\mathcal{V}$, on a $AB \in X^*\mathcal{V}$. Perrot a montré que toute variété fermée par produit est <u>littérale</u> i.e. pour tout X et tout $x \in X$, $\{x\} \in X^*\mathcal{V}$; (3) proposition 2.8.

<u>Théorème 2</u>. <u>Soit $\mathcal{V}$ une L-variété et V la M-variété correspondante; $\mathcal{V}$ est fermé par produit si et seulement si pour tous $M,N \in V$, $M \diamond N \in V$.</u>

<u>Preuve</u>. Si $\mathcal{V}$ est fermée par produit, soient $M,N \in V$. D'après le th. 1, pour tout alphabet X, tout langage L sur X reconnu par $M \diamond N$ est dans $X^*\mathcal{V}$.
Donc le monoïde syntactique M_L de L est dans V, par définition de la correspondance $\mathcal{V} \to V$. Or, il existe un nombre fini de langages $L_1,\ldots,L_n$ reconnus par $M \diamond N$ tels que $M \diamond N$ divise le produit $M_{L_1} \times \ldots \times M_{L_n}$ (cf. (2) prop. VII. 1. 6.) Par suite $M \diamond N \in V$. Pour la réciproque voir (2) th. IX. 1.2.

Rappelons qu'un monoïde est dit <u>apériodique</u> si tous les groupes qu'il contient sont triviaux.

<u>Corollaire 1</u>. <u>Un monoïde fini est apériodique si et seulement s'il divise un des monoïdes de la suite (M_n) avec $M_1 = \{1\}$, $M_{n+1} = M_n \diamond \{1\}$.</u>

<u>Preuve</u>. Comme $M \times N$ est quotient de $M \diamond N$, la classe des monoïdes finis qui vérifient la condition ci-dessus est une M-variété V. Soit $\mathcal{V}$ la L-variété correspondante : d'après th. 2, $\mathcal{V}$ est la plus petite L-variété non vide fermée par produit. Donc d'après (3) corollaire 2.7., V est la M-variété des monoïdes finis apériodiques.□

On vérifie aisément que le produit de Schützenberger n'est pas associatif. Cependant le théorème 1 a pour conséquence le

<u>Corollaire 2</u>. <u>Soient M_1, M_2, M_3 des monoïdes finis. Alors $M_1 \diamond (M_2 \diamond M_3)$ et $(M_1 \diamond M_2) \diamond M_3$ engendrent la même M-variété.</u>

<u>Preuve</u> Ceci découle du th. 1 et du fait que si M-reconnaît A, N reconnaît B et $x \in X$, alors $M \diamond N$ reconnaît $A\,x\,B$.□

<u>Définition</u> Soit $\mathcal{V}$ une L-variété. $\mathcal{V}$ est <u>fermée par substitution finie inverse</u> (resp. <u>par morphisme strictement alphabétique</u>) si pour tous alphabets X et Y et toute substitution finie $\varphi : X^* \to X^*$ (resp. tout morphisme strictement alphabétique

$\psi : X^* \to Y^*$) on a : $L \in Y^*\mathcal{V} \Rightarrow \varphi^{-1}(L) \in X^*\mathcal{V}$

(resp. $L \in X^*\mathcal{V} \Rightarrow \psi(L) \in Y^*\mathcal{V}$).

Exemple : la L-variété des langages dont le monoïde syntactique est commutatif cf. (3) exemple 2.10.

Rappelons qu'une substitution finie $\varphi: X^* \to Y^*$ est un homomorphisme de X^* dans le monoïde des parties finies de Y^*, que si $L \subset Y^*$, $\varphi^{-1}(L)$ désigne le langage $\{w \in X^* | \varphi(w) \cap L \neq \emptyset\}$, et qu'un morphisme strictement alphabétique $\psi : X^* \to Y^*$ est un morphisme vérifiant $\psi(X) \subset Y$.

Si M est un monoïde, $\mathcal{P}(M)$ est muni d'une structure de monoïde de manière naturelle : $A, B \in \mathcal{P}(M)$, $AB = \{ab | a \in A, b \in B\}$.

Théorème 3 Soient $\mathcal{V}$ une L-variété et V la M-variété correspondante. Les conditions suivantes sont équivalentes.

(i) $\mathcal{V}$ est fermée par substitution finie inverse

(ii) $\mathcal{V}$ est fermée par morphisme strictement alphabétique

(iii) $\forall M \in V$, $\mathcal{P}(M) \in V$.

Nous avons besoin d'un lemme.

Lemme 2 Soit $\mathcal{V}$ une L-variété fermée par morphisme strictement alphabétique et $M \in V$. Alors pour tout $P \subset M$ et tout homomorphisme $\varphi : X^* \to \mathcal{P}(M)$, on a $L = \{w \in X^* | \varphi(w) \cap P \neq \emptyset\} \in X^*$.

Preuve. Soit Z_x un alphabet en bijection avec $\varphi(x)$; $\alpha_x : Z_x \to \varphi(x)$ est une bijection. On suppose les Z_x disjoints. Soit $Z = \bigcup_{x \in X} Z_x$ et $\psi : Z^* \to X^*$, $\psi(z) = x$ si $z \in Z_x$. Soit $\gamma : Z^* \to M$, $\gamma(z) = \alpha_x(z)$ si $z \in Z_x$. Alors $\gamma^{-1}(P) \in Z^*$, donc $\psi(\gamma^{-1}(P)) \in X^*$. Or il est immédiat que $L = \psi(\gamma^{-1}(P))$. □

Preuve du théorème 3 (i) ⇒ (ii) Soit $\varphi : X^* \to Y^*$ un morphisme strictement alphabétique et $L \in X^*\mathcal{V}$; soit ψ la substitution finie $Y^* \to X^*$, $\psi(y) = \varphi^{-1}(y)$, $\forall y \in Y$.

Comme φ est strictement alphabétique, on a : $\forall w \in Y^*$, $\varphi^{-1}(w) = \psi(w)$.

Par suite : $w \in \varphi(L) \Leftrightarrow \exists\, u \in L$ tel que $w = \varphi(u) \Leftrightarrow \varphi^{-1}(w) \cap L \neq \emptyset \Leftrightarrow w \in \psi^{-1}(L)$.

Donc $\varphi(L) = \psi^{-1}(L) \in Y^*$.

(ii) ⇒ (iii) Soit $\varphi : X^* \to \mathcal{P}(M)$ un homorphisme et $P \subset (M)$. On est ramené à $\mathrm{Card}(P) = 1$, i.e. P est constitué d'un élément $\{m_1,\ldots,m_n\}$ de $\mathcal{P}(M)$. Soit $Q = M \setminus P$. On a : $\varphi(w) \in P \Leftrightarrow \forall i,\ m_i \in \varphi(w)$ et $\varphi(w) \cap Q = \emptyset$

$\Leftrightarrow w \in L_1 \cap \ldots \cap L_n \setminus K$ avec $L_1 = \{w | \varphi(w) \cap \{m_i\} \neq \emptyset\}$ et $K = \{w | \varphi(w) \cap Q \neq \emptyset\}$

D'après le lemme 2, les L_i et K sont dans X^* , donc $\varphi^{-1}(P)$ est dans X^* ; ceci étant vrai pour tout $P \subset \mathcal{P}(M)$, on a $\mathcal{P}(M) \in V$.

(iii) ⇒ (i) Soit φ une substitution $X^* \to Y^*$ et $L \in Y^*\mathcal{V}$. Soit $M \in V$ un monoïde reconnaissant L : il existe un morphisme $\psi : Y^* \to M$, une partie P de M telle que $L = \psi^{-1}(P)$. ψ se prolonge en $\bar{\psi} : \mathcal{P}(Y^*) \to \mathcal{P}(M)$.

Soit $\mu : X^* \to \mathcal{P}(M)$, $\mu = \psi \circ \varphi$ et $Q \subset \mathcal{P}(M)$, $Q = \{P' \subset M \mid P' \cap P \neq \emptyset\}$

Alors $\varphi^{-1}(L) = \mu^{-1}(Q)$, donc $\varphi^{-1}(L) \in X^* \mathcal{V}$. □

Remarque On a montré en fait que les trois conditions sont équivalentes encore à : $\mathcal{V}$ est fermée par substitution (même infinie) inverse.

Corollaire Si $\mathcal{V}$ est fermée par morphisme strictement alphabétique, $\mathcal{V}$ est fermée par produit de Hurwitz.

Preuve Celà découle de (3) lemme 2.16. □

Références

(1) Brzozowski J.A. : Hierarchies of aperiodic languages, RAIRO-Informatique Théorique 10 (1978) 33-49.

(2) Eilenberg, S. : Automata, languages and machines, B, Academic Press (1976) New York.

(3) Perrot, J.F. : Variétés de langages et opérations, Theor. Comput. Science 7 (1978) 197-210.

(4) Reutenauer, C. : Algèbres et séries formelles (en préparation).

(5) Schützenberger, M.P. : On finite monoïds having only trivial subgroups, Information and Control 8 (1965) 190-194.

(6) Simon, I. : Piece wise testable events, in Automata Theory and Formal Languages, 2nd GI Conference, Lecture Notes in Computer Science 33 (1975) 214-222.

AUTOMATEN IN PLANAREN GRAPHEN

H.A. Rollik

Abstract: For any finite set of automata there is a planar graph which the automata together cannot search.

1. Einleitung

Wir untersuchen in dieser Arbeit das Verhalten von endlichen Automaten in planaren Graphen. Eine endliche Menge von endlichen Automaten durchsucht einen Graphen, wenn jeder Punkt von einem Automaten der Menge mindestens einmal betreten wird. H. Müller konnte in [4] zeigen, daß man zu jedem endlichen Automaten einen planaren Graphen angeben kann, den der Automat nicht durchsuchen kann. L. Budach hat in [3] bewiesen, daß man zu jedem endlichen Automaten einen endlichen Teilgraphen des 2-dimensionalen Gitternetzes konstruieren kann, den der Automat von einem vorgegebenen Ausgangspunkt nicht bewältigen kann. M. Blum und D. Kozen haben in [1] einen Automaten mit 2 Marken angegeben, der jeden endlichen Teilgraphen des 2-dimensionalen Gitternetzes durchsuchen kann. Diese Arbeit zeigt, daß ein ähnliches Resultat für planare Graphen nicht gilt. Es gibt keine endliche Menge von endlichen Automaten, die alle planaren Graphen durchsuchen kann. Dies beweist eine Vermutung von W. Paul und R.E. Tarjan. Für Mengen von 2 und 3 Automaten haben M. Blum und D. Kozen das Ergebnis in [1] bewiesen.

2. Definitionen

$\mathbb{N}$ bezeichne die Menge der natürlichen Zahlen $\mathbb{N} = \{1,2,...\}$. Für endliche Mengen A bezeichne /A/ die Anzahl der Elemente von A. Ein abzählbarer Graph G ist eine höchstens abzählbare Menge V(G) von Punkten zusammen mit einer Menge E(G) von ungeordneten Paaren verschiedener Punkte aus V(G). Die Elemente aus E(G) heißen Kanten. Ein Punkt P inzidiert mit einer Kante k, wenn P in k enthalten ist. Jeder Punkt inzidiert nur mit endlich vielen Kanten. 2 Kanten inzidieren, wenn sie mindestens einen Punkt gemeinsam haben. Eine l-Kantenfärbung von G ist eine Abbildung f von E(G) nach $\{1,2,...,l\}$, so daß für inzidierende Kanten k und k' mit $/k \wedge k'/ = 1$ die Bilder f(k) und f(k') verschieden sind. Der Grad eines Punktes P sei die Anzahl der Kanten, mit denen er inzidiert. Der Grad eines abzählbaren Graphen sei definiert als das Supremum über die Grade der Punkte. Für jeden l-gefärbten Graphen G definieren wir die Valenz eines Punktes P durch $val(P) = \{j \in \{1,2,\ldots,l\} /$ es existiert eine Kante $\{P,Q\} \in E(G)$, die j-gefärbt ist.$\}$

Eine endliche oder unendliche Folge von Punkten aus G heißt Pfad, wenn je zwei aufeinanderfolgende Punkte durch eine Kante verbunden sind. Sei $q = P_0, P_1, \ldots, P_t$ ein endlicher Pfad in G. q heißt geschlossen, wenn $P_0 = P_t$ gilt. t heißt die Länge von q und wird mit l(q) bezeichnet. l(q) ist gleich der Anzahl der Kanten, die zu q gehören, wobei mehrfach auftretende Kanten mehrfach gezählt werden. Für unendliche Pfade q ist l(q) nicht definiert. Die Länge des kürzesten Pfades zwischen zwei Punkten P und Q in einem Graphen G bezeichnen wir als den Abstand von P und Q in G.

Sei G ein planarer Graph, der so in die Ebene eingebettet ist, daß sich zwei Kanten nur in Punkten schneiden, mit denen sie gemeinsam inzidieren und $q = \{P_i\}_{l=o}^{t}$ sei ein geschlossener Pfad in G mit der Eigenschaft:

$$P_i \neq P_j \text{ für } i,j \in \{1,\ldots,t\} \text{ und } i \neq j$$

q heißt Kreis. Durch jeden Kreis wird die Ebene in zwei zusammenhängende Komponenten eingeteilt. q wird mit zum Äußeren gerechnet. Für eine feste Einbettung von G sei I die Menge aller Punkte, die im Innern eines Kreises q liegen. Ein Punkt von G aus dem Komplement von I heißt Randpunkt.

Wir betrachten endliche Automaten, die sich in kantengefärbten Graphen bewegen. Diese Automaten haben eine endliche Menge von Zuständen zusammen mit einer partiellen Übergangsfunktion δ. In jedem Punkt P eines kantengefärbten Graphen stellt ein solcher Automat fest, wie die Kanten gefärbt sind, die mit P inzidieren und in welchem Zustand die anderen Automaten sind, die sich auch in P befinden. Diese Informationen bilden die Eingabe für den Automaten. In Abhängigkeit von seinem Zustand und der Eingabe gibt δ an, in welchem Zustand der Automat übergeht und bestimmt die Kante, über die der Automat den Punkt verläßt. Alle diese Aktionen bilden einen Schritt des Automaten. Formal werden k endliche Automaten mit n Zuständen, die sich zusammen in einem Graphen bewegen, spezifiziert durch ein (k+2)-Tupel $(S, X, \delta_1, \ldots, \delta_k)$. Hierbei bezeichnet S die Zustandsmenge der Automaten und X das Ausgabealphabet. X enthält die Zeichen 1,2,3 und '+' P(X) bezeichnet die Potenzmenge von X. Sei S_1 gleich $S \cup \{\perp\}$. Die Funktionen $\delta_i : S_1^k \times P(X) \to S \times X$ sind partielle Funktionen und heißen Übergangsfunktionen. δ_i bezeichnet die Übergangsfunktion des i-ten Automaten. $\delta_i(s_1, \ldots, s_k, X')$ ist nur für $s_i \neq \perp$ und nichtleere Mengen X', die das Zeichen '+' nicht enthalten, definiert.

$\delta_i(s_1, \ldots, s_k, X') = (s_i', r)$ bedeutet: Wenn der i-te Automat im Zustand s_i einen Punkt P mit $val(P) = X'$ betritt und in P g Automaten, $g \leq k-1$, trifft, die sich in den Zuständen $s_{i_1}, \ldots, s_{i_g}$, $i_l \in \{1, \ldots, k\}$, befinden, wobei $s_{i_j} = \perp$ bedeutet, daß der Automat A_{i_j} nicht in P ist, so geht der i-te Automat in den Zustand s_i' über und verläßt P über die mit r gefärbte Kante. Im Fall $r = +$ bleibt der i-te Automat in P.

3. Konstruktion von Fallen für einzelne Automaten

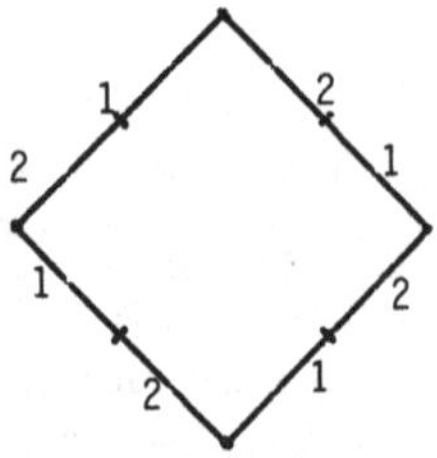

Fig. 1

H sei der Graph aus Figur 1. Die Zahlen geben die Färbung der Kanten an. Sei T' ein abzählbar unendlicher Baum, in dem jeder Punkt Grad 4 hat. Wir konstruieren einen neuen Graphen T, indem wir alle Punkte in T' durch einen Kreis H ersetzen wie in Figur 2 angegeben.

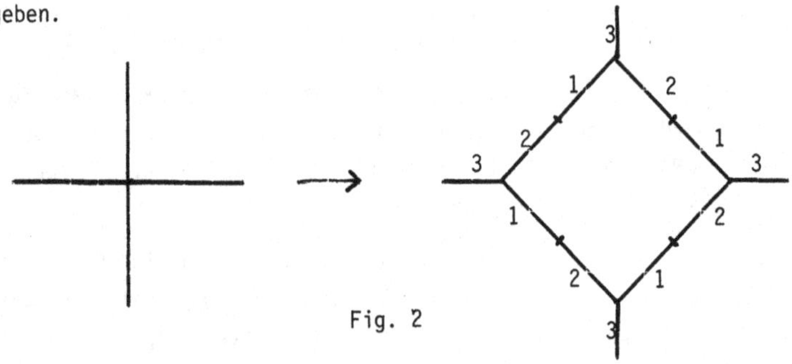

Fig. 2

Wir beschreiben 2 Methoden aus 3-kantengefärbten Graphen neue 3-kantengefärbte Graphen zu gewinnen. G und G' seien zwei 3-kantengefärbte Graphen und G' habe 2 ausgezeichnete Punkte P und Q mit val(P) = val(Q) = {1,2}. Wir sagen G'' entsteht durch Einsetzung von G' in G wenn G" aus G hervorgeht, indem jede Kante in G mit Farbe 3 durch Figur 3 ersetzt wird.

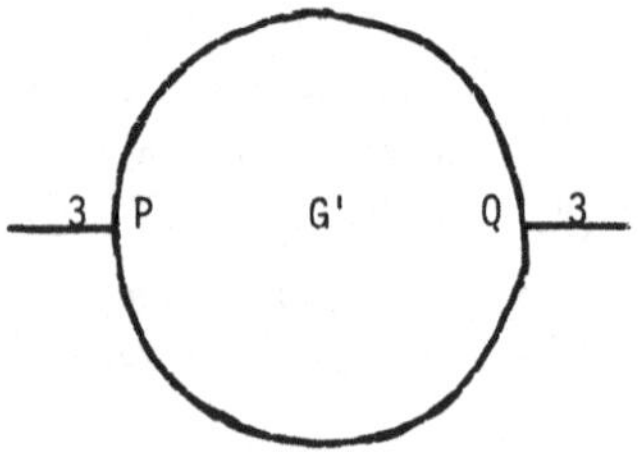

Fig. 3

Im allgemeinen können durch Einsetzung von G' in G viele verschiedene Graphen entstehen. Dies wird im folgenden keine Rolle spielen. Ist G ein Graph mit zwei ausgezeichneten Punkten P und Q mit val(P) = val(Q) = {1,2}, so bezeichnen wir mit G_{2P} den Graphen aus Figur 4. Die beiden Kopien von Q sind ausgezeichnete Punkte von G_{2P}.

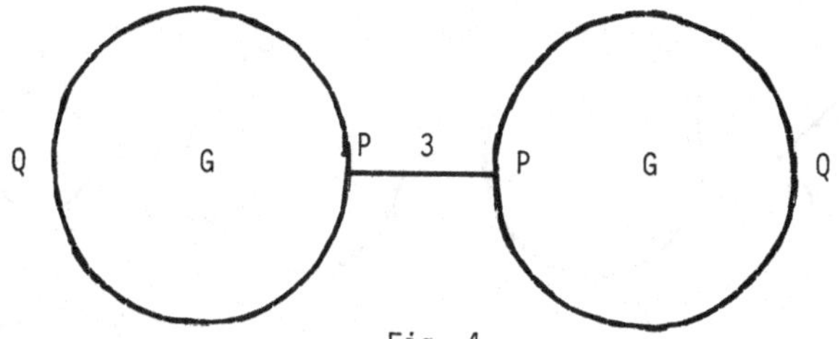

Fig. 4

Zu allen endlichen 3-kantengefärbten planaren Graphen G, die mindestens zwei Punkte mit Valenz {1,2} haben, bilden wir die Graphen G_{2P} für alle Punkte P mit Valenz {1,2}. Die Graphen G_{2P} setzen wir nach der ersten Methode in den Graphen T ein. Die Menge aller Graphen, die wir so erhalten, nennen wir $\mathcal{T}$. Der Graph T soll auch zu $\mathcal{T}$ gehören. Sei P ein Punkt aus irgendeinem der Graphen $G \in \mathcal{T}$. Hat P Grad 3 und gehört nicht zu den eingesetzten Graphen, so nennen wir P einen H-Punkt. H-Punkte desselben Kreises H' sind in H' nur durch Pfade verbunden, die aus 1- und 2-gefärbten Kanten bestehen. Alle Pfade in Graphen aus T lassen sich durch Farbfolgen beschreiben, indem den Kanten des jeweiligen Pfades ihre Farbe zugeordnet wird. Ist der Anfangspunkt eines Pfades gegeben, so ist der Pfad durch die zugeordnete Farbfolge eindeutig bestimmt.

Definition: Sei B eine endliche Menge von Automaten. Eine B-Falle ist ein 4-Tupel (G,P_0,P,Q), wobei gilt:

(3.1) G ist ein planarer 3-kantengefärbter Graph.

(3.2) P_0,P, und Q sind Randpunkte von G mit Valenz {1,2}. Kein Automat findet von P_0 nach P oder Q.

(3.3) Sämtliche Kanten mit Farbe $\neq 3$ liegen auf Kopien des Kreises H. Kopien des Kreises H sind mit Kanten der Farbe 3 verbunden.

Mit A(n) bezeichnen wir die Menge aller Automaten mit n Zuständen, wobei wir Automaten, die durch Umbenennung von Zuständen auseinander hervorgehen, identifizieren.

Lemma 1: Für jede Menge $B \subseteq A(n)$ gibt es B-Fallen.

Beweis durch Induktion über /B/.

Der Kreis H ist eine $\emptyset$-Falle. Für $/B/ \geq 1$ sei $A \in B$ und G eine (B-{A})-Falle. T_1 entstehe durch Einsetzen von G_{2P} in T. Figur 5 zeigt einen Ausschnitt aus T_1.

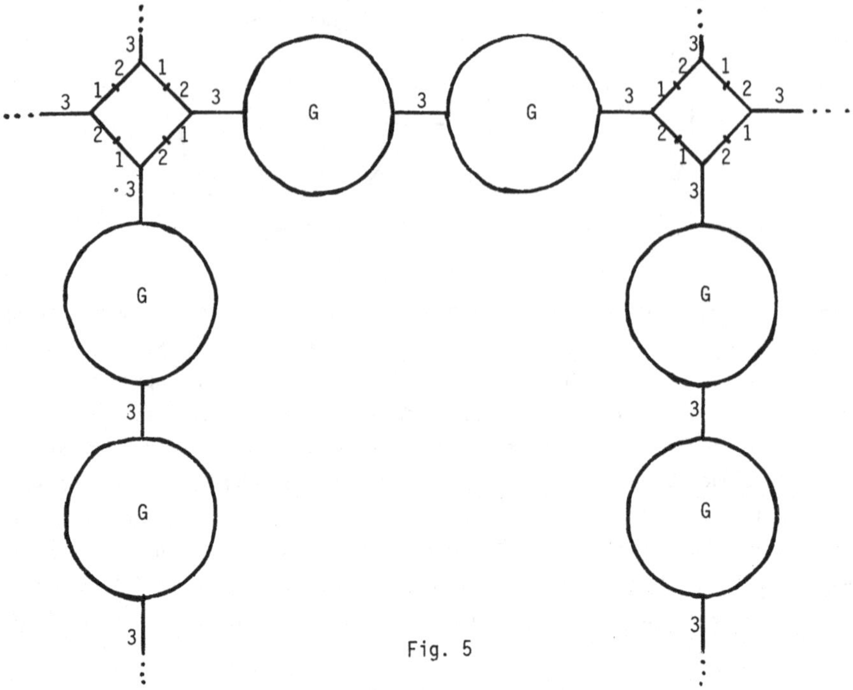

Fig. 5

Fall 1: Auf dem Weg von A in T_1 liegen nur endlich viele Punkte. M sei eine Zahl, die größer ist als die Anzahl der Punkte in G_{2P}.
U sei die Menge aller Punkte aus T_1, die zu mindestens einem Punkt auf dem Weg von A einen Abstand kleiner gleich M haben. Wir definieren einen Graphen L, dessen Punktmenge die Menge U ist und in dem 2 Punkte genau dann durch eine f-gefärbte Kante verbunden sind, wenn sie auch in T_1 durch eine f-gefärbte Kante verbunden sind. Durch die Wahl von M haben wir erreicht, daß der Graph G_{2P} in L enthalten ist. Wenn der Automat A in L in P_0 startet, erreicht er keine Punkte, die er von P_0 aus in T_1 nicht betreten hat. Es ist klar, daß es Randpunkte Q und Q' gibt, die A nicht findet und daß L eine B-Falle ist.

Fall 2: Auf dem Weg von A liegen unendlich viele Punkte.
$A \in A(n)$ kann jeden Punkt höchstens n-mal betreten. Unter den unendlich vielen Punten, die A besucht, sind unendlich viele H-Punkte. Unter diesen gibt es unendlich viele, die der Automat zuerst über eine Kante mit Farbe $\neq 3$ erreicht und zuletzt über eine Kante mit Farbe 3 verläßt. Diese Punkte nennen wir D-Punkte. Aus den Symmetrien der Graphen aus T folgt: spätestens beim Erreichen des (n+1)-ten D-Punktes wiederholt sich ein Zustand, der früher beim Erreichen eines D-Punktes angenommen wurde. Sei P_t der Punkt, den A nach t Schritten erreicht. P_{t_0} bezeichne den ersten der beiden D-Punkte, R die durchlaufende Farbfolge, t_1 die Länge dieser Folge und $P_{t_0+t_1}$ den letzten der beiden D-Punkte. Für $F = f_1 \ldots f_s, f_i \in \{1,2,3\}$, bezeichnen wir die Umkehrung $f_s \ldots f_1$ von F mit $\bar{F}$. F^* bezeichne die unendliche Farbfolge FF... . Wir indenti-

fizieren im folgenden Farbfolgen mit den zugehörigen von P_{t_0} ausgehenden Pfaden. $\{1,2,3\}^+$ bezeichne die Menge aller Folgen aus den Zeichen 1,2 und 3.

Lemma 2: $\bar{R}^*$ berührt unendlich viele Punkte und hat nur endlich viele Punkte mit R^* gemeinsam.

Beweis: $R = G_1H_1 \ldots G_sH_s, G_i, H_i \in \{1,2,3\}^+$, sei eine Dekomposition von R, so daß die zu den G_i gehörenden Pfade zwischen zwei H-Punkten verlaufen, die nur durch einen Graphen G_{2P} getrennt sind. Die zu den H_i gehörenden Pfade verlaufen bis auf Exkursionen in die 4 benachbarten Graphen G_{2P} im gleichen Kreis H'. Es folgt, daß $\bar{R} = \bar{H}_s\bar{G}_s \ldots \bar{H}_1\bar{G}_1$ eine ebensolche Dekomposition ist.
R' entsteht wie folgt aus R:

i) Alle G_i werden durch 3 ersetzt und
ii) aus allen H_i werden Exkursionen in Graphen G_{2P} gestrichen.

Ebenso entstehe $\bar{R}'$ aus $\bar{R}$.
R' und $\bar{R}'$ definieren in naheliegender Weise Pfade in T. R'' entstehe aus R', indem solange wie möglich Farbfolgen, die zum gleichen Punkt zurückführen, gestrichen werden. Ebenso enstehe $\bar{R}''$ aus $\bar{R}'$. Daraus folgt:
$(R'')^*$ berührt unendlich viele Punkte; berührt $(\bar{R}'')^*$ unendlich viele Punkte so auch $\bar{R}^*$; haben $(R'')^*$ und $(\bar{R}'')^*$ nur endlich viele Punkte gemeinsam, so auch R^* und $\bar{R}^*$.

Nach Konstruktion von R'' und $\bar{R}''$ berührt keiner dieser beiden Pfade einen Punkt zwischen Startpunkt und Endpunkt zweimal. Wäre der Startpunkt gleich dem Endpunkt, so würde R^* nur endlich viele Punkte berühren. Weil R" in D-Punkten beginnt und endet, beginnt R'' mit Farbe 3 und $\bar{R}''$ mit Farbe $\neq 3$. Es folgt, daß $(R'')^*$ und $(\bar{R}'')^*$ nur P_{t_0} gemeinsam haben. Würde $(\bar{R}'')^*$ nur endlich viele Punkte berühren, so auch $(R'')^*$ und damit R^*. Damit ist Lemma 2 bewiesen.

Sei $P_{t_0+t_1}$ der Punkt, der von P_{t_0} aus über die Farbfolge R erreicht wird und Q_{t_1} der Punkt, der von P_{t_0} aus über die Farbfolge $\bar{R}$ erreicht wird. Q_{t_1-1} sei der Punkt, den man von Q_{t_1} über die Kante der Farbe 3 erreicht. Diese existiert, denn die Farbfolge $\bar{R}$ endet mit 3. T_1' bezeichne den Graphen, den man erhält, wenn man aus T_1 die von $P_{t_0+t_1}$ und Q_{t_1-1} ausgehenden Kanten mit Farbe 3 entfernt und $P_{t_0+t_1}$ und Q_{t_1-1} mit einer Kante der Farbe 3 verbindet. Der Graph T_1' ist planar, denn die neue Kante verbindet Punkte, die in T_1 Randpunkte waren. Der Automat A bewegt sich nach t_0 Schritten nur noch auf dem Zyklus $P_{t_0}, \ldots P_{t_0+t_1}, Q_{t_1-1}, \ldots, P_{t_0}$. Entfernen aller Punkte in einem genügend großen Abstand von diesem Zyklus liefert einen endlichen Graphen T_2 mit den gewünschten Eigenschaften. T_2 kann immer so in die Ebene eingebettet werden, daß P_0 ein Randpunkt bleibt. Der Graph, den man so erhalten hat ist eine B-Falle.

Wir bemerken, daß in den oben konstruierten Fallen alle Kanten mit Farbe $\neq 3$ auf Kreisen H liegen.

4. Konstruktion von Fallen für Automaten, die sich gleichzeitig in einem Graphen bewegen

Definition: Ein (n,k)-Labyrinth ist ein Graph G, für den gilt:

(4.1) Es gibt einen planaren 3-kantengefärbten Graphen G' mit 2 ausgezeichneten Punkten P und Q, die Valenz {1,2} haben, so daß $G = G'_{2P}$. (vergleiche Figur 4)

(4.2) Ist J ein 3-kantengefärbter planarer Graph, der wie in Figur 6 mit G verbunden ist und starten $g \leq k$ Automaten in Knoten von J, so benutzt kein Automat jemals die Kante zwischen den beiden Kopien von P.

(4.3) Jede Kante von G mit Farbe $\neq 3$ liegt auf einer Kopie des Kreises H. Kopien von H sind durch Kanten mit Farbe 3 verbunden.

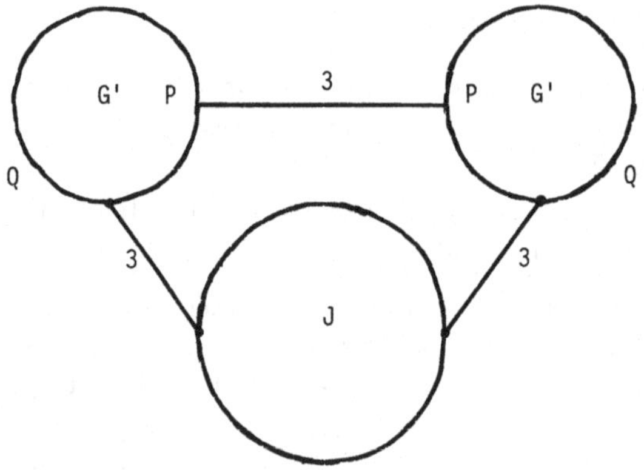

Fig. 6

Unser Hauptergebnis ist der folgende,

Satz: Es gibt (n,k)-Labyrinthe für alle n und k.

Der Beweis wird durch Induktion über k geführt. Mit der gleichen Technik läßt sich ein ähnliches in [2] angekündigtes Ergebnis über Automaten in 3-dimensionalen Gitternetzen beweisen.

Wählt man G' = H, so kann man leicht ein (n,0)-Labyrinth bauen. Der Satz sei richtig für 0,1,...,k-1 und alle n.

Sei L_1 ein (n,k-1)-Labyrinth. L_1 bestehe aus 2 Kopien eines Graphen L_1'. P_1 und P_2 seien die ausgezeichneten Punkte von L_1.

L_2 bestehe aus einer Kette von k Kopien von L_1 wie in Figur 7 angegeben.

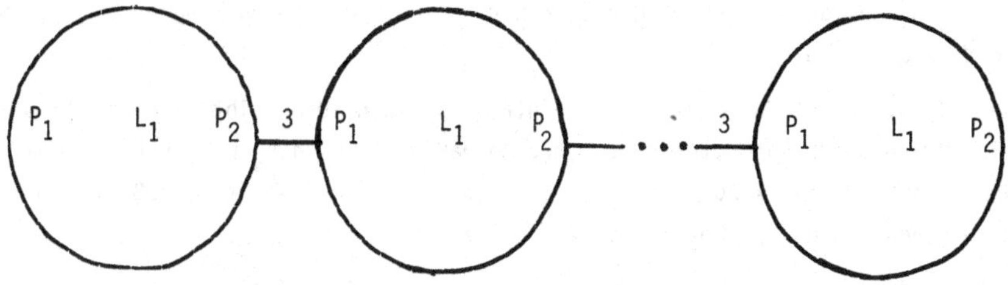

Fig. 7

$L_3 = (G_3,P_3,P_4,P_5)$ sei eine A(m)-Falle, wobei m später bestimmt wird.
L_4 entstehe durch Einsetzen von L_2 in L_3.
L_5 bestehe aus 2 Kopien von L_4 wie in Figur 8 angegeben.

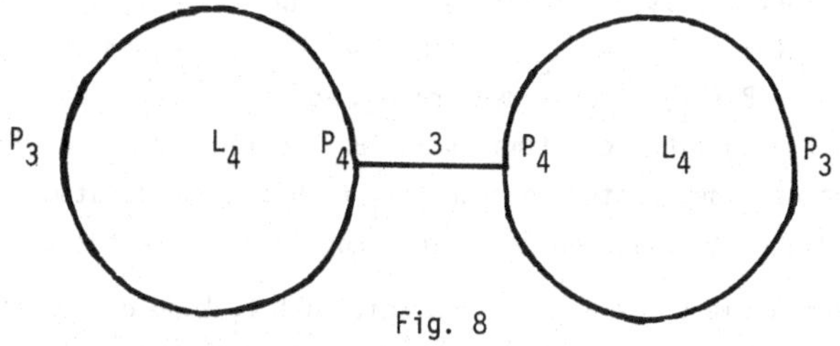

Fig. 8

Wir zeigen, daß L_5 für große m ein (n,k)-Labyrinth ist.

Definition: Eine l-Konfiguration von k Automaten $A_1,\dots,A_k$ bezüglich eines Automaten A_1 in einem 3-kantengefärbten Graphen ist ein 2k-Tupel $(s_1,\dots,s_k,\mathrm{val}(P),N_2,\dots,N_k)$, wobei gilt:

- s_i ist der Zustand des Automaten A_i
- P ist der Punkt, in dem sich der Automat A_1 befindet
- $N_i, i \geq 2$, ist die Menge aller Farbfolgen, die zu Pfaden von Automat A_i nach P gehören und deren Länge kürzer als l ist. N_i ist leer, falls sich der Automat A_i in P befindet oder alle Pfade von A_i nach P länger als l sind.

Definition: Sei G ein Graph mit Knotenmenge V. $V' \subseteq V$ heißt getrennt, wenn es eine Partition von V' in nichtleere Mengen V_1 und V_2 gibt, so daß jeder Pfad zwischen V_1 und V_2 durch eine Kopie von L_1 (und zwar zwischen P_1 und P_2) verläuft. Eine Menge von Automaten heißt getrennt, wenn ihre Standpunkte getrennt sind.

Sei G die Menge aller Graphen, die man durch Einsetzen von L_2 in Graphen, die (3.3) bzw. (4.3) erfüllen, erhält. Sei l(k) das Supremum über den Abstand (=Länge des kürzesten Pfades) zwischen Punkten in nicht getrennten Mengen der Mächtigkeit k in Graphen aus G. Wegen (3.3) bzw. (4.3) ist l(k) endlich. Mit k_1 = Anzahl der Knoten in L_1 gilt $l(k) \leq (k_1+1)k+4$.

Sei m' die Anzahl der 1(k)-Konfigurationen von nicht getrennten Mengen von k Automaten in Graphen aus $\underline{G}$.

Wir nehmen an, L_5 sei für $m \geq m'+1$ kein (n,k)-Labyrinth. Dann gibt es einen Graphen J und eine Menge von k Automaten $A_1,\ldots,A_k$, so daß gilt: Wird L_5 wie in Figur 7 mit J verbunden, so kann man k Automaten mit n Zuständen so in J starten, daß einer die Kante zwischen den beiden Kopien von P_4 benutzt.

O.B.d.A. sei dies der Automat A_1. Dann muß sich A_1 in einer Kopie von L_4 von P_3 nach P_4 bewegen.

Lemma 3: Sind die Automaten in irgendeinem Zeitpunkt t getrennt, so durchkreuzt nach t kein Automat mehr eine Kopie von L_1, in dem zum Zeitpunkt t kein Automat war.

Beweis: Zum Zeitpunkt t gibt es eine Menge S von Kopien von L_1 und eine Partition der Menge der Automaten in B_1 und B_2, so daß jeder Weg von einem Automaten in $B_1(B_2)$ zu einem Automaten in $B_2(B_1)$ durch einen Graphen aus S verläuft. Wir zeigen zuerst, daß Automaten aus B nach t keine Automaten aus B_2 treffen und umgekehrt. Geschieht dies doch, so gibt es einen ersten Zeitpunkt t_1 nach t, wo ein Automat in einem Graphen L_1 aus S die Kante zwischen den beiden Kopien von L_1' benutzt.

O.B.d.A. ist dieser Automat aus B_1. Bis zum Zeitpunkt t_1 kann die Existenz der Automaten aus B_2 für die Automaten aus B_1 ignoriert werden. Da L_1 aber ein (n,k-1)-Labyrinth ist und B_1 höchstens aus k-1 Automaten besteht, kann kein Automat aus B_1 ohne Hilfe von Automaten aus B_2 die besagte Kante benutzen.

Aus dem oben Gesagten folgt, daß nach t der Effekt von Automaten aus B_1 auf Automaten aus B_2 ignoriert werden kann. Daraus folgt - wieder, weil L_1 ein (n,k-1)-Labyrinth ist - die Behauptung des Lemmas.

Sei t' nun der letzte Zeitpunkt, zu dem A_1 eine Kopie von P_3 in Figur 8 trifft, bevor A_1 eine der Kopien von P_4 in Figur 8 erreicht. Nach Lemma 3 ist zur Zeit t' die Menge der Automaten nicht getrennt. Wir geben einen Automaten A mit Zustandsmenge Z und Übergangsfunktion δ an.

$Z' = \{C/C$ ist eine 1(k)-Konfiguration von $A_1,\ldots,A_k$ bezüglich A_1 in $L_5\}$ und
$Z = Z' \cup \{0\}$.

Für $z \in Z'$ wird $\delta(z,K) = (z',r)$ nur für solche z erklärt, wo sich A_1 auf einem Knoten v von einem der Kreise H außerhalb von Kopien von L_2 befindet und $K = \mathrm{val}(v)$ gilt.
In diesem Fall wird (z',r) wie folgt bestimmt:
Man starte $A_1,\ldots,A_k$ in Konfiguration C in J. Sei t_2 der erste Zeitpunkt, zu dem A_1 einen von v verschiedenen Punkt v' auf einem Kreis außerhalb einer Kopie von L_2 betritt und sei z' die 1(k)-Konfiguration der Automaten zur Zeit t_2. Sind v und v' durch eine Kante mit Farbe $f \in \{1,2\}$ verbunden, so sei $r = f$, andernfalls sind v und v' durch eine Kopie von L_2 getrennt und wir setzen $r = 3$.

Sei z_0 die 1(k)-Konfiguration von $A_1,\ldots,A_k$ zur Zeit t'. Aus Lemma 3 und der Annahme folgt, daß der Automat A, gestartet im Zustand z_0 im Punkt P_3 des Graphen aus Figur 9, den Punkt P_4 erreicht, ohne vorher P_3 wieder zu betreten.

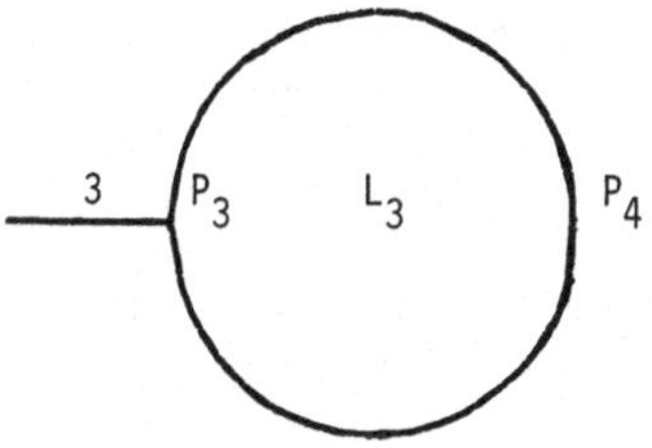

Fig. 9

Setzt man noch $\delta(0,\{1,2\}) = \delta(z_0,\{1,2,3\})$, so findet A in L_3 von P_3 nach P_4. Aber L_3 ist eine A(m)-Falle für $m \geq /Z/$. Widerspruch!

Korollar: Zu jeder Menge von k Automaten mit n Zuständen gibt es einen planaren 3-kantengefärbten Graphen L und einen Stratpunkt für die Automaten, so daß die Automaten, wenn sie in P starten, nicht alle Punkte in L besuchen.

Beweis: G sei ein (n,k)-Labyrinth, das aus zwei Kopien eines Graphen G' besteht. G' sei wie in Figur 6 mit einem planaren 3-kantengefärbten Graphen verbunden. Ersetzt man die Kante zwischen den beiden Kopien von G' durch

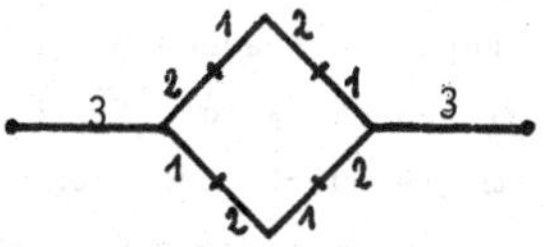

so hat der Graph, den man damit erhält, die gewünschte Eigenschaft.

5. Literatur

1. M. Blum, D. Kozen, "On the power of the compass", 19th IEEE FOCS 1978
2. M. Blum, W. Sakoda, "On the capability of finite automata in 2 and 3 dimensional space", Proc. 17th IEEE Conf. (1977), 147-161
3. L. Budach, "Automata and labyrinths", unveröffentlichtes Manuskript, 1974
4. H. Müller, "Endliche Automaten und Labyrinthe", EIK 7(1971) 4, 261-264.

THEOREME DE TRANSVERSALE RATIONNELLE POUR LES AUTOMATES A PILE DETERMINISTES

Jacques Sakarovitch

Let A be a deterministic pushdown with X as input alphabet and ω be the mapping of X^* into the set of configurations of A which maps a word w of X^* onto the configuration reached by A when reading w . It is shown that for any rational subset R of X^* there exists a rational subset T of R such that ω is one-to-one from T onto $\omega(R)$. A new necessary condition for the determinism of context free languages is then derived.

Soient X^* un monoïde libre et f une application de X dans un ensemble E ; nous dirons que l'application f possède la *propriété de transversale rationnelle* si, par définition, elle satisfait la condition suivante : pour tout ensemble rationnel R de X^* il existe un ensemble rationnel T inclus dans R qui soit une transversale de R pour f , c'est-à-dire qui soit un ensemble de représentants, inclus dans R , des éléments de R modulo l'équivalence d'application de f , ou encore tel que f soit une bijection entre T et f(R) . Métonymie naturelle, nous dirons qu'un monoïde M possède la propriété de transversale rationnelle si, pour tout monoïde libre X , tout homomorphisme de X^* dans M possède la propriété de transversale rationnelle. S. Eilenberg a montré ([4], Théorème IX.7.1) que tout monoïde libre possède la propriété de transversale rationnelle.

Le but de cette communication est de montrer que l'application définie par un automate à pile déterministe, c'est-à-dire l'application qui fait correspondre à un mot la configuration de l'automate après la lecture de ce mot, possède la propriété de transversale rationnelle (Théorème 5). On en déduit alors l'énoncé d'une condition que doivent satisfaire les langages algébriques déterministes (Corollaire 2) et qui n'est pas, comme le sont d'habitude les conditions nécessaires de ce type, un théorème d'itération. A titre d'exemple on utilisera le corollaire 2 pour donner une nouvelle preuve de ce que le langage $L=\{a^nb^n|n\in N\}\cup\{a^nb^{2n}|n\in N\}$ n'est pas déterministe.

Le théorème 5 repose sur deux résultats. Le premier assure que le groupe libre et le monoïde polycyclique possèdent la propriété de transversale rationnelle (Théorème 3 et Corollaire 1) ; il forme le point central de ce travail et est exposé à la section 2. Ce théorème 3 repose lui-même sur un théorème fondamental, dû à M. Benois [1] et que nous rappelons d'abord à la section 1. Le second résultat décrit une représentation des automates à pile par des transductions rationnelles à valeur dans le monoïde polycyclique et est dû à M. Nivat [8]. On le trouvera, ainsi que le théorème 5, à la section 3.

1. LES SIMPLIFICATIONS DE DYCK

Nous inspirant d'une remarque de M.P. Schützenberger pour définir d'un même mouvement les congruences de Dyck et de Dyck restreinte (cf. [2]), nous posons la définition suivante :

Définition 1 : Soient X un alphabet et S un sous-ensemble de X^2. Nous appelons *simplification de Dyck* associée à S l'application θ de X^* dans lui-même définie par :

i) $\theta(1_{X^*}) = 1_{X^*}$;

ii) $\forall f\in X^* \ \forall x\in X \quad \theta(fx) = g$ si $\theta(f) = gy$ et $yx\in S$

$\theta(fx) = \theta(f)x$ sinon

On vérifie aisément, en en démarquant la preuve dans [7] par exemple, que toute simplification de Dyck θ sur X^* vérifie :

$$\forall f,\ g\in X^* \quad \theta(fg) = \theta(\theta(f)g) \tag{1}$$

Il s'ensuit que l'équivalence d'application de θ est régulière à droite et que $\theta(X^*)$ est un ensemble de représentants pour cette équivalence.

Soit X un ensemble ; nous noterons $\tilde{X}$ l'union de X et de $\bar{X}$, copie de X , disjointe de X . Pour chaque lettre z de $\tilde{X}$ nous noterons $\bar{z}$ la lettre qui correspond à z dans la bijection canonique entre X et $\bar{X}$, lettre barrée ou non barrée suivant que z appartient à X ou à $\bar{X}$. On appelle classiquement réduction de Dyck (resp. réduction de Dyck restreinte) la simplification ρ (resp. ρ') associée à $D = \{z\bar{z} \mid z \in \tilde{X}\}$ (resp. $D' = \{z\bar{z} \mid z \in X\}$). Les réductions ρ et ρ' vérifient aussi :

$$\forall f,g \in \tilde{X}^* \quad \rho(fg) = \rho(\rho(f)\rho(g)) \tag{2}$$

Ainsi, les équivalences d'applications associées à ρ et à ρ' sont des congruences. Il est classique (cf. [7]) que le quotient de $\tilde{X}^*$ par ρ est le groupe libre de base X , que nous noterons $X^{\circledast}$. Le quotient de $\tilde{X}^*$ par ρ' a été appelé "free half-group" par E. Shamir [13] et monoïde involutif par M. Fliess [5].

En généralisant un résultat de M. Benois [1] on peut énoncer :

Théorème 1 : *L'image d'un ensemble rationnel par une simplification de Dyck est un ensemble rationnel.*

Ce résultat(restreint aux seules réductions ρ et ρ') a aussi été prouvé par M. Fliess [5] d'une manière directe et élégante, en utilisant la définition des parties rationnelles par les représentations du monoïde libre par des matrices booléennes. Pour démontrer le théorème 1 nous suivrons les mêmes étapes que celles de la démonstration de [1]. Nous les adaptons d'une part à la généralisation du résultat, d'autre part en faisant apparaître explicitement une construction qui nous servira pour démontrer le théorème de transversale rationnelle. La démonstration de [5] ne se prête pas, semble-t-il, à ces transformations.

Lemme 1 ([1]) : *Soient θ une simplification de Dyck de X^* et φ un homomorphisme strictement alphabétique de A^* dans X^*. Il existe alors une simplification de Dyck λ de A^* telle que $\varphi \circ \lambda = \theta \circ \varphi$*

Preuve : Soient S le sous ensemble de X^2 associé à θ et $T = \varphi^{-1}(S)$; comme φ est strictement alphabétique, T est un sous ensemble de A^2. T définit une simplification de Dyck λ sur A^* et on vérifie, par récurrence sur $|f|$, que $\varphi(\lambda(f)) = \theta(\varphi(f))$ pour tout f dans A^*. ∎

Lemme 2 ([1]) : *L'image d'un ensemble rationnel local par une simplification de Dyck est un ensemble rationnel local, éventuellement augmenté du mot vide.*

Preuve : *Soient* θ une simplification de Dyck de X^* et L un langage local de X^* c'est-à-dire

$$L = AX^* \cap X^*B \backslash X^*VX^* \qquad \text{avec } A,B \subset X \text{ et } V \subset X^2$$

Nous commençons par construire une application μ de X^* dans lui-même, qui jouera aussi un rôle capital dans la démonstration du théorème 3.

a) Pour chaque lettre x de X soit $\delta(x)$ le mot f de X^* le plus court tel que :

i) $fx \in AX^* \setminus X^*VX^*$

ii) $\theta(fx) = x$

Si un tel mot f n'existe pas, $\delta(x) = \emptyset$.

b) Pour chaque lettre x de X soit $\gamma(x)$ le mot f de X^* le plus court tel que :

i) $xf \in X^*B \setminus X^*VX^*$

ii) $\theta(xf) = x$

Si un tel mot f n'existe pas, $\gamma(x) = \emptyset$.

c) Pour chaque couple (x,y) de lettres de X soit $\tau(x,y)$ le mot f de X^* le plus court tel que :

i) $xfy \in X^* \setminus X^*VX^*$

ii) $\theta(xfy) = xy$

Si un tel mot f n'existe pas, $\tau(x,y) = \emptyset$

L'application μ est alors définie par :

i) $\mu(1_{X^*})$ est égal au mot f de L le plus court tel que $\theta(f) = 1_{X^*}$ et est égal à l'ensemble vide si un tel mot f n'existe pas.

ii) si $w = w_1 w_2 \ldots w_n$ est un mot de X^* avec $w_i \in X$ alors

$$\mu(w) = \delta(w_1)w_1\tau(w_1,w_2)w_2 \ldots w_{n-1}\tau(w_{n-1},w_n)w_n\,\gamma(w_n).$$

L'application μ est une transduction rationnelle fonctionnelle (partielle).
Soit L' le langage local défini par :

$$L' = A'X \cap X^*B' \setminus X^*V'X^*$$

avec $A' = \{x \in X \mid \delta(x) \neq \emptyset\}$, $B' = x \in X \mid \gamma(x) \neq \emptyset\}$, et $V' = \{xy \in X^2 \mid \tau(x,y) = \emptyset\}$. On pose alors $L'' = L'$ si $\mu(1_{X^*}) = \emptyset$ et $L'' = L' \cup \{1_{X^*}\}$ si $\mu(1_{X^*}) \neq \emptyset$.

On vérifie alors, par récurrence sur $|w|$, les deux implications :

$$w \in L'' \Rightarrow \mu(w) \in L \qquad (3)$$

$$w \in L'' \Rightarrow \theta(\mu(w)) = w \qquad (4)$$

ce qui entraine l'inclusion $L'' \subset \theta(L)$. L'inclusion inverse se vérifie, elle aussi par récurrence, et le lemme est démontré. ■

Démonstration du théorème 1 [1] : Soient θ une simplification de Dyck de X^* et R un ensemble rationnel de X^*. Posons $R' = R \setminus \{1_{X^*}\}$; il est classique (cf. [2] par exemple) qu'il existe un alphabet A, un homomorphisme strictement alphabétique φ de A^* dans X^* , et un langage local L de A^* tels que $\varphi(L) = R'$.

D'après le lemme 1, il existe une simplification de Dyck λ de A^* telle que $\theta \circ \varphi = \varphi \circ \lambda$. D'après le lemme 2, l'image de L par λ est un ensemble rationnel K . Ainsi $\theta(R')$ est rationnel puisque :

$$\theta(R') = \theta(\varphi(L)) = \varphi(\lambda(L)) = \varphi(K)$$

L'image de R par θ , égale à $\theta(R')$ éventuellement augmentée du mot vide est un ensemble rationnel.

c.q.f.d.

2. GROUPES LIBRES ET AUTRES MONOIDES

Rappelons tout d'abord le théorème de S. Eilenberg :

Théorème 2([4], Théorème IX.7.1) : *le monoïde libre possède la propriété de transversale rationnelle.*

Nous sommes maintenant en mesure de montrer :

Proposition 1 : *Toute simplification de Dyck possède la propriété de transversale rationnelle.*

Démonstration : La figure suivante permet de suivre plus facilement la preuve

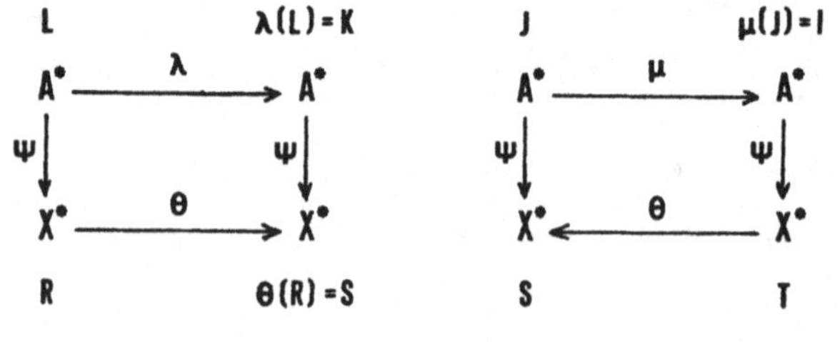

Figure 1

Soit θ une simplification de Dyck sur X^* et soit R un ensemble rationnel de X^* qui ne contient pas le mot vide. Comme dans la démonstration du théorème 1, soient ψ homomorphisme strictement alphabétique de A^* sur X^*, L ensemble rationnel local tel que $\psi(L) = R$, et λ simplification de Dyck de A^* telle que $\psi \circ \lambda = \theta \circ \psi$. Posons $\lambda(L) = K$ et $\theta(R) = S$; on a $\psi(K) = S$.

Appliquons le théorème 2 : il existe J , transversale rationnelle de K pour ψ .

Soit μ la transduction rationnelle fonctionnelle construite à partir de L et λ comme dans la démonstration du lemme 2. Posons $I = \mu(J)$ et $T = \psi(I)$. T est un ensemble rationnel. Comme J est inclus dans K, I est inclus dans L (implication (3)), et T est inclus dans R. De plus, comme $\theta \circ \psi = \psi \circ \lambda$ on a $\theta \circ \psi \circ \mu = \psi \circ \lambda \circ \mu$; et comme $\lambda \circ \mu$ est l'identité sur K (implication (4)) on a $\theta(T) = \psi(J) = S$. Enfin, comme $\psi \circ \mu$ est surjectif de J sur T et ψ injectif de J sur S, θ est injectif de T sur S : T est une transversale rationnelle de R pour θ.

On peut remarquer dès maintenant, mais on ne s'en servira que dans la preuve du corollaire 1, que la bijection θ de T sur S — et donc aussi son inverse que nous noterons ν — et une transduction rationnelle fonctionnelle. En effet $\nu = \psi \circ \mu \circ \tau_J \circ \psi^{-1}$ où τ_J désigne l'intersection avec le rationnel J.

Si R est un ensemble rationnel de $\tilde{X}^*$ qui contient le mot vide on construit comme ci-dessus une transversale rationnelle T' de $R \setminus \{1_{X^*}\}$ et $T = (T' \setminus \nu(1_{X^*})) \cup \{1_{X^*}\}$ est une transversale rationnelle de R. ∎

Théorème 3 : *Le groupe libre possède la propriété de transversale rationnelle.*

Démonstration : Soit $X^{\circledast}$ le groupe libre de base X ; l'équivalence d'application de l'homomorphisme canonique γ de $\tilde{X}^*$ sur $X^{\circledast}$ est identique à celle de ρ la réduction de Dyck sur $\tilde{X}^*$, qui est une simplification de Dyck particulière.

Soit α un homomorphisme d'un monoïde libre quelconque A^* dans $X^{\circledast}$. L'homomorphisme α se factorise en $\alpha = \gamma \circ \beta$ où β est un homomorphisme de A^* dans $\tilde{X}^*$. Soient R un ensemble rationnel de A^* et K son image par β. D'après la proposition 1 il existe L transversale rationnelle de K pour γ. Posons $S = R \cap \beta^{-1}(L)$, ensemble rationnel de A^* ; d'après le théorème 2 il existe T , transversale rationnelle de S pour β . B est une bijection entre T et $\beta(T) = \beta(S) = L$; γ est une bijection entre L et $\gamma(L) = \gamma(K) = \varphi(R)$; T est donc une transversale de R pour φ . c.q.f.d.

De même, *le monoïde involutif possède la propriété de transversale rationnelle.* On va en déduire la même propriété pour le monoïde polycyclique.

Le *monoïde polycyclique* de base X , défini par M. Nivat en [8] pour formaliser le fonctionnement des automates à pile (cf. théorème 4 ci-dessous), est isomorphe au quotient de Rees du monoïde involutif de base X par son idéal propre maximum I ; nous le noterons $X^{\boxtimes}$ (cf. [10] pour plus de détails).

Corollaire 1 : *Le monoïde polycyclique possède la propriété de transversale rationnelle.*

Preuve : Si l'on identifie les éléments du monoïde involutif de base X avec les éléments de $\rho'(\tilde{X}^*)$ l'image de I, idéal propre maximum, est

$$J = \tilde{X}^* \{x\bar{y} \mid x,y \in X ,\ x \neq y\} \tilde{X}^* \cap \rho'(\tilde{X}^*) \text{ ensemble rationnel de } \tilde{X}^*.$$

Soit R un ensemble rationnel de $\tilde{X}^*$; soit S' son image par ρ' et T' la transversale rationnelle de R pour ρ' construite dans la démonstration de la proposition 1. La bijection entre S' et T' ainsi définie est une transduction rationnelle fonctionnelle ν'. Si $S' \cap J$ est vide, posons $T = T'$; sinon soit z un élément de $S' \cap J$ et posons $T = \nu'((S' \setminus J) \cup \{z\})$. Dans les deux cas T est une transversale rationnelle de R pour l'homomorphisme canonique de $\tilde{X}^*$ sur $X^{\circledast}$. La fin de la preuve du corollaire 1 est alors identique à la preuve du théorème 3. ■

3. AUTOMATES A PILE DETERMINISTES

On reprend pour l'essentiel les définitions et les notations de [6].
Soit $A = \langle X,Q,Y,\delta,q_-,y_- \rangle$ un automate à pile classique, mais sans états terminaux, avec X alphabet d'entrée, Y alphabet de pile, Q ensemble d'états, δ fonction de transition, et (q_-,y_-) configuration initiale. La notation

$$(f,q_-,y_-) \overset{*}{\underset{A}{\vdash}} (1_{X^*},q,w) \qquad (5)$$

exprime qu'un calcul conduit l'automate A , à partir de la configuration initiale et du mot f sur la bande d'entrée, à la configuration (q,w) après la lecture complète de f .
Si l'automate A est *déterministe* la notation $(f,q_-,y_-) \overset{d*}{\underset{A}{\vdash}} (1_{X^*},q,w)$ exprime que (5) est vérifiée et qu'il n'existe pas dans A d'ε-transition à partir de la configuration (q,w) .

Nous aurons aussi besoin de la notion de transduction (pour plus de détails cf [2] ou [4]) :

Soit un monoïde M . On appelle *transduction* toute application, multivoque,d'un monoïde libre X^* dans M ; une transduction est dite *rationnelle* si son graphe est une partie rationnelle du monoïde $X^* \times M$. Le théorème de Kleene-Schützenberger énonce qu'une transuction τ de X^* dans M est rationnelle si, et seulement si, il existe un entier N , un homomorphisme μ de X^* dans le monoïde des matrices carrées de dimension N à coefficients dans les parties rationnelles de M , un vecteur ligne λ et un vecteur colonne ν de dimension N à coefficients dans les parties rationnelles de M , tels que pour tout mot f de X^* on ait

$$\tau(f) = \lambda.\mu(f).\nu .$$

En [8] et [9], M. Nivat a établi le résultat suivant, qui précise un théorème de E. Shamir [13] :

Théorème 4 (Shamir-Nivat) : *Soit* $A = \langle X,Q,Y,\delta,q_-,y_- \rangle$ *un automate à pile. Pour chaque* q *dans* Q *l'application* θ_q *définie par :*

$$\forall f \in X^* \quad \theta_q(f) = \{w \mid (f,q_-,y_-) \overset{*}{\underset{A}{\longmapsto}} (1_{X^*},q,w)\}$$

est une transduction rationnelle de X^* *dans* $Y^{\circledast}$, *le monoïde polycyclique engendré par* Y. *Si, de plus, l'automate* A *est déterministe l'application* ω_q *définie par:*

$$\forall f \in X^* \quad \omega_q(f) = \{w \mid (f,q_-,y_-) \overset{d*}{\underset{A}{\longmapsto}} (1_{X^*},q,w)\}$$

est une transduction rationnelle fonctionnelle de X^* *dans* $Y^{\circledast}$.

Cette représentation des automates à pile à l'aide de transductions à valeur dans le monoïde polycyclique est bien entendu essentielle à notre propos. Elle permet, d'une façon plus générale, d'utiliser pour l'étude des automates à pile et des langages algébriques la puissance et la souplesse de la notion de transductions (cf [12] par exemple). Nous nous contenterons d'utiliser ici le résultat suivant, généralisation d'un résultat de [3].

Lemme 3 : *Soit* M *un monoïde possédant la propriété de transversale rationnelle. Toute transduction rationnelle fonctionnelle de* X^* *dans* M *possède la propriété de transversale rationnelle.*

La simple succession des corollaire 1, lemme 3, et théorème 4 permet alors d'énoncer :

Théorème 5 : *Soit* A *un automate à pile déterministe sur l'alphabet d'entrée* X *. L'application qui fait correspondre à un mot* f *de* X^* *la configuration de l'automate* A *après la lecture de* f *et toutes les* ε*-transitions possibles, possède la propriété de transversale rationnelle.*

En effet, les propositions citées établissent que chaque ω_q (avec les notations du théorème 4) possède la propriété de transversale rationnelle.

Soit ω l'application visée par le théorème 5 ; on a :

$$\omega = \sum_{q \in Q} (q,\omega_q)$$

On remarque alors que les domaines des ω_q sont disjoints deux à deux et donc que ω est la somme d'applications dont les domaines et les images sont respectivement disjoints deux à deux et qui chacune possède la propriété de transversale rationnelle ; ω possède la propriété de transversale rationnelle.

c.q.f.d.

Corollaire 2 : *Soit* L *un langage algébrique déterministe de* X^*. *Il existe une équivalence régulière droite* ω *de* X^* *qui sature* L *et telle qu'il existe une transversale rationnelle de* L *pour* ω .

Preuve : Soit $A = \langle X,Q,Y,\delta,q_-,y_-, F \rangle$ un automate à pile déterministe, "loop-free" (cf [6]), avec un ensemble F d'états finaux, qui reconnaît le langage L par état final. Avec les notations des théorèmes 4 et 5 on peut écrire

$\omega = \omega_F + \omega_N$ avec

$$\omega_F = \sum_{q \in F} (q,\omega_q) \quad \text{et} \quad \omega_N = \sum_{q \notin F} (q,\omega_q)$$

Le domaine de ω est X^* tout entier puisque A est "loop-free" ; l'équivalence d'application de ω est régulière à droite. Les domaines et les images de ω_F et ω_N sont disjoints ; le domaine de ω_F est L, donc ω sature L. Comme ω, ω_F possède la propriété de transversale rationnelle. Soit T une transversale rationnelle de X^* pour ω_F ; T est une transversale du domaine de ω_F pour ω_F ; ω coïncide avec ω_F sur son domaine ; donc T est transversale de L pour ω. ∎

Le corollaire 2 énonce une propriété que doit nécessairement satisfaire un langage pour être algébrique déterministe. En ce sens il ressemble à un lemme d'itération. En fait il permet, dans certaines preuves, de se ramener à l'application d'un lemme d'itération pour les langages rationnels, au lieu d'avoir à utiliser un lemme d'itération pour les langages algébriques déterministes.

A titre d'exemple nous allons montrer que le langage

$$L = \{a^n b^n \mid n \in N\} \cup \{a^n b^{2n} \mid n \in N\}$$

n'est pas déterministe. On conviendra que ce résultat n'est pas, à proprement parler, nouveau ; on conviendra aussi que les preuves qu'on en a jusqu'ici utilisent soit un lemme d'itération pour les langages algébriques déterministes [11], soit une preuve sur les automates qui revient à établir ce lemme d'itération dans un cas particulier [6].

Soit ρ_L l'équivalence régulière à droite de $\{a,b\}^*$ la plus grossière qui sature L ; il est aisé de vérifier que chaque mot $a^n b^m$, avec $m \leq n$, est seul dans sa classe modulo ρ_L.

Supposons L déterministe. Soient ω l'équivalence régulière à droite qui sature L et T la transversale rationnelle de L pour ω données par le corollaire 2. Puisque ω est plus fine que ρ_L, par définition de ρ_L, chaque mot $a^n b^m$, avec $m \leq n$, est seul dans sa classe modulo ω et T contient l'ensemble $\{a^n b^n \mid n \in N\}$.

Puisque T est rationnel, et grâce au lemme de l'étoile, il contient un mot $a^{n+k} b^n$ qui, par ailleurs, ne peut appartenir à une transversale de L pour ω puisqu'il n'appartient pas à L ; d'où la contradiction.

BIBLIOGRAPHIE

[1] M. Benois - Parties rationnelles du groupe libre, *C.R. Acad. Sci. Paris* A. 269, 1969, 1188-1190.

[2] J. Berstel - *Transductions and context free languages*, Teubner, 1978.

[3] C. Choffrut - *Contribution à l'étude de quelques familles remarquables de fonctions rationnelles*, Thèse Sci. Math., Univ. Paris VII, Paris, 1978.

[4] S. Eilenberg - *Automata, Languages, and Machines*, Vol. A, Academic Press, 1974.

[5] M. Fliess - Deux applications de la représentation matricielle d'une série rationnelle non commutative, *J. of Algebra* 19, 1971, 344-353.

[6] S. Ginsburg and S. Greibach-Deterministic context free languages, *Inform. and Control* 9, 1966, 620-648.

[7] W. Magnus, D. Karass, and S. Solitar - *Combinatorial Group Theory*, J. Wiley, 1966.

[8] M. Nivat - Transductions des langages de Chomsky, *Ann. Inst. Fourier* 18, 1968, 339-445.

[9] M. Nivat - Sur les automates à mémoire pile, in Proceedings of International Computing Symposium 70 (W. Itzfeld edt.), 1973, 655-663.

[10] M. Nivat et J-F. Perrot - Une généralisation du monoïde bicyclique, *C.R. Acad. Sci. Paris* A 270, 1970, 221-228.

[11] W. Ogden - Intercalation theorems for pushdown store and stack languages, Ph. D. Thesis, Standford, 1968.

[12] J. Sakarovitch - On the recognition of languages by pushdown automata, to appear.

[13] E. Shamir - A representation theorem for algebraic and context-free power series in non commuting variables, *Inform. and Control* 11, 1967, 239-254.

ON THE ADDITIVE COMPLEXITY OF POLYNOMIALS AND SOME NEW LOWER BOUNDS

C.P. Schnorr

Abstract For each $w \in N$ we establish polynomials $R_{w,j}$ $j \in N$ with $(w+1)(w+2)/2$ variables and $\deg R_{w,j} \leq 2wj+1$ such that the coefficient vectors $(a_j | j \in N)$ of all polynomials $\Sigma_j a_j (x-\eta)^j$ which can be computed with $\leq w$ additions/subtractions and arbitrarily many mult./div., are contained in the image of $(R_{w+1,j} | j \in N)$. As a consequence we prove $C^t_{0,1}(n) \geq n/(81d(n)+4)-1$ (this bound is sharp up to a constant factor), $C^{ns}_{0,1}(n) \geq \frac{1}{4}\sqrt{n/(1d(2n))} - 2$ and $C^+_{0,1}(n) \geq \sqrt{n}/(41d\ n)$. Hereby $C^t_{0,1}(n)$, $C^{ns}_{0,1}(n)$ and $C^+_{0,1}(n)$ are the maximal number of arithmetical operations, non-scalar operations and add./sub. respectively that are necessary to evaluate n degree polynomials with 0-1 coefficients. We specify n-degree polynomials with algebraic coefficients that require n additions/subtractions no matter how many mult./div. are used. As a first non-trivial lower bound on a single specific polynomial with integer coefficients we prove $L_{ns}(\Sigma^k_{i=1} x^n_i y^i) \geq k\ 1d\ n/(1d\ k+1d\ 1d\ n)$.

1. Introduction and Notation

Sections 1-3 are an extended abstract of results which have been independently discovered by the author [12] and Van de Wiele [14] and which will be published as a common paper in TCS [17]. In section 4 we establish a new lower bound on the number of nonscalar operations that are necessary to evaluate polynomials like $\Sigma^k_{i=1} x^n_i y^i$. These lower bounds are based on Bezout's theorem for affine algebraic varieties.

It is well known that the evaluation of a polynomial $\Sigma^n_{j=0} a_j x^j$ with algebraically independent coefficients a_j requires n/2 mult./div. and n add./sub. even if arbitrary constants can be used without cost. However, the polynomials that are of interest do not have algebraically independent coefficients. In order to prove lower bounds on the arithmetical complexity of more specific polynomials one needs more information on the structure of those polynomials that are easy to compute. A major step into such an analysis has been done by Strassen [13].

Strassen gave specific representations for those polynomials that can be computed with few arithmetical operations. This analysis has been carried on by Borodin and Cook [2], Hyafil and Van de Wiele [5] and Schnorr [11].

In particular Schnorr [11] specified polynomials $Q_{w,j}$ in $(w+1)^2$ variables and $\deg Q_{w,j} \leq 2wj+1$ such that the coefficient vectors $(a_j | j \in N)$ of all polynomials $\Sigma_j a_j (x-\eta)^j$ which can be computed with $\leq w$ nonscalar operations (and arbitrarily many scalar operations) are contained in the image of $(Q_{w+1,j} | j \in N)$. In this paper we introduce polynomials $R_{w,j}$ in $(w+1)(w+2)/2$ variables and $\deg R_{w,j} \leq 2wj+1$ such that the coefficient vectors $(a_j | j \in N)$ of all polynomials $\Sigma_j a_j (x-\eta)^j$ which can be computed with $\leq w$ add./sub. (and arbitrarily many mult./div.) are contained in the image of $(R_{w+1,j} | j \in N)$. This representation which is established in theorem 1, section 2 uses many ideas contained in the above mentioned previous papers [2], [5], [11], [13].

Theorem 2 gives a representation for all those polynomials that can be computed with $\leq w$ arithmetical operations in total. In theorem 3 we establish the existence of a polynomial $H \in Q[y_0, \ldots, y_n]$, $H \neq 0$ with small degree such that $H(a_0, \ldots, a_n) = 0$ for all $a_0, \ldots, a_n$ where $\Sigma_{j=0}^{n} a_j x^j$ can be computed with given bounds for the number of add./sub. and for the total number of operations. This yields

$$C^t_{0,1}(n) \geq n/(8 \mathrm{ld}(n)+4)-1$$

where $C^t_{0,1}(n)$ is the maximal number of arithmetical operations necessary to evaluate n-degree polynomials with 0-1 coefficients. This bound is sharp up to a constant factor, since Savage [10] proved $C^t_{0,1}(n) \leq O(n/\mathrm{ld}\ n)$. This also implies

$$C^{ns}_{0,1}(n) \geq \frac{1}{4} \sqrt{n/(\mathrm{ld}(n)+1)} -2$$

where $C^{ns}_{0,1}(n)$ is the maximal number of nonscalar operations necessary to evaluate n-degree polynomials with 0-1 coefficients. This improves previous bounds $C^{ns}_{0,1}(n) \geq \Omega(n^{1/4}/\mathrm{ld}\ n)$ by Lipton [6], $C^{ns}_{0,1}(n) \geq \Omega(n^{1/3}/\mathrm{ld}(n))$ by Hyafil and Van de Wiele [5] and $C^{ns}_{0,1}(n) \geq \sqrt{n}/(4 \mathrm{ld}\ n)$ by Schnorr [11]. It also follows that

$$C^{+}_{0,1}(n) \geq \sqrt{n/(4 \mathrm{ld}\ n)}$$

where $C^{+}_{0,1}(n)$ is the maximal number of add./sub. necessary to evaluate n-degree polynomials with 0-1 coefficients. This improves a previous bound $C^{+}_{0,1}(n) \geq \Omega(n^{1/3}/ld(n))$ in [5]. In corollary 6 we show how to improve a result of Lipton, Stockmeyer [7] on the existence of hard factors of easy polynomials.

In section 3 we specify n-degree polynomials with algebraic coefficients that require n add./sub. no matter how many mult./div. are used. Whereas the methods of section 3 are elementary we should note that Joos Heintz (Universität Frankfurt) has recently developed a more powerful and rather elegant method for proving lower bounds on polynomials with algebraic coefficients. However, the method of Heintz requires some algebraic geometry.

In section 4 we combine Strassen's degree bound [16] with the results of Schnorr [11]. This yields a nontrivial lower bound on the number of nonscalar operations which are necessary to evaluate single specific multivariate polynomials p with integer coefficients. This lower bound is nonlinear both in the number of variables and in ld deg p. In particular we prove $L_{ns}(\Sigma^{k}_{i=1} x_i y^i) \geq k\ ldn/(ld\,k + ld\ ld\ n)$. This bound is rather tight since $L_{ns}(\Sigma^{k}_{i=1} x_i^n y^i) = O(k\ ld\ n)$.

In the following let $\mathbb{K}$ be any field that contains the field Q of rational numbers. Let x be a variable over $\mathbb{K}$. A <u>computation</u> is a sequence of computation steps S_i $i = 1,..,l$ such that either (1) $S_i \in \mathbb{K} \cup \{x\}$ or (2) $S_i = S_j o S_k$ with $j,k<i$ and $o \in \{+,-,/,*\}$ and $S_k \neq 0$ if o is /. Thus the S_i are rational functions, $S_i \in \mathbb{K}(x)$ and they are called the <u>results</u> of the computation. A step $S_i = S_j o S_k$ is called <u>nonscalar</u> provided o is * and both S_j, S_k are not in $\mathbb{K}$ or o is / and $S_k \notin \mathbb{K}$. For $p \in \mathbb{K}(x)$ let (1) $L_+(p)$, (2) $L_{ns}(p)$, (3) $L_t(p)$ be the minimal number of (1) add./sub., (2) nonscalar steps, (3) arithmetical operations in total, in any computation for p. We identify $p \in \mathbb{K}(x)$ with its power series $p = \Sigma^{\infty}_{i=0} a_i(\eta)(x-\eta)^i$ provided η is not a pole of p. N denotes the set of natural numbers and Z the set of integers. Throughout the paper subscript o means $0 \in N$.

2. The arithmetical complexity of 0-1 polynomials

Most polynomials that are of practical interest have small integer coefficients, whereas polynomials with algebraic independent coefficients do not occur at all. In this section we determine the maximal arithmetical complexity of n-degree polynomials with 0-1 coefficients: $C^{t}_{0,1}(n) := \max\{L_t(\Sigma^{n}_{i=0} b_i x^i) \mid b_i \in \{0,1\}\}$. We prove

$C^t_{1,o}(n) \geq n/(8ld(n)+4)-1$, whereas $C^t_{1,o}(n) \leq O(n/ld(n))$ is known from Savage [10].

Theorem 1 There exist polynomials $R_{r,j} \in Q[z_1,..,z_{m(r)}]$ $r,j \in N$, $m(r) := (r+1)(r+2)/2$ with $\deg R_{r,j} \leq 2rj+1$ such that for every $p \in K(x)$ with $L_+(p) \leq w$ and for all but finitely many $\eta \in K$ there exists $\underline{\gamma} \in K^{m(w+1)}$ such that $p \equiv \Sigma_{j\geq 0} R_{w+1,j}(\underline{\gamma})(x-\eta)^j$.

Proof: Following Belaga [1] every computation β for p with $\leq w$ add./sub. can be transformed into a scheme (1) by collecting mult./div. steps and by normalizing add./sub. steps $aR(x)+bS(x)$ as $a/b+S(x)/R(x)$:

$$(1)\qquad \begin{aligned} P_o &= x \\ P_r &= c_r + \prod_{i=0}^{r-1} P_i^{u_{i,r}} \qquad \text{for } r = 1,..,w \\ p &= c_{w+1} \prod_{i=0}^{w} P_i^{u_{i,w+1}} \\ &\text{with } u_{i,r} \in Z, c_r \in K \end{aligned}$$

Let $\eta \in K$ be such that $P_r(\eta) \neq 0$ for $r = 0,1,..,w$ then we can use the polynomials $\bar{P}_r = P_r/P_r(\eta)$ instead of the P_r by changing the c_r appropriately. This yields a scheme for p as

$$(2)\qquad \begin{aligned} \bar{P}_o &= x/\eta = 1+\eta^{-1}(x-\eta) \\ \bar{P}_r &= 1-c_r+c_r \prod_{i=0}^{r-1} P_i^{u_{i,r}} \qquad \text{for } r = 1,..,w \\ p &= c_{w+1} \prod_{i=0}^{w} P_i^{u_{i,w+1}} \qquad \text{with } c_{w+1} = p(\eta) \end{aligned}$$

We abbreviate $y = \eta^{-1}(x-\eta)$. By the Taylor series $\Sigma_{\mu=0}^{\infty} \binom{s}{\mu} y^\mu = (1+y)^s$ for $s \in Z$ we have

$$\begin{aligned} \bar{P}_1 &= 1-c_1+c_1(1+y)^{u_{o,1}} \\ &= 1-c_1+c_1[1+\Sigma_{\mu=1}^{\infty} \binom{u_{o,1}}{\mu} y^\mu] \end{aligned}$$

If $c_1, u_{o,1}$ are considered as variables then the last line can be written as

$$1+\Sigma_{\mu=1}^{\infty} R^*_{1,\mu} y^\mu \text{ with } R^*_{1,\mu} = c_1 \binom{u_{o,1}}{\mu} \in Q[c_1,u_{o,1}]$$

Then by induction on r we define the polynomials

$$R^*_{r,j} \in Q[c_\nu, u_{i,\nu} | 0 \leq i \leq \nu \leq r] \quad \text{by}$$

$$(3)\quad \begin{aligned} 1+\Sigma_{j\geq 1}R^*_{r,j}y^j &= 1-c_r+c_r\prod_{i=o}^{r-1}(1+\Sigma_{j\geq 1}R^*_{i,j}y^j)^{u_{i,r}} \\ &= 1-c_r+c_r\prod_{i=o}^{r-1}[1+\Sigma_{\mu=1}^{\infty}\binom{u_{i,r}}{\mu}(\Sigma_{j\geq 1}R^*_{i,j}y^j)^{\mu}) \end{aligned}$$

In addition we set $R^*_{r,o} = c_r$ then the construction implies $p\equiv\Sigma_{j\geq o}R^*_{w+1,j}(\underline{\gamma}^*)\mu^{-j}(x-\mu)^j$ where $\underline{\gamma}^*$consists of the values $c_r, u_{i,r}$ which have been used in (2). The polynomials $R_{r,j}$ in theorem 1 are obtained as $R_{r,j} = R^*_{r,j}z^j$ and $\underline{\gamma} = (\underline{\gamma}^*, \eta^{-1})$. Note that we obtain a definition by induction of the $R_{r,j}$ by substituting $\eta^{-1}z$ for y in (3).

The number of variables of the polynomials $R_{r,j}$ $j = 0,1,..$ is counted as follows. There are $r(r+1)/2$ variables $u_{i,\nu}$ for $0\leq i\leq\nu\leq r$ and $r+1$ variables for $c_1,..,c_r,\eta^{-1}$. This yields a total of $(r+1)(r+2)/2 = m(r)$ variables that are called $z_1,..,z_{m(r)}$ in theorem 1. In particular $R_{w+1,j}$ $j = 0,1,...$ depend on $(w+2)(w+3)/2 = m(w+1)$ variables.

Finally we prove by induction on r that $\deg R_{r,j}\leq 2rj+1$ which is clear for $r = 1$ since

$$R_{r,j} = R^*_{r,j}z^j = c_1\binom{u_{o,1}}{j}z^j \in \mathbb{Q}[c_1,u_{o,1},z].$$

For any power series P let $\deg_k P$ be the degree of the polynomial which is the coefficient of y^k. The induction hypothesis $\deg R_{i,j}\leq 2ij+1$ for $i<r$ implies

$$\begin{aligned} \deg_k(\Sigma_{j\geq 1}R_{i,j}y^j)^{\mu} &\leq \max\{\mu+\Sigma_{\nu=1}^{\mu}2ij_{\nu} \mid \Sigma_{\nu=1}^{\mu}j_{\nu}=k, j_{\nu}\geq 1\} \\ &\leq \mu+2ik \text{ with } \mu\leq k. \end{aligned}$$

It follows

$$\begin{aligned} \deg_k\binom{u_{i,r}}{\mu}(\Sigma_{j\geq 1}R_{i,j}y^j)^{\mu} &\leq 2\mu+2ik \text{ with } \mu\leq k \\ &\leq 2rk \text{ since } i<r \end{aligned}$$

Hence the definition (3) of the $R_{r,j}$ implies

$$\begin{aligned} \deg R_{r,j} &\leq 1+\max\{\Sigma_{\nu} 2rk_{\nu} \mid \Sigma_{\nu} k_{\nu} = j\} \\ &\leq 1+2rj. \end{aligned}$$

Here +1 counts the factor c_r. ∎∎

In the following we also use the above polynomials $R^*_{r,j}$ with $R_{r,j}=R^*_{r,j}z^j$ and we always denote $m(r) := (r+1)(r+2)/2$ and $m^*(r) := m(r)-1$. In particular we have proved that for all $p\in\mathbb{K}(x)$ with $L_+(p)\leq w$ and for all but finitely many $\eta\in\mathbb{K}$ there exists $\underline{\gamma}^*\in\mathbb{K}^{m^*(w+1)}$ such that

$$p\equiv\Sigma_{j\geq 0}R^*_{w+1,j}(\underline{\gamma}^*)\eta^{-j}(x-\eta)^j.$$

In fact the above parameter vector $\underline{\gamma}^* = (c_r, u_{i,r}|0\leq i<r\leq w+1)$ does not range over the entire set $\mathbb{K}^{m^*(w+1)}$ but over countably many (w+1)-dimensional subsets which will be called (w+1)-fibres. With every pair $(\underline{i},\underline{\gamma}) = ((i_1,..,i_{m-1}),(\gamma_1,...,{}_{m-1}))\in N^{m-1}\times Q^{m-1}$ such that $1\leq i_1<...<i_{m-1}\leq m$ we associate an <u>l-fibre</u> $F(\underline{i},\underline{\gamma})\subset K^m$ as

$$F(\underline{i},\underline{\gamma}) := \{(y_1,..,y_m)\in\mathbb{K}^m|y_{i_\nu} = \gamma_\nu \text{ for } \nu = 1,..,m-1\}.$$

Thus an l-fibre $F\subset\mathbb{K}^m$ is a fibre with respect to a projection $pr: \mathbb{K}^m \to \mathbb{K}^{m-1}$ and a point $\underline{\gamma}\in Q^{m-1}$: $F = pr^{-1}(\underline{\gamma})$, $\dim(F) = 1$. Clearly the parameter vector γ^* in the representation

$$p\equiv\Sigma_j R^*_{w+1,j}(\underline{\gamma}^*)\eta^{-j}(x-\eta)^j$$

of all p with $L_+(p)\leq w$ ranges over countably many (w+1)-fibres of $\mathbb{K}^{m^*(w+1)}$. Moreover, we show that $\underline{\gamma}^*$ in this representation ranges over at most $16^w w!$ (a+1)-fibres F_ν provided that there is a computation β for p with $\leq$a add./sub. and $\leq$w operations in total. The upper bound on the number of (a+1)-fibres is obtained by counting all equivalence classes of computations β with $\leq$a add./sub. and $\leq$w operations in total. Here two computations are called equivalent iff they merely use different constants in $\mathbb{K}$. In fact each such equivalence class corresponds to some of these fibres F_ν.

<u>Theorem 2</u> Let $a,w\in N$ and $m = m^*(w+1)$, then there exist (a+1)-fibres $F_\nu\subset K^m$ $\nu=1,..,16^w w!$ such that for every $p\in\mathbb{K}(x)$ which is computable with $\bar{a}$ add./sub. and $\bar{n}$ nonscalar steps $a\leq\bar{a}$, $\bar{a}+\bar{n}\leq w$ the following holds: for all but finitely many $\eta\in Q$ there exists $\underline{\gamma}^*\in\bigcup_\nu F_\nu$ such that $p\equiv\Sigma_{j\geq 0}R^*_{w+1,j}(\underline{\gamma}^*)\eta^{-j}(x-\eta)^j$.

Let $P\in Q[z_1,..,z_m]$ and $F(\underline{i},\underline{\gamma})\subset K^m$ be some l-fibre with $\underline{i} = (i_1,..,i_{m-1})$, $\underline{\gamma} = (\gamma_1,..,\gamma_{m-1})$. Then by definition $P|_{F(\underline{i},\underline{\gamma})}$ is the polynomial obtained from P by fixing z_{i_ν} to $\gamma_\nu\in Q$ for $\nu = 1,..,m-1$. $P|_{F(\underline{i},\underline{\gamma})}$ is in $Q[z_1,..,z_m]$ and depends on at most l variables.

Observe that

$$\deg_{c_i}(R^*_{r,j}) \le \begin{cases} j & \text{for } i<r \\ 1 & \text{for } i=r \\ 0 & \text{for } i>r \end{cases}$$

can easily be seen by straightforward induction on r over the recursive definition (3) of the $R^*_{r,j}$. Now let F_ν be some (a+1)-fibre as in theorem 2. $\deg R^*_{w+1,j}|F_\nu$ is the degree of $R^*_{w+1,j}$ with respect to a+1 of the variables $c_1,..,c_{w+1}$. This implies

$$(4) \qquad \deg R^*_{w+1,j}|F_\nu \le \begin{cases} j(a+1) & \text{for } j\ge 1 \\ 1 & \text{for } j=0 \end{cases}$$

Setting $R_j := R^*_{w+1,j}|F_\nu$ where $F_\nu \subset K^{m^*(a+1)}$ is the (a+1)-fibre corresponding to a computation ß for p with ≤a add./sub. and ≤w operations in total then we have proved the following corollary which is the base of some interesting results due to J. Heintz [4].

<u>Corollary 1</u> Let $p \in \mathbb{K}(x)$ with $L_+(p) \le a$ then there exist $R_j \in \mathbb{Q}[z_1,..,z_{a+1}]$ with $\deg R_j \le j(a+1)$ such that for all but finitely many $\eta \in \mathbb{K}$ there exists $\underline{\gamma} \in \mathbb{K}^{a+1}$ such that $p \equiv \Sigma_{j\ge 0} R_j(\underline{\gamma})\eta^{-j}(x-\eta)^j$.

One proves by standard methods of linear algebra:

<u>Lemma 1</u> Let $P_1,..,P_q \in \mathbb{Q}[z_1,..,z_m]$ and $F_\nu \subset K^m$ $\nu=1,..,k$ be 1-fibres with $\deg P_i|F_\nu \le c$. Then $\exists\, H \in \mathbb{Q}[y_1,..,y_q]$, $H \not\equiv 0$ such that $H(P_1,..,P_q)|\cup_\nu F_\nu \equiv 0$ and $\deg H \le g$, provided $\binom{g+q}{q} > \binom{gc+1}{1}\cdot k$.

By applying Lemma 1 to theorem 2 one obtains after some careful calculations:

<u>Theorem 3</u> Let $0<\varepsilon\le 1, n\ge 1, b\ge 1/n$. Then there exists $H \in \mathbb{Q}[y_0,..,y_n]$, $H\not\equiv 0$, $\deg H \le \lceil n^{(2-\varepsilon)/\varepsilon}(8bn)^{b/\varepsilon}\rceil$ such that $H(a_0,..,a_n) = 0$ for all $p \equiv \Sigma_{i\ge 0} a_i x^i$ which can be computed with $\le(1-\varepsilon)n-1$ add./sub. and bn-1 steps in total.

By some standard calculations theorem 3 yields as an immediate consequence the following corollaries:

<u>Corollary 2</u>

For all ε and n with $1/n \le 1-\varepsilon < 1$ $\exists\, a_0,..,a_n \in \mathbb{N}$, $0 \le a_i \le \lceil n^{1/\varepsilon}[8(1-\varepsilon)n^2]^{(1-\varepsilon)/\varepsilon}\rceil$ such that $L_t(\Sigma_{j\ge 0} a_j x^j) \ge (1-\varepsilon)n$.

Corollary 3 $C^{t}_{0,1}(n) \geq n/(8ld(n)+4)-1$ with $C^{t}_{0,1}(n) := \max\{L_t(\sum_{i=0}^{n} b_i x^i) \mid b_i = 0,1\}$.

This lower bound on $C^{t}_{0,1}(n)$ is sharp up to a constant factor, since there is an upper bound $C^{t}_{0,1}(n) \leq O(n/ld(n))$ which has been proved by Savage [10].

We consider $C^{ns}_{0,1}(n) := \max\{L_{ns}(\Sigma^{n}_{i=o} b_i x^i) \mid b_i = 0,1\}$ the maximal number of nonscalar operations that is necessary for evaluating n-th degree polynomials with 0-1 coefficients. In [11] we proved $C^{ns}_{0,1}(n) \geq \sqrt{n}/(4\ \mathrm{ld}\ n)$. This lower bound can still be improved by applying Corollary 3. Any computation for p with $\leq w$ nonscalar steps can be transformed by collecting scalar steps into the following recursion scheme with $u_{r,i}, v_{r,i} \in \mathbb{K}$, $c_r \in \{0,1\}$:

$$P_{-1} \equiv 1, \quad P_0 = x$$

for r = 1,..,w:

$$P_r = \Sigma^{r}_{i=-1} u_{r,i} P_i [c_r S_r + (1-c_r)/S_r]$$

$$\text{with } S_r = \Sigma^{r-1}_{i=-1} v_{r,i} P_i$$

$$p = \Sigma^{w}_{i=-1} u_{w+1,i} P_i \quad \text{with } u_{w+1,i} \in \{0,1\} \text{ for } i \geq 1$$

Now the total number of operations to compute p can be bounded as follows: we need $\Sigma^{w}_{r=1} r = w(w+1)/2$ scalar mult. and $\Sigma^{w}_{r=1} r = w(w+1)/2$ add./ to compute $\Sigma^{r-1}_{i=-1} u_{r,i} P_i$ for r = 1,..,w. The same number of operations is required to compute $\Sigma^{r-1}_{i=-1} v_{r,i} P_i$ for r = 1,2,..,w. In addition we have w nonscalar mult./div. and the computation of $\Sigma^{w}_{i=-1} u_{w+1,i} P_i$ requires w+2 scalar steps. This yields $2w(w+1)+2w+2 = 2(w+1)^2$ operations in total. Hence

$$(5) \qquad L_t(p) \leq 2(L_{ns}(p)+1)^2 \qquad \text{for all } p \in \mathbb{K}(x)$$

It follows from Corollary 3

$$C^{ns}_{0,1}(n) \geq \sqrt{C^{t}_{0,1}(n)/2} - 1 \geq \sqrt{n/(16\ \mathrm{ld}(n)+8)} - 2$$

Thus we have proved

Corollary 4 $C^{ns}_{0,1} \geq \frac{1}{4}\sqrt{n/(\mathrm{ld}(2n))} - 2$

We observe that theorem 1 can be used to prove lower bounds on

$$C^{+}_{0,1}(n) := \max\{L_{+}(\Sigma^{n}_{i=o} b_i x^i) \mid b_i = 0,1\}.$$

Corollary 5 $\quad \forall\, n \ge n_o : C^{+}_{0,1}(n) \ge \sqrt{n}/(4 \text{ ld } n)$

The proof of this corollary is almost the same as the proof of the following

Theorem (Schnorr [11]) $\forall\, n \ge n_o : C^{ns}_{0,1}(n) \ge \sqrt{n}/(4 \text{ ld } n)$.

The reason is that theorem 1 of this paper is essentially the same as theorem 1 in [11] however with L_+ substituted for L_{ns}. The number $(r+1)(r+2)/2$ of variables of the polynomials $R_{r,j}$ $j = 0,1,..,$ is even smaller than that of the corresponding polynomials $Q_{r,j}$ $j = 0,1,..$ in [11] which is $r^2 + 2r$. The degree bounds for $Q_{r,j}$ and $R_{r,j}$ are the same. Therefore the proof for L_{ns} in [11] holds a fortiori for L_+.

We finally show that theorem 3 can be used to generalize a result of Lipton, Stockmeyer [7] on the existence of hard factors of easy polynomials. Using their method and theorem 3 we improve theorem 3.1 and 3.4 in [7].

Corollary 6 $\forall\, p \in \mathbb{K}[x]$ with at least m distinct roots $\exists f \in \mathbb{K}[x]$ with $f|p$ and (1) $L_t(f) \ge m/(9 \text{ ld } m))$, (2) $L_{ns}(f) \ge \sqrt{m/(18 \text{ ld}(m))} - 1$.

3. Polynomials that require n additions / subtractions

In this section we specify polynomials with algebraic coefficients that require n additions/subtractions, no matter how many multiplications/divisions are used. These results are obtained by applying Theorem 1 and Lemma 1. The method of proof uses the same technique as has been applied in Schnorr [11] where we counted the number of necessary mult./div. no matter how many add./sub. are used.

Theorem 4

Suppose $L_+(p) < b$, $p = \Sigma^{\infty}_{i=0} a_i x^i \in \mathbb{K}(x)$ and let $0 \le \delta_1 < \delta_2, .., \delta_q \le n$. Then there exists $H \in \mathbb{Q}[y_1,..,y_q]$, $H \not\equiv 0$ such that $H(a_{\delta_1},..,a_{\delta_q}) = 0$ and $\deg H \le g$ provided $\binom{g+q}{q} > \binom{b(gn+1)}{b}$.

Let $[\mathbb{K}_1 : \mathbb{K}_2]$ be the degree of $\mathbb{K}_1$ over $\mathbb{K}_2$. Then Theorem 5 can be proved by using Lemma 2 and Theorem 4.

Lemma 2 (Strassen [13]

Let $\tau_1,..,\tau_q \in \mathbb{K}$ such that $\forall k : [\mathbb{Q}(\tau_1,..,\tau_k) : \mathbb{Q}(\tau_1,..,\tau_{k-1})] \ge g$. Then there is no $H \in Q[y_1,..,y_q]$, $H \neq 0$ such that deg $H<g$ and $H(\tau_1,..,\tau_q) = 0$.

Theorem 5

Let $\tau_1,..,\tau_n \in \mathbb{K}$ and $0 \leq \delta_1 < ... < \delta_q \leq n$ such that $\forall k: [Q(\tau_{\delta_1},..,\tau_{\delta_k}):Q(\tau_{\delta_1},..,\tau_{\delta_{k-1}})] \geq (qn)^q$. Then $L_+(\Sigma_{j=0}^{n} \tau_j x^j) \geq q-1$.

As typical corollaries one obtains

Corollary 7

$L_+(\Sigma_{k=0}^{n} \exp(2\pi i/2^{f(k)})x^k) \geq n$ provided that $\forall k$: $f(k) \in N$, $f(k) \geq f(k-1)+2(n+1)\,ld(n+1)$, $f(0) \geq 1$.

Corollary 8 $L_+(\Sigma_{j=0}^{n} \exp(2\pi i/2^j)x^j) \geq \lfloor n/(6\ ld\ n) \rfloor$

The corollaries 7 and 8 correspond to corollary 3 in Schnorr [11] where the following has been proved:

(1) $L_{*/}(\Sigma_{j=0}^{n} \exp(2\pi i/2^{f(k)})x^k) \geq n/2$

provided $\forall k: f(k) \geq f(k-1)+2n\,ld(2n)$, $f(k) \in N$, $f(0) \geq 1$

(2) $L_{*/}(\Sigma_{k=0}^{n} \exp(2\pi i/2^k)x^k) \geq \lfloor n/(12\ ld\ n) \rfloor$

Thus these polynomials require many add./sub. no matter how many mult./div. are used. They also require many mult./div. no matter how many add./sub. are used.

4. A new application of Bezout's theorem

We consider multivariate polynomials p with variables $x_1,..,x_k,y$ and y as a main variable, i.e. $p \in \mathbb{K}[x_1,..,x_m,y]$ is represented as $p = \Sigma_{i=1}^{k} p_i(x_1,..,x_m)y^i$ with $p_i \in \mathbb{K}[x_1,..,x_m]$.

Let $W(\underline{p}) := \overline{\text{graph}(p_1,..,p_k)}$ be the affine variety over $\mathbb{K}$ which is the closure of the graph of the mapping $\underline{p} = (p_1,..,p_k): \mathbb{K}^m \to \mathbb{K}^k$. $\preccurlyeq$ denotes $\leq$ up to a constant factor.

Theorem 6 $L_{ns}(\Sigma_{i=1}^{k} p_i(x_1,..,x_m)y^i)+k \succcurlyeq ld\ deg\ W(\underline{p})/ld\ ld\ deg\ W(\underline{p})$

As a corollary this yields $L_{ns}(\Sigma_{i=1}^{\lceil ld\,n \rceil} x_i^n y^i) \succcurlyeq (ld\ n)^2/ld\ ld\ n$.

Observe that $x_i^n = 1$ for $i = 1,..,k$ has n^k solutions which proves that deg $W(\underline{p}) \geq n^k$ for $\underline{p} = (p_1,..,p_k)$ with $p_i = x_i^n$.

Sketch of the proof: Let β be a computation for p with $v := L_{ns}(p)$

nonscalar operations. Let β_1 be the maximal initial part of β which does not use the variable y. β_1 computes certain rational functions $\gamma_1,..,\gamma_r \in \mathbb{K}(x_1,..,x_m)$. In particular the γ_i $i = 1,..,r$ contain all variables $x_1,..,x_m$ and all constants in $\mathbb{K}$ which are used in β. Let β_2 be the remaining part of β. We consider β_2 as a computation with inputs $\gamma_1,..,\gamma_r,y$. Suppose that there are v_i nonscalar operations in β_i, $v_1+v_2 = v$. We associate with β_1,β_2 the mappings $\varphi_1: \mathbb{K}^m \to \mathbb{K}^r$, $\varphi_2: \mathbb{K}^r \to \mathbb{K}^k$ which are given by

$$\varphi_1:(x_1,..,x_m) \mapsto (\gamma_1,...,\gamma_r) \qquad \varphi_2:(\gamma_1,...,\gamma_r) \mapsto (p_1,..,p_k)$$

We consider the affine algebraic varieties $\overline{\text{graph}(\varphi_1)}$ and $\overline{\text{graph}(\varphi_2)}$ which are the closure of $\text{graph}(\varphi_1)$ and $\text{graph}(\varphi_2)$. Using Bezout's theorem for affine varieties it is not difficult to prove

(6) $$\deg \overline{\text{graph}(\varphi_1)} \le 2^{v_1}.$$

This is the core of Strassen's degree bound in [16]. On the other hand by applying Bezout's theorem and the technique in the proof of theorem 2.5 in Schnorr [11] we can prove

(7) $$\deg \overline{\text{graph}(\varphi_2)} \le (2v_2k)^k \, 2^{3v_2}$$

<u>Sketch:</u> In Schnorr [11] we proved that any computation β_2 for p with $\le v_2$ nonscalar operations and which uses the field elements $\gamma_1,..,\gamma_r$ as parameters can be normalized to $\tilde{\beta}$ which uses the field elements $\tilde{\gamma}_1,..,\tilde{\gamma}_r$ as parameters such that there exists polynomials $Q_j \in \mathbb{Z}[\tilde{\gamma}_1,...,\tilde{\gamma}_r]$ with $\deg Q_j \le 2v_2 j$ and

(8) $$\bar{p} = \Sigma_{j\ge 1} Q_j(\tilde{\gamma}_1,..,\tilde{\gamma}_r)(y-\eta)^j.$$

Such a normalisation $\tilde{\beta}$ of β_2 exists for each fixed $\eta \in \mathbb{K}$ with only finitely many $\eta \in \mathbb{K}$ excluded.

By (8) it follows from Bezout's theorem that the mapping $\psi_1:(\tilde{\gamma}_1,...,\tilde{\gamma}_r) \mapsto (p_1,..,p_k)$ has the degree bound $\deg \overline{\text{graph}(\psi_1)} \le (2v_2k)^k$. Moreover the degree of the mapping $\psi_2:(\gamma_1,...,\gamma_r) \mapsto (\tilde{\gamma}_1,...,\tilde{\gamma}_r)$ which normalizes the parameters can easily be bounded as $\deg \overline{\text{graph}(\psi_2)} \le 2^{3v_2}$. Since $\varphi_2 = \psi_1 \circ \psi_2$ this proves (7).

Since $W(\underline{p}) = \overline{\text{graph}(\varphi_2 \circ \varphi_1)}$ it follows from (6) and (7) that

$$\deg W(\underline{p}) \le 2^{v_1}(2v_2k)^k 2^{3v_2}$$

This implies $\text{ld} \deg W(\underline{p}) \le (v+k)\,\text{ld}(v+k)$ which yields $v+k \ge \text{ld} \deg W(\underline{p}) / \text{ld}\,\text{ld} \deg W(\underline{p})$. ∎

References

1. Belaga, E.G.: (1958) Some problems involved in the computation of polynomials. Dokl. Akad. Nauk. 123, 775-777

2. Borodin, A. and Cook, S.: (1976) On the number of additions to compute specific polynomials, Siam J. Comput. 5, 146-157

3. Borodin, A. and Munro, I.: (1975) The complexity of algebraic and numeric problems. American Elsevier, New York

4. Heintz, J.: (1978) A new method for proving lower bounds for polynomials which are hard to compute. This symposium

5. Hyafil, L. and Van de Wiele, J.P.: (1976) Bornes Inférieures pour la complexité des polynomes à coefficients 0-1. IRIA Rapport No. 192

6. Lipton, R.J.: (1975) Polynomials with 0-1 coefficients that are hard to compute. in: Proceedings of the 16th Annual IEEE Symposium on the Foundations of Computer Science, New York

7. Lipton, R.J. and Stockmeyer, L.J.: (1978) Evaluation of polynomials with super-preconditioning. Journal of Comp. and System Sciences 16, 124-139

8. Motzkin, T.S.: (1955) Evaluation of polynomials and evaluation of rational functions Bull. Amer. Math. Soc. 61, 163

9. Paterson, M.S. and Stockmeyer, L.J.: (1973) On the number of nonscalar multiplications necessary to evaluate polynomials. Siam J. Comput. 2, 60-66

10. Savage, J.E.: (1974) An algorithm for the computation of linear forms. Siam J. Comput. 3, 150-158

11. Schnorr, C.P.: (1977) Improved lower bounds on the number of multiplications/divisions which are necessary to evaluate polynomials. in: Proceedings of the 6th International MFCS Symposium, High Tatras. Springer: Lecture Notes in Computer Science 53, 135-147. to appear in TCS (1978)

12. Schnorr, C.P.: (1978) On the additive complexity of polynomials. preprint Universität Frankfurt

13. Strassen, V.: (1974) Polynomials with rational coefficients which are hard to compute. Siam J. Comput. 3, 128-149

14. Van de Wiele, J.P.: (1978) An optimal lower bound on the number of total operations to compute 0-1 polynomials over the field of complex numbers. Proceedings of the 19th Annual Symposium on Foundations of Computer Science

15. Winograd, S.: (1970) On the number of multiplications necessary to compute certain functions. Comm. Pure Appl. Math. 23, 165-179

16. Strassen, V.: (1973) Die Berechnungskomplexität von elementarsymmetrischen Funktionen und von Interpolationskoeffizienten. Numerische Mathematik 20, 238-251

17. Schnorr, C.P. and Van de Wiele, J.P.: On the additive complexity of polynomials. To appear in TCS.

REMARKS ON THE NONEXISTENCE OF SOME COVERING GRAMMARS

Esko Ukkonen

Abstract. The problem of covering context-free grammars by grammars in some normal forms is considered. It is shown that certain example grammars cannot be covered by grammars which are in ε-free form or in Greibach normal form or in Chomsky normal form. The results are generalized using a concept called the structural similarity of context-free grammars. Finally, a grammatical transformation method for constructing ε-free covers is given.

1. Introduction

A context-free grammar is said to cover another one if both grammars generate the same language and if parses in the covered grammar are homomorphic images of parses in the covering grammar [1,2]. The problem whether it is possible to cover a given grammar by different normal form grammars has both theoretical and practical interest and contains several open questions [3,4]. For example, no grammatical conditions are known which specify precisely those context-free grammars that have a covering grammar in ε-free form or in Greibach normal form or in Chomsky normal form. Moreover, optimal transformations into covering grammars of these forms are not yet presented. Some related results have appeared in [1,2,3,4,5,7], sometimes informally.

The main purpose of this paper is to prove that some example grammars cannot have covering grammars of the forms mentioned. No similar nontrivial examples have been verified in the literature so far.

The transitivity of covering relations implies that the nonexistence of a cover can sometimes be proved by reducing to our examples. We will illustrate this technique. We also provide a generalization of the examples. In fact, we will introduce the concept of structural similarity of context-free grammars and use it to isolate from some of our example grammars those syntactical structures that imply the nonexistence of the cover in question.

As a more positive result we give a method to construct ε-free covering grammars and show that the method is in a sense optimal.

In Section 2 different grammatical covers are defined. In addition to the usual covering relation we introduce a related notion called weak covering, which allows us to formulate the results more generally. In Section 3 we consider unambiguous and in Section 4 ambiguous example grammars. Our method for constructing ε-free covers is presented in Section 5. Some proofs are omitted in this paper, particularly in Sections 4 and 5.

We conclude the present section by giving our notations and basic definitions. We mainly follow [1]; all definitions and notations not explicitly given are as in this reference.

A (context-free) grammar is denoted by a quadruple $G = (N,\Sigma,P,S)$, where N, Σ, P and S denote the nonterminals, the terminals, the productions and, respectively, the start symbol of G. The language generated by grammar G is denoted L(G), and the language generated by a string α in $(N \cup \Sigma)^*$ is denoted $L(\alpha)$. The empty string is denoted ε.

Grammar G is *ε-free* if it has no *ε-productions* (productions of the form $A \to \varepsilon$) except possibly the production $S \to \varepsilon$ in which case S does not appear on the right hand side of any production of G. Grammar G is said to be in *Greibach normal form (GNF)* if G is ε-free and each non-ε-production of G is of the form $A \to a\alpha$ with A in N, a in Σ, α in N^*. Grammar G is said to be in *Chomsky normal form (CNF)* if G is ε-free and each non-ε-production of G is of the form $A \to BC$ or $A \to a$ with A, B, C in N and a in Σ.

For α, β in $(N \cup \Sigma)^*$, a leftmost derivation of β from α is denoted $\alpha \overset{\pi}{\Rightarrow}_L \beta$ where π is the sequence of productions of G which are used, in the proper order, in the derivation. Analogously, we use $\alpha \overset{\pi}{\Rightarrow}_R \beta$ for a rightmost derivation of β from α in G. If $S \overset{\pi}{\Rightarrow}_L \alpha$ then π is a *left parse (l-parse)* of α, and if $S \overset{\pi}{\Rightarrow}_R \alpha$ then the reverse of π is a *right parse (r-parse)* of α in G.

All grammars in this paper are *reduced*, that is, every nonterminal of a grammar is used in a derivation of a terminal string from the start symbol.

2. Grammatical covers

For the sake of completeness, let us recall the well-known covering concepts called the right, left, right-to-left and left-to-right covering (r|r-covering, l|l-covering, r|l-covering, l|r-covering, for short). Definitions similar to the following have appeared e.g. in [1-3].

Let $G = (N,\Sigma,P,S)$, $G' = (N',\Sigma,P',S')$ be grammars, and let x|y denote r|r, l|l, r|l, or l|r. Grammar G' is said to x|y-cover grammar G if there is a homomorphism $h : P'^* \to P^*$ such that for all strings w in Σ^*:

(C1) if π' is an x-parse of w in G', $h(\pi')$ is a y-parse of w in G, and

(C2) if π is a y-parse of w in G, there exists an x-parse π' of w in G' such that $h(\pi') = \pi$.

Clearly, if G' x|y-covers G then $L(G') = L(G)$.

Next, let us introduce a less restrictive covering relation. Using this cover type, it is possible to present our results in a more general form.

Let grammars $G = (N,\Sigma,P,S)$ and $G' = (N',\Sigma',P',S')$ be such that $\Sigma \subset \Sigma'$. Then grammar G' is said to *weakly* x|y-cover grammar G if there is a homomorphism $h : P'^* \to P^*$ such that for all strings w in L(G) conditions (C1) and (C2) are valid.

If G' weakly x|y-covers G then obviously L(G) ⊂ L(G'). In addition, covers clearly have the following elementary properties.

Proposition 1. If G' x|y-covers G then G' weakly x|y-covers G.

Proposition 2. (transitivity)
(i) If G'' weakly x|y-covers G' and G' weakly y|z-covers G then G'' weakly x|z-covers G.
(ii) If G'' x|y-covers G' and G' y|z-covers G then G'' x|z-covers G.

In the sequel, the nonexistence of certain covers will be shown by proving that the corresponding weak cover does not exist.

3. Examples of noncoverable unambiguous grammars

In this section we prove that some unambiguous grammars cannot have covering grammars in certain normal forms. There are in the literature some related remarks. In [1,2] it is stated that a grammar S → S0 | S1 | 0 | 1 , which resembles our examples, cannot be right covered by a grammar in Greibach normal form. Nijholt [3], however, shows that such a cover exists.

We first consider the following grammars G_1 - G_4 for the language $\{0^n1^m \mid n,m > 0\}$:

G_1:	*1.*	$S \to LS1$
	2.	$S \to LR1$
	3.	$R \to LR0$
	4.	$R \to 0$
	5.	$L \to \varepsilon$

G_2:	*1.*	$S \to 0SL$
	2.	$S \to 0RL$
	3.	$R \to 1RL$
	4.	$R \to 1$
	5.	$L \to \varepsilon$

G_3:	*1.*	$S \to L0S$
	2.	$S \to L0R$
	3.	$R \to L1R$
	4.	$R \to 1$
	5.	$L \to \varepsilon$

G_4:	*1.*	$S \to S1L$
	2.	$S \to R1L$
	3.	$R \to R0L$
	4.	$R \to 0$
	5.	$L \to \varepsilon$

Covering of grammars G_1 - G_4 by ε-free grammars (ε-free covering, for short) is not always possible.

Theorem 1. (i) Grammar G_1 has no weak ε-free right cover.
(ii) Grammar G_2 has no weak ε-free left cover.
(iii) Grammar G_3 has no weak ε-free left-to-right cover.
(iv) Grammar G_4 has no weak ε-free right-to-left cover.

Proof. The proofs of different claims (i) - (iv) are quite similar. We shall therefore consider in detail claim (i) only.

(i) The proof is by contradiction. Suppose there is an ε-free grammar $Q = (N_Q, \{0,1\}, P_Q, S_Q)$ that weakly right covers G_1 under a homomorphism mapping right parses in Q to equivalent right parses in G_1. Then a reverse homomorphism h must also exist which maps reverses of right parses in Q to reverses of right parses in G_1.

Consider the derivation of strings $0^{n+1}1^{m+1}$. Let $S_Q \overset{\pi}{\Rightarrow}_R 0^{n+1}1^{m+1}$ in Q. Then $h(\pi) = \mathit{1}^m\mathit{2}\mathit{3}^n\mathit{4}\mathit{5}^{n+m+1}$ where the numbers refer to productions of G_1. Without loss of generality, let $\pi = \rho\sigma$ such that $h(\rho) = \mathit{1}^m\mathit{2}\mathit{3}^n\mathit{4}$, $h(\sigma) = \mathit{5}^{n+m+1}$ and

(1) $$S_Q \overset{\rho}{\Rightarrow}_R \alpha A u \overset{\sigma}{\Rightarrow}_R vu = 0^{n+1}1^{m+1}$$

where $\alpha \in (N_Q \cup \{0,1\})^*$, $A \in N_Q$, $u \in \{0,1\}^*$. Our goal is now to prove that, for some n and m, derivation (1) can be chosen so that the structure of the corresponding derivation tree is as shown in Fig. 1. The tree has the essential property of containing recursive nonterminals B and C such that B generates a portion of string 0^{n+1} and C generates a portion of string 1^{m+1}.

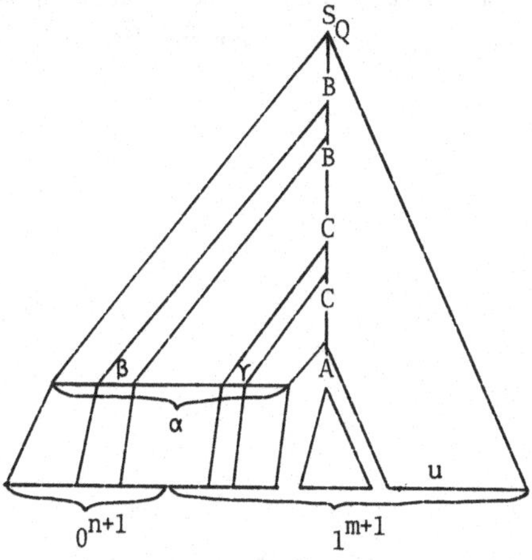

Fig. 1.

To confirm the situation in Fig. 1 we first note that the final string $0^{n+1}1^{m+1}$ generated in (1) is uniquely determined already by productions ρ since $h(\rho) = \mathit{1}^m\mathit{2}\mathit{3}^n\mathit{4}$. Let $\alpha A = X_t X_{t-1} \cdots X_0$ where $X_t, X_{t-1}, \ldots, X_0 \in N_Q \cup \{0,1\}$. Uniqueness then implies that each X_i generates in Q only one terminal string x_i. Consequently, $v = x_t \cdots x_1 x_0$. Each length $|x_i| > 0$ because Q is ε-free. On the other hand, lengths $|x_i|$ also have an upper bound; otherwise by the Pumping Lemma for context-free grammars [1], the language of X_i would be infinite. Moreover, we may write $\sigma = \sigma_0\sigma_1 \cdots \sigma_t$ such that for $i = 0, \ldots, t$, $X_i \overset{\sigma_i}{\Rightarrow}_R x_i$. Now, if $X_i \overset{\tau}{\Rightarrow}_R x_i$ for some τ, then $h(\tau)$ must always be equal to $h(\sigma_i)$ because $h(\sigma) = h(\sigma_0 \cdots \sigma_{i-1}\tau\sigma_{i+1} \cdots \sigma_t)$. So we may assume in the sequel that each σ_i is chosen from possible sequences τ such that $|\sigma_i|$ is minimal. Then lengths $|\sigma_i|$ have an upper bound since lengths $|x_i|$ are bounded and a derivation sequence σ_i of minimal length cannot use recursion. (Note that if $|\sigma_i|$ is not minimal, the recursion which may occur in σ_i must be of the "chain" type $Y \overset{+}{\Rightarrow}_R Y$.)

Next, we let k be an index such that $x_t \ldots x_{k+1} \in 0^*$ and $x_{k-1} \ldots x_1 \in 1^*$. Thus $\alpha_0 = X_t \ldots X_{k+1}$ generates a string of 0's and $\alpha_1 = X_{k-1} \ldots X_1$ a string of 1's. We now show that α_0 and α_1 can be generated of any length by choosing n and m large enough. First, since $h(\sigma) = 5^{n+m+1}$, $|\sigma|$ must have a lower bound which increases with m. But since each $|\sigma_i|$ is bounded and $\sigma = \sigma_0 \sigma_1 \ldots \sigma_t$, we may increase t, the length of $X_t \ldots X_1$ by increasing m. Moreover, when m is so large that $k \geq 1$, $|\alpha_0|$ has a lower bound which increases with n since lengths $|x_i|$ have an upper bound. Noting in addition that $|\alpha_0| \leq n+1$ since each $x_i \neq \varepsilon$, we see that $|\alpha_0| = t-k$ and $|\alpha_1| = k-1$ can be increased over any finite limit by first choosing a sufficiently large n and then increasing m.

Therefore, for some n and m, $|\alpha_0|$ and $|\alpha_1|$ are $\geq (\nu-1)(\mu-1)$ where ν is the number of nonterminals of Q, and μ is the maximum length of the right hand sides of the productions of Q. Then the generation of α_0 and α_1 must be so long that it involves recursion. More precisely, there are nonterminals B and C such that using notations $\rho = \rho_1 \rho_B \rho_2 \rho_C \rho_3$, $\alpha = \delta_1 \beta \delta_2 \gamma \delta_3$, $u = v_3 y v_2 x v_1$, the part corresponding to ρ in (1) can be written as

$$S_Q \overset{\rho_1}{\Rightarrow}_R \delta_1 B v_1 ,$$

$$B \overset{\rho_B}{\Rightarrow}_R \beta B x ,$$

$$B \overset{\rho_2}{\Rightarrow}_R \delta_2 C v_2 ,$$

$$C \overset{\rho_C}{\Rightarrow}_R \gamma C y ,$$

$$C \overset{\rho_3}{\Rightarrow}_R \delta_3 A v_3 .$$

Here $\beta \neq \varepsilon$ is a portion of α_0 and $\gamma \neq \varepsilon$ a portion of α_1. Thus for these n and m, derivation (1) is as portrayed in Fig. 1.

Now we are in position to complete the proof. Let 0^p be the string generated by β and 1^q the string generated by γ; $p,q > 0$. Then $h(\rho_B)$ must contain 3^p, and $h(\rho_C)$ must contain 1^q in order for the number of *3*'s and *1*'s to be correct in $h(\rho_1 \rho_B^r \rho_2 \rho_C^s \rho_3)$ when r and s are varied. But then $h(\rho)$ has some *3*'s to the left of *1*'s, that is, the relative order of *3*'s and *1*'s cannot be correct. This contradiction accomplishes the proof that G_1 has no weak ε-free right cover.

(ii) The proof that G_2 has no weak ε-free left cover is symmetric to the proof of (i) above: left and right must be exchanged, and a left cover homomorphism must be used.

(iii) This proof has the same basis as the proof of (i). The main technical differences are outlined below.

To derive a contradiction, suppose an ε-free grammar Q weakly left-to-right covers G_3 under a homomorphism h, and let $S_Q \overset{\pi}{\Rightarrow}_L 0^{n+1}1^{m+1}$. Then $h(\pi) = 5^{n+m+1}43^m21^n$. Let $\pi = \rho\sigma$ such that $h(\rho) = 5^{n+m+1}4$. Then

(2) $$S_Q \overset{\rho}{\Rightarrow}_L uA\alpha \overset{\sigma}{\Rightarrow}_L uv = 0^{n+1}1^{m+1}$$

for some $u \in \{0,1\}^*$, $A \in N_Q$, $\alpha \in N_Q^*$. When n is sufficiently larger than m, the string u must be in 0^*. Then $u = 0^k$ for some k, and the length of the string generated from $A\alpha$ must be n+m+2-k. This implies that $|\alpha|$ can be increased by increasing n+m. Furthermore, it can be shown, as in the case (i), that for some n and m, portions β and γ of α, where β generates only 0's and γ generates only 1's, must be so long that they involve recursion. In fact, there are n and m such that the derivation tree corresponding to (2) is as in Fig. 2.

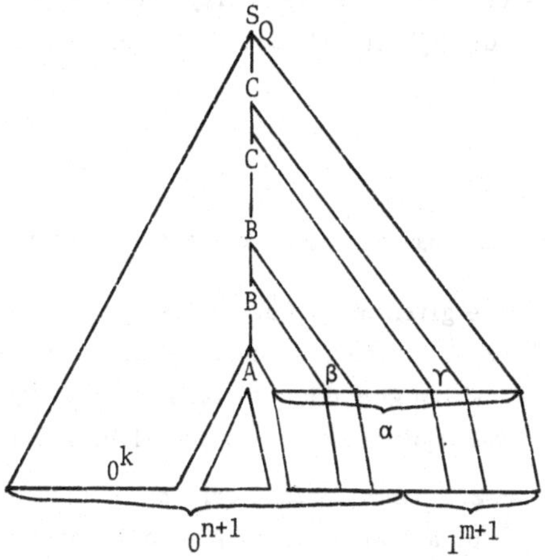

Fig. 2.

Then we may write $\sigma = \sigma_1\sigma_\beta\sigma_2\sigma_\gamma\sigma_3$ where σ_β is applied to β and σ_γ to γ, and $\beta \overset{\sigma_\beta}{\Rightarrow}_L 0^p$, $\gamma \overset{\sigma_\gamma}{\Rightarrow}_L 1^q$. Here p,q > 0 because Q is ε-free. Finally, it is straightforward to see that $h(\sigma_\beta)$ must contain 1^p and $h(\sigma_\gamma)$ must contain 3^q in order for the number of terminals 0 and 1 generated and the number of productions *1* and *3* in the image under h to be consistent in derivations in which the number of recursive parts starting from C and B in Fig. 2 are varied. But this means that in $h(\pi)$ some *1*'s are before all *3*'s, that is, the relative order of *1*'s and *3*'s is not correct.

(iv) The proof that G_4 has no weak ε-free right-to-left cover is symmetric to the proof of (iii): left and right must be exchanged. Moreover, instead of the right-to-left cover homomorphism the reverse of it should be used. □

Next we present some consequences of Theorem 1, or more precisely, consequences of assertion (i). A similar analysis is also possible for assertions (ii) - (iv).

First, it clearly follows from (i) that G_1 has no ε-free right cover. Moreover, since a grammar with no (weak) ε-free right cover has no (weak) right cover in GNF or CNF, grammar G_1 has no (weak) right cover in GNF or CNF. This means because G_1 is a cycle-free grammar that, contrary to some claims in the literature [1, p. 280], every cycle-free grammar cannot be right covered by a grammar in CNF.

Noting the transitivity of covers stated in Proposition 2 we see that the non-existence of a cover can sometimes be proved by reducing to Theorem 1. For example, if a grammar G weakly right or left-to-right covers G_1 then by transitivity, G has no (weak) ε-free right or, respectively, right-to-left cover. As illustrations of this technique, let us consider first a grammar with productions

$$S \to LS0 \mid LS1 \mid 0 \mid 1$$
$$L \to \varepsilon$$

Since this grammar weakly right covers grammar G_1, as is easily seen, it has no ε-free right cover. This confirms a conjecture of Nijholt [4]. Similarly, an ε-free grammar

$$S \to SA \mid SB \mid 0 \mid 1$$
$$A \to 0$$
$$B \to 1$$

left-to-right covers G_1. Hence this grammar has no ε-free right-to-left cover.

A generalization of Theorem 1 will be given next. Our purpose is to isolate those syntactic structures inherent in our example grammars which imply the nonexistence of the covers. We introduce first a concept which we call structural similarity, and which is closely related to the structural equivalence of context-free grammars [6].

For a grammar $G = (N,\Sigma,P,S)$, the *simple parenthesized version* of G is a grammar $(G_\varepsilon) = (N, \{(,)\}, P', S)$ where P' consists of all productions $A \to (\alpha_\varepsilon)$ such that $A \to \alpha$ is in P and α_ε is obtained from α by replacing every element of Σ by the empty string ε.

Two grammars, G and G', are *structurally similar* if their simple parenthesized versions (G_ε) and (G'_ε) generate the same language.

Now we may formulate the generalization. Only grammar G_1 is considered here; similar results may also be obtained for grammars G_2 - G_4.

Grammar G_1 has derivations of the form $A \Rightarrow^* \alpha A \beta$ where $\alpha \neq \varepsilon$, $\beta \neq \varepsilon$, and $\alpha \Rightarrow^* \varepsilon$. This grammatical structure is noncoverable by ε-free grammars in the following sense.

Corollary 1. If in a grammar G there is a derivation of the form $A \Rightarrow^* \alpha A \beta$ where α and β are nonempty strings and $\alpha \Rightarrow^* \varepsilon$, then there exists a grammar G', which is structurally similar to G and which does not generate the empty string, such that G' cannot be (weakly) right covered by an ε-free grammar.

Proof (outline). It is straightforward (we omit the details) to construct on the basis of G a structurally similar grammar G', $\varepsilon \notin L(G')$, which weakly right covers G_1.

Then by Proposition 2 and Theorem 1 (i), G' has no (weak) ε-free right cover. □

As further examples of noncoverable grammars we will then consider the following ε-free grammars G_5 and G_6 for the language $\{0^n1^m0^k \mid n,k \geq 0,\ m > 0\}$:

G_5:	1. $S \to S0$	G_6: 1. $S \to 0S$
	2. $S \to K$	2. $S \to K$
	3. $K \to 0K$	3. $K \to K0$
	4. $K \to L$	4. $K \to L$
	5. $L \to 1L$	5. $L \to L1$
	6. $L \to 1$	6. $L \to 1$

Theorem 2. (i) Grammar G_5 has no weak left cover in GNF.
(ii) Grammar G_6 has no weak left-to-right cover in GNF.
(iii) Grammar G_5 has no weak ε-free right-to-left cover.

Proof. The proof is similar to the proof of Theorem 1. Some technical differences are caused by the structure of G_5 and G_6 and the fact that covering by grammars in GNF is in question.

(i) To derive a contradiction, suppose grammar Q in GNF weakly left covers G_5. Let $S_Q \overset{\pi}{\Rightarrow}_L 0^n1^{m+1}0^k$ in Q. Then $h(\pi) = 1^k23^n45^m6$ where h is a left cover homomorphism. Denote $\pi = \rho\sigma$ such that $|\rho| = n+m+1$. Then

(3) $$S_Q \overset{\rho}{\Rightarrow}_L 0^n1^{m+1}A\alpha \overset{\sigma}{\Rightarrow}_L 0^n1^{m+1}0^k$$

for some $A \in N_Q$, $\alpha \in N_Q^*$ because Q is in GNF. When k is sufficiently larger than n+m, $h(\sigma)$ must contain the suffix 23^n45^m6 of $h(\pi)$. Now write $A\alpha = \alpha_1\alpha_2\alpha_3\alpha_4\alpha_5$, and let the corresponding decomposition of σ be $\sigma = \sigma_1\sigma_2\sigma_3\sigma_4\sigma_5$, that is, productions σ_i are applied to α_i. Strings α_2 and α_4 are chosen as the maximal substrings of α such that $h(\sigma_2)$ is a sequence of 3's and, respectively, $h(\sigma_4)$ is a sequence of 5's. On the basis of ρ, $h(\sigma)$ must contain precisely n 3's and m 5's. Hence lengths $|\alpha_2|$ and $|\alpha_4|$ can be increased by increasing n and m. So recursion must occur in the derivation of α_2 and α_4 for some n and m. More precisely, the derivation tree corresponding to (3) is as shown in Fig. 3, that is, there are nonterminals B and C such that using notations $\rho = \rho_1\rho_2\rho_3\rho_4\rho_5$, $0^n1^{m+1} = u_1vu_2wu_3$, $\alpha = \delta_3\beta\delta_2\gamma\delta_1$, the part corresponding to ρ in (3) can be written as

$$S_Q \overset{\rho_1}{\Rightarrow}_L u_1C\delta_1,$$

(4) $$C \overset{\rho_2}{\Rightarrow}_L vC\gamma,$$

$$C \overset{\rho_3}{\Rightarrow}_L u_2B\delta_2,$$

(5) $$B \overset{\rho_4}{\Rightarrow}_L wB\beta,$$

$$B \overset{\rho_5}{\Rightarrow}_L u_3 A \delta_3 .$$

Here $\beta \neq \varepsilon$ is a part of α_2 and $\gamma \neq \varepsilon$ a part of α_4. Now let σ_β be the part of σ_2 which is applied to β and, respectively, σ_γ the part of σ_4 which is applied to γ. In addition, we may choose β and γ so that $h(\sigma_\beta)$ and $h(\sigma_\gamma)$ are nonempty. Hence $h(\sigma_\beta) = 3^p$, $h(\sigma_\gamma) = 5^q$ for some $p,q > 0$. But this implies that $v = 1^q$, $w = 0^p$ in order for the number of terminals 1 and 0 generated and the number of productions *3* and *5* in the image under h to be consistent in derivations in which the number of recursive parts (4) and (5) are varied. So we find that in 0^n1^{m+1} some 1's should be to the left of 0's. This contradiction completes the proof of (i).

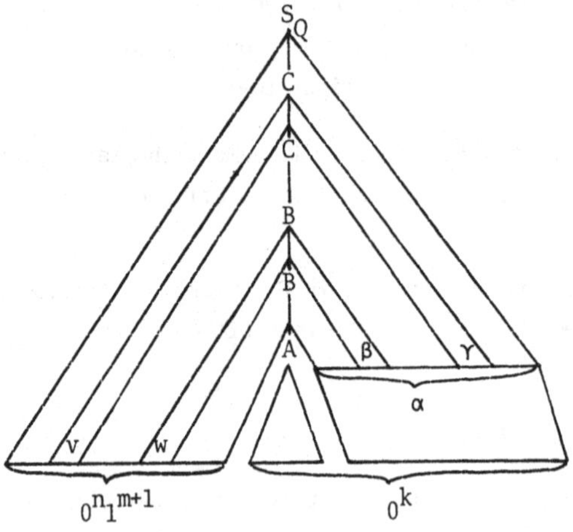

Fig. 3.

(ii) Suppose grammar Q in GNF weakly left-to-right covers G_6 and $S_Q \overset{\pi}{\Rightarrow}_L 0^n1^{m+1}0^k$ in Q. Then $h(\pi) = 65^m43^k21^n$ where h is a left-to-right cover homomorphism. Write $\pi = \rho\sigma$ where $|\rho| = n$. Suppose that n is so much larger than m+k that $h(\rho)$ must contain 65^m43^k. Now a contradiction may be derived as in the proof of Theorem 1 (ii). It can be shown that in $h(\rho)$ some *3*'s must be before *5*'s for some n,m,k.

(iii) Suppose an ε-free grammar Q weakly right-to-left covers G_5 and $S_Q \overset{\pi}{\Rightarrow}_R 0^n1^{m+1}0^k$ in Q. Then $h(\pi) = 65^m43^n21^k$, where h is the reverse of a right-to-left cover homomorphism. Write $\pi = \rho\sigma$ such that $h(\rho) = 65^m43^n2$. Now a contradiction may be derived as in the proof of Theorem 1 (i). It can be shown that in $h(\rho)$ some *3*'s must be before *5*'s for some m,n,k. □

We conclude this section with a remark on grammar G_6 and assertion (ii) of Theorem 2. When productions *2* - *5* of G_6 are replaced by productions

$S \rightarrow 0K$	$M \rightarrow 0$
$K \rightarrow 0KM$	$L \rightarrow 1L$
$K \rightarrow 0L$	

the resulting grammar G_6' is in GNF. It is easy to see that the proof of Theorem 2 (ii), with minor modifications, can be used to show that G_6' cannot have a weak left-to-right cover in GNF. Hence we obtain:

Corollary 2. The class of context-free grammars which have a weak left-to-right cover in GNF does not contain all the GNF grammars.

4. Examples of noncoverable ambiguous grammars

The simplest example of a grammar which does not have an ε-free cover is a grammar in which the empty string ε has more than one derivation tree [3]. We consider here the following ambiguous grammars for language {0}:

G_7: *1.*	$S \to LS$	G_8: *1.*	$S \to SL$
2.	$S \to 0$	*2.*	$S \to 0$
3.	$L \to \varepsilon$	*3.*	$L \to \varepsilon$

Theorem 3. (i) Grammar G_7 has no weak ε-free right or left-to-right cover.
(ii) Grammar G_8 has no weak ε-free left or right-to-left cover.

Proof. We prove the first claim of (i). The other proofs are similar.

To derive a contradiction suppose there is an ε-free grammar $Q = (N_Q, \{0\}, P_Q, S_Q)$ that weakly right covers G_7 and h is a cover homomorphism mapping right derivations of 0 in Q to right derivations of 0 in G_7. Let $S_Q \Rightarrow_R^{\pi} 0$ in Q. Then $h(\pi) = 1^k 2 3^k$ for some $k \geq 0$. Without loss of generality, let $\pi = \rho\sigma$ such that $h(\rho) = 1^k$. Since S_Q is ε-free, derivation $S_Q \Rightarrow_R^{\rho} \delta$ must be of the form

$$S_Q = X_o \Rightarrow_R^{\rho_1} X_1 \Rightarrow_R^{\rho_2} X_2 \Rightarrow_R^{\rho_3} \cdots \Rightarrow_R^{\rho_n} X_n = \delta$$

for some $X_1, \ldots, X_n \in N_Q$, $\rho = \rho_1 \ldots \rho_n$. Clearly, if k is large enough, $X_i = X_j$ for some $i < j$, and $h(\rho_{i+1} \ldots \rho_j) \neq \varepsilon$. Hence $h(\rho_{i+1} \ldots \rho_j) = 1^{k'}$ for some $k' > 0$. Now $\tau = \rho_1 \ldots \rho_i \rho_{j+1} \ldots \rho_n \sigma$ must also be a righmost derivation of 0 in Q. However, $h(\tau) = 1^{k-k'} 2 3^k$ where $k-k' \neq k$. This is a contradiction because such an $h(\tau)$ cannot be a rightmost derivation of 0 in G_7. □

It is easily seen that Theorem 3 can be generalized as follows:

Corollary 3. (i) If in a grammar G there is a derivation of the form $A \Rightarrow^* \alpha A$ where α is nonempty and $\alpha \Rightarrow^* \varepsilon$, then G has no weak ε-free right or left-to-right cover.

(ii) If in a grammar G there is a derivation of the form $A \Rightarrow^* A\alpha$ where α is nonempty and $\alpha \Rightarrow^* \varepsilon$, then G has no weak ε-free left or right-to-left cover.

5. Constructing ε-free covers

The standard methods for elimination of ε-productions from a context-free grammar do not yield a grammar that covers the original one, e.g. [1, p. 148]. In this section we present a method to eliminate ε-productions such that the resulting grammar is a cover. For simplicity, we only deal with the right covering. Similar results may be obtained also for other cover types.

Algorithm 1. Let $G = (N,\Sigma,P,S)$ be a grammar. We write $i.A \to \alpha$ to express that the unique reference number of a production $A \to \alpha$ in P is i. The algorithm yields an ε-free grammar $G' = (N',\Sigma,P',S')$ and a homomorphism $P'^* \to P^*$. Productions in P' are given in the form $A \to \alpha$ $<\pi>$ where $A \to \alpha$ is the production and $\pi \in P^*$ is its image under the homomorphism. If $<\pi>$ is missing, the image is the empty string. Productions P' and nonterminals N' are defined by the following rules 1 - 3.

1. Initially, N' contains the new start symbol S'. If $S \overset{\pi}{\Rightarrow}_R \varepsilon$ in G, add $S' \to \varepsilon$ $<\pi>$ to P'. If G does not generate a nonempty string, the algorithm terminates. Otherwise add $S' \to [\underline{S}]$ to P' and $[\underline{S}]$ to N', and then repeat steps 2 - 3 until no changes are possible.

2. For each element $[\gamma\underline{A}]$ in N' and for each production $i.A \to \alpha$ of G such that $L(\alpha) \neq \{\varepsilon\}$, add to P' all productions constructed as follows. Suppose that α can be represented as $\alpha = \alpha_0 X_1 \alpha_1 X_2 \ldots \alpha_{n-1} X_n \alpha_n$, $n > 0$, where each $X_i \in N \cup \Sigma$ is such that $L(X_i) \neq \{\varepsilon\}$, $i = 1,\ldots,n$, and each $\alpha_i \in N^*$ is such that $\varepsilon \in L(\alpha_i)$, $i = 0,\ldots,n$. For each such representation of α, add to P' the production $[\gamma\underline{A}] \to Z_1 Z_2 \ldots Z_n$ $<i>$, where

$$Z_1 = \begin{cases} [\gamma\alpha_0\underline{X_1}\alpha_1], & \text{if } \gamma\alpha_0\alpha_1 \neq \varepsilon \text{ or } X_1 \in N; \\ X_1, & \text{otherwise,} \end{cases}$$

and for $i = 2,\ldots,n$

$$Z_i = \begin{cases} [\underline{X_i}\alpha_i], & \text{if } \alpha_i \neq \varepsilon \text{ or } X_i \in N; \\ X_i, & \text{otherwise.} \end{cases}$$

3. Let $j.B \to \beta$ be a production of G such that $\varepsilon \in L(\beta)$. For each nonterminal $[\gamma\underline{X}\alpha B]$ in N' where $\alpha,\gamma \in N^*$ and $X \in N \cup \Sigma$, if $\gamma\alpha\beta \neq \varepsilon$ or $X \in N$, add the production $[\gamma\underline{X}\alpha B] \to [\gamma\underline{X}\alpha\beta]$ $<j>$ to P' and the nonterminal $[\gamma\underline{X}\alpha\beta]$ to N', and otherwise, that is, if $\gamma\alpha\beta = \varepsilon$ and $X \in \Sigma$, add to P' the production $[\gamma\underline{X}\alpha B] \to X$ $<j>$. Similarly, for each nonterminal $[\gamma B\underline{X}]$ in N' where $X \in \Sigma$ and $\gamma \in N^*$, if $\gamma\beta \neq \varepsilon$, add the production $[\gamma B\underline{X}] \to [\gamma\beta\underline{X}]$ $<j>$ to P' and the nonterminal $[\gamma\beta\underline{X}]$ to N', and otherwise, add the production $[\gamma B\underline{X}] \to X$ $<j>$ to P'. □

Example. When Algorithm 1 is applied to a grammar with productions

1. $S \to LAB$	4. $B \to BL$
2. $L \to \varepsilon$	5. $B \to \varepsilon$
3. $A \to La$	6. $B \to b$

the resulting grammar has the following productions:

$S' \to [\underline{S}]$	$[L\underline{A}] \to [LL\underline{a}]$ <3>
$[\underline{S}] \to [L\underline{A}][\underline{B}]$ <1>	$[LL\underline{a}] \to [L\underline{a}]$ <2>
$[\underline{S}] \to [L\underline{A}B]$ <1>	$[L\underline{a}] \to a$ <2>
$[\underline{B}] \to [\underline{B}L]$ <4>	$[L\underline{A}B] \to [L\underline{A}]$ <5>
$[\underline{B}] \to b$ <6>	$[L\underline{A}B] \to [L\underline{A}BL]$ <4>
$[\underline{B}L] \to [\underline{B}]$ <2>	$[L\underline{A}BL] \to [L\underline{A}B]$ <2>

Theorem 4. The grammar G' produced by Algorithm 1 is ε-free and right covers the original grammar G under the homomorphism defined by the algorithm if and only if

(i) there is at most one π such that $S \overset{\pi}{\Rightarrow}_R \varepsilon$ in G, and

(ii) there is in G no derivation of the form $A \Rightarrow^* \alpha A \beta$, where α is nonempty and $\alpha \Rightarrow^* \varepsilon$.

If condition (i) of Theorem 4 is not true, Algorithm 1 cannot define the cover homomorphism uniquely, and if condition (ii) is not true, Algorithm 1 does not halt.

It is evident that a grammar G not satisfying condition (i) of Theorem 4 has no ε-free right cover. Moreover, a grammar not satisfying condition (ii) has by Corollary 3 no ε-free right cover, or by Corollary 1, there is a structurally similar grammar satisfying (i) but not having an ε-free right cover. In other words, for a grammar G satisfying condition (i), Algorithm 1 produces an ε-free right cover if and only if every grammar, which is structurally similar to G and satisfies condition (i), has an ε-free right cover.

A grammar with productions $S \to LS1 \mid 1,\ L \to \varepsilon$ is an example of a grammar for which an ε-free right cover cannot be produced by Algorithm 1 although such a cover exists. This grammar is structurally similar to the noncoverable grammar G_1 given in Section 3.

References

1. Aho,A.V. and J.D.Ullman: The Theory of Parsing, Translation, and Compiling, Vol.I: Parsing. Prentice-Hall, Englewood Cliffs, N.J., 1972.
2. Gray,J.N. and M.A.Harrison: On the covering and reduction problems for context-free grammars. J. Assoc. Comput. Mach. 19 (1972), 675-698.
3. Nijholt,A.: Cover results and normal forms. In: Proc. 6th Int. Symp. on Mathematical Foundations of Computer Science (ed. J.Gruska), Lect. Notes in Computer Science 53, pp. 420-429, Springer-Verlag, Berlin-Heidelberg-New York, 1977.
4. Nijholt,A.: On the covering of left-recursive grammars. Conf. Record of the Fourth ACM Symposium on Principles of Programming Languages, pp. 86-96, 1977.
5. Nijholt,A.: Structure preserving transformations on non-left-recursive grammars. Report IR-39, Vrije Universiteit Amsterdam, 1978.
6. Salomaa,A.: Formal Languages. Academic Press, New York and London, 1973.
7. Ukkonen,E.: Transformations to produce certain covering grammars. In: Proc. 7th Int. Symp. on Mathematical Foundations of Computer Science (ed. J.Winkowski), Lect. Notes in Computer Science 64, pp. 516-525, Springer-Verlag, Berlin-Heidelberg-New York, 1978.

ZUR KOMPLEXITÄT DER PRESBURGER ARITHMETIK UND DES ÄQUIVALENZPROBLEMS EINFACHER PROGRAMME

Kai Wöhl

1. Einführung

Zu der interessanten Klasse von entscheidbaren Problemen, die dicht an der Nicht-Entscheidbarkeitsgrenze liegen, gehört auch die Frage, ob eine Formel der Presburger Arithmetik /9/ - das ist die Theorie der ganzen Zahlen unter der Addition - wahr oder falsch ist. Durch Aufnahme nur eines weiteren monadischen Prädikats in die Theorie geht die Entscheidbarkeit verloren /3/. Als untere Komplexitätsschranke für nicht-determinierte Entscheidbarkeitsalgorithmen haben Fischer und Rabin die Größenordnung $2^{2^{cn}}$ (n Formellänge, c Konstante) nachgewiesen /5/. Die obere Abschätzung von Oppen /8/ basiert auf dem Algorithmus von Cooper /2/ und liegt um eine Potenzstufe höher bei $2^{2^{2^{cn}}}$.

Durch Einbettung in die Presburger Arithmetik läßt sich auch die Entscheidbarkeit des Äquivalenzproblems erweiterter, über den ganzen Zahlen interpretierter Loop-1-Programme zeigen. Die Änderung der Schleifenschachtelungstiefe von 1 auf 2 führt auch hier direkt aus dem entscheidbaren Bereich hinaus /7/,/11/,/12/.

Im Folgenden sollen die Formeln, die aus dem Äquivalenzproblem durch Abbildung in die Presburger Arithmetik entstehen, sowie dazugehörige Entscheidbarkeitsalgorithmen näher untersucht werden. Es zeigt sich,daß diese Formelklasse zunächst grob durch eine geringe Anzahl von Quantorenwechsel in der Prenexnormalform charaktersisiert ist. Der Algorithmus von Cooper läßt sich bzgl. dieser Eigenschaft so weiterentwickeln, daß $2^{2^{cn^{(q+4)}}}$ (q Anzahl der Quantorenwechsel) eine neue obere Komplexitätsschranke wird /10/,/12/. Ferner gelingt es, mit dem neuen Algorithmus das Äquivalenzproblem in $2^{2^{cn}}$ determiniert zu entscheiden. Berücksichtigt man, daß die untere Schranke für nicht-determinierte Algorithmen nach Fischer und Rabin dieselbe Größenordnung besitzt, so liegt die starke Vermutung nahe, daß das Äquivalenzproblem eine geringere Komplexität als das Entscheidbarkeitsproblem der Presburger Arithmetik besitzt.

Bem.: Die Arbeit /10/ von Reddy und Loveland war dem Autor erst nach Annahme des Vortrags zugänglich.

2. Entscheidbarkeitsalgorithmen der Presburger Arithmetik

Die Presburger Arithmetik $\mathcal{PA}$ ist eine axiomatische Theorie auf der Grundlage der Prädikatenlogik 1. Stufe mit Gleichheit und Operationssymbolen. Die nicht logischen Konstanten sind:

0, 1	Individuenkonstanten
-	unäres Operationssymbol
+	binäres Operationssymbol
>0,2|,3|,...	unäre Prädikatenkonstanten

Es gelten zusätzlich zu den Axiomen des Prädikatenkalküls die Axiome der kommutativen Gruppe, der totalen und der diskreten Ordnung sowie Teilbarkeitsaxiome (siehe / 6/). Zur vereinfachten Schreibweise werde die Infixnotation verwendet. Die Zahlzeichen 2,3,4... seien Abkürzungen für die Ausdrücke (1+1),((1+1)+1),(((1+1)+1)+1),... . Neben der Notation $t_1 - t_2$ für $t_1+(-t_2)$ können auch die Symbole $>, <, \leq, \geq, 2\nmid, 3\nmid, \ldots$ stellvertretend benutzt werden. Die Standardinterpretation $I = (\mathbb{Z}, \mathfrak{f}, \mathfrak{P}, \sigma)$ bildet die Symbole der Presburger Arithmetik in die schon durch die Schreibweise angedeuteten Konstanten $0,1 \varepsilon \mathbb{Z}$, Operationen +,- und Prädikate =,>0,2|,3|,4|,... über $\mathbb{Z}$ ab (n|... teilt nachfolgenden Term).

Ein Entscheidbarkeitsalgorithmus der Presburger Arithmetik transformiert die zu analysierende Formel durch Quantorelimination in eine äquivalente quantorfreie Formel. Enthält die Eingabeformel keine freien Variablen, so besteht anschließend die quantorfreie Ausgabeformel nur aus Konstanten und kann anhand der Standardinterpretation unmittelbar zu wahr oder falsch ausgewertet werden. Diese Quantorelimination entspricht dem Substitutionsverfahren, das bei der Lösung linearer Gleichungssysteme verwendet wird. Während man es dort mit Formeln des einfachen Typs $\exists x_1 \exists x_2 \ldots \exists x_n \; a_{11}x_1 + \ldots + a_{1n}x_n = b_1 \wedge \ldots \wedge a_{n1}x_1 + \ldots + a_{nn}x_n = b_n$ zu tun hat, kommt bei allgemeinen Formeln der Presburger Arithmetik hinzu, daß in $\mathbb{Z}$ keine Divisionsoperation zur Verfügung steht - Teilbarkeitsbedingungen müssen in die Formel mitaufgenommen werden -, daß die Formeln neben Gleichungen auch Gößer/Kleiner- und Teilbarkeitsrelationen enthalten und daß diese durch die logische v-Operation verknüpft sein können. Allquantoren lassen sich durch $(\forall x \; F \equiv \neg \exists x \; \neg F)$ stets in Existenzquantoren umwandeln. Negationen in einer quantorfreien Teilformel können durch Änderung der Prädikate eliminiert werden $(\neg a=b \equiv a<b \vee b<a)$.

Der spezielle Algorithmus von Cooper /2/ vereinfacht die Struktur der Formeln weiter. So werden Gleichungen in Größer/Kleiner-Relationen überführt (a=b≡a<b+1 b<a+1). v-Verknüpfungen werden vom Algorithmus genau wie $\wedge$-Operationen behandelt. Die Eliminierung der Quantoren bzw. der gebundenen Variablen erfolgt iterativ beginnend mit der jeweils innersten Teilformel $\exists x \; F(x)$, wobei F quantorenfrei ist. Nach Erweiterung der Relationen in F auf einen einheitlichen x-Koeffizienten λ wird die

Teilformel $\exists x\ F(\lambda x)$ durch Variablentransformation in $\exists x\ (\lambda|x \wedge F(x))$ überführt. Diese enthält dann nur noch Relationen der Art: $x<a_i$ $x>b_i$ $\delta_i|x+c_i$ $\varepsilon_i \nmid x+d_i$, wobei $\delta_i, \varepsilon_i \in N$ und a_i, b_i, c_i, d_i x-freie Ausdrücke sind. Sei F' nun $(\lambda|x \cdot \wedge F(x))$ und γ das kgV der δ_i und ε_i-Konstanten sowie $F_{-\infty}$ die Formel, die aus F' durch Ersetzung der x-abhängigen <-Relationen durch wahr und der >-Relationen durch falsch entsteht, so kann die Teilformel $\exists x\ F(x)$ durch die äquivalente x-freie Formel

$$\bigvee_{j=1}^{\gamma} F_{-\infty}(j) \vee \bigvee_{j=1}^{\gamma} \bigvee_{b_i} F'(b_i+j)$$

ersetzt werden. Sollte die Anzahl der Relationen vom Typ $x<a$ geringer sein, so kann auch

$$\bigvee_{j=1}^{\gamma} F_{+\infty}(j) \vee \bigvee_{j=1}^{\gamma} \bigvee_{a_j} F'(a_i-j)$$

benutzt werden. Dieser determinierte Algorithmus besitzt nach der Arbeit von Oppen /8/ die obere Zeit- und Platzkomplexitätsschranke $2^{2^{2^{cn}}}$ (n Formellänge, c Konstante).

Optimierungsmöglichkeiten bestehen zum einen darin, die für die Aufblähung der Formel verantwortliche Konstante γ zu verkleinern, sowie zum anderen in der Beschränkung des Substitutionsprozesses auf ausgewählte Teilformeln.

Reddy und Loveland erreichen ersteres in /10/, indem sie zunächst darauf verzichten, die x-Koeffizienten in der Formel zu normalisieren. Stattdessen ersetzten sie jeweils die Teilformel $\exists x\ F(x)$, die Relationen der Art $\alpha x \leq a, \alpha x \geq b, \delta|\alpha x+c, \varepsilon|\alpha x+d$ enthält, unmittelbar durch

$$\bigvee_{j=0}^{\sigma-1} F'_{-\infty}(j) \vee \bigvee_{b} \bigvee_{j=0}^{\sigma-1} [F((b+j) \swarrow \alpha x) \wedge \alpha|(b+j)]$$

bzw. die analog über a gebildete Disjunktion. $F((b+j) \swarrow \alpha x)$ bezeichnet darin die Formel, in der alle Vorkommen von αx durch $(b+j)$ ersetzt werden ($\beta x = \alpha x + \ldots + \alpha x$). Falls ein x-Koeffizient β kein Vielfaches von α ist, erfolgt vorher eine Erweiterung der entsprechenden Relation mit α. σ ist das kgV von α und den Konstanten δ, ε aller x-abhängigen Teilbarkeitsrelationen in F. Diese Optimierung wird dadurch verstärkt, daß alle Existenzquantoren vor die neu entstandenen disjunktiv verknüpften Teilformeln gezogen werden können ($\exists x\ (F \vee F') \equiv \exists x\ F \vee \exists x\ F'$). Somit sind die Substitutionsprozesse auf Teilformeln beschränkt. Ein Quantorenwechsel, die Aufeinanderfolge von Existenz- und Allquantor, bedeutet jedoch, daß während der Iteration eine Negation aufgelöst werden muß, die alle bis dahin erzeugten v-Operationen in Konjunktionen umwandelt und somit obigen Effekt zerstört. Sei q die Anzahl der Quantorenwechsel innerhalb der Prenexnormalform einer Formel F, so kann nach /10/ für eine determinierte Maschine die Zeitkomplexität mit

$$2^{2^{cn^{(q+4)}}}$$

und die Platzkomplexität unter Berücksichtigung des Ergebnisses von Ferrante und Rackoff /4/ mit $2^{cn^{(q+4)}}$ abgeschätzt werden.

Zu gleichem Ergebnis kommen wir, wenn lediglich bei der Substitution nach Cooper die $\wedge,\vee$-Verknüpfungsstruktur der Formel berücksichtigt wird. Wie man leicht nachweist, ist eine Substitution nur jeweils in jenen Relationen notwendig, die konjunktiv mit der Relation verknüpft sind, aus der der zu ersetzende Term b stammt. Sei z.B. F' eine Teilformel, in der die Variable x mit Hilfe der Relation $\alpha x \geq b$ eliminiert werden soll (linker Syntaxbaum in Abb.). Die Substitution muß dann nur in den mit $\alpha x \geq b$ konjunktiv verknüpften Relationen erfolgen, dargestellt im rechten Syntaxbaum der Abb.:

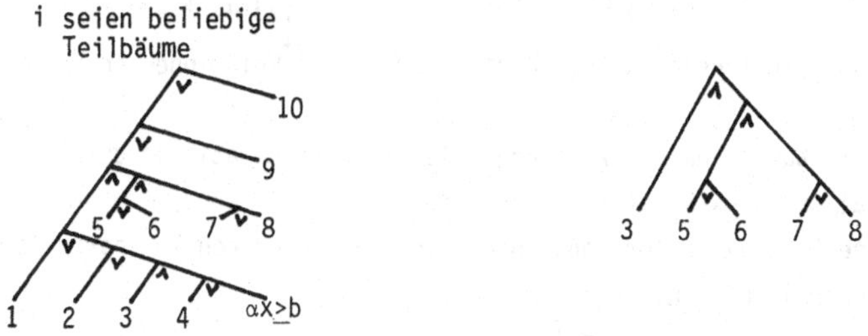

Diese Änderung des Algorithmus wirkt sich für die Abschätzung wie bei Reddy und Loveland aus, da, wie oben bereits gesehen, der Algorithmus die Formel nur durch $\vee$- Operationen aufbläht. Für eine praktische Nutzung jedoch hat die Sonderbehandlung von Gleichungen die größere Bedeutung, denn in einer Teilformel, die mit einer Gleichung konjunktiv verknüpft ist, muß nur eine einzige Substitution erfolgen, d.h. die Formel vergrößert sich nur maximal mit der Anzahl der Gleichungen, kann sich aber auch je nach Verknüpfungsstruktur verkleinern. Insbesondere dadurch gelingt es, eine Reihe von Formeln, die praktisch interessierende Probleme beschreiben, mit noch vertretbarem Aufwand an Rechenzeit und Speicherplatz zu entscheiden /12/.

Der nachfolgende Algorithmus ist die Weiterentwicklung des Algorithmus von Cooper mit den beschriebenen Optimierungen aus /10/ und /12/:

1. Ersetze in F alle Teilformeln $\forall x$ F' durch $\neg\exists x(\neg F')$;
2. <u>Solange</u> F nicht quantorenfrei, <u>tue</u>
   - 2.1. Lokalisiere Teilformel $\exists x$ F'(x) mit F'(x) quantorenfrei;
   - 2.2. Eliminiere alle logischen Negationen in F';
   - 2.3. Setze F_{neu}:= <u>falsch</u>;

     {Substitution durch Gleichungen}
   - 2.4. Bringe alle x-abhängigen Gleichungen in F' auf die Form

     $\alpha x = t$ mit $\alpha \in \mathbb{N}$, t x-freier Term;

2.5. <u>Solange</u> F' eine x-abhängige Gleichung $g \equiv (\alpha x = t)$ enthält, <u>tue</u>

- 2.5.1. Bestimme Formeln G^g und I^g, die g nicht enthalten, so daß gilt:
  $F' = (g \wedge G^g) \vee I^g$ und
  G^g enthält minimale Anzahl von Relationen,
  d.h. G^g ist die minimale Konjunktion der Teilformeln von F', die mit g konjunktiv verknüpft sind;
- 2.5.2. Setze $F_{neu} := F_{neu} \vee (G^g(t \diagup \alpha x) \wedge \alpha | t)$;
- 2.5.3. Ersetze g in F' durch <u>falsch</u> und vereinfache;

{Substitution durch $<, \geq, >, \geq, \neq$-Relationen}

2.6. Bringe alle x-abhängigen Relationen in F' auf eine der Formen:

I. $\alpha x \begin{bmatrix} < \\ \leq \\ \neq \end{bmatrix} t$ II. $\alpha x \begin{bmatrix} > \\ \geq \\ \neq \end{bmatrix} t$ III. $\delta \begin{bmatrix} | \\ \nmid \end{bmatrix} \alpha x + t$

2.7. <u>Falls</u> Anzahl der Typ-I-Relationen > Anzahl der Typ-II-Relationen in F' <u>dann</u>

- 2.7.1. Bilde $F'_{-\infty}$ aus F' durch Ersetzung aller $<, \leq, \neq$-x-Relationen durch <u>wahr</u>, aller $>, \geq$-x-Relationen durch <u>falsch</u>;
- 2.7.2. Berechne das kgVσ aller Konstanten δ der x-abhängigen Teilbarkeitsrelationen in $F'_{-\infty}$ und setze

$$F_{neu} := F_{neu} \vee \bigvee_{j=0}^{\sigma-1} F'_{-\infty}(j)$$

- 2.7.3. <u>Für alle</u> Typ-II-Relationen $r \equiv (\alpha x \begin{bmatrix} > \\ \geq \\ \neq \end{bmatrix} t)$ <u>tue</u>
  - 2.7.3.1. Bilde G^r aus F' analog zu 2.5.1.;
  - 2.7.3.2. Berechne das kgVσ aus α und allen Konstanten δ der x-abhängigen Teilbarkeitsrelationen in G^r und setze

$$F_{neu} := F_{neu} \vee \bigvee_{j=0}^{\sigma-1} \begin{cases} G^r((t+j) \diagup \alpha x) \wedge \alpha | t+j, & \text{falls } r \geq \text{-Relation} \\ G^r((t+j+1) \diagup \alpha x) \wedge \alpha | t+j+1, & \text{sonst} \end{cases}$$

<u>sonst</u>

- analog zu 2.7.1. - 2.7.3. für entsprechendes $F'_{+\infty}$ und Substitution mittels Typ-I-Relationen

2.8. Ersetze $\exists x\, F'(x)$ in F durch F_{neu} und vereinfache;

3. Äquivalenzproblem erweiterter Loop-1-Programme

Def. 3.1.: Ein erweitertes Loop-n-Programm $P \varepsilon \mathcal{P}(EL_n)$ ist

$$P = (R, IN, OUT, BF) \quad \text{mit}$$

R ist eine endliche, geordnete Menge von Registern ($r = \#R$)

$IN \subseteq R$ ist die Menge der Eingaberegister ($in = \#IN$)

$OUT \subseteq R$ ist die Menge der Ausgaberegister ($out = \#OUT$)

BF ist eine endliche Befehlsfolge von

X:=X+1, X:=X-1, X:=0, X:=Y X,YεR

und den Schleifen LOOP X... END sowie LOOP-X ... END, die höchstens n-mal geschachtelt sind.

Def. 3.2.: $\phi = (\mathbb{Z}, \psi)$ ist die Interpretation der erweiterten Loop-Programme, wobei $\psi: \mathcal{P}(EL_n) \to \{f: \mathbb{Z}^{in} \to \mathbb{Z}^{out} / \ in, out \in \mathbb{N}_0\}$, $\psi(P)(x_1, \ldots, x_{in}) = (y_1, \ldots, y_{out})$ ist, $x_1, \ldots, x_{in}$ sind die Inhalte der Eingaberegister vor Programmausführung, alle anderen Register aus $R \setminus IN$ sind mit 0 initialisiert. $y_1, \ldots, y_{out}$ sind Werte der Ausgaberegister nach der Ausführung. Die Programmbefehle besitzen ihre übliche Bedeutung. Die Befehlsfolge in den Schleifen wird (X)-mal bzw. -(X)-mal iteriert, sofern (X)>0 bzw. -(X)>0 ist. (X) sei der Inhalt des Schleifenregisters X vor Schleifenbeginn.

Die von Meyer und Richie in /7/ ursprünglich definierten Loop-Programme wurden über den natürlichen Zahlen interpretiert. Es fehlten der Befehl X:=X-1 und die Schleife LOOP-X... END. Für jene Loop-1-Programmklasse wies Tsichritzis in /11/ die Entscheidbarkeit des Äquivalenzproblems ($P_1 \equiv P_2 \iff \psi(P_1) = \psi(P_2)$) über die von den Programmen berechneten Funktionen nach. Das Äquivalenzproblem der erweiterten Loop-1-Programme aus Def. 3.1. soll hier zunächst auf das Äquivalenzproblem spezieller erweiterter Loop-0-Programme reduziert und anschließend durch Einbettung in die Presburger Arithmetik entschieden werden.

Def. 3.3.: Die erweiterte Loop-n-Programmklasse $\mathcal{P}(EL_n(+,-,if,\div k))$ sei definiert wie in Def. 3.1. mit den zusätzlichen Befehlen

$X:=X+Y$, $X:=-X$, $X_1:=$ if $Y>0$ then X_2 else X_1, $X:=X\div 2$, $X:=X\div 3, \ldots$

Die Interpretation $\phi = (\mathbb{Z}, \psi)$ werde entsprechend erweitert.

Satz 3.1.: Die Loop-Programmklassen $\mathcal{P}(EL_1)$ und $\mathcal{P}(EL_0(+,-,if,\div k))$ sind bzgl. $\phi = (\mathbb{Z}, \psi)$ äquivalent.

Beweisskizze: " <=" Die zusätzlichen Befehle lassen sich durch einfache Loop-1-Programme ausdrücken.

"=> ": Sei f die von der Schleife LOOP X_K A END berechnete Funktion und g die der Befehlsfolge A, so gilt:

$f,g: \mathbb{Z}^r \to \mathbb{Z}^r$

$f(x_1,\dots,x_r) = g^{x_k}(x_1,\dots,x_r)$

$g(x_1,\dots,x_r) = (a_1 x_{i_1}+c_1, a_2 x_{i_2}+c_2,\dots,a_r x_{i_r}+c_r)$

mit $a_j \in \{0,1\}$, $c_j \in \mathbb{Z}$, $i_j \in \{1,\dots,r\}$

Nach einer konstanten Anzahl von Iterationen, die durch if-Abfragen ausgedrückt werden können, werden die Anfangswerte von einigen Variablen nur noch zyklisch permutiert und um die Summe der zugehörigen Konstanten c_j erhöht. Über die konstante Zykluslänge können die Endwerte der Variablen nach Abbruch der Schleife mit Hilfe ganzzahliger Divisionsbefehle berechnet werden.

Satz 3.2.: Für alle $\underline{in} \in \mathbb{N}$ gibt es eine Konstante $c = c(\underline{in})$ und einen determinierten Algorithmus, der jedes Äquivalenzproblem $P_1 \equiv P_2$ der Länge n von Loop-1-Programmen $P_1, P_2 \in \mathfrak{P}(EL_1)$ mit $\underline{in}$ Eingaberegistern in $2^{2^{cn^2}}$ Berechnungsschritten entscheidet.

Lemma 3.1.: Es gibt einen determinierten Algorithmus, der jedes Loop-1-Programm $P \in \mathfrak{P}(EL_1)$, das m Anweisungen besitzt, polynomial in ein äquivalentes Loop-0-Programm $P' \in \mathfrak{P}(EL_0(+,-,if,\div k))$ übersetzt, das folgenden Abschätzungen für eine hinreichend große Konstante c genügt:

1) die Anzahl der Anweisungen $m' < cm^2$
2) die maximale Divisionskonstante $k < m$
3) die Anzahl der if-Anweisungsfolgen mit gleicher Bedingung $m'_{if} < cm$
4) die Anzahl der Divisionsanweisungen $m'_{\div k} < m$

Beweis: Satz 3.1. und Abschätzung in /12/.

Lemma 3.2.: Es gibt einen determinierten Algorithmus, der zu jedem Loop-1-Programm $P \in \mathfrak{P}(EL_1)$ mit m Anweisungen und $\underline{in}$ Eingaberegistern in 2^{cm} eine geschlossene Formel F mit 0-beschränktem Quantorenwechsel der Presburger Arithmetik erzeugt, so daß gilt:

$$\forall x_1,\dots,x_{in} \in \mathbb{Z} \quad \psi(P)(x_1,\dots,x_{in}) = (0,\dots,0) \iff F$$

und F besitzt folgende Eigenschaften für eine Konstante c:

1) $(a+b) < 2^{cm}$, wenn $(a+b)$ Anzahl der Relationen ist,
2) $g < m^m$, wenn g die maximale Konstante in F ist,
3) $v = \underline{in}$, wenn v die Anzahl der gebundenen Variablen ist.

Beweisidee: Das Loop-1-Programm P wird zunächst mit Lemma 3.1 in das äquivalente Loop-0-Programm P' transformiert, das ohne Beschränkung der Allgemeinheit nur ein Ausgaberegister X_1 besitze. Mit Hilfe der Abbildung β werde die Formel

$F = \beta(P', x_1 = 0) = \beta(P', x_1+1>0 \wedge (-x_1)+1>0)$ konstruiert, so daß gilt:

$$\beta(P', x_1+1>0 \wedge (-x_1)+1>0)$$
$$\Longleftrightarrow \forall x_1 \forall x_2 \ldots \forall x_{in} \quad \psi(P')(x_1,\ldots,x_{in}) = 0$$
$$\Longleftrightarrow \neg \exists x_1 \exists x_2 \ldots \exists x_{in} \neg \psi(P')(x_1,\ldots,x_{in}) = 0$$

β ist definiert durch

$$\beta: \mathcal{P}(EL_0(+,-,if,\div k)) \times \mathcal{PA} \rightarrow \mathcal{PA}$$
$$\beta((R,IN,OUT,\ ),F) = \neg \exists x_1 \exists x_2 \ldots \exists x_{in} \neg F(0/x_{in+1}, 0/x_{in+2}, \ldots, 0/x_r)$$
$$\beta((R,IN,OUT,BF\ X_i := X_i+1),F) = \beta((R,IN,OUT,BF), F((x_i+1)/x_i))$$
$$\beta((R,IN,OUT,BF\ X_i := X_i-1),F) = \beta((R,IN,OUT,BF), F((X_i-1)/x_i))$$
$$\beta((R,IN,OUT,BF\ X_i := 0),F) = \beta((R,IN,OUT,BF), F(0/x_i))$$
$$\beta((R,IN,OUT,BF\ X_i := X_j),F) = \beta((R,IN,OUT,BF), F(X_j/x_i))$$
$$\beta((R,IN,OUT,BF\ X_i := X_i+X_j),F) = \beta((R,IN,OUT,BF), F((x_i+x_j)/x_i))$$
$$\beta((R,IN,OUT,BF\ X_i := -X_i),F) = \beta((R,IN,OUT,BF), F((-x_i)/x_i))$$
$$\beta((R,IN,OUT,BF\ X_i := \text{if } X_j>0 \text{ then } X_1 \text{ else } X_i),F) =$$
$$\begin{cases} \beta((R,IN,OUT,BF), (x_j>0 \wedge F_1(x_1/x_i)) \vee ((-x_j)+1>0 \wedge F_2)) \\ \qquad \text{falls } F = (x_j>0 \wedge F_1) \vee ((-x_j)+1>0 \wedge F_2) \\ \beta((R,IN,OUT,BF), (x_j>0 \wedge F(x_1/x_i)) \vee ((-x_j)+1>0 \wedge F)) \\ \qquad \text{sonst} \end{cases}$$
$$\beta((R,IN,OUT,BF\ X_i := X_i \div k),F) =$$
$$\beta((R,IN,OUT,BF), (x_i>0 \wedge kF((-x_i)/k(-x_i), (x_i-k+1)/kx_i))$$
$$\vee ((-x_i)+1>0 \wedge kF(((-x_i)-k+1)/k(-x_i), x_i/kx_i)))$$

Die Abschätzung siehe in /12/.

<u>Beweisskizze zu Satz 3.2.:</u> Sei $P_1 \equiv P_2$ das Äquivalenzproblem der Länge n mit $P_1, P_2 \in \mathcal{P}(EL_1)$ und <u>in</u> als Anzahl der Eingaberegister. Für die Anzahl der Anweisungen in P_1 und P_2 m_1 und m_2 gilt dann: $m_1+m_2<n$. Zu P_1 und P_2 läßt sich ein Loop-1-Programm P mit m Anweisungen konstruieren, so daß gilt:

$$P_1 \equiv P_2 \Longleftrightarrow \forall x_1 \ldots x_{\underline{in}} \quad \psi(P)(x_1,\ldots,x_{\underline{in}}) = (0,\ldots,0)$$
$$\text{und } m<c\,(m_1+m_2)$$

Nach Lemma 3.2. kann aus P in 2^{cm} eine geschlossene Formel F mit 0-beschränktem Quantorenwechsel erzeugt werden, so daß gilt:

$$a + b < 2^{cm} \qquad g < m^m \qquad v = \underline{in}$$

Die Zeit- und Platzkomplexität des weiterentwickelten Quantor-Eliminations-Algorithmus besitzt nach der Abschätzung in /12/ für Formeln der Presburger Arithmetik mit 0-beschränktem Quantorenwechsel die Größenordnung $g^{(a+b)^{cv}}$ für eine hinreichend große Konstante c. Da hier die Anzahl der Eingaberegister <u>in</u> = v mit in die Konstante c eingeht, erhalten wir für das Äquivalenzproblem erweiterter Loop-1-Programme das Abschätzungsergebnis:

$$(m^m)^{(2^{c'm})^{c''(\underline{in})}} \quad \text{oder} \quad 2^{2^{cn}}.$$

4. Schlußbemerkung

Erste Erfahrungen mit einer Implementation des vorgestellten Algorithmus der Presburger Arithmetik lassen trotz des superexponentiellen Aufwands praktische Anwendungsmöglichkeiten für einige Probleme aus dem Bereich der Verifikation und lokalen Optimierung von Programmteilen erwarten insbesondere dann, wenn der Algorithmus weiter an die speziellen Eigenschaften der zu bearbeitenden Formelklasse angepaßt wird. So stellten Cherniavsky und Kamin in ihrer Arbeit /1/ ein vollständiges und widerspruchsfreies Hoare'sches Axiomensystem für Loop-1-Programme vor, in dem die Presburger Arithmetik als zugrundeliegender logischer Kalkül benutzt wird.

5. Literatur

/1/ J.Cherniavsky, S.Kamin: A complete and consistent Hoare axiomatic for a simple programming language, Conf. Report of 4th ACM-Symposium on Principles of Programming Languages, 1977

/2/ D.C.Cooper: Theorem proving without multiplication, Machine Intelligence 7, S. 91-99, Edinburgh 1972

/3/ P.C.Downey: Undecidability of Presburger Arithmetic with a single monadic letter, Center for Research in Computing Technologie, Harvard University, 18-72, 1972

/4/ J.Ferrante, C.Rackoff: A decision procedure for the first order theory of real addition with order, SIAM J.Comp., Vol. 4 No. 1, 1975

/5/ M.J.Fischer, M.O.Rabin: Super-exponential complexity of Presburger Arithmetic, SIAM-AMS Proceedings Vol. 7, 1974

/6/ G.Kreisel, J.L.Krivine: Elements of mathematical logic, North-Holland, Amsterdam 1971

/7/ A.R.Meyer, D.M.Ritchie: Computation complexity and program structure, IBM Research Report RC 1817, 1967

/8/ D.C.Oppen: An upper bound on the complexity of Presburger Arithmetic JCSS 16, 323-332, 1978

/9/ M.Presburger: Über die Vollständigkeit eines gewissen Systems der Arithmetik ganzer Zahlen, in welchem die Addition als einzige Operation hervortritt, Comptes-Rendus du Congrès des Mathématiciens des Pays Slaves, Warsaw 1930, S. 99-101, 395

/10/ C.R.Reddy, D.W.Loveland: Presburger Arithmetik with bounded quantifier alternation, Conf. Report of 10th ACM-Symposium on Theory of Computing, 1978

/11/ D.Tsichritzis: The equivalence problem of simple programs, JACM Vol. 17, No.4, S. 729-738, 1970

/12/ K.Wöhl: Äquivalenzuntersuchungen an einfachen Programmen (Dissertation), Bericht Nr. 56/78, Abteilung Informatik, Universität Dortmund, 1978

Autorenverzeichnis

BEAUQUIER, Joffroy

L.I.T.P. 248 et Institut de Programmation
Université Pierre et Marie Curie (Paris VI)
4, Place Jussieu
F-75230 PARIS Cedex 05 / Frankreich

BENNISON, Victor L.

Bell Laboratories
Warrenville-Naperville Road
NAPERVILLE, Ill. 60540 / USA

BLUM, Norbert

Universität des Saarlandes
Fachbereich 10
D-6600 SAARBRÜCKEN

BOASSON, L.

5, Allée G. Rouault
F-75020 PARIS / Frankreich

BOUDOL, Gérard

Université Paris VII
VER de Mathematiques, CNRS
9, Rue Marrier
F-77300 FONTAINEBLEAU / Frankreich

von BRAUNMÜHL, Burchard

Universität Bonn
Institut für Informatik
Wegelerstr. 6
D-5300 BONN

van EMDE BOAS, Peter

University of Amsterdam
Dept. of Mathematics
Roetersstraat 15
NL-1018 WB AMSTERDAM / Niederlande

FRIEDE, Dietmar

Universität Hamburg
Fachbereich Informatik
Schlüterstr. 70
D-2000 HAMBURG 13

GÁCS, Pêter

Universität Frankfurt
Fachbereich Mathematik
Robert-Mayer-Str. 6-10
D-6000 FRANKFURT / MAIN

GANZINGER, Harald

Technische Universität München
Institut für Informatik
Arcisstraße 21
D-8000 MÜNCHEN 2

GUESSARIAN, Irêne

CNRS Université Paris 7
Tour 45-55 - 5ème étage
2, Place Jussieu
F-75221 PARIS Cêdex 05 / Frankreich

GREIF, Irene

Massachusetts Institute of Technology
Laboratory for Computer Science
545, Technology Square
CAMBRIDGE, Mass. 02139 / USA

HEINTZ, Joos

Universität Frankfurt
Fachbereich Mathematik
Robert-Mayer-Str. 6-10
D-6000 FRANKFURT / MAIN

JANTZEN, Matthias

Universität Hamburg
Fachbereich Informatik
Schlüterstr. 70
D-2000 HAMBURG 13

KANDA, Akira

University of Leeds
Dept. of Computer Studies
LEEDS, LS2 9JT / UK

LATTEUX, Michel

Université de Lille I
UER d'IEEA Service Informatique
B.P. 36
F-59650 VILLENEUVE D'ASCQ / Frankreich

van LEEUWEN, Jan

University of Utrecht
Dept. of Computer Science
Budapestlaan 6
NL-3508 TA UTRECHT / Niederlande

MAJSTER, Mila

Technische Universität München
Institut für Informatik
Postfach 202420
D-8000 MÜNCHEN 2

MAURER, H.

Technische Universität Graz
Institut für Informationsverarbeitung
Steyrergasse 17
A-8010 GRAZ / Österreich

MEHLHORN, Kurt

Universität des Saarlandes
Fachbereich Angewandte Mathematik und Inform
D-6600 SAARBRÜCKEN

MEYER, A.

Massachusetts Institute of Technology
Laboratory for Computer Science
545 Technology Square
CAMBRIDGE, Mass. 02139 / USA

MILNER, Robin

University of Edinburgh
Dept. of Computer Science
EDINBURGH, EH9 3JZ / UK

OTTMANN, Th.

Universität Karlsruhe
Institut für Angewandte Informatik und
Formale Beschreibungsverfahren
D-7500 KARLSRUHE

PARK, David

University of Warwick
Dept. of Computer Studies
COVENTRY, CV4 7AL / UK

PAUL, W.J.

Universität Bielefeld
Fakultät für Mathematik
Postfach 8640
D-4800 BIELEFELD

PIN, J.E.

CNRS Université Paris VI
Tour 55-65 - 4e étage
4, Place Jussieu
F-75230 PARIS Cedex 05 / Frankreich

PRIESE, Lutz

Universität Dortmund
Fachgebiet Systemtheorie und Systemtechnik
Postfach 500500
D-4600 DORTMUND

REISCHUK, R.

Universität Bielefeld
Fakultät für Mathematik
Postfach 8640
D-4800 BIELEFELD

REISER, Angelika

Technische Universität München
Institut für Informatik
Postfach 202420
D-8000 MÜNCHEN 2

REUTENAUER, Christophe

Université Pierre et Marie Curie
Institut de Programmation et CNRS LA 248
4, Place Jussieu
F-75230 PARIS Cedex 05 / Frankreich

ROLLIK, Hans-Anton

Universität Bielefeld
Fakultät für Mathematik
Postfach 8640
D-4800 BIELEFELD

ROSENBERG, A.L.

IBM T.J. Watson Research Center
Mathematical Sciences
YORKTOWN HEIGHTS, N.Y. 10598 / USA

SAKAROVITCH, Jacques

Université Paris VI CNRS
Laboratoire d'Informatique Théorique et Programmation
2, Place Jussieu
F-75221 PARIS Cedex 05 / Frankreich

SCHNORR, Claus Peter

Universität Frankfurt
Fachbereich Mathematik
Robert-Mayer-Str. 6-10
D-6000 FRANKFURT / MAIN

SCHÖNHAGE, A.

Universität Tübingen
Mathematisches Institut
Auf der Morgenstelle 10
D-7400 TÜBINGEN 1

SIX, H.W.

Universität Karlsruhe
Institut für Angewandte Informatik und
Formale Beschreibungsverfahren
D-7500 KARLSRUHE

UKKONEN, Esko

University of Helsinki
Dept. of Computer Science
Tukholmankatu 2
SF-00250 HELSINKI 25 / Finnland

VALINAT, Leslie G.

University of Edinburgh
Dept. of Computer Science
EDINBURGH EH9 3JZ / UK

VERBEEK, Rutger

Universität Bonn
Institut für Informatik
Wegelerstr. 6
D-5300 BONN

WÖHL, Kai

Universität Dortmund
Abteilung für Informatik
August-Schmidt-Str.
D-4600 DORTMUND-HOMBURCH

WOOD, D.

McMaster University
Dept. of Applied Mathematics
HAMILTON, Ontario L8S 4K1 / Kanada

ɪl. 49: Interactive Systems. Proceedings 1976. Edited by A. Blaser d C. Hackl. VI, 380 pages. 1976.

ɪl. 50: A. C. Hartmann, A Concurrent Pascal Compiler for Mini-mputers. VI, 119 pages. 1977.

ɪl. 51: B. S. Garbow, Matrix Eigensystem Routines – Eispack uide Extension. VIII, 343 pages. 1977.

ɪl. 52: Automata, Languages and Programming. Fourth Colloquium, niversity of Turku, July 1977. Edited by A. Salomaa and M. Steinby. 569 pages. 1977.

ɪl. 53: Mathematical Foundations of Computer Science. Proceed-gs 1977. Edited by J. Gruska. XII, 608 pages. 1977.

ɪl. 54: Design and Implementation of Programming Languages. roceedings 1976. Edited by J. H. Williams and D. A. Fisher. X, 96 pages. 1977.

ɪl. 55: A. Gerbier, Mes premières constructions de programmes. , 256 pages. 1977.

ɪl. 56: Fundamentals of Computation Theory. Proceedings 1977. lited by M. Karpiński. XII, 542 pages. 1977.

ɪl. 57: Portability of Numerical Software. Proceedings 1976. Edited W. Cowell. VIII, 539 pages. 1977.

ɪl. 58: M. J. O'Donnell, Computing in Systems Described by Equa-ns. XIV, 111 pages. 1977.

ɪl. 59: E. Hill, Jr., A Comparative Study of Very Large Data Bases. 140 pages. 1978.

ɪl. 60: Operating Systems, An Advanced Course. Edited by R. Bayer, M. Graham, and G. Seegmüller. X, 593 pages. 1978.

ɪl. 61: The Vienna Development Method: The Meta-Language. lited by D. Bjørner and C. B. Jones. XVIII, 382 pages. 1978.

ɪl. 62: Automata, Languages and Programming. Proceedings 1978. lited by G. Ausiello and C. Böhm. VIII, 508 pages. 1978.

ɪl. 63: Natural Language Communication with Computers. Edited Leonard Bolc. VI, 292 pages. 1978.

ɪl. 64: Mathematical Foundations of Computer Science. Proceed-gs 1978. Edited by J. Winkowski. X, 551 pages. 1978.

ɪl. 65: Information Systems Methodology, Proceedings, 1978. lited by G. Bracchi and P. C. Lockemann. XII, 696 pages. 1978.

l. 66: N. D. Jones and S. S. Muchnick, TEMPO: A Unified Treat-ent of Binding Time and Parameter Passing Concepts in Pro-amming Languages. IX, 118 pages. 1978.

l. 67: Theoretical Computer Science, 4th GI Conference, Aachen, arch 1979. Edited by K. Weihrauch. VII, 324 pages. 1979.

This series reports new developments in computer science research and teaching – quickly, informally and at a high level. The type of material considered for publication includes:

1. Preliminary drafts of original papers and monographs
2. Lectures on a new field or presentations of a new angle in a classical field
3. Seminar work-outs
4. Reports of meetings, provided they are
   a) of exceptional interest and
   b) devoted to a single topic.

Texts which are out of print but still in demand may also be considered if they fall within these categories.

The timeliness of a manuscript is more important than its form, which may be unfinished or tentative. Thus, in some instances, proofs may be merely outlined and results presented which have been or will later be published elsewhere. If possible, a subject index should be included. Publication of Lecture Notes is intended as a service to the international computer science community, in that a commercial publisher, Springer-Verlag, can offer a wide distribution of documents which would otherwise have a restricted readership. Once published and copyrighted, they can be documented in the scientific literature.

Manuscripts

Manuscripts should be no less than 100 and preferably no more than 500 pages in length.
They are reproduced by a photographic process and therefore must be typed with extreme care. Symbols not on the typewriter should be inserted by hand in indelible black ink. Corrections to the typescript should be made by pasting in the new text or painting out errors with white correction fluid. Authors receive 75 free copies and are free to use the material in other publications. The typescript is reduced slightly in size during reproduction; best results will not be obtained unless the text on any one page is kept within the overall limit of 18 x 26.5 cm (7 x 10½ inches). On request, the publisher will supply special paper with the typing area outlined.
Manuscripts should be sent to Prof. G. Goos, Institut für Informatik, Universität Karlsruhe, Zirkel 2, 7500 Karlsruhe/Germany, Prof. J. Hartmanis, Cornell University, Dept. of Computer-Science, Ithaca, NY/USA 14850, or directly to Springer-Verlag Heidelberg.

Springer-Verlag, Heidelberger Platz 3, D-1000 Berlin 33
Springer-Verlag, Neuenheimer Landstraße 28–30, D-6900 Heidelberg 1
Springer-Verlag, 175 Fifth Avenue, New York, NY 10010/USA

ISBN 3-540-09118-1
ISBN 0-387-09118-1